DATE DUE

MY 9'05			
MY 25'05			

DEMCO 38-296

LAW OFFICE
MANAGEMENT

LAW OFFICE MANAGEMENT

SECOND EDITION

JONATHAN S. LYNTON
TERRI MICK LYNDALL
DONNA MASINTER

WEST PUBLISHING

an International Thomson Publishing company I(T)P®

Albany • Bonn • Boston • Cincinnati • Detroit • London • Madrid
Melbourne • Mexico City • Minneapolis/St. Paul • New York • Pacific Grove
Paris • San Francisco • Singapore • Tokyo • Toronto • Washington

CE TO THE READER

he products described herein or perform any independent analysis in
contained herein. Publisher does not assume, and expressly disclaims,
ther than that provided to it by the manufacturer.

nal tool, not a practice book. Since the law is in constant change, no
ied upon for any service to any client. The reader should always refer
v. If legal advice or other expert assistance is required, the services of

The publisher makes no representations or warranties of any kind, including but not limited to, the warranties of fitness for particular purpose or merchantability, nor are any such representations implied with respect to the material set forth herein, and the publisher takes no responsibility with respect to such material. The publisher shall not be liable for any special, consequential, or exemplary damages resulting, in whole or in part, from the readers' use of, or reliance upon, this material.

Background by Jennifer McGlaughlin
Design by Douglas J. Hyldelund/Linda C. DeMasi

Delmar Staff:

Acquisitions Editor: Christopher Anzalone
Project Editor: Eugenia L. Orlandi
Developmental Editor: Jeffrey D. Litton

Production Coordinator: Jennifer Gaines
Art & Design Coordinator: Douglas J. Hyldelund

COPYRIGHT © 1996
By West Publishing
an imprint of Delmar Publishers
a division of International Thomson Publishing Inc.

The ITP logo is a trademark under license.

Printed in the United States of America

For more information, contact:

Delmar Publishers
3 Columbia Circle, Box 15015
Albany, New York 12212-5015

International Thomson Publishing Europe
Berkshire House 168 - 173
High Holborn
London WC1V7AA
England

Thomas Nelson Australia
102 Dodds Street
South Melbourne, 3205
Victoria, Australia

Nelson Canada
1120 Birchmount Road
Scarborough, Ontario
Canada M1K 5G4

International Thomson Editores
Campos Eliseos 385, Piso 7
Col Polanco
11560 Mexico D F Mexico

International Thomson Publishing GmbH
Königswinterer Strasse 418
53227 Bonn
Germany

International Thomson Publishing Asia
221 Henderson Road
#05 - 10 Henderson Building
Singapore 0315

International Thomson Publishing - Japan
Hirakawacho Kyowa Building, 3F
2-2-1 Hirakawacho
Chiyoda-ku, Tokyo 102
Japan

2 3 4 5 6 7 8 9 10 XXX 01 00 99 98 97

Library of Congress Cataloging-in-Publication Data

Lynton, Jonathan S.
    Law office management/Jonathan S. Lynton, Terri Mick Lyndall, Donna
Masinter.—2nd ed.
        p.   cm.
    Rev. ed. of: Law office management for paralegals. 1992.
    Includes index.
    ISBN 0-8273-7139-X
    1. Law offices—United States. 2. Legal assistants—United
States. I. Lyndall, Terri Mick. II. Masinter, Donna.
III. Lynton, Jonathan S. Law office management for paralegals.
IV. Title.
KF318.Z9L96 1996
340'.068—dc20

                                                        95-25317
                                                        CIP

DEDICATION

From Jonathan:

To my wife, Kim,
who continues to blossom before my eyes,

To my mom, Joan S. Lynton,
who has always been there for me, through thick and thin,

and to
Mark D. Jacobs,
friend and brother, then and now

From Terri:

To my children, Stuart and Morgan,
with love and affection

From Donna:

To Michael, my best friend

This book is also dedicated to the memory of Alexander:

*" ... little else of life shall we demand
than the fortune such friendship as ours to find."*

Delmar Publishers' Online Services

To access Delmar on the World Wide Web, point your browser to:
http://www.delmar.com/delmar.html
To access through Gopher: gopher://gopher.delmar.com
(Delmar Online is part of "thomson.com", an Internet site with information on
more than 30 publishers of the International Thomson Publishing organization.)
For more information on our products and services:
email: info@delmar.com
or call 800-347-7707

CONTENTS

PART I
THE LEGAL PROCESS AND THE LAW OFFICE

IIII CHAPTER 1:   The Work of the Paralegal   3

IIII CHAPTER 2:   Malpractice Avoidance Through Law Office Systems   32

PART II
LAW OFFICE ADMINISTRATION

IIII CHAPTER 8:   Records Management   212

IIII CHAPTER 9:   The Law Library and Other Office Management Systems   235

PART III
COMPUTERS AND TECHNOLOGY IN THE LAW OFFICE

IIII CHAPTER 10: Computers and Paralegals: A Working Relationship   263

IIII CHAPTER 11: Word and Data Processing   279

IIII **CHAPTER 12: Telecommunications and Office Equipment   296**

IIII **CHAPTER 13: Technical Applications for Legal Practice   314**

PART IV
PROFESSIONALISM

IIII **CHAPTER 14: Legal Ethics and Professional Responsibility   341**

IIII Appendices

FOREWORD

When Donna Masinter first approached me about writing a foreword for this book, I thought that it would be simply another law office management book for paralegal students. That is, an overview of file management, billing techniques, office decorum, and tips on dressing for success. What a pleasant surprise it was to see that this book provides so much more.

Law Office Management is the first book that I know of that addresses the role of the paralegal in today's modern law office. This book finally addresses the full array of challenges and opportunities facing paralegals in their professional lives. I found the chapters on "Coping with Stress," "The Art of Communication," and "Professional Development" to be particularly useful and reflective of the maturity of the paralegal profession. I also felt that the emphasis placed by the authors on malpractice avoidance as an overriding concern of modern legal practice is highly appropriate. As full members of the legal team, paralegals must understand the potential that their actions have for contributing to malpractice situations and how to avoid such situations. I also found the author's emphasis on ethics and professional responsibility timely and a helpful contribution to the book's overall theme of professionalism for today's paralegal.

Of course, many of the usual subjects are also discussed in this book, such as law office structure, time records, and computers in the law office. These topics, however, are covered in greater depth than in most such books, and the information provided concerns the latest techniques for law office management. Introducing the paralegal to zero-based budgeting and management of law firm growth was particularly interesting and unique.

In short, I found *Law Office Management* to be an indispensable tool for those educators who are truly interested in preparing their students for the realities of today's paralegal practice.

Albert Greenstone
President, The National Center for
  Paralegal Training
Atlanta, Georgia
April 1991

PREFACE TO THE SECOND EDITION

We are gratified at the excellent reception the first edition of this book has had and are pleased to provide, in this second edition, a much expanded text that includes a number of new features. Discussion and response from across the country since publication of the first edition have confirmed our belief that the effective paralegal and law office employee must master the systems and processes of law office management to be successful. This text focuses on how the law, and the business of law, gets done. As such, it is of vital importance to anyone who wants to develop a career working in the legal field.

This second edition includes a number of topics that have emerged as critical issues for law office management. These include drug testing, responding to HIV/AIDS, the application of Total Quality Management, team building, new technical developments (including multimedia, computer animation, and the Internet), cultural diversity in the workplace, and conflict resolution.

In addition to discussion of these newly emerging issues, we have expanded our guest editorials. This edition includes new editorials by experts such as Susan Goodman, on contract employment as a career option; Doug Cohen, on presentation graphics for legal applications; and Lynne Z. Gold-Bikin, on avoiding stress by identifying difficult clients. Other new editorials focus on the quality movement and conflict management. A new and valuable feature in Chapter 13 takes you screen-by-screen through O.N.E. Ware, an integrated system for law office management.

We have continued and expanded our problems at the end of each chapter so that you can apply the concepts presented in the text to a simulated client.

Finally, we have expanded our "On Point" features. We hope you will be amused by these scenarios, each of which contains issues, activities, or behaviors relevant to the concepts presented in that chapter. Not only will you have some fun with these features, but they will also introduce you to the tradition of using hypothetical (and hopefully humorous) situations in the presentation of legal problems for discussion or examination.

Today more than ever, the effective paralegal must complement knowledge of the law with a knowledge of the systems and processes that constitute the environment in which legal work is done. We all need to be aware that it is not just *what* you do, it is *how* you do it that matters. This text is designed to help you in your work as a paralegal by introducing you to the systems, processes, issues, and vocabulary encountered in the field of law office management. This knowledge will help you develop a strong foundation for excellence and efficiency in your work, which in turn will increase both your productivity at work and the satisfaction you derive from work.

We are again indebted to our entire editorial team for their support and encouragement. We are also especially appreciative of Brooke Graves, whose editorial scrutiny and keen eye have surely made this a better book, as well as the efforts of Jehanne Schweitzer and Graphics West, Inc.

Jonathan S. Lynton
Donna Masinter
Terri Mick Lyndall

Atlanta, Georgia
October 1995

PREFACE TO THE FIRST EDITION

Law Office Management is a practical textbook designed to familiarize paralegals with their roles, activities, and responsibilities in the workings of a law office. Paralegals need to understand and appreciate more than the technical components of paralegal work; they need to understand the context in which their skills fit and the organization of which they are a part. It is essential that today's paralegals understand law office management in order to take advantage of the tremendous opportunities available to them. Only by combining technical paralegal skills with the organizational, administrative, and professional skills necessary to succeed in the contemporary law office can the paralegal truly be prepared to succeed in the workplace.

The purpose of this book is to give the student a comprehensive introduction to the different facets of law office management by integrating practical examples, case studies, and applications with the explanatory material. The student will be exposed to each of the major areas of law office management, and each section is tied together by the most important theme for law offices of the 1990s: malpractice avoidance. Effective law office management goes far beyond efficiency and organization; it also includes a sensitivity to the ethical and legal parameters that define legal practice. *Law Office Management* not only explores this important dimension in general, but also provides unique "On Point" case studies in each chapter that relate malpractice avoidance to the themes and processes discussed in that chapter.

Each of the four major sections of *Law Office Management* introduces the reader to related groups of office management systems. By the completion of the book, the reader will have gained a thorough understanding of law office management and will be prepared to be an effective and productive contributor to a law office.

Section 1, "The Legal Process and the Law Office," introduces the reader to the various realities of working in a law office. This section will help the student learn about the realities of paralegal work and the structure of the legal profession, areas that are frequently neglected in paralegal education and areas which are essential for the paralegal to understand if he or she is to be an involved contributor in the law office. Chapter 1, "The Work of the Paralegal," uses interviews with actual paralegals to introduce the reader to the work opportunities and activities that characterize paralegal work. By starting with paralegal work, the book's orientation becomes clear: The perspective is that of the paralegal. Chapter 2 introduces the reader to a major unifying theme of the book. malpractice avoidance. This chapter orients the student to the many different dimensions of malpractice. from how it is committed, to its repercussions, to its avoidance. This featured emphasis on malpractice contributes to the practical orientation of the book; it also imparts the serious consequences of legal work and unites the disparate systems and processes discussed in the book by relating them to malpractice avoidance.

The third chapter in this section introduces the student to the vocabulary used to describe and define the types of law firms and the positions commonly found in law firms. It also acquaints the student with the real workings of a law firm by describing both its activities and its economics. This chapter provides an acculturation into the world of the law firm and an introduction to the vocabulary that is used to describe the structures and people in a law firm. The final chapter of the section concerns law firm growth. By introducing the student to marketing, strategic planning, and the trends that will characterize the law firm of the future, this chapter broadens the paralegal's perspective of paralegal work. The chapter shows how paralegals can contribute to law firm growth by being an active participant in the marketing effort and preparing for future developments through awareness and continued education.

These four chapters lay the foundation for effective law office management for paralegals. They provide the information and perspective that enables the student to understand the context for and the reality of being a paralegal, both in the law office of today and in the developing law office of the future.

The second section of the book, "Law Office Administration," describes the major systems used in the actual administration of a law firm. In addition to being introduced to these systems, the student will apply the systems to actual clients described in the "Problems & Activities" section of each chapter. By complementing the theoretical knowledge with actual applications, the student will gain a highly practical understanding of the major systems used in the administration of a law firm. Chapter 5 introduces the student to the general idea of systems in an office, and the following four chapters in this section each concern a specific administrative area. Chapter 6 concerns accounting systems and covers both manual and computerized accounting systems. It also introduces the student to zero-based budgeting. Chapter 7 focuses on time management and its tremendous importance in a law office. The student is introduced to different methods of thinking about and documenting time; charts and examples illustrate timekeeping methods. Chapter 8 describes records management, and takes the student through the actual process of opening, maintaining, and closing a file. Chapter 9 examines the library, one of the key resources for a paralegal, and describes other office management systems such as office manuals, mailrooms, and other support systems. Through this section, the student will gain exposure to all of the administrative systems used in a law office, and, by doing the problems and activities in each section, will apply the systems discussed to actual clients. Additionally, the theme of malpractice avoidance runs through this section to emphasize that the systematic administration of a law office is one of the most important ways to avoid malpractice claims.

The third section of the book, "Computers and Technology in the Law Office," features a thorough discussion of technical applications found in the modern law firm. The successful paralegal must be aware of and use numerous technical applications and equipment, and this section features a comprehensive introduction to the various technical systems that a paralegal might be exposed to. Chapter 10 provides the foundation for this section by describing the relationship between paralegals and computers as a working partnership. The following three chapters discuss the major technical systems found in a legal practice: word and data processing, telecommunications and office equipment, and technical systems and applications designed for legal work. This detailed exposure to technical applications is a tremendous benefit to the paralegal because of the high degree of automation found in the contemporary law office. The successful paralegal of the future must not merely be able to use existing technology; he or she must also be willing and able to learn new applications as they are developed and used. This section imparts both the knowledge to use technology productively and the motivation to see technology as an integral part of the work of a law office.

The final section of the book, "Professionalism," complements the book's preceding focus on law office systems with an exploration of the systems an individual paralegal will use to develop his or her professional identity and abilities. Chapter 14 introduces the student to the highly important area of legal ethics, oriented to the specific ethical issues that the paralegal most frequently faces: giving legal advice, maintaining confidentiality, and avoiding conflict of interest. This emphasis on professional responsibility. combined with the theme of malpractice avoidance, sensitizes the student to the ethical parameters that define the realities of paralegal work. Chapter 15 describes achieving professionalism through communications. By understanding general principles of effective communication as well as specific communications issues that arise in the course of legal work. the student will learn how to communicate effectively with other paralegals, lawyers, and clients, and how to avoid the errors and misunderstandings that so frequently arise in human communication. Chapter 16 looks at the professional's ability to handle stress effectively. The student learns about the sources of stress in legal work and develops strategies to cope effectively with the stress that accompanies the hectic pace so frequently found in law offices. Chapter 17 concerns professional development. It takes the student through an actual paralegal job search and features examples of résumés and a detailed examination of all phases in the job search. The student is also introduced to the idea that professional development requires the continued learning of new skills and knowledge, and the text encourages the student to develop his or her career potential through professional development.

Law Office Management is an indispensable guide to the office systems that create the context for paralegal work. Only by learning about the realities of working in a law firm and the methods through which the work of the law can proceed in an efficient, profitable, and ethical manner, can the paralegal truly be prepared to be a productive member of the legal team.

ACKNOWLEDGMENTS

The authors offer their sincere thanks and appreciation to the following people and organizations for their valuable contributions to this book:

Brenda DeSimone, Joanna Moylan, Teri Pinyan, and the entire team of paralegals at Drew, Eckl & Farnham, for their excellent suggestions, illustrations, and advice;

Michael Masinter, Shannon Selfridge, Allison Daniel, Marcy Kushner, and Mark Masinter, for their support and encouragement;

Doug Cohen of TrialGraphix, for his support, illustrations, and outstanding guest editorial;

Susan L. Goodman and her partner, Anne H. Whitaker, for their support of this project and for providing such an excellent guest editorial;

John Aflin of O.N.E. Ware, for providing the materials to create a superb feature on computerized law office support software;

James Keane, Lynn Gold-Bikin, Saul Cohen, and all the other writers of guest editorials, for their much-appreciated participation in this project;

Carl Puls and Kathy Jarman, for their friendship, encouragement, camaraderie, and support during the preparation of the revision of this manuscript;

Paige Belote, Ann Lindsey, Gail Burns, Sherri Godwin, Dick Roe, Bob Seel, David Dean, Jimmy Z, Jay and Agatha, and the whole crew at Mick's/Decatur, for providing the freshest and friendliest atmosphere anywhere;

Dean Nick Vitterite, Dean Ray Bass, and President Ron Bush of DeVry Institute in Decatur, for their continued support and encouragement;

The Law Firm of Hartley & Puls, for allowing us to take photographs of their office;

Cathy Alterman, for her support, friendship, and advice;

Professor Michael S. Harper, for continued friendship and inspiration;

Candy Lesher, the most fabulous secretary in the world;

Charles Sheetrock, for whom I have the greatest respect and admiration;

Mr. Tom Collins and all the people at Juris, Inc., for their generous sharing of materials and illustrations;

Ms. Lauri Kohn of STUDIOS, for cheerfully providing information and photographs of law office interiors;

Holly Pritchard and Pennie Rundle, for their excellent matchmaking skills;

DeeDee Murphy and Heide Evans, for their many contributions to the care of the Lynton household, and Carol Willingham for her care of the Lyndall household;

Ken Hyry, for his outstanding photographs which appear throughout the book;

The law firm of Savell and Williams, and especially John Parker, for their involvement in the project;

Nancy Gibson Cowles, for her support and encouragement;

The Honorable Don A. Langham, for his wise guidance;

Professor Roy Sobelson, of Georgia State University, for sharing his knowledge of the law, offering valuable advice, and being a wonderful friend and mentor;

Georgia State Law professors James Bross, Steven Kaminshine, Paul Milich, Patrick Wiseman, and William Gregory, for generously sharing their time and motivating us to pursue our study of the law;

Irving Green, President of Skan Technologies, Inc., for his interest in the project and contribution on optical imaging;

Wayne Eley and Judy Hickey of MicroPatent, who supplied materials and enthusiastically supported this work;

Atlanta Legal Copies, Inc., for their contribution of forms to this manuscript;

Tom Holbrook and Christine Arruda of Aspen Systems Corporation, for providing information and resources on litigation support;

All of the people whose photographs appear in the text;

The law firm of Hurt, Richardson, Garner, Todd, and Cadenhead for their cooperation and assistance;

John Gormley and Sharon Semmons, for their contributions;

Our editorial teams at Delmar and The Lawyers Cooperative, and especially our editor, Chris Anzalone, and his assistant, Judy Roberts, whose patience, support, encouragement, and sense of humor have made the project a joy to work on;

Jerry Percifield, Phil Lewin, Dennis Grady, Jim Holcomb, Felix Love, and Bob Bouwman: "You get by with a little help from your friends";

Joan S. Lynton, who set high standards and expectations for her son, and then gave him the means and encouragement to achieve them;

John and Gabie Mick, whose patience and understanding are greatly appreciated;

Nick and Aaron Lynton, and Stuart and Morgan Lyndall, whose love and support has made all things possible;

Julian E. and Joan L. Lynton, who are always there with love and encouragement;

Vicki Sendele, who has always supported and encouraged me;

Bob and Mary Beth Bova, who make it easy to remember the Sixties, as well as the reasons I practice law;

Bud Siemon, for his friendship, encouragement, and advice;

Steve Reighard, appellate lawyer extraordinaire, who is always there with a helping hand;

Bruce Cross, master carpenter, whose meticulous work and careful construction are much appreciated;

David Ryback, for encouragement, extended invitations, and wonderful conversations.

We also express our appreciation to the reviewers whose thoughtful commentary has made this a better book:

Anneta Buster
    Johnson County Community College
    Overland Park, KS

Suzanne Sheldon
    Woodbury College
    Montpelier, VT

Delores Grissom
    Samford University
    Birmingham, AL

Laura St. George
    Champlain College
    Burlington, VT

INTRODUCTION

We welcome you in your quest to learn about an essential yet often neglected area of paralegal education, that of law office management. Paralegal work exists in the context of both the legal process and the law office, yet too often paralegals mistakenly believe that their work is limited to the specific activities a paralegal is trained to perform. What is true is that a paralegal is a highly valuable member of a legal team, whose responsibilities extend far beyond technical paralegal skills to include, among other things, keeping time records, meeting billable hour requirements, managing records, maintaining a zero-based budget, resolving ethical conflicts, and pursuing professional development. These activities provide a context in which paralegal work fits, and, without the ability to manage yourself and your work in a law office, it will be difficult for you to perform your work well or to be prepared to take advantage of future opportunities.

This book will help you learn about the systems used in law offices, and you will appreciate that only through a systematic approach to managing the activities of a law office will you be able to achieve the level of efficiency and professionalism that must characterize legal work. We have tried to cover all of the systems and issues that you will encounter in the process of working in a law office to give you a comprehensive overview of what to expect. We have also tried to write our ideas in a clear, easy-to-understand style so that the reading is both informative and enjoyable.

The textual material is complemented by many illustrations, case studies, and examples that will make it easy for you to relate the ideas to the actual reality of working in a law office. Additionally, we cover issues such as malpractice avoidance, ethics, stress management, and effective communication techniques, topics that are universally seen as critically important, yet topics that are frequently not covered by other texts. Taken together, the features of the book are intended to give you information that will make you an active, professional participant in a law firm who is well aware of the different systems and skills necessary to achieve success. Equipped with both the skills necessary to perform paralegal activities and the skills necessary to work effectively in a law office, you will be well prepared to achieve excellence in your work and to successfully meet the challenges that your work will offer.

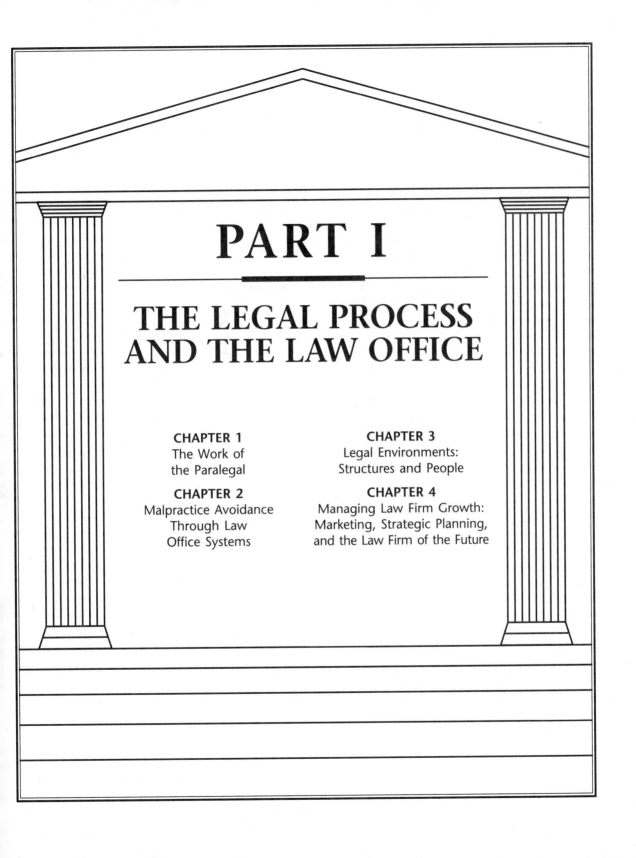

PART I

THE LEGAL PROCESS AND THE LAW OFFICE

PART I OVERVIEW

Chapter 1: The Work of the Paralegal

An examination of what a paralegal does, offered from the perspective of practicing paralegals. An overview of paralegal work and how it fits into the legal process, including descriptions of paralegal activities and specializations.

Chapter 2: Malpractice Avoidance Through Law Office Systems

An introduction to the concept of malpractice and the critical role of malpractice avoidance, with an emphasis on avoiding malpractice by using office management systems. How malpractice might arise across the spectrum of legal work, with discussions of methods to avoid malpractice claims and allegations.

Chapter 3: Legal Environments: Structures and People

A review of the types of firms and environments in which the law is practiced, including private firms, corporations, and the government. Description of people and positions in a law firm. Different environments are compared to help readers make a fit between their interests and abilities and the environment in which they are most happy and productive. Special features include sections on law firm design and moving a law office.

Chapter 4: Managing Law Firm Growth: Marketing, Strategic Planning, and the Law Firm of the Future

A comprehensive introduction to various aspects of law firm growth, including marketing techniques and strategies and the application of strategic planning to law offices. A look forward into the law office of the future gives the reader an idea of the trends that will characterize law firms of the future.

CHAPTER 1

THE WORK OF
THE PARALEGAL

OBJECTIVES

By the completion of this chapter, you should:

- understand the types of activities that the paralegal performs;

- learn about areas of specialization for paralegals;

- learn about paralegal associations; and

- understand how the paralegal can make a significant contribution to the workings of the legal process.

ON
POINT   *SAM CHOOSES A CHALLENGING CAREER*

Sam Malone, ex-owner of Cheers, has grown tired of the bar business and sold the bar to Carla. He has decided to pursue a career as a paralegal or a law office manager and has just enrolled in a paralegal program. Uncertain about what particular direction his new career should take, Sam drops by the bar for some advice on the kind of career path he should pursue.

Cliff tells him that government work is the best. "It's not too hard and you just sit behind a desk," he says.

"I don't know," replies Sam, "I was just over at the DA's office and those paralegals had so many cases they needed a cart to carry all the files. Anyway, I don't know if I want to prosecute cases … you just never know if they are guilty."

"That part doesn't matter," says Norm, "it just matters that you don't have to work late hours so you can see us here at Cheers, Sammy boy."

"The money, Sam. The money," offers Carla. "That's what you should be looking for."

"Now, Sam," says Diane, "this is the only time in your life you can do something for others. I think you should try to get a position at the Legal Clinic for the Homeless or become a child advocate. Now that is something you could be proud of."

"Wait a second," says Sam. "I'm a little overwhelmed by all of these choices. I think I want to be in litigation—being in court appeals to my competitive instincts."

"Yeah, you could be like Conrad on 'Matlock,' " offers Carla.

Cliff chimes in, "No, no, no, you could prosecute postal fraud. It's a very big problem, you know."

"Oh, Sam," sighs Diane, "you would look so very nice in those beautiful suits those big firm lawyers wear."

"Thanks for your thoughts, guys, but I can see I'm going to have to learn for myself about my choices and opportunities before I figure out the direction I take with my new career. I just hope I find a situation just like Cheers," he says, smiling coyly, "you know, where everybody knows my name!"

The Work of the Paralegal: An Introduction

The paralegal profession is one of the most rapidly growing professions in the country. As legal costs increase, firms are learning that one of the best ways to contain these costs is to hire paralegals. Not only can legal assistants do much of the same work as lawyers, but they are also less expensive, both for the firm and the client than attorneys. You have chosen a truly exciting and challenging career.

Apart from challenge and excitement, the paralegal profession offers a wide variety of opportunities in many different types of environments. This book introduces you to the process of law office management, which is important to the aspiring paralegal for two reasons.

First, all paralegal positions require both paralegal skills and office management skills. Regardless of your specialty or the type of environment in which you work, you will need skills and information to deal with all the facets of your job. The field of law office management will teach you about areas such as malpractice avoidance, types of legal environments, practice management, law offices moves, law office accounting, billable hour requirements, records management, ethical guidelines, and effective communication. These areas, among others, provide the context in which paralegal work is done. By understanding these areas, you will be able to complement your legal skills, such as performing research writing, and interviewing witnesses, with office management skills. If you are going to achieve excellence in the legal field, you will need to attend to both of these aspects of your work.

Second, law office management represents a career path that might be very attractive to paralegals. Law firms of all sizes hire law office managers or administrators to handle the operation of the firm. Although some firms use professional managers for this position, many firms promote paralegals from within the firm to this type of work.

As a first step in being able to manage paralegal work, whether your own or that of others, you will want to understand what a paralegal does. The truth is that there is no single definition of paralegal work. In part because of the newness of the paralegal profession, there are a wide variety of views toward paralegals and the work they can perform. Like any new field, the paralegal profession is still growing, developing, and finding its niche. Although some attorneys appreciate paralegals and integrate them as much as possible into the process of doing legal work, others remain uncertain as to how best to utilize these paraprofessionals. Nonetheless, the prospects for the paralegal profession remain bright, even though the concept of paralegalism, and paralegals' position in the legal community, is an evolving one.

It is not unusual, therefore, for you to have questions about the identity and role of the paralegal: Exactly what is it like to be a paralegal in the "real world"? What do they do and how are they perceived by attorneys? What are the differences between corporate and litigation legal assistants? How would paralegals describe their "typical" days? In an effort to answer these questions

and give you a practical idea of what being a paralegal means, we have interviewed several paralegals specializing in different areas and in different types
of firms. By hearing from actual paralegals, you will get a realistic picture of
their work.

John Gormley is a paralegal in a small Atlanta firm that specializes in bankruptcy. Unlike many of his counterparts, John has worked in almost all areas of
the law, from litigation to probate work. With this unique background, John
was able to give us a good idea of how being a paralegal has changed over the
years:

> Until recently the role of the paralegal in the American legal system was
> viewed as a "glorified secretary." Although secretaries serve a vital role in the le-
> gal industry, the functions of the paralegal and the secretary are separate and
> distinct jobs. Due to the highly specialized nature of the law, there are parale-
> gals, like attorneys, who possess skills tailored to one or several particular areas
> of the law. There are probate, bankruptcy, litigation, corporate, and admiralty
> paralegals. Although the expertise of each may differ, a common thread runs
> through them. Today's paralegal is intimately involved in every aspect of a case.
> He/She plays a role in the substantive and procedural decisions made during
> the several phases of a lawsuit, filing of a bankruptcy petition, corporate take-
> overs, or the administration of a decedent's estate.
>
> A litigation paralegal's expertise is most useful during the discovery phase of
> a lawsuit. By drafting interrogatories, requests for production of documents,
> and other discovery requests, the paralegal helps to narrow the issues for trial
> and makes preparation for trial a much less complicated task. In many in-
> stances, the litigation paralegal is responsible for interviewing witnesses, pre-
> paring for depositions, monitoring compliance with discovery requests, and, if
> necessary, drafting motions to compel and motions for sanctions for violations
> of the discovery rules.
>
> The bankruptcy paralegal performs a vital role in Chapters 7, 11, and 13 fil-
> ings. The bankruptcy paralegal is one of the few who can attend court hearings
> without the aid of an attorney, for many bankruptcy hearings are administra-
> tive in nature and do not require an attorney. In many cases, the bankruptcy
> paralegal attends Section 341 hearings, propounds questions to the debtor, and
> reports to the attorney the developments of the debtor's case. In some bank-
> ruptcy filings, there exist secured creditors. Law firms representing these clients
> often seek relief from the stay imposed by the Bankruptcy Code. The paralegal
> is often responsible for drafting motions to lift the stay and, if the motion is
> granted, taking the necessary steps to pursue their client's remedies. In repre-
> senting a debtor, the paralegal often meets with the client and assists in deter-
> mining their assets and liabilities in preparation of the schedules and statement
> of financial affairs.
>
> The corporate paralegal is often involved in the intricacies of incorporating
> a business. Once the business is incorporated, the paralegal often assists the
> client in preparing for stockholder's meetings and meetings of the board of di-
> rectors. In several cases, the paralegal will sit as an officer or director of a com-
> pany to provide some guidance and expertise.
>
> The probate paralegal prepares wills, powers of attorney, and trust agree-
> ments. He/She is frequently involved in locating all assets and potential bene-
> ficiaries of a decedent's estate and ensuring that the administration of the

estate progresses smoothly. There are close contacts with the executors of the estate, real estate agencies, banks, and appraisers.

A paralegal's day consists of performing many tasks and communicating with different people involved in the legal process. Being a paralegal is a challenge, and it is a position of great responsibility. As you can see from John's description, the role of the legal assistant varies according to the type of law the paralegal chooses to specialize in. Although the specific tasks and responsibilities may vary, common skills are needed by paralegals no matter what their specialization. These skills include organization, drafting, research, and communication skills; even though they may be utilized in different ways, they are nonetheless required of all paralegals. (See Figure 1-1.) As we examine a day-in-the-life of various paralegal specialties, you will see that working in the paralegal profession is truly like wearing a "coat of many colors. " (See Figures 1-2 and 1-3.)

A real estate paralegal at the Atlanta firm of Hurt, Richardson, Garner, Todd, and Cadenhead made the following observations and comments:

> When I was first asked about a typical day in the life of a real estate paralegal, I was just winding up a 5-day, 56-hour work week. Believe me, the idea of recapping any one of the days I had just struggled through was definitely not appealing. Given this hectic schedule, before I begin I want to make one thing clear: the next attorney who greets me with the words "I hear the real estate market is dead," will be summarily executed.
>
> My career as a real estate paralegal began approximately 15 years ago. Luckily it began with a small firm and I had the opportunity to work with a very knowledgeable, patient attorney, which made my initial learning experience a

FIGURE 1-1 Paralegals communicate directly with attorneys ...

FIGURE 1-2   ... interview witnesses, including police officers ...

very positive one. Also, during my employment with this firm, the real estate market went into a real slump, and I had the opportunity to assist in other areas of the law, including litigation, domestic relations, wills and estates, and bankruptcies. It didn't take me very long to realize that real estate was definitely the area I wanted to remain in, but I did appreciate the exposure to various types of legal work.

My first seven years consisted primarily of residential real estate transactions. My day usually consisted of receiving title and survey orders from lenders and pulling any abstracts available that would assist the law clerks in doing the actual title searches. I would then proceed with reviewing completed title searches, clearing any title exceptions, preparing the closing documents, submitting closed loan packages to the lender, and preparing final title opinions and policies.

The opportunity presented itself to move to a larger town and work for a larger firm. With the move, I left the residential area behind and moved into working on commercial transactions. A typical day now consists of a great variety of duties. I work with many clients, including major banks, insurance companies, and developers. Also, I have the opportunity to work with approximately 80 attorneys, 11 of whom make up the real estate department. There is a great deal of client contact, over the telephone and in person. I enjoy this part of my job the most. There are always questions from clients as well as from attorneys that have to be answered immediately. In a given day, I may assist with as many as four or five different transactions in progress. Initially, checklists have to be prepared. All due diligence items have to be accumulated and reviewed. Documents have to be drafted, negotiated, and revised, and title exceptions have to be cleared.

It is very important that I be flexible in my job, due to the fact that at any given time it may be necessary to work from three or four files at once. Patience is also necessary, not only with clients, but with attorneys.

I hope I have given an accurate description of a typical day in the life of a real estate paralegal. Actually, when I give it some thought, I can't really think of any other profession I would enjoy more. Maybe I would like to go on to law school and become an attorney. I'll give it some thought, but I don't think they have classes that begin at 11:00 P.M. and end in time for me to go home, take a shower, and drive to the office.

Compare the real estate paralegal's description with the following description from Sharon Semmons, a paralegal coordinator at the Atlanta firm of Savell and Williams:

I am a paralegal coordinator for a midsize downtown law firm in Atlanta, Georgia, which specializes in insurance defense litigation. The senior partner with whom I work concentrates on defending workers' compensation cases, representing uninsured employers, and, on occasion, claimant's cases. I am also responsible for managing the flow of paralegal work in the firm and interviewing prospective paralegal applications. Thus, my "typical" day is an eclectic mix of legal and administrative responsibilities.

Among the many different tasks I perform regularly, one of the most ubiquitous and important ones is the investigation of new cases that are forwarded to us for defense. The attorney I work with reviews and summarizes the cases, making an initial evaluation of each case. He then forwards the file to me with an initiating memo specifying the work to be done. Typically this includes indexing the claimant's records at the state board of workers' compensation for

FIGURE 1-3 ... and organize documents for trial.

claims history; requesting copies of any claims; initiating discovery through requesting the claimant's medical records; and setting the claimant's deposition and contacting the employer for records and to obtain statements.

The initial contact with the insured is often quite important. We may not know very much about the nature of the alleged accident or injury or how it occurred, including whether there were any witnesses; whether the claimant has received Medicare; whether the insured has a properly posted panel of physicians; or whether the claimant has returned to work for the insured or another employer. I also need to make a preliminary determination regarding the insured's compliance with certain provisions of Georgia's Workers' Compensation Act. For example, does the insured have a properly posted panel of physicians, and have they properly informed their employees of their rights under the act? I request copies of the claimant's personnel and payroll records and see if there are any defenses or whether there is a possible claim against the Subsequent Injury Trust Fund. I prepare an average weekly wage statement and check to see if the claimant has filed any claims with a group health insurer or Social Security disability, or whether the claimant has filed an unemployment claim.

In addition to requesting and reviewing the claimant's employment records, I also often obtain statements from the claimant's supervisors and co-employees, who may have relevant information regarding not only the alleged accident but also the claimant's past history or current activities. These statements help us to determine the basis for our defense of the claim: they can suggest the utility of surveillance, or they can point to the need to resolve the claim on a compromise basis. Obtaining the accurate and complete knowledge statements from potential witnesses, either adverse or defense, is one of the important aspects of my job.

Once the initial investigation has been completed, the attorney will take the claimant's deposition, review the medical and other discovery responses, and make a secondary evaluation of the claim and the viability of any defenses. Normally, additional discovery and investigation is warranted, and I assist in this process. As well, I begin to control and manage the flow of documents to make sure all the information that has been and continues to be requested is received by the hearing or deposition date. The rule of thumb in workers' compensation defense is organization. We generally have very little time to prepare a defense, obtain the necessary documents and records, and properly serve witnesses. Consequently, calendar control on the paralegal's part is essential.

As the hearing approaches, potential exhibits are carefully examined and, in some cases, where the records are voluminous, summarized and indexed. Exhibits must be prepared for the administrative law judge, and copies must be provided to the opposing counsel. It is also my job to make sure that our witnesses are properly served and have been interviewed prior to the hearing. This may involve the use of skip tracing services and/or process servers if the witnesses prove to be difficult to locate or serve through the U.S. mail. It often occurs that a witness who has been extremely helpful and cooperative during the course of the investigation becomes increasingly reluctant as the hearing date approaches. One of my functions is to assess when the use of a process server is warranted, depending on the attitude of a particular witness.

In addition to my paralegal duties, I also have certain administrative responsibilities as our firm's paralegal coordinator. I am required to make sure the work of the paralegals is equitably and efficiently distributed. In our firm, the paralegals work in clusters with, usually, two to three attorneys and one or more secretaries. Some paralegals may have substantially more work during any given week or month than others. Part of my job is to distribute overflow work and make suggestions regarding potential changes in the makeup of the clusters when it appears that the work may be unevenly distributed.

One of my most enjoyable tasks as paralegal coordinator is the opportunity to interview and train new paralegals. I learn a great deal about the way in which new entrants into the field view their chosen profession as well as the suggestions that veterans have for improving the manner in which we perform the many aspects of our job. There are many opportunities for paralegals to expand their level of responsibility, and one of the many reasons I enjoy working for Savell and Williams is the way that the partnership encourages paralegals to develop their full professional potential. Additionally, the attorneys I work with encourage us to take responsibility for case management.

I feel strongly that this is an aspect of working for a smaller firm that is often overlooked by paralegals. We have a large client base and a large volume of work. Our clients appreciate the extensive use of paralegals because it is cost-efficient. The paralegals enjoy the level of responsibility we can attain as our skills and experience develop.

It would be impossible to provide a description of every variation of the paralegal profession. However, these interviews should give you a general idea of what being a paralegal is about. A corporate attorney at Hurt, Richardson, Garner, Todd and Cadenhead gave the following observations about the paralegal profession:

> Competent corporate paralegals make possible systems of monitoring and contacting clients regarding annual meetings of shareholders and directors, corporate registrations, etc. Paralegals can monitor the lists of corporations and can provide follow-up contacts with clients and accountants, ensure proper filings, draft minutes/consents, and otherwise make these systems work without significant need for lawyer involvement or oversight. The result is that client status is maintained, efficient client contact is continued, and current fees are generated on an ongoing basis.
>
> An almost endless variety of services can be performed by paralegals at lower hourly rates and costs. Examples of areas in which paralegal drafting is extremely helpful, when little lawyer review time is needed, are employment agreements and shareholder agreements. The more obvious areas where virtually all required time and effort can be accomplished at the paralegal level are incorporation, name changes, dissolutions. and similar filing documents. I have relied on a paralegal I consider both experienced and especially intelligent to draft certain purchase and sale agreements. In some circumstances, a partner and a paralegal can form the most efficient team for undertaking a corporate transaction—the paralegal can perform most of the work otherwise detailed to an associate while the more expensive partner time is kept relatively minimal.
>
> In a complex transaction, with the partner focused on business negotiations and junior or other lawyers dealing with various tax, real estate, environmental, securities, or corporate issues, the work of the lawyers can be facilitated and the entire transaction process made smoother and more efficient with the

input of corporate paralegals. Routinely, paralegals prepare ancillary documents ranging from minutes/consents to supporting certificates and articles of merger, dissolution, etc. In addition, the paralegals can assume the duty of organization of exhibits, schedules, and the numerous transaction documents themselves. By initiating the closing agenda and taking responsibility for tracking the various items, the administrative burden of a complex closing is assumed by the paralegal, thereby improving the nature and efficiency of the legal service provided, not to mention the frame of mind of the responsible partner. After having conducted a closing on my own by having the parties sign an Exhibit A instead of the contract itself, my own rule is never to undertake a closing without the presence of a corporate paralegal whom I trust to ensure that everything is signed on the proper page.

The following story from Jean Weathers illustrates both the changes that occur in legal practice and the immense satisfaction that can be derived from paralegal work.

TWO DECADES WITH THE SAME LAWYER

In the early 1970s the term "paralegal" was brand new, and the definition of that term was debatable.

I worked in Peachtree Center for a small insurance defense firm consisting of 15 lawyers, 15 secretaries, and 1 bookkeeper. I was secretary to one of the senior partners who was so exceedingly busy that I didn't even see him for the first two weeks of my employment. I had enough work, however, to keep me busy the entire time.

That firm had vision, and by 1975 it had more than doubled in size, with the addition of 15 new lawyers, as many new secretaries, 2 assistant bookkeepers, and an office manager. And they were contemplating a paralegal staff.

Neither Atlanta nor the state of Georgia had a paralegal training center at the time, so the decision was whether to advertise for paralegals or to look within the firm for suitable candidates for training in a preceptor/didactic type of program. I was happy to be one of the four secretaries selected for this program. Over the next several months, I and my three counterparts participated in a number of paralegal courses and seminars, including an intense legal research course given by the law librarian at Emory Law School. We were allowed to work full time while attending these afternoon-evening classes, and utilized on the job the training we were receiving. This was an easy transition for me, since I was already familiar with our files, office procedures, and clients. My responsibilities did increase tremendously, and fairly soon we hired a secretary to work for both of us.

Extracurricularly, I was an active member of the Georgia Association of Legal Assistants. I was elected vice president and chairman of the Continuing Legal Education Committee one year, and the following year I was nominated for president, which I unfortunately had to decline due to work and home demands.

Nineteen years later, I am still working for that same lawyer, and our faithful secretary is also still with us, but we have seen some phenomenal changes over the years—the purchase and restoration of a "dream" building, a major split in the firm, the creation of a brand new firm, the purchase (and eventual sale) of a building, the purchase of yet another building, and the explosive growth of this newly created law firm. All the while, we were easing into the world of high technology. .

My title, too, has changed to "Senior Legal Assistant." We all have desktop computer terminals (which we actually understand and use), and the system is upgraded frequently.

Though the hours are long and the work is intense, I love my job. Working in insurance defense involves investigating claims, serving subpoenas, interviewing witnesses, preparing for hearings, etc. Of course, there are the not-so-thrilling but necessary tasks of answering interrogatories, organizing trial exhibits and ordering and reviewing millions and millions of medical records. The fun and exciting duties outweigh those, however.

I never know from day to day if I'll be in or out of the office because at a moment's notice I may be dispatched to a judge's, doctor's, or attorney's office, or to attend a client luncheon.

I have represented my attorney at administrative hearings. I have given my deposition and had my statement taken. I have attended numerous depositions and hearings and have performed discreet "surveillance." Each day is different from the one before, and, as you can probably tell, I truly enjoy being a major component of my lawyer's (and the firm's) team as we begin our third decade together.

One final story illustrates the career path of a paralegal who realized she was more interested in the business and administrative side of law firms than in actually doing paralegal work.

I am law office manager for a 10-person firm in San Diego, California. As an undergraduate, I majored in criminal justice and worked for several years as a probation officer. After several years, I became disenchanted with my position and attended paralegal school at night, specializing in business transactions. I knew I wanted to stay in the legal profession, but wanted to work in some environment not directly involving the court system.

After graduating from paralegal school, I found a position with a small firm that specialized in representing small businesses. My supervising attorney was the senior partner and gave me as much responsibility as I wanted. My responsibilities included preparing the bills for clients and purchasing office supplies and equipment, as well as other nonlegal administrative duties. My administrative duties began to consume more and more of my time; therefore, another paralegal was retained to assist me with the drafting of articles of incorporation, etc.

When the firm later decided to merge with another firm, I was responsible for arranging the logistics of the merger, including ordering letterheads, assigning offices and support staff, and merging of two computer networks. The senior partner realized how efficiently I had handled the merger, and when I expressed to him that I really enjoyed the administrative end of practicing law more than actually doing "paralegal" work, he suggested that he would talk with his partners and see if a position could be created for me as office manager. At that time I had two assistant paralegals helping me with my paralegal duties.

The firm voted to hire me as the office manager. I have been employed in this capacity for fifteen years and could not imagine having another job. My paralegal background helps me implement systems and programs that are compatible with the legal environment. Without my paralegal training I do not think I would be as effective a law office manager. I am able to understand billing as well as the needs of the attorneys and support staff from a practical perspective.

These statements from working paralegals and attorneys should give you a good idea of what being a paralegal is all about. A common thread that runs through all of the commentary is that paralegal work is interesting and exciting and also offers the opportunity to develop skills and increase one's career options.

What Is a Paralegal?

The American Bar Association has defined a *paralegal,* or *legal assistant,* as:

[A] person, qualified through education, training, or work experience, who is employed or retained by a lawyer, law office, governmental agency, or other entity in a capacity or function which involves the performance, under the ultimate direction and supervision of an attorney, of specifically designated substantive legal work, which work, for the most part, requires a sufficient knowledge of legal concepts that, absent such assistant, the attorney would perform the task.

The National Association of Legal Assistants (NALA) has defined the role of the paralegal as follows:

Under the supervision of a lawyer, the legal assistant shall apply knowledge of law and legal procedures in rendering direct assistance to lawyers, clients and courts; design, develop and modify procedures, techniques, services and processes; prepare and interpret legal documents; detail procedures for practicing in certain fields of law; research, select, assess, compile and use information from the law library and other references; and analyze and handle procedures and problems that involve independent decisions.

The National Federation of Paralegal Associations (NFPA) defines the term *paralegal,* or *legal assistant,* as follows:

[A] person, qualified through education, training or work experience, to perform substantive legal work that requires knowledge of legal concepts and is customarily, but not exclusively, performed by a lawyer. This person may be retained or employed by a lawyer, law office, governmental agency or other entity, or may be authorized by administrative, statutory, or court authority to perform this work.

As you can see, each of these definitions attempts to be thorough and comprehensive, but they are difficult to apply in reality. Essentially, paralegals are nonlawyers who do legal work. Paralegal work must be performed under the supervision of an attorney; this supervisory requirement gives attorneys the ultimate responsibility for all work the paralegal performs, thus assuring the public of quality service.

A paralegal can perform many of the activities that lawyers have traditionally performed. Generally, paralegals are prohibited from giving legal advice, representing clients in court, or accepting or terminating a case on behalf of a firm. Other than these limitations, which are discussed more fully in Chapter 14, paralegals can perform an almost infinite number of activities and services. (See Figures 1-4, 1-5, and 1-6.)

The challenge for law firms and lawyers who recognize the benefits of integrating paralegals into the legal team is to develop a culture where paralegals are used effectively and recognized and respected as professionals. If lawyers do not respect paralegals and see them merely as secretaries; if roles and duties of paralegals are unclear; if there does not exist a firm-wide effort to use paralegals effectively, it will be difficult for paralegals to make the kind and level of contribution that is possible. If, in contrast, paralegals are used effectively, law firms can increase both the quality and the cost-effectiveness of their services. Approaches to using paralegals effectively include:

- Treating paralegals like professionals rather than clerical workers

- Developing job responsibilities and salary classifications that differentiate paralegals from clerical workers, placing them between support staff and lawyers in salary

FIGURE 1-4 Being a paralegal involves working with computers ...

FIGURE 1-5   ... being detail-oriented with documents ...

- Involving paralegals in client meetings
- Involving paralegals in firm decisions
- Developing orientation and training programs and supporting professional development for paralegals.

FIGURE 1-6   ... and performing legal research.

The Growth and Development of the Paralegal Profession

The paralegal profession began its astronomical growth in the 1970s. Simultaneous with the growth of the paralegal profession—and a possible reason for the growth of the profession—was the rapidly rising cost of legal services. The costs for legal services began to rise due to increased overhead costs for such items as rent, secretarial salaries, health insurance, copying costs, and the costs of upgrading technology in law firms (for instance, installing computer systems). Also, the increased costs of associate salaries greatly impacted the rise in legal costs.

Once legal fees started rising significantly, firms began to look for ways to cut these expenses so that they could continue to provide their clients with excellent legal services at reasonable costs. The alternative became the paralegal, a paraprofessional, like a paramedic, who could do many of the routine tasks performed by attorneys for lower costs. Paralegals could be paid less than attorneys, but could do much of the same work; therefore, the pragmatics of hiring paralegals became clear.

One case from Texas, *Reich v. Page & Addison,* No. 3:91-CV-2655-P (N.D. Tex. 1992), suggests the evolving professionalism of the paralegal profession. That case concerned the status of paralegals as exempt or nonexempt employees. The Department of Labor has classified paralegals as not exempt from the overtime requirements of the Fair Labor Standards Act, a classification that many find demeaning because it does not differentiate paralegals from nonprofessional support staff. In the *Reich* case, however, a jury found that paralegals at the law firm of Page & Addison were given enough discretion and independence such that they should be exempt from the overtime provisions. Although the pocketbooks of the paralegals might have suffered from this opinion, the prestige of paralegals was surely enhanced.

The profession is split over the questions of whether paralegals should receive overtime pay or whether they should be treated as exempt, salaried employees, with the attendant prestige and professionalism that comes from that status. This type of question is characteristic of an evolving profession attempting to find its niche. As the paralegal profession advances into the next century, we expect that paralegal compensation will increase, not through overtime pay, but through the development of compensation programs and packages that acknowledge the emerging professionalism of the paralegal.

Paralegals: A Good Bottom Line

Firms as well as public agencies have realized the economic advantages of using paralegals. Paralegals can do much of the repetitive drafting, research, and document organization ordinarily done by young associates, yet paralegals are less expensive than attorneys. Because paralegal salaries are lower, both the costs to the firm and the costs to the client are reduced. In addition, paralegals free attorney time so that new clients can be cultivated and the firm can expand without adding attorneys.

As you may have read in recent data concerning job growth in the United States, paralegal jobs are projected to increase by 125 percent over the next few years. This growth is due to three factors: first, the increasing cost of providing good legal representation to clients; second, the increased awareness of attorneys of how invaluable and cost-efficient paralegals are; and third, the ability of firms to obtain good, qualified, and trained paralegal candidates who have had a formal education in paralegal studies.

There are two factors to keep in mind in order to take advantage of these employment opportunities. First, attorneys are generally very poor people managers. Second, attorneys have not been taught in law school how to effectively use a paralegal. By recognizing these realities, you can work productively with them, rather than become frustrated by them.

To deal with the fact that most attorneys are poor people managers, one must understand that attorneys have been educated not to be intuitive, like social workers or psychologists, but rather to be detail- and fact-oriented. When dealing with attorneys, present your conclusions and be sure to support them with facts. (See Figure 1-7.)

The lack of training on how to utilize paralegals is, for the most part, the burden of paralegals. Naturally, many firms already recognize the value of paralegals and have developed effective training programs. However, many attorneys still do not know how to use legal assistants effectively. By training the attorneys you work with as to how to use your skills, your job will not only be

FIGURE 1-7 A paralegal discusses details of a case with her supervising attorney.

CASE STUDY   **THE GROWTH OF THE PARALEGAL PROFESSION**

As you have learned thus far in your paralegal education, paralegals are capable of doing most of the work attorneys do except for highly specialized professional areas like giving legal advice or representing clients in judicial proceedings. The following example illustrates how paralegals have helped keep legal fees reasonable.

Michael West, the president of Bagby Manufacturing Company, wants to incorporate his company. Mr. West goes to the firm of Brown, Smith & Jones, where Mr. West has most of his legal work done. The firm does the incorporation and sends Mr. West the following bill:

Brown, Smith & Jones
Attorneys at Law
3736 Broad Street
Somerset, New Jersey 12200
Telephone: (908) 555-1212
Facsimile No.: (908) 555-1213

INVOICE FOR LEGAL SERVICES

To: Mr. Michael West
Bagby Manufacturing Company
323 Plantation Avenue
Somerset, New Jersey 12200

RE: Incorporation of Bagby Manufacturing Company
Our File No. 96-245

DATE	DESCRIPTION OF WORK PERFORMED	ATTY	RATE	HRS.	TOTAL
1–30–96	Draft Articles of Incorp.	HHB	$200.00	2.5	$500.00
2–3–96	Research: tax consequences	TMS	$150.00	3.0	$450.00
2–6–96	Revise Articles of Incorp.	HHB	$200.00	1.5	$300.00
2–8–96	File Articles w/Secy of State; travel to and from Secy of State's Office	HHB	$200.00	2.0	$400.00

TOTAL AMOUNT DUE: $1,650.00

Mr. West is quite upset by the enormity of the legal bill incurred for the fairly simple incorporation he wanted. He decides never to use the firm of Brown, Smith & Jones again because his bill was, he felt, too much. However, much of the work done by Mr. Brown could have been done by a paralegal, which would have greatly reduced Mr. West's bill. Compare the first bill with the following bill, in which a paralegal, John Stills, did a significant portion of the work on the case.

Brown, Smith & Jones
Attorneys at Law
3736 Broad Street
Somerset, New Jersey 12200
Telephone: (908) 555-1212
Facsimile No.: (908) 555-1213

INVOICE FOR LEGAL SERVICES

To: Mr. Michael West
      Bagby Manufacturing Company
      323 Plantation Avenue
      Somerset, New Jersey 12200

RE: Incorporation of Bagby Manufacturing Company
      Our File No. 96-245

DATE	DESCRIPTION OF WORKPERFORMED	ATTY	PL	RATE	HRS.	TOTAL
1–30–96	Draft Articles of Incorp.		JS	$ 50.00	3.0	$150.00
2–3–96	Research: tax consequences	TMS		$150.00	3.0	$450.00
2–6–96	Revise Articles of Incorp.	HHB		$200.00	1.5	$300.00
2–8–96	File Articles w/Secy of State; travel to and from Secy of State's Office		JS	$ 50.00	2.0	$100.00

TOTAL AMOUNT DUE: $1,000.00

With John's assistance, all of the necessary work was completed, but the client was much happier, for his bill was cut by almost a half. Obviously, the pragmatic effects of paralegals will keep the paralegal profession a growing and thriving one.

---

more challenging, but your marketability and success will also be significantly increased. To train your attorneys, you must be assertive but not abusive. You cannot always ask the attorney to define the parameters of your job, but must define them for yourself. This means you must thoroughly understand what a paralegal can and cannot do and must master the skills you have learned through your paralegal education.

As the preceding billing example in the case study indicated, one major way for legal assistants to contribute to the success of the firm is by making a positive impact on the bottom line: profitability. As an additional example of the significance of this impact, consider this scenario. If a matter takes 17 hours, with some delegation to paralegals, the matter might be billed as follows:

12 attorney hours @ $160/hr.	=	$1,920
5 paralegal hours @ $60/hr.	=	300
TOTAL	=	$2,220

With greater delegation, and allowing for increased time because of the delegation, it might look like this:

5 attorney hours @ $160/hr.	=	$ 800
15 paralegal hours @ $60/hr.	=	900
TOTAL	=	$1,700

As you look at this analysis, you can clearly see a substantial savings to the client, which is plain good business—but note also the hidden opportunities for increased revenue, which come from two sources. First, the firm in the example could raise attorney rates without increasing the cost to the client. Second, spending five rather than twelve lawyer hours on a case enables the lawyer to handle more cases, thereby increasing the overall revenue of the firm.

In a fixed-fee case, the savings provided by legal assistants can also be dramatic. Suppose that it takes one hour to draft a revised will, the fixed charge for which is $200. Using the rates from the example, the profit if the attorney does the work is $40, but if the paralegal does it, the profit is $140, more than three times as much. These examples should convince you of the many economic advantages flowing from effective use of paralegals in the law office.

One additional way in which paralegals can make a significant positive impact on the firm's bottom line is through client relations. As we mentioned earlier, many attorneys are essentially analytical, rather than humanistic, in their approach. This is a natural and expected phenomenon, as legal training emphasizes analytical skills. However, it tends to create a situation where attorneys' client development and maintenance skills are not as developed as their legal skills. This creates an opportunity for the paralegal to make an impact by doing things to make the client feel comfortable and cared for. Of course, what the paralegal does to foster client relations must be approved by the supervising attorney, but paralegals can certainly attend to clients and client communications and interactions in a way that makes the attorney's clients feel well cared for. If clients stay with a firm in part due to the efforts of the paralegals, that is clear evidence of legal assistants' effect on the firm's profitability.

In this vein, consider the findings of the American Society for Quality Control (ASQC), based on its 1995 study of why companies lose customers or clients. The study showed that:

4% of the clients die or move away

5% of the clients are influenced by friends to change

9% of the clients are lured away by the competition

14% of the clients are dissatisfied with the product or service

68% of the clients changed because of the indifference of company employees; clients did not like the way they were treated

If law firms are to become more businesslike in their approach, they will need to learn from the experience of other businesses, and the lesson of the ASQC survey is clear: to keep your clients and customers, you have to care for and nurture their loyalty through commitment and involvement. It is not only the attorney who can do the kinds of things and act in the kind of way that promotes client development and loyalty. All members of the legal team can play a big part in this important process, and paralegals can make an especially important contribution because of their frequent interaction with clients. By treating clients well, all of the employees of the law firm can increase and solidify their value to the firm, as well as assist the firm in its efforts to remain both successful and profitable.

Paralegal Activities

As previously discussed, paralegals are capable of doing an almost limitless amount of legal work. The three strict exceptions, which are discussed in more detail in Chapter 14, are representing clients in court, giving legal advice, and accepting or declining cases. Beyond these three prohibitions, the parameters that delineate the work of the paralegal are tremendously flexible. The following list is not conclusive, but is an attempt to give you some idea of the specific things a paralegal can do in the legal process.

1. Draft discovery responses, such as interrogatories, requests for production of documents, and requests for admission.
2. Draft complaints and answers.
3. Set up, summarize, and attend depositions.
4. Interview witnesses.
5. Locate witnesses.
6. Locate assets.

7. Organize file materials.
8. Prepare trial notebooks and oral argument notebooks.
9. Attend trials.
10. Summarize and analyze data received in response to discovery requests.
11. Attend Section 341 hearings in bankruptcy court to question the debtor.
12. Draft bankruptcy petitions.
13. Draft articles of incorporation and minutes of the meetings of stockholders.
14. Perform title examinations (see Figure 1-8).
15. Draft documents for real estate closings.
16. Perform legal research.
17. Draft wills and codicils.
18. Prepare documents for the probating of wills.
19. Draft visa and citizenship papers.
20. Explain to clients how the legal process pertaining to their particular problem works.

Although this list is by no means all-inclusive, it will give you an idea of the tasks routinely performed by paralegals. Practically, the percentage of legal work that must be done exclusively by an attorney is very small. This fact, combined with the large number of tasks paralegals can perform, should leave you assured that the paralegal profession is not only a challenging field but a growing one as well.

FIGURE 1-8 Paralegals must often go to the courthouse for various tasks.

To take advantage of the growth of the paralegal profession and the opportunities available to paralegals generally, you will want your work to be characterized by a high degree of excellence and professionalism. Remember that it is the attorney who bears the ultimate responsibility for his or her staff's work, and that the work that goes out under the attorney's name is a reflection on the attorney. The more an attorney trusts you to do professional work, the greater will be the amount and variety of activities and level of responsibility that you receive.

Specialization of Paralegals

Just like lawyers, paralegals are beginning to specialize. Although the various paralegal specializations have many things in common—namely, the parameters of their work defined by ethics—the exact tasks each type of paralegal performs is unique to that specialty. For example, all paralegals draft legal documents, but the types of documents drafted by each specialty varies. Litigation paralegals draft motions, complaints, answers, and discovery, whereas paralegals specializing in the probate/estate planning area draft wills, codicils, and trust documents. Thus, all types of paralegals draft documents, communicate with clients, do research, and generally assist the attorneys. However, it is elementary to becoming a successful paralegal to learn the particularities of the area in which you specialize.

Legal Administrators and Paralegal Coordinators

Although *law office management* refers to the skills and abilities required by all workers in an office environment, there do exist specific positions in law firms which have the management of the law office as their explicit function. The position most commonly established in law firms to meet this management need is that of *law office administrator,* also called *law office manager* or *paralegal coordinator.*

Law Office Administrator

A law office administrator, like any office administrator, is primarily responsible for the day-to-day and long-term administrative operations of an organization. By handling administrative, personnel, and other related matters, law office administrators liberate attorneys to do what they do best—practice law and delegate the administrative and operations functions of the law office.

Note that in law firms there are actually two kinds of management: practice management and operations management. *Practice management,* which is not the focus of this book, refers to the type of legal work a firm performs. Practice management refers to the mix of types of legal work and types of clients that the firm takes; literally speaking, it is the management of the type of practice the firm pursues.

Operations management refers to the entirety of administrative, organizational, and technological systems, processes, and applications that a firm uses to run its business. As its name suggests, operations management concerns the management of the operation of a law firm. It is this type of management which is the focus of this book and the type of management in which all legal assistants can expect to be involved. The law office administrator or manager would be in charge of all aspects of operations management.

The National Association of Legal Administrators (NALA) is a national organization that provides training and support for law office managers. The Legal Assistant Management Association (LAMA), with national headquarters in Overland Park, Kansas, provides similar services for legal assistants who are in management positions in law firms.

Law office administrators come from a wide variety of backgrounds, but most have experience as managers, accountants, legal secretaries, or paralegals. Certainly all who choose the career path of law office administration have excellent communication skills, are highly organized, delegate and supervise well, plan effectively, manage time efficiently, and can work productively with all types of people to achieve results.

Paralegal Coordinator

The role of a paralegal coordinator, sometimes called a legal assistant manager, is multifaceted and is particularly important in firms where a significant number of paralegals are on staff. This position need not be added at the cost of a new employee, but rather can be assigned to an existing, experienced, senior paralegal or attorney who will become directly involved with allocation of work assignments, training, and utilization. The coordinator must be someone who believes in the paralegal approach to completing the work product and is interested in the professional development of the firm's paralegals. The coordinator must also be supportive, sympathetic, and willing to spend the time necessary to "champion" the group.

Paralegal coordinators possess supervisory responsibility for the work performance and development of paralegals within the firm. In some firms, the coordinator is also responsible for hiring and recruiting activities, such as placing advertisements in newspapers; direct contact with paralegal schools; screening and interviewing candidates; checking references; and making recommendations to the person who is actually in charge of hiring.

The coordinator should also be forward-thinking and make it a practice to educate the firm's attorneys on how best to utilize and benefit from their paralegals. In addition, he or she must keep a keen eye on the volume and quality of work performed by each paralegal and constantly work with the group on professional development. Seminar notices should be reviewed constantly and recommendations made as to who should attend.

Most likely, the Human Resources Department will call upon the coordinator to submit written performance evaluations of each paralegal when it is time for performance review. In each instance, the coordinator must remain professional, honest, and candid.

Some firms choose not to have a paralegal coordinator but instead to develop a committee, sometimes called a *paralegal review committee,* comprised of attorneys, the Human Resource Director, and any other involved individuals. The committee takes on the activities and responsibilities noted for a coordinator, as well as salary administration, performance evaluation, grievance hearings, and employee discipline and termination. A firm with a paralegal review committee is generally committed to a strong paralegal program, and will use this committee to provide a forum for communication about issues relevant to the paralegals, such as work environment, billable hours, work flow, or work allocation. The committee may also give feedback to paralegals about their work performance. Additionally, the paralegal review committee may develop continuing education programs on relevant topics.

Freelance Paralegals

Some paralegals choose not to work as full-time employees in a law firm, corporation, or governmental agency, and instead work on an as-needed basis. This approach to being a paralegal is cost-effective for the organization and flexible for the individual. As long as the paralegal's work is being supervised by an attorney, there are no ethical problems with this arrangement. However, when a paralegal performs work that requires a licensed attorney, the paralegal might be engaging in the unauthorized practice of law.

Some people believe that certain tasks should be reserved for lawyers, who are licensed and regulated professionals, citing protection of the public as the primary reason. Others argue that lawyers should not have an economic monopoly and that lawyers have not fulfilled their obligation to provide legal representation for the lower economic class. They also argue that there are a number of areas of the law where paralegals can perform at least as competently, and probably less expensively, than lawyers. You will learn more about this issue in a detailed study of the unauthorized practice of law in your legal ethics class.

Several states are experimenting with permitting various types of exceptions to the unauthorized practice of law doctrine. Paralegals who act as independent contractors are attempting to carve out a niche for paralegals to perform activities that up to now have been reserved for attorneys. These paralegals call themselves *freelance paralegals, independent paralegals,* or *legal technicians.* One approach to the use of freelance paralegals allows them to perform standard procedures in areas such as divorce or probate. Another tends to allow the work if it is motivated by an authentic desire to bring legal services to those who otherwise could not afford it. One of the challenges for the legal community is to find ways to utilize the knowledge and abilities of these freelance paralegals without jeopardizing the quality of legal services provided to the public.

Paralegal Associations and Organizations

There are two national paralegal associations, the National Federation of Paralegal Associations (NFPA) and the National Association of Legal Assistants (NALA). NFPA consists of a group of paralegal organizations throughout the country, whereas NALA is an organization of individual legal assistants nationwide. Both organizations are oriented toward advancing the legal profession. NALA favors certification for paralegals and provides a Certified Legal Assistant (CLA) and Certified Legal Assistant Specialist (CLAS) program culminating in certification. In contrast, NFPA does not have an overall certification program, but believes that paralegals should have primary control for the creation and development of standards for the paralegal profession. To that end, NFPA supports limited licensing as well as direct service by paralegals in specialized fields. Each organization has its own committee structure and provides seminars, newsletters, salary surveys, and job placement assistance. For more information, you can contact the organizations at the following addresses:

National Federation of Paralegal Associations
P.O. Box 33108
Kansas City, MO 64114
Telephone: (816) 941-4000

National Association of Legal Assistants
1420 South Utica
Tulsa, OK 74014
Telephone: (918) 587-6828

The Complete Paralegal

Because most of the preparation to become a paralegal and the visible work of most paralegals concerns doing legal work, it is tempting to believe that paralegals need only legal skills to perform their work. This is only a partial view of being a paralegal. One of the main ideas of this book, and a concept that you should embrace in your quest to be successful, is that paralegals perform work in an environment and in a context. That context demands that the successful paralegal combine organizational, administrative, and business skills with legal skills to fulfill the demands of being a complete paralegal. Figure 1-9 gives you a visual image of the complete paralegal.

As you can see, the complete paralegal combines four major skill areas. First, *legal skills,* such as research, writing, and analysis, are required. Second, *business skills* are required. These refer to an understanding of law firm economics, billable hours, and profitability. Business skills also extend to group dynamics, communication skills, and marketing activities, as well as any activities that may contribute to the image of the firm. *Technical skills* refer to the ability to use computers and technology effectively and efficiently; as you will see, law offices make many varied uses and applications of modern technology. Finally, the complete paralegal has to have *administrative and organizational skills* to be able to prioritize and account for work that is accomplished and to avoid errors that might lead to claims of malpractice against the firm.

By having this broader, more complete view of what it means to be a successful paralegal, you will have the most accurate view of the work that paralegals perform. You will thereby be well prepared to make a significant and positive contribution to the organization or firm in which you work.

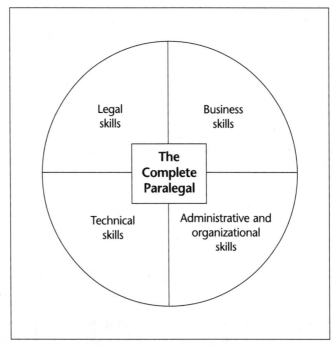

FIGURE 1-9 The complete paralegal combines four major skill areas.

Working in the Legal Field

As we conclude this introduction to the work of the paralegal, it is important to emphasize an obvious but frequently overlooked point: being a paralegal enables you to work in the legal profession, a profession that is intellectually challenging, socially productive, and personally rewarding. Few fields offer as many opportunities for performing satisfying, valuable work as does the law. As a member of the legal services team, you will experience many of the positive and pleasurable aspects of working in the legal profession. It is important to acknowledge and appreciate that working in the legal profession is both challenging and fulfilling, and that the people who work in the legal profession are, for the most part, intelligent, caring, dedicated professionals.

The following guest editorial by attorney Saul Cohen is a light look at some of the pleasures that come from working in the legal field. Naturally, his perspective is that of an attorney, but most of the positive factors he cites are experienced by many nonlawyers who work in the legal profession.

G U E S T   E D I T O R I A L

The Pleasures of Law Practice

Saul Cohen

Saul Cohen is a partner in the Albuquerque and Santa Fe, N.M., law firm of Sutin, Thayer & Browne. This article is reprinted with the permission of the Bar Bulletin *of the State Bar of New Mexico.*

So much has been written lately about the pain of law practice. Surveys show lawyer dissatisfaction with their careers to be widespread and large numbers of lawyers who would change careers if they could. Aggravation with clients or opposing counsel is commonplace and malpractice suits multiply.

Are there no pleasures in the practice of law? It seems to me that there are and I have tried to list some in no particular order:

Being with other lawyers, a good bunch on the whole.

The challenge of wrestling with a difficult problem and solving it.

Following through on a line of inquiry without knowing where it will lead.

Being a champion for someone who is unable to fight his or her own battle.

Helping someone to make his or her dream come true.

The compliment implied in being asked to act as an arbitrator or mediator.

Being asked by a lawyer or firm to represent them.

Finding the right case, one on all fours with your case, is a particular source of pleasure. If it's an opinion by an important court, or even the Supreme Court, so much the better.

Having a colleague ask you a question and being able to refer her to the exact case or statutory provision she needs.

Giving good advice to clients is always a satisfaction, especially when you know you are giving good advice, and even more so when the client knows you are giving good advice.

Being told by clients that regardless of the result, they are pleased with the job you did.

Being told that the law is against you, but checking the Supplement or the Pocket-Part and finding that the law has been changed and that the change applies to your case.

Reviewing an associate's pleading and suggesting changes that improve it markedly.

Coming up with a creative solution to break an impasse at which all parties were facing enormous expense and stress.

Hearing the judge say that your motion is granted, any motion, although summary judgment is best. The simple fact is that winning is better.

Waiting for the jury to bring in its verdict, and then having them walk in with several jurors looking at you and smiling.

Knowing that the argument you just made was a good argument.

Being told that "that was the best oral argument we've ever heard," or, "that was the best brief ever filed with this court" (this hasn't happened yet).

Negotiating a settlement when your client would have been willing to pay more or accept less.

When you convey the bad news that the case has been lost and your client says, "That's the way it goes sometimes; there's no point in our aggravating ourselves."

Telling people what you do for a living, although this pleasure seems to be fading slightly in today's world.

Being your own boss, independent, a professional.

Getting a substantial new client with an interesting case and the ability to pay a substantial retainer when you are sitting at your desk wondering if anyone will ever call again.

Being told that some client had spoken very highly of you, or that someone said you handled a matter brilliantly, or that your reputation was certainly good.

Making a substantial contribution to your community.

The Payment Principle

Prompt payment is a pleasure. Prompt payment with a note saying the services were worth twice as much is an even greater pleasure.

Other pleasures: Sending a bill to a client's office and sending him a copy in England where he is working so that he will know what is happening, and receiving two checks within the next 10 days. Sending a bill to a client and having it returned with note saying this bill is obviously in error, please send a new statement for x-amount, x being substantially more than the amount you billed. (This actually happened to me once, in 38 years of practice.)

Back in the days when we billed only when the job was done, and not with ongoing monthly statements, I was asked by a client what he owed me at the conclusion of the first matter that I had handled for him, which took approximately eight months. I pulled out the prepared bill. (Time records were not customarily used in those days, but simply a narrative statement of the services performed.) The bill was for $7,500.

The client did not look happy, and I asked if anything was wrong. He told me it was larger than he anticipated. I said I valued him as a client, wanted him to be happy, and was more concerned with our future relationship than the money involved, and he could send me any amount whatsoever and it would be accepted as payment in full. He said he would discuss the matter with his board of directors (composed of his wife, daughter, son-in-law, secretary and plant manager.)

He called me a couple of weeks later and said he had asked the board, all of whom were familiar with the work I had done, to write on a piece of paper what they thought a fair fee would be. He told me that each of them had written a higher figure than the actual bill and so he was simply paying the bill. We had a long and fruitful relationship until his untimely death.

Dealing with lawyers, dealing with clients, using your skills to help others, doing a good job, having your good work recognized—these are not small pleasures.   ▐▌▐▌

The Work of the Paralegal: A Summary

The paralegal profession is continually growing and changing. You are at the frontier of a new, exciting profession. By immersing yourself in your education, determining what type of legal environment is best suited to you, and continuing to grow professionally, you will become a leader in the world of legal assistants. The types of jobs and personalities involved in the paralegal profession are compatible with all the varieties of personalities who attend paralegal school. By understanding yourself and understanding the varieties of environments in the legal process, you will best be able to find a position compatible with your needs.

Key Terms

freelance paralegal
independent paralegal
LAMA
law office administrator
National Association of Legal
  Administrators (NALA)
National Association of Legal Assistants
  (NALA)

National Federation of Paralegal
  Associations (NFPA)
operations management
paralegal activities
paralegal coordinator
paralegal specializations
practice management

Problems and Activities

1. Interview one or two paralegals to learn about their activities.

2. Generate a list of possible paralegal specializations. Begin to learn what each involves with an eye towards choosing an area of interest for yourself.

3. Write to both the national and state paralegal associations and get information on membership and services offered.

4. Interview several paralegals who are not employed at law firms. Find out the advantages and disadvantages of being employed in a nontraditional legal environment.

CHAPTER 2

MALPRACTICE AVOIDANCE THROUGH LAW OFFICE SYSTEMS

OBJECTIVES

By the completion of this chapter, you should:

- understand the idea of malpractice and the importance of malpractice avoidance;

- understand the major areas in law office management where malpractice issues are most likely to arise;

- understand how systems in law firms can contribute to malpractice avoidance; and

- understand how to handle situations that might result in a malpractice claim.

What Is Malpractice?

Ballentine's Law Dictionary defines *malpractice* as "the violation of a professional duty to act with reasonable care and good faith without fraud or collusion." Essentially, this means that malpractice is committed when a professional's work falls below the standards to which she is held by the profession and the community. It is a way of protecting the public from those whose lack of skill, training, or diligence might cause harm to their clients. In the legal context, malpractice might occur when the legal professional—the lawyer or the paralegal—fails to apply those principles of professional conduct, learned in school, or through experience, and a client is damaged because of that failure. For example, if a client's claim was barred because suit had not been filed within the statute of limitations, the client was injured because of counsel's failure to perform her job properly. A malpractice claim might well follow.

It is generally the lawyer, not the paralegal, who can be found liable for malpractice. The attorney is the state-licensed practitioner, under direct control of state rules; the attorney is also able to get malpractice insurance, which assures that clients who become victims of attorney incompetence or error can receive compensation for their injuries. Although liability has been imputed to a paralegal in some situations, it is the attorney who generally has to answer a malpractice suit.

The lawyer might be directly liable because of her own action or inaction, or the lawyer might be liable on a theory of vicarious liability for the negligent acts of others. Under the theory of vicarious liability, also known as *respondeat superior,* the principal is responsible for the acts of her agents because she is required to train and supervise their work. A lawyer, therefore, can be found liable for the negligent acts or omissions of a paralegal.

Malpractice is clearly behavior to be avoided. Not merely is your client or your firm injured when you commit malpractice, but you and your career will be severely affected, for even the allegation of malpractice can cloud your professional life for many years. Should one be charged and found guilty of malpractice, there are possible criminal and civil penalties. Thus, a paralegal who commits malpractice could be subject to the revocation of her license, if the jurisdiction in which she practices licenses paralegals, or even imprisonment or fines. She might become a defendant in a lawsuit, and her job would surely be jeopardized. Without question, the consequences of malpractice are significant.

Although malpractice—behavior that falls below the standards of acceptable conduct—occurs frequently, it can nonetheless be avoided. By using the systems set forth in this book, you can take a significant step toward avoiding behaviors and practices that frequently set the stage for allegations of malpractice. Systems are implemented by law firms not only to effectively manage the business of practicing law, but also to prevent malpractice. For example, by using standard accounting procedures, the firm can be certain that client escrow funds are not deposited in the firm's regular operating account, thus opening the firm to the allegation of misappropriation of client funds.

Each chapter in this book introduces you to an area in which mistakes or negligence might open you up to an allegation of malpractice. By understanding how malpractice relates to each area, and by applying the systems and techniques discussed in each chapter, you will appreciate how using systems in law firms not only contributes to organization and efficiency in performing legal work, but also contributes to malpractice avoidance. Developing an understanding of the importance of malpractice prevention and a commitment to using systems designed to prevent malpractice claims will also help you define yourself as an ethical and effective professional.

The following hypothetical situation illustrates how the failure to use systems in the practice of law can lead to disastrous results.

The Case of the Negligent Paralegal

Jessica is a litigation paralegal with a large metropolitan firm that has offices throughout the United States and Canada. She is in charge of the documents to be used in a huge case involving alleged patent and trademark infringement. As part of her job, she must docket all documents; ensure that documents covered by the attorney-client privilege are not released to opposing parties; keep all documents organized and readily accessible; ensure that when responding to requests for the production of documents, only those specific portions of documents are released; and ensure that her client's account is properly reimbursed when the opposing party pays for copies of documents. Additionally, because this case is so highly sensitive, due to the trade secret and patent information involved, Jessica is subject to a gag order issued by the United States District Court for the Northern District of Kentucky. This gag order provides that no person except the judge and those individuals specifically listed in the order may view the documents; the listed individuals are to keep the information totally confidential or they will be subject to contempt charges by the court.

The attorneys and legal assistants in the firm's New York and Los Angeles offices are helping with the case. It is common practice for documents to be faxed between these offices. Jessica has been asked by one of the attorneys in the New York office to fax the patent for the machine at issue in the case. It is ordinary office policy for all faxes to be accompanied by a cover sheet stating the following: "The information contained herein is covered by the attorney-client privilege and is confidential and privileged information. The information is intended for the attention of the addressed person ONLY." In her haste to send the patent to the New York attorney, Jessica does not attach a cover sheet to the document and merely writes at the top of the copy of the patent "To Attorney A from Jessica." Little does Jessica know that the patent is being faxed not to the New York offices of her firm, but to the offices of the opposing party's counsel, where the attorney from her firm is taking a deposition. The fax is obtained by a secretary not covered in the protective order, whose husband has a manufacturing company that manufactures machines used in the same industry as the machine covered in the patent. The secretary makes copies of the fax before taking it to Attorney A and takes it home to her husband.

On this very same day, Jessica receives a check from the opposing party's law firm for copies of documents that her firm produced in response to a request for production of documents. The check is for $5,000. While chatting on the telephone with her best friend Paige, Jessica makes out a deposit slip for the check. Because the check is for the reimbursement of copying expenses, it should be deposited in the client's escrow account, so that when the client is billed for the copies, the client can see that opposing counsel reimbursed the firm for the expenses. This amount should be taken by the firm from the escrow account. Jessica subsequently takes the check and the deposit slip not to Accounting, the normal procedure in the firm, but to a courier known for his $5,000-per-day crack habit. Needless to say, the check does not make it to Accounting.

Because the case that Jessica is working on is covered by a gag order, all word processing for the case is done by two individuals, Maxine and Lula, and is coded so that access is limited. These two individuals also do work on hundreds of other cases, so they must be told when something should have limited access or when it should be on the network for the use of the entire firm in all cities. The firm uses a special form to indicate to Maxine and Lula when "limited access" is to be attached to a document. Jessica is working on a status memo to her supervising attorney and asks Maxine to transcribe her dictation, but does not tell Maxine that the document should be coded for limited access, and fails in her haste to use the proper form to indicate that access should be limited on the document. Every individual in the firm has a terminal on his or her desk, so information is freely passed from one to another.

Maxine finishes the memo and puts it on the firm's network, sending an electronic mail (e-mail) message to Jessica's attorney to look at the memo. It just so happens that the lead attorney for the opposing party is in Jessica's boss's office and sees the e-mail message on the screen. Knowing that the memo could really help his case, he accesses the document (the word processing equipment is just like the equipment used in his firm) and reads it, taking careful notes. All this is completed by the time Jessica's boss returns to the office from a confidential telephone call in another room.

Because of Jessica's failure to apply the systems set in place in her firm for telecommunications, accounting, and word processing, her duty of total confidentiality of information has been breached. She has not only violated office policy, but has also broken the attorney-client privilege doctrine and violated the provisions of the court's gag order, setting up the firm for potential contempt charges.

Even though these are extremely serious breaches of her duties as a legal professional, they could have been avoided by applying the established systems in her office. These systems, which provide the framework and foundation for effective, ethical legal representation, must be established and used by all legal professionals if they are to avoid malpractice. This is one of the most important contributions of paralegals to a successful law firm. Although paralegals will generally not be held directly liable for malpractice, paralegals are directly involved with many activities that, if performed negligently, might result in a malpractice claim. Paralegals are therefore able to contribute in a major way to the duty of the legal team to provide efficient, professional legal help.

In the following sections, you will learn how malpractice might arise while using the various systems in a law firm and how to avoid allegations of malpractice by dealing systematically with law office activities.

Malpractice Avoidance Across the Legal Spectrum

The possibilities for malpractice exist in all phases of legal work, many of which the paralegal performs. The effective paralegal will therefore become sensitized to the types of acts, or omissions, which might occur in all phases of paralegal activities. The following overview introduces you to various aspects of law office management and how an understanding of malpractice relates to that area. In each of the following chapters, the theme of malpractice avoidance is picked up in the "On Point" features, which give case examples of malpractice and its avoidance. Taken together, these discussions of malpractice avoidance will prepare you to deal effectively with this important and serious aspect of law office management.

Malpractice and Marketing

Marketing refers to the activities undertaken by a law firm to generate business. Under First Amendment law, marketing, which is a form of commercial speech, is permissible unless it is untruthful or deceptive. However, marketing and advertising by attorneys has its own history. Formerly, most states barred attorney advertising because it was considered unprofessional and undignified; also, fears of attorney overreaching or intimidation fueled moves to place limits on attorney advertising.

Today, state bar associations promulgate rules and guidelines to establish the parameters for ethical advertising and marketing of professional services. Law firms can avoid unethical solicitation through the development of good business practices that do not violate ethical guidelines concerning solicitation.

In general, attorneys and their agents may attempt to develop business unless their solicitation involves face-to-face or telephone communication. In those areas, attorneys are limited, and they are also limited if their advertising is false, misleading, or deceptive. For example, an attorney or his agent, a paralegal, cannot go to the welfare office handing out cards and asking people about to file for bankruptcy to hire the attorney as their lawyer. Attorneys cannot go to a funeral home or the emergency room of a hospital soliciting clients, but they certainly can offer classes, send out brochures, or receive referrals. Naturally, any advertisement regarding legal services must be truthful. An attorney cannot advertise that she will represent a client for no cost, even if there is a contingency fee arrangement, because there are court costs and other fees that the client must pay. Apart from these restrictions, attorneys have a great deal of latitude in how they attract business.

The potential problem of improper marketing techniques that violate ethical considerations can be avoided by developing a comprehensive marketing plan that has been analyzed for ethical concerns and is followed by everyone in the firm. By developing and following a comprehensive plan, it is unlikely that the firm's marketing efforts could be regarded as solicitation. It is when firm members do not follow a thoroughly researched marketing plan that the question of solicitation arises. Chapter 4 discusses the systems necessary for a successful marketing plan. However, at this point, it is imperative to realize that these systems are necessary to ensure that marketing of the business of law will not be considered malpractice.

Malpractice and Accounting

The vast majority of malpractice and ethical complaints against attorneys are filed by clients who have had their money embezzled by attorneys. A fundamental ethical principle for attorneys and paralegals is that client funds must be kept separate from the attorney's money and must also be accounted for accurately and completely. Therefore, one must learn and use a structured accounting system so that there will be no possibility that a client's funds will be commingled with either the funds of the firm or those of the attorney.

Of course, funds that belong solely to the client must be kept in a separate account and be accounted for accurately (see Figure 2-1). In addition, any monies that a client pays for the legal services offered by the attorney must also be accurately accounted for. For instance, if a client has hired an attorney for representation in four matters, the check that comes in to pay for those cases must be posted to the correct accounts. If inaccurate accounting procedures are used, the client might question the attorney's ethics or competence, and that client is probably lost. Accurate accounting of income must also take into consideration specialized reporting procedures, such as those governing cash payments of more than $10,000. In some cash payment situations, an attorney must complete and file federal Form 8300, indicating responses to all requested information. If you are responsible for bookkeeping functions, you will need to be aware of these special procedures, some of which may be unique to your jurisdiction.

Additionally, mishandling client funds by depositing them in improper accounts can lead to problems with the local bar association. Many bar associations require that trust accounts be interest-bearing and that the interest be forwarded directly to the bar for the indigent defense fund or other bar activities. If the proper monies are not deposited in these accounts, or the interest is not forwarded to the bar, ethical violations as well as possible malpractice issues will arise.

Malpractice and Time Management

All legal activities occur within a framework of time. Court dates must be adhered to; causes of action must be commenced in a timely fashion; responses to discovery must comply with time requirements; even opening statements in a trial must comply with the time limitations established by the court. Additionally, the actual practice of law can be hectic and stressful—everyone always seems to be in a time crunch—and learning to prioritize activities and manage time effectively is an absolute necessity.

There are a number of habits to develop to manage time effectively and avoid an error or omission that could create liability for the firm. Developing and using a tickler system, for example, is crucial for keeping track of important dates and times. Learning to prioritize, keep good records, set goals, and calendar effectively are all essential to the avoidance of malpractice. (See Figure 2-2.)

It is also unethical to provide inaccurate or inflated time records. By using the methods for keeping accurate time records set forth in Chapter 7, you are unlikely ever to run into this problem. However, in firms that require a minimum annual billing figure for paralegals, it is a real temptation to pad your hours. Situations that should be avoided include adding the time for your personal telephone calls to the time billed for a client. Although it is unlikely that you will be caught, inflating your time records not only is unethical and unprofessional, but also makes you appear less efficient than you actually are.

```
REPORT DATE    02/29/91                    Bachman, Wilson & Juris                        PAGE  1
REPORT NUMBER TA161-000056          TRUST ACCOUNT BANK BALANCE REPORT
SORTED BY BANK                            Third American Bank                        PRINTED BY TDD
RANGE SELECTED: 02/01/91 TO 02/12/91
```

TRANS DATE	CLIENT MATTER REPORTING NAME	CHECK NUMBER	BALANCE	RECEIPTS AMOUNT	DISBURSEMENTS AMOUNT	ADJUSTMENT AMOUNT
02/01/91	BEGINNING BALANCE		.00			
02/11/91 000100 00004	Abbey Industries 1985 IRS Received from client for potential IRS liability		1,892.00	1,892.00		
000150 00003	Fischer, Schrebenski vs. Received from client		21,892.00	20,000.00		
02/12/91 000150 00003	Fischer, Schrebenski vs. Patient # 45925-87 Invoice 4601 Medical Bills for Mr. Schrebinski Methodist Hospital 2201 Church Street Nashville, TN 37210	010026	20,360.00		1,532.00	
	Police Report #87-12884 Metropolitan Police Department P.O. Box 9999 Franklin, TN 37064-9999	010027	20,320.00		40.00	
	Disbursed to plaintiff Harold R. Schrebenski c/o Ardman, Phillips & Clay, P.C. 600 Lewisburg Pike, Suite 600 Franklin, TN 37064	010028	1,892.00		18,428.00	
	BANK TOTALS		1,892.00	21,892.00	20,000.00	.00

FIGURE 2-1 Trust account bank balance report assures that the firm has handled client funds accurately and ethically.

FIGURE 2-2 Effective time management is crucial in avoiding malpractice claims.

Malpractice and Records Management

Every client and every issue undertaken by a law firm must be effectively documented (see Figure 2-3). The files and records established by a law firm in the representation of its clients must be managed effectively because they form the written record of the legal representation undertaken. Documents are the cornerstone of the practice of law; development and maintenance of effective records management systems are critical not only for effective representation of clients, but also for avoidance of allegations of malpractice.

Documents can be proof of assertions or allegations; they can establish time; they can be proof of notice or knowledge. They are always important.

Learning to effectively organize, retrieve, and destroy documents is a fundamental way to avoid malpractice. Being unable to retrieve an important document can be devastating to any attorney. This is especially true if the document is one of a kind, such as a passport or stock certificate. To keep this situation from ever occurring, effective and comprehensive records management systems must be established.

The issues of complete client loyalty, preservation of client confidences and secrets, and protection of the attorney-client privilege all arise in the context of records management. A records management system must support the privacy and confidentiality requirements regarding legal documents. These issues arise not only in the context of document security used in current cases, but also in the context of the destruction of documents from closed cases. By developing

FIGURE 2-3 Effective records management is necessary to avoid malpractice.

and utilizing a system for records management, it is easy to preserve the attorney-client privilege and to ensure that legal documents remain confidential. Systems establish steps to be followed in all situations; therefore, it is unlikely that consistently following the same steps for opening and closing files will result in malpractice.

An important aspect of records management specifically set up to avoid malpractice is the check for conflicts of interest. Most firms have conflicts of interest checked when a new file is set up. Conflict of interest arises when an attorney sues a former client or represents a person formerly sued by the attorney. Such conflicts of interest are in and of themselves malpractice. By setting up and using a system to check for conflicts of interest in records management, malpractice can be avoided.

The following guest editorial addresses malpractice avoidance by an understanding of the work product privilege, which concerns whether items prepared in anticipation of litigation must be given to the opposing party. This is an extremely important area for paralegals to comprehend because paralegals are frequently responsible for responding to discovery requests from opposing attorneys. You must properly understand work product privilege before you can comply properly with those requests.

The editorial also serves several other purposes. First, it is a good example of an in-house presentation to paralegals. One way in which firms provide continuing education for their paralegals is to have attorneys come in and speak on relevant topics. This editorial was originally given in that kind of environment at the law firm of Drew, Eckl & Farnham, in Atlanta, Georgia. Second, you can see how thoroughly you must understand the language of the law to succeed as an attorney or paralegal. In this article, the author uses phrases such as "disclosure of purported work product," or "when hostile witnesses are available"—and expects his audience to understand the terminology. Third, you can see how specific and detailed the thinking of the law is when it comes to an issue. Your work will have to be characterized by a high level of detail and accuracy as well. Finally, the article gives you a good idea of the level of knowledge you must have to be a successful paralegal.

GUEST EDITORIAL

The Work Product Privilege—Avoiding Malpractice

Lucian Gillis and Fred Hubbs

I. What Is Attorney Work Product?

Attorney work product can be any document, chart or tangible item prepared by an attorney or his representative in anticipation of litigation. The work product doctrine was first established in *Hickman v. Taylor,* 329 U.S. 495 (1947). The doctrine is codified in Fed. R. Civ. P. 26(b)(3), which provides:

> A party may obtain discovery documents and tangible things otherwise discoverable under subdivision (b)(1) of this Rule and prepared in anticipation of litigation or for trial for another party or for that other party's representative ... only upon a showing that the party seeking the discovery has *substantial need* of the materials in the preparation of the party's case and that the party is unable without *undue hardship* to obtain the substantial equivalent of the materials by other means. ... The court shall protect against the disclosure of the *mental impressions, conclusions, opinions or legal theories of an attorney or other representative or a party concerning litigation* ... .

The purpose of the work product privilege is to "create a zone of privacy in which an attorney can investigate, prepare, and analyze a case." *In re Grand Jury Subpoena,* 622 F.2d 933, 935 (6th Cir. 1980); *In re Grand Jury,* 599 F.2d 504, 511 (2d Cir. 1979).

Work product immunity is only meant to protect documents, charts, graphs, etc. ... (tangible items). Facts or opinions contained on the document may still be discoverable. *Hickman v. Taylor, supra;* Fed. R. Civ. P. 26(b)(3), Advisory Committee Notes ("[o]ne party may still discover relevant facts known or available to the other party, even though such facts are contained in a document which is not itself discoverable").

In addition, documents or materials which are prepared or assembled in the ordinary course of business or for other nonlitigation purposes are not protected. This is essentially meant to cover documents which are prepared as part of a routine practice and not necessarily prepared in anticipation of litigation. For instance, in *Miles v. Bell Helicopter Co.,* 385 F. Supp. 1029 (N.D. Ga. 1974), the northern district [court] determined that accident reports prepared immediately after a helicopter crash were not prepared in anticipation of litigation but instead routinely prepared in the event that litigation may arise.

Simply because the document is in the possession of an attorney does not necessarily make the document privileged; and if the work product is not privileged in the hands of someone else, it is not privileged when placed in the hands of an attorney. *Fisher v. United States,* 425 U.S. 391, 404 (1976); *United States v. Davis,* 636 F.2d 1028 (5th Cir. 1981). The burden of establishing that the materials are work product is on the one asserting the privilege. *Cedrone v. Unity Savings Ass'n,* 103 F.R.D. 423, 426 (E.D. Pa. 1984).

In short, attorney work product can take any form as long as it is a document or tangible item.

While the document itself may be protected, information contained on the document may not necessarily also be protected.

II. Types of Work Product

Work product can be divided into two general categories: (1) ordinary or "factual" work product and (2) opinion work product. Ordinary work product generally includes client's notes, investigator's (adjuster's) reports, witness statements, etc. Ordinary work product is generally afforded a lesser degree of protection than opinion work product, and often the party seeking disclosure can obtain the document by showing that: (a) the information is not otherwise available; and (b) the information is necessary for preparation of the party's case. Consequently, ordinary work product receives only qualified immunity.

[A] higher showing is required if the disputed documents contain opinion work product. *Upjohn Co. v. United States,* 449 U.S. 383, 401 (1981). Generally, opinion work product is afforded absolute immunity against disclosure. *In re International Systems & Controls Corp. Securities Litigation,* 693 F.2d 1235, 1240 (5th Cir. 1982) ("almost absolute protection"); *In re Murphy,* 560 F.2d 326, 336 (8th Cir. 1977) ("nearly absolute immunity" and only discoverable only in "rare and extraordinary circumstances"). Opinion work product usually includes items such as deposition summaries, chronologies, opinion letters, reports to clients, etc.

III. Requirement for Immunity

Work product [includes] those documents or tangible items prepared *in anticipation of litigation* or for trial. It is not necessary that litigation have been commenced or be imminent, but merely that the "primary motivating purpose behind the creation of the document was to aid in possible future litigation." *United States v. Davis, supra; Osternick v. E.P.T. Barwick Industries,* 82 F.R.D. 81, 87 (N.D. Ga. 1979). *See also,* C. Wright & A. Miller, *Federal Practice and Procedure* § 2024 (1970). This includes materials not only prepared by the attorney but also prepared by an attorney's representative. *United States v. Nobles,* 422 U.S. 225, 238–39 (1975); Fed. R. Civ.

P. 26(b)(3). A "representative" can be an investigator or adjuster.

It is not necessary that litigation have already commenced or be imminent, *but* "the mere possibility of litigation is not enough to invoke work product protection." *Home Insurance Co. v. Bellenger Corp.,* 74 F.R.D. 93, 101 (N.D. Ga. 1977). Also, there is no work product immunity for documents prepared in the regular course of business rather than for the purposes of litigation. C. Wright & A. Miller, *Federal Practice and Procedure* § 2024 (1970). *See also Simon v. G.D. Searle,* 816 F.2d 397, 401 (8th Cir. 1987). Information or material that serves both business and litigation purposes generally is not privileged. *Fine v. Facet Aerospace Product Co.,* 133 F.R.D. 439 (S.D.N.Y. 1990) (risk management report that was created for business purposes was discoverable although focus was associated with prospects of litigation).

Whether a document was prepared "in anticipation of litigation" is probably the biggest gray area in the doctrine of work product immunity. The simple suggestion when it comes to determining whether a document is a protected work product is: **When in doubt, don't give it out.** Often it is easy to make an argument that a document was prepared in anticipation of litigation. Make the other side work as hard as we do in preparing the case, provided your actions are made in good faith.

IV. Piercing Work Product Immunity

A party seeking disclosure of purported work product must show two things: (1) he has a *substantial need* for the material; and (2) he cannot obtain the substantial equivalent without *undue hardship*. These two hurdles are often difficult to overcome and usually turn on the specific facts of the case.

Many different grounds have been held to constitute substantial need. A frequently encountered situation constituting substantial need is the unavailability of a witness. *Hickman v. Taylor, supra.* Another such instance has been where a witness has a faulty memory. *In re International Systems & Controls Corp. Securities Litigation;* and *Xerox v. IBM,* 64 F.R.D. 367, 382 (S.D.N.Y. 1974). However, a party who needs a witness's prior statement simply for impeachment or corroboration does not have a substantial need. *United States v. Chatham City Corp.*, 72 F.R.D. 640, 644 (S.D. Ga. 1976); *see Hickman v. Taylor, supra.*

[Most] courts are unwilling to award a lack of initiative in preparing one's case by allowing the discovery of work product. Therefore, disclosure will not be awarded if this same information can be acquired by the movant's own discovery. *See, e.g., Castle v. Sangamo Weston, Inc.* 744 F.2d 1464, 1466 (11th Cir. 1984); *In re International Systems & Control Corp. Securities Litigation, supra.* A lapse in time between the commencement of a case and the time a statement is taken will not generally constitute undue hardship for the party seeking disclosure. *Almaguer v. Chicago, Rock Island & Pacific Railroad*, 55 F.R.D. 147 (D. Neb. 1972). However, a court may find "undue hardship" when hostile witnesses are available for deposition but the quality of information obtainable from them is not substantially equivalent. *Almaguer v. Chicago, Rock Island & Pacific Railroad, supra; Long's Drug Stores v. Howell*, 657 P.2d 412 (1983).

Courts may consider the cost involved in securing substantially equivalent information as one factor in the "undue hardship" determination, *In re International Systems & Controls Corp. Securities Litigation, supra;* but "the cost or inconvenience of taking depositions is not in and of itself sufficient to meet the undue hardship requirement." *United States v. Chatham City Corp., supra.*

V. Expert Witnesses

[D]ocuments prepared in anticipation of litigation by an attorney, and then disclosed to that attorney's testifying expert, are protected work product. *McKinnon v. Smock*, 209 Ga. App. 647, 430 S.E.2d 92 (1993), *aff'd.*, 264 Ga. 375, 445 S.E.2d 526 (1994). The same holds true in federal courts as well. *Bogosian v. Gulf Oil Corp.*, 738 F.2d 587 (3d Cir. 1984); *United States v. 215.7 Acres of Land*, 719 F. Supp. 273 (D. Del. 1989); *Hamel v. General Motors Corp.*, 128 F.R.D. 281 (D. Cal. 1989); and *Hydromar, Inc. v. General Dynamics Corp.*, 119 F.R.D. 367 (E.D. Pa. 1988). Also, materials disclosed to experts who are informally consulted but not specifically

retained or expected to testify are also protected. *Ager v. Jane C. Stormant Hospital & Training School for Nurses*, 622 F.2d 496 (10th Cir. 1980); *Weiner v. Bache Halsey Stewart, Inc.*, 76 F.R.D. 624 (S.D. Fla. 1977); 4 J. Moore, W. Taggart & J. Wicker, *Moore's Federal Practice* § 26.66[4].

However, since the opposing party is entitled to a "thorough and sifting cross-examination" of an expert and his opinions, the party seeking discovery often has a good argument that he has a "substantial need" to know as much as possible about the thoughts and conclusions of his opponent's expert. Furthermore, an expert's notes or any documents upon which he relies are rarely available by other means. Therefore, one should always be aware that any work product shown to an expert might be discoverable. Documents provided to experts should be carefully selected.

VI. Investigative Files

Generally, ... state courts are fairly protective of investigator/adjuster's files and will not allow this discovery without a showing of substantial need and undue hardship. *Lowe's of Georgia, Inc. v. Webb*, 180 Ga. App. 755, 350 S.E.2d 292 (1986); *Tobacco Road, Inc. v. Callahan*, 174 Ga. App. 539, 330 S.E.2d 769 (1985); *Howell v. U.S. Fire Insurance Co.*, 185 Ga. App. 154, 363 S.E.2d 560 (1987). It is safe to say that, more likely than not, any insurance investigator's or adjuster's files are usually protected work product within the state courts ... .

However, federal courts have been reluctant to offer such blanket protection to investigative files. Instead, local federal courts have generally held that whether investigative files are protected by work product privilege turns on the facts of each case. *Carver v. Allstate Insurance Co.*, 94 F.R.D. 131 (1982); *Miles v. Bell Helicopter Co.*, 385 F. Supp. 1029, 1033 (N.D. Ga. 1974). [Some hold that] the work product does not protect the materials resulting from an insurance investigation at all. *Atlanta Coca-Cola Bottling Co. v. TransAmerica Insurance Co.*, 61 F.R.D. 115 (N.D. Ga. 1972). The distinction the federal courts make is that insurance investigation materials are presumed to have been made in the ordinary course of business rather than in anticipation of litigation, and thus may not be afforded work product protection. *Miles v. Bell Helicopter Co., supra.* It appears from the conflicting nature of these decisions that, at the very least, if you want to argue that something is protected by work product, you would not be subject to a bad faith claim in doing so.

VII. Conclusion

When in doubt, don't give it out. If it is a close call, it is probably better to assert that the document or material the other side is requesting is work product. Chances are greater for malpractice for giving out a document that you should not have than for not giving out one you should have. If you can assert in good faith that the document is work product, then make the other side earn his nickel and show that he has a substantial need for the document and cannot obtain the same information without undue hardship. More often than not, as a paralegal you will be confronted with these questions when it comes to responding to discovery (i.e., interrogatories and requests for production). ...

Here are some suggestions for dealing with possible attorney work product:

(1) Designate privileged and protected documents by categories.
(2) Create a database or index including all privileged and protected documents.
(3) Be constantly sensitive to privilege (attorney-client and work product) issues, not just when discovery requests are received:
    (a) Stamp or type "Privileged," "Confidential," or "Attorney Work Product" on appropriate documents;
    (b) File privileged or protected documents in different places from nonprivileged documents.
    (c) Bates-stamp documents produced during litigation with a special code for documents produced under claim of privilege (assuming [you] are forced to produce them at all). ▒

Malpractice and Technology

The law office today uses more and more sophisticated technology to perform a wide range of applications. These technological developments give a new angle to the issue of malpractice. The old devices and systems used to protect client confidences and secrets and to preserve the attorney-client privilege are no longer adequate. For instance, merely locking the file cabinets with the file, talking behind closed doors, and closing the door for private telephone conversations are no longer sufficient. The development of new technology requires that new systems be developed and used to prevent malpractice.

As the law office becomes more computerized, and as more and more information and communications are transmitted electronically, computer security becomes an increasingly significant concern. If the issues of computer security are not addressed and effectively dealt with, malpractice problems may arise, especially in areas related to confidential communications and unauthorized use of information.

One way to avoid malpractice is to implement a systems approach for computer security. Documents that are privileged and should not be available to everyone within the firm should be coded so that access is limited. Further, everyone in the firm should be required to sign on to the firm's computer system using a password. These two simple steps, as part of comprehensive computer security procedures, should alleviate potential malpractice issues.

The widespread use of the facsimile machine to transmit messages to various locations also brings up malpractice issues. Because the information is being transmitted to a number rather than a specific person, care must be taken to ensure that the information is seen only by that person. (See Figure 2-4.) A high percentage of legal documents have aspects of the attorney-client privilege and confidentiality pertaining to them. Such simple steps as always enclosing a cover sheet with the fax, specifying that the information contained within is covered by the attorney-client privilege, can help to avoid potential malpractice. (See Figure 2-5.)

Finally, the telephone has given rise to new issues of malpractice. Depending on what type of telephone you are using, the conversation taking place over that phone may not be a protected communication. For example, the widespread use of cellular telephones means that others may be able to intercept your telephone calls. The United States Supreme Court has held that communications over a cellular telephone are not afforded the same privacy rights as conversations over a traditional telephone.

Malpractice and Communication

Effective communication is the cornerstone of malpractice prevention. A vast majority of malpractice allegations arise because of miscommunication between the attorney and the client. By keeping the client informed about what

FIGURE 2-4 Following fax protocol and procedures is necessary to malpractice avoidance.

is happening in her case, not overestimating a client's case, letting only attorneys give legal advice, and returning telephone calls, most malpractice complaints arising from miscommunication can be avoided. By understanding and following the communication practices outlined in Chapter 15 of this book, you should never have a miscommunication problem become the basis of a malpractice claim.

ANNE H. WHITAKER, ESQ.
SUSAN L. GOODMAN, ESQ.

IN-HOUSE COUNSEL, INC.

SPECIALIZING IN CONTRACT PLACEMENT
FOR LAWYERS ~ BY LAWYERS

333 SANDY SPRINGS CIRCLE, SUITE 209
ATLANTA, GEORGIA 30328
FAX (404) 256-6599
(404) 256-9099

FAX TRANSMISSION MEMO

CONFIDENTIALITY NOTE:

The information contained in this facsimile message is legally privileged and confidential information intended only for the use of the individual or entity named below. If the reader of this message is not the intended recipient, you are hereby notified that any dissemination, distribution or copy of this telecopy is strictly prohibited. If you have received this telecopy in error, please immediately notify us by telephone and return the original message (and any copies) to us at the above address via the United States Postal Service. Thank you.

DATE: February 6, 1995   TIME:11:20 a.m.

TO: Jonathan Lynton   FAX #: 292-2321

FROM: Susan Goodman

RE: Guest Editorial

NUMBER OF PAGES SENT (INCLUDING THIS SHEET): 3

REASON FOR TRANSMITTAL:

(X) FOR YOUR INFORMATION
(X) FOR YOUR ACTION
(   ) FOR YOUR COMMENTS, PLEASE
(   ) REVIEW AND CALL ME ASAP
(   ) REVIEW AND REPLY
(   ) REVIEW AND FORWARD TO:
(X) SIGN AND RETURN TO ME VIA: fax (404) 256-6599

ADDITIONAL COMMENTS OR INSTRUCTIONS FROM SENDER:

FIGURE 2-5 A fax cover sheet specifying that the material contained within is covered by attorney-client privilege is necessary to avoid malpractice.

Malpractice and Stress

Effectively organizing one's time and prioritizing work assignments can greatly reduce stress and avoid malpractice problems that might arise as a result of stress. People deal with stress in different ways—some destructive and others beneficial. The mechanisms set forth in Chapter 16, outlining ways to avoid stress and handle stress effectively, are essential to malpractice avoidance. If you are under severe stress, you increase your chances of making mistakes, missing deadlines, confusing issues or clients, or performing in a host of ways that might constitute negligent behavior.

It is the attorney's obligation to every client to represent that client's case zealously and completely. This also applies to each member of the legal team who will be providing services to that client. To fulfill your responsibilities as a team member, and to protect your client's interests as fully and completely as possible, you need to give her case the benefit of your knowledge and expertise. If you are unable to fulfill your responsibilities because you are overly stressed, you will not only jeopardize your job, but you might also be alienating or negligently representing the client.

Malpractice and Substance Abuse

One of the major causes of malpractice claims can be traced to something that plagues not merely the legal profession but society as well: the use and abuse of alcohol and drugs. It is certainly understandable that those in a high-stress, high-responsibility profession such as the law would need a way to relax and get away from the pressures of work. Unfortunately, when a person turns to alcohol or drugs, she opens the door to the possibility of abuse, which in turn may affect the person's performance. Impaired performance inevitably leads to threats of malpractice.

The individual, the law firm, and bar associations can take steps to assure that a person does not become a victim of substance abuse. The individual person must learn to cope with stress and to find appropriate outlets to deal with the pressures of a highly competitive and pressure-filled profession. Law firms can also aid in the fight against substance abuse by developing policies and procedures to guard against the use and abuse of drugs and alcohol. Local and state bar associations can also provide committees, peer support, or prevention and rehabilitation programs to aid in drug and alcohol abuse prevention. You will find a discussion of substance abuse and an example of a firm's substance abuse policy in Chapter 5.

Malpractice and Professional Development

Professional development is also an important aspect of malpractice avoidance. Only by keeping abreast of current legal issues and developments will you be able to develop the requisite skill and knowledge to perform your professional responsibilities as a paralegal. You will be expected to be aware of the current law and of currently litigated issues in your area of specialization, and the client must be informed about the law relative to her case. Although ultimate responsibility for legal advice must come from the attorney, the paralegal, as a member of the legal team, also has an obligation to help the attorney keep informed of relevant information that must be provided to the client. For example, if your client is seeking advice in estate planning, and in conference with your client you hear your supervising attorney omit reference to a recently decided case that might impact the client's options and choices, you should—in the privacy of the attorney's office and with just you and the attorney present—ask if she is aware of the case. If she is, but does not think it is relevant, you have done your job. If the attorney for some reason was unaware of the case, you will earn high praise. In either case, you will have performed ethically and professionally.

Handling Ethical Dilemmas

It is difficult and stressful to be faced with ethical dilemmas or to witness or become party to behavior that might be considered malpractice. If, for example, your supervising attorney is mishandling client funds, what should you do?

As you might surmise, figuring out how to handle an ethical dilemma is itself an ethical dilemma! If you confront your boss, you might get fired or demoted. If you do not tell your boss, you yourself might be implicated. What should you do?

There are not very many choices. You can communicate with the individual whose work you believe might violate ethical principles or lead to a malpractice claim. This discussion should probably be held in privacy, between the two of you. You can talk with your supervising attorney or the paralegal supervisor. You can call the bar association in your state. Remember, however, that each of these solutions puts you in the position of being perceived as a "whistle blower," and, especially if you are in an at-will employment state, your job will not be protected by the courts.

You might get advice from an expert in ethics, such as an experienced attorney or ethics professor. (See Figure 2-6.) By talking to an expert who also is objective about your situation, you might be able to see your situation more clearly and to develop responses that are appropriate under the circumstances.

FIGURE 2-6   A paralegal discusses an ethical dilemma with an objective third party to determine her best course of action.

Finally, there is always the option of doing nothing and going along with the practice or saying nothing about it. This may not feel very comfortable, but in many cases it might be the best approach for keeping your job. Of course, if the situation is highly offensive to you, you can always try to find a position with another firm or organization, and in some cases that might well be the best solution.

Malpractice Avoidance: A Summary

One of your personal professional goals, and one of the major goals of a law firm, should be the development of systems, procedures, and approaches to handle situations that might lead to legal malpractice. The possibilities of committing malpractice extend to all facets of legal work. By identifying possible pitfalls, developing and using a systematic approach to legal work, and responding ethically and appropriately to possible malpractice situations, you will be well prepared to avoid allegations of malpractice. Additionally, paralegals who understand the significance of malpractice claims and who actively assist the firm by developing and using effective systems will surely be appreciated and recognized for their efforts in this area.

Key Terms

direct liability	malpractice avoidance	vicarious liability
malpractice	substance abuse	work product privilege

Problems and Activities

1. Contact your bar and paralegal associations to see if your jurisdiction has adopted any ethical guidelines for paralegals.

2. You know that your supervising attorney has nearly doubled her hours on a bill sent out to a client. How would you handle this situation?

3. At dinner with a friend, you, a paralegal, see your supervising attorney looking amorously into the eyes of his dinner companion, who is the estranged spouse of the attorney's client in a divorce action. What should you do?

4. Suppose you were told by your supervising attorney to engage in unethical conduct, such as drafting a settlement letter to clients informing them that their case had settled for $10,000 less than it actually did. How would you handle such a situation?

5. Do you think that paralegals should be licensed by states, as other professionals such as doctors and lawyers are? Why or why not?

6. You are asked to notarize a signature that you did not actually witness. What should you do?

CHAPTER 3

LEGAL ENVIRONMENTS: STRUCTURES AND PEOPLE

CHAPTER OUTLINE

OBJECTIVES

By the completion of this chapter, you should:

- understand the different types of legal environments;

- understand the categories of lawyers and nonlawyers who work in a law office;

- learn about law office design considerations; and

- understand the process of moving the law firm.

Legal Environments: An Introduction

One of the most exciting aspects of the legal profession is the variety of environments in which an attorney or paralegal can work. It is important for all legal practitioners to become aware of the different ways of organizing law offices; not only will this help you choose an environment for yourself that fits your interests, but it will also enable you to communicate and interact effectively in the future when you come into contact with other forms. A vocabulary has evolved to describe legal environments and those who work in them. This chapter introduces you to the environments in which law is practiced and the people who work together who constitute the legal team.

Private Law Firms

Perhaps the most typical environment for paralegals is the private law firm. Each private law firm has its own personality, style, and ambience. The size varies, from the sole practitioner to the very large, multioffice firm. They may be partnerships, corporations, or professional corporations (P.C.s), or limited liability corporations (L.L.C.s). The following review of the types of law firms is intended to give you an idea of the different issues that are related to the size of a firm. You will find that each firm, although providing legal services, has a definite identity regardless of its size. Although it will take some effort to find a work environment that fits your needs and interests, you can be assured that there are opportunities for paralegals in all different environments.

The Sole Practitioner

The sole practitioner works on his own; his law firm is his own business (Figure 3-1). In many ways sole practitioners are the entrepreneurs of the legal world: both entrepreneurs and sole practitioners have high self-confidence and like the responsibility of being the leader. They may be mavericks, being successful in the system while operating on its fringes. They are both high achievers possessing excellent problem-solving capabilities. They both need to be in charge and, in many instances, have the skills and abilities to lead with excellence.

The sole practitioner's office differs from even the smallest law firm. Because of the size of the business, the sole practitioner does not have to run his business in the same way demanded of larger firms, but must be sophisticated from a business aspect in order to compete for business and make a reasonable profit. The sole practitioner's office is truly a reflection of the individual attorney, and there are as many variations as there are personalities. It is clear, however, that sole practitioners differ from larger firms in a number of categories. The following is a list of possible differences between a sole practitioner and a larger law firm:

Instead of:

Signing a lease for a large amount of office space, he may rent a small suite of offices (Figure 3-2);

FIGURE 3-1 Sole practitioners experience both the freedom and the responsibilities of running their own law practices.

FIGURE 3-2 Often sole practitioners lease office space with other sole practitioners.

Keeping time through an elaborate, computerized, time-and-billing system, he may keep time manually or on a personal computer;

Hiring a large, permanent staff of clericals and professionals, he may hire independent contractors on an as-needed basis;

Hiring a paralegal, receptionist, and secretary, he may hire one person who is qualified to handle all three functions—often called a girl Friday in the past, now known as an administrative assistant;

Buying office supplies in bulk from a variety of vendors, he may choose to go to an office supply store and select the items that he needs as supplies dwindle;

Purchasing computers, photocopiers, telephones, and other such office equipment, he may choose to rent or lease with an option to purchase;

Answering to a managing partner or management committee, the sole practitioner makes all of his own decisions about the practice—he is his own boss!

The personality of the sole practitioner's office will vary from very casual to very formal. It all depends upon the sole practitioner, the type of practice, and the image(s) he chooses to project.

Often, great opportunities exist for paralegals within the framework of the office of the sole practitioner. Because the sole practitioner is generally financially limited and can only employ a certain number of individuals, he may ask the paralegal to take on a role of greater responsibility. In this scenario, a paralegal may be asked to:

Do legal research and writing

Go to the courthouse to file documents and/or obtain copies of documents

Deal directly with vendors when purchasing supplies or negotiating equipment leases

Recruit, interview, test, and hire clerical employees

Input time and prepare bills for clients

Establish and maintain an open and closed file plan

Assist with an office move

Analyze new software for the computer system

Help with marketing efforts by planning receptions, seminars, and other client development programs

Contact clients on behalf of the attorney and generally have more client contact than a paralegal in a larger firm.

In reality, the list could be endless. It is important to mention that in this environment the paralegal must be interested in handling a variety of administrative projects in addition to paralegal work. It calls for a person who is highly creative, energetic, and interested in all aspects of the law office. Like the sole practitioner, the paralegal working with a sole practitioner is generally not specialized and is able to handle everything from litigation to corporate work. Although some sole practitioners do specialize, they specialize in a different sense than do lawyers in larger firms. For example, a sole practitioner may specialize in litigation, but do every type of litigation from civil to criminal, whereas an attorney in a larger firm would tend to specialize not only in litigation, but in a particular type of litigation, such as commercial litigation.

The Boutique Firm

The boutique firm is small, with a highly specialized practice focusing either on a particular area of the law (i.e., labor or employee relations) or a particular type of clientele (i.e., sports, entertainment, or entrepreneurial business practice). A typical boutique firm is composed of one or more partners (generally not more than three or four) and two to four associates.

The group might take an impressive, but not necessarily large, suite of offices. The image must fit the type of clients the firm is seeking and will, to a large degree, determine the personality and ambience of the firm. In the boutique firm, a receptionist-typist may be seated in the entry office. This person is responsible for answering and routing all incoming calls, arranging for conference calls, and handling routine typing. He may also be responsible for making appointments for the various attorneys in the office. Because of the size of a boutique firm, many of the same possibilities that exist with a sole practitioner's office also exist here. The paralegal's role may again be broader here than at the medium or large law firm. Often, boutique law firms seek high visibility within the business and legal community. They market their services widely and aggressively. For example, a paralegal who has specialized training beyond a paralegal degree, such as nursing, may choose to work in a boutique firm specializing in medical malpractice. Boutique firms permit paralegals with specialized skills to utilize both their paralegal and their specialized skills.

The Small Firm

A small law firm, depending upon its geographic location, might have 15 or fewer attorneys, some of whom are partners and the balance of whom are either associates, contract lawyers, law clerks, or independent contractors. These categories of lawyers are discussed in detail later in this section.

Generally, the small law firm has a person who is designated as the office manager. The office manager differs from the director of administration in that he handles the routine running of the business, but usually is not responsible for the overall management of the firm. Accounting management, including budgeting and hiring and firing decisions, may not be a part of this job description. The office manager, who could be a paralegal, may be responsible for many of the functions discussed regarding the office of the sole practitioner. It is a very interesting position for the person who likes to deal with the nuts and bolts of the law firm on a daily basis. Each day is different and challenging. Other positions that may be available in the small firm are:

legal secretaries
law clerks
courier/photocopier operators
bookkeepers

The small law firm may be less formal in setting and personality than the medium or large law firm. Often, attorneys and staff are on a first-name basis.

The computer system, whether made up of personal computers or mini-computers, often is more sophisticated than in the firm of the sole practitioner or the boutique firm, as the need for more in-depth reports exists. A structured time-and-billing system is generally used, and the emphasis on specific recordation of billable time is greater.

As the number of professionals and clericals increases, the amount of space required to house the firm also increases. A firm of 15 or so may be interested in purchasing a small building or a suite in an office cooperative, but generally a firm of this size leases space. The office space is then divided into defined areas, such as:

reception room
attorney offices
paralegal offices
secretarial areas

photocopy/supply room
law library
file storage room
conference room(s)
break room

The Medium-Size Firm

Greater differences are noticeable when you consider the medium-size firm. Again, depending upon geographical locations, a medium-size firm may range from 15 to 75 attorneys. More administrative support staff is required in medium-size firms (Figure 3-3). Positions vary, but may include:

Director of administration
Assistant to director of administration
Personnel director
Computer systems manager
Bookkeeper and bookkeeping assistant(s)
Facilities manager
Law librarian
Data and word processors
Receptionists/Telephone operators
Couriers/Mailroom personnel

In addition to a larger administrative staff, there may also be a sizeable group of paralegals, summer and winter law clerks, and various categories of lawyers. One may find the atmosphere in a medium-size law firm more formal than in the firms previously discussed, and there is a definite chain of command.

FIGURE 3-3 An office administrator is responsible for managing a law firm.

Everything becomes more structured in a medium-size firm. Roles of each individual are more clearly delineated; more rules exist and are more strictly enforced; the recordation of billable and nonbillable hours is extremely important; marketing is done on a grander scale; in-house continuing legal education programs may be presented for the benefit of the lawyers and paralegals; a continuing legal education budget may be given to each lawyer and paralegal for attendance at outside seminars; free legal work, known as *pro bono* work, may be expected of each professional; participation in client development activities is most likely expected as part of the professional's overall work effort; and participation on firm committees may be mandatory for both lawyers and paralegals.

Additionally, there may be multiple locations, with some of the professionals transferring between offices (Figure 3-4). If the offices are within the same city, the smaller offices are generally referred to as *satellite offices*. Couriers may shuttle documents, mail, and other information among the offices; computers may link the offices together for word and data processing purposes. Salary of nonpartner lawyers and paralegals, as well as the share of profits, otherwise known as "points," of partners, is often directly related to the achievement of billable hour goals.

FIGURE 3-4 A medium- or large-size law firm might own its own building.

The Large Firm

The large law firm is generally very structured and, as with the medium-size firm, rules are plentiful and are enforced. The same expectations (if not more) of the professional in the medium firm exist in the large firm. In most cases, the large law firm operates on a more formal level. Again, there is a defined chain of command that structures authority and decision making in the office. (See Figure 3-5 for one example of an organizational chart.)

A very large law firm may have multiple locations, both in this country and abroad. The offices are linked through very complex, sophisticated communications systems. Often the lawyers and paralegals are transferred from one office to another. Achievement of billing goals plays a major role in the remuneration of lawyers and paralegals.

In addition to the administrative positions defined for the medium-size firm, large firms may also have the following additional personnel:

> Executive director
> Chief financial officer/Comptroller
> Marketing director
> Training director
> Support services director
> Human resources director
> Paralegal coordinator(s)
> Director of paralegal program
> Satellite office managers
> Communications director

One thing that is apparent from the discussion of all types and sizes of private law firms is that there are many career paths for the paralegal who is bright, ambitious, and willing to work hard. All law firms are expected to give the highest quality service to the client for a reasonable fee. Quality, service, ethics, and fair price are the key objectives for the private law practice of the 1990s, and the paralegal can play an important role in achieving all of these objectives.

Now that we have discussed private law practices and how they differ, we should note that there are other environments in which the lawyer and the paralegal play major roles.

In-House Counsel: The Corporate Environment

In-house counsel works within the framework of a corporation, rather than in a private law practice. These lawyers have the same training as private law firm attorneys and must have passed the bar. In-house counsel is no less important than a private attorney, but has chosen to work directly for a corporation and is devoted to the concerns of that corporation. The corporate counsel may be the only in-house lawyer and, in that situation, may have the role of general counsel. There may be a general counsel, who has other lawyers acting as corporate counsel working directly under him. The corporate counsel plays a major role in all corporate activities and works closely on strategic planning—both present and future. Within the in-house legal department, positions are usually

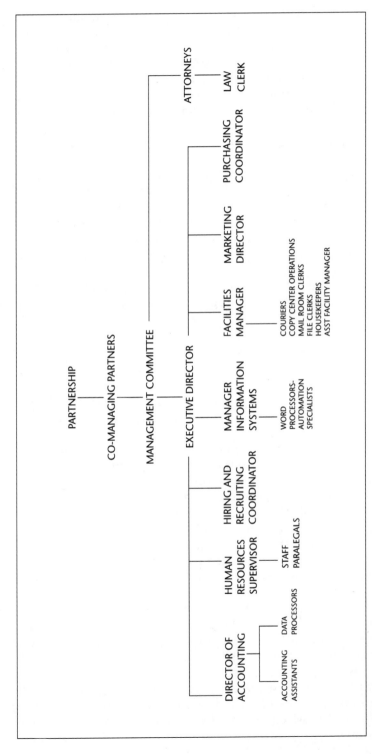

FIGURE 3-5 In general, larger law firms will have a structured chain of command.

available for legal secretaries and paralegals, but administrative needs are met by those in similar positions within the corporation. Traditionally, corporate counsel and paralegals do not record billable hours, because they work as employees of the corporation, thereby eliminating the need for time and billing systems. However, the present trend is toward keeping time records even in corporate legal departments. Many corporate departments maintain timekeeping records of hours spent, whether on litigation projects, projecting budgets for litigation, recovering attorney fees based on hours spent, and evaluating the need for a legal department. If they find they need expertise that they do not have, or if they do not find that maintaining in-house counsel is cost-effective, they may engage lawyers from private law firms on an hourly fee or per-project arrangement. Many companies have found that hiring corporate counsel can greatly reduce their overall budget for legal services. Also, they have found it very helpful to have these talented people as part of the corporate team, as they often see potential problems in time to prevent the occurrences.

Large, in-house legal departments are usually organized on the same basis as medium- to large-size private firms. Lawyers usually specialize in litigation, corporate, patent/trademark, or labor law. Corporations with smaller legal departments, in contrast, are organized more like a sole practitioner's office, in that a lawyer must be more of a generalist.

Government Attorneys: The Public Environment

Lawyers work for the government in a variety of roles. They are paid according to their government classification, and their roles are clearly defined. There are tiers of authority within the government, and those tiers exist for lawyers as well. The government also has many positions for paralegals and they, too, are paid according to their classification. The government is highly structured and, of course, billable hours are not counted. However, in some states where the attorney general's office represents all state agencies, the attorneys will keep time so that each particular agency can pay for its legal services. This system makes agencies accountable for their legal work and prevents abuse of the system.

Involvement in government work is involvement with public law, which might include working in the office of the district or prosecuting attorney, the county or town attorney, the public defender, or legal aid. Lawyers in government service may also be found clerking for judges, working as assistant attorney generals, or working for administrative law judges or administrative agencies. Some attorneys and paralegals in government service may have more of an administrative than legal role. Of course, numerous attorneys are employed by law schools and by the legislatures of both the federal and state governments.

Lawyer Classifications

To operate effectively in a law firm, you must understand the different classifications of practicing attorneys. Perhaps the major distinction among lawyers working in a law firm is between partners and associates. Partners own shares in the law-firm partnership; associates do not. Thus, partners are like the owners of a business, and associates are the hired managers. Frequently, associates aim to become partners, and partners aim to bring promising associates into the firm (Figure 3-6). When a young attorney is on track for partnership, the associate must not only meet the billable hours requirement and do excellent legal work, but must also show the partners that he has the ability to bring in clients.

The following classifications will help you understand various categories of attorneys.

Equity Partner

The equity partner, if not one of the original owners, is generally voted into the practice by the existing partners. The word *equity* means that the partner shares in the profits and losses of the practice according to the amount of shares, otherwise known as *points,* that he owns in the practice. He may take part in the management of the firm, and attends all partnership meetings, at which he has a full vote. The equity partner is responsible for payment for all

FIGURE 3-6 A partner is an owner of a law firm and shares in its profits and losses.

of his own benefits, such as insurance, pension plan, and the like. He is also expected to make capital contributions as needed and is jointly and severally liable with the other partners.

Nonequity Partner

The word *nonequity* means that this type of partner works for a salary and does not share in the profits or losses of the firm. Benefits may be paid for him by the firm. He may attend partnership meetings, but has no vote. The nonequity partner may take part in some aspects of firm management and is usually expected to participate on committees within the firm. The nonequity partner may or may not have a contract with the firm. Even with these differences, for all intents and purposes, he is considered a partner by clients and the firm alike.

Associate Attorney

The associate attorney (Figure 3-7) is an employee at will and works for the firm for a salary. The associate may not have a contract. He may be asked for opinions, but has no vote and is not included in partnership meetings unless by express invitation. An associate attorney is considered on track for partnership. The current law-firm practice time frame for associates before being eligible for partnership is in the range of five to nine years, depending upon the law firm. Generally, the larger the law firm, the longer the partnership track.

FIGURE 3-7 An associate works on her cases.

Senior Attorney

A senior attorney is an employee at will who works for a salary and has no contract. The senior attorney is not considered to be on track for partnership, which means that it is not anticipated that he would ever be voted into the partnership. A variety of reasons account for this situation. In some circumstances, a lawyer may not want to devote the long hours that are expected of associate attorneys. He also may not have all of the qualities that are sought by the partnership. This status is being used more and more by working attorneys with small children who enjoy practicing law but do not want to work full time. The senior attorney does not attend partnership meetings, nor does he have a vote.

Managing Partner

The managing partner may be elected by the partnership to make decisions on behalf of the firm. He regularly reports to a management committee or the partnership as a whole. The length of the managing partner's term varies with the structure of the law firm, but often it is for a two-year period. He generally can have a repeat term if elected.

Senior Partner(s)

This term is reserved for the partners who are highest on the firm's letterhead, which is generally designed based upon seniority. Being a senior partner does not make one a managing partner. Senior partners' names usually appear in the name of the firm. However, if the number of senior partners becomes too high, firms may elect not to include these partners' names in the firm name.

Nonlawyer Partner

The legal establishment has long opposed nonlawyers being partners in a law firm, fearing a loss of independence and compromise on professional standards. On January 1, 1991, the first nonlawyer partner was named: Abe Isenberg, an accountant and chief administrator, is now a partner with the Washington firm of Howrey & Simon. At present, Washington is the only state that permits nonlawyers to become partners; as such, it is being watched by other states as its laws allow changes in the structures of law firms.

Contract Attorney

A contract attorney works for a salary under a contract for a specific term. He is considered an independent contractor, meaning that he is responsible for his own taxes and benefits.

Of Counsel

This title is a little more vague. The attorney who works in the of-counsel position may or may not have a contract and may or may not be a pending partner. In any event, the attorney in this category does not share in the profits and losses of the partnership, nor in firm management. He may attend partnership meetings by invitation of the partnership only. Often firms hire partner-level attorneys away from other firms in the hopes of making them partners of the hiring firms after a brief (one to two years) look at each other. Such an attorney might clearly fall into the of-counsel role. Another situation that may call for this category is the hiring of a well-known figure, such as a retired judge or chief executive officer (CEO) (with law degree) of a major corporation, who does not want to spend the long hours required of an equity partner, but who can lend his name and expertise for the good of the law firm (Figure 3-8). The role of these well-known of-counsel attorneys is generally to bring in new business for the firm. A common vernacular name for these types of attorneys is "rainmaker," for, by bringing in new clients, the rainmaker is making it rain so that the "harvest" can flourish.

FIGURE 3-8
Of-counsel attorneys offer prestige and contacts to the law firm.

Freelance Attorney

This attorney works for an hourly wage with no contract and no paid benefits. He is an independent contractor and is responsible for his own taxes. The term of employment may be for an indefinite duration.

Law Clerks

Law clerks are attorneys who have generally just graduated from law school and passed the bar, who work for judges. These attorneys help judges with legal research and assist in the drafting of orders and opinions. These positions are usually limited to one to two years; however, in some instances, especially at the state level, some law clerk positions are permanent.

Other Law Office Staff Terms

In addition to the preceding designations, it is helpful to know several terms commonly used to describe situations that occur in legal environments with legal personnel. The following list introduces you to some of those terms.

Lateral Hire

A lateral hire happens when an established attorney is hired by another firm with the understanding that he will be placed in the same position (based upon years of experience) in the new law firm. In other words, the lateral hire is not expected to start at the bottom of the letterhead ranking.

Parachuting

This term is reserved for one who "parachutes" into the firm by receiving increased salary and/or credit to partnership over other new hires or those already working with the firm, who may or may not have equal or greater experience. Many firms recognize the value to the firm as a whole of having the flexibility to offer increased salary and/or credit to partnership to a potential new attorney who has extraordinary capability or experience. Parachuting a new attorney should occur only when the attorney has a substantial degree of proven skill, and the firm should consider the loyalty and commitment to the firm exhibited by those who have joined the firm without the benefit or expectation of any advance credit or additional money.

Associate Sharing

More and more, law firms are encouraging, if not enforcing, the rule of associate sharing. This means that an associate is assigned to more than one section so that he can have exposure and experience under similar but differing types of practice and under the leadership of different partners.

Associate Mentor Program

Many firms have found value in assigning a mentor to work directly with an associate when the associate first arrives at the firm. This mentoring program may last as long as three years, and involves a partner taking the new associate under his tutelage and acting as a sponsor or guide. He encourages the associate to become involved in firm activities and committees, including social experiences.

Clerkship Program

Clerks are law school students who are in their first or second year, and who can work part or full time in the summer or winter to assist the various categories of lawyers with research and writing projects. It is also an opportunity for law firms to take a look at potential new hires before they have finished law school. Law clerks are expected to meet certain billable hour goals and are given secretarial support as deemed necessary by the firm.

Legal Team

This term refers to all of the people necessary to do a task for a client from start to finish (see Figure 3-9). By way of example, consider the following hypothetical situations:

Mr. Joe Smith, a client of the firm of Ball and Sloan, seeks the advice of his attorney, Bill Peters, with regard to an arson matter. Mr. Smith's case requires not only Mr. Peters's assistance, but that of Peters's two associates, Jeff Lewis and Kim Porter. Lewis and Porter then ask for the assistance of paralegals Joan Day, Drew Stone, and Betty Kelly. Because of the type of case, a decision is made to engage the services of an arson investigator, Brent Land, and a photographer, Craig Jones. This group would be considered the legal team of Mr. Smith. In addition to this defined team, scores of others may work on the case: legal secretaries, couriers, photocopy operators, law clerks, and so on.

FIGURE 3-9 A legal team discusses the strategy for a case.

On the same day that Mr. Smith met with Mr. Peters to discuss his arson case, Michael Swarthmore called Layton Jones, a tax lawyer at the firm of Ball and Sloan, to discuss his possible problems with the Internal Revenue Service. Jones found it necessary, due to the complexity of the situation, to bring his partner, Bob Forbes, and three associates, Allison Michon, Shannon Moore, and Marcy Mast, into the project. Additionally, Sylvia Browne and Andy Curtis, junior and senior paralegals, respectively, were asked to devote 100 percent of their time to the case. Midway through the matter, Jones engaged Princeton Bray, a highly experienced CPA, to work with the legal team. Again, a number of legal secretaries, law clerks, photocopy operators, and couriers helped achieve a favorable end result.

Committees

One of the ways in which law firms operate is by committee. Depending upon the size, type, and leadership structure of the law firm, a variety of committees may be formed. Here we briefly discuss a few that you might find in a typical law firm.

Management Committee or Executive Committee This is a group of partners, usually between three and five, who are voted into power by the partnership to assist with the overall leadership of the firm. The length of term varies according to the wishes of the partnership.

Hiring and Recruiting Committee This committee is very important and is most often chaired by a partner. Both partners and senior associates (those associates with seniority) may serve on the committee to actively recruit and hire new attorneys for the firm. They may interview on law school campuses, as well as in the law firm. They also entertain recruits and try to give them a feeling for the firm's personality, desires, and demands.

Library Committee This committee also may be chaired by a partner, with both associates and partners actively participating. If books, periodicals, microfiche, or other such materials are desired by a lawyer or paralegal, they may send their requests to this committee for consideration. The committee should have an annual budget for such purchases.

Social Committee This committee may be composed of partners, associates, and staff members and exists for the sole purpose of planning social activities for the firm.

Continuing Legal Education Committee This committee may be composed of partners, associates, and paralegals for the purpose of planning and presenting in-house, continuing legal education seminars. They may also inform lawyers and paralegals of outside educational opportunities.

Paralegal Review Committee   This committee, comprised of attorneys and other managers, develops and directs the paralegal program at a firm. The goal is to effectively integrate the paralegals into the firm and give them a forum to gain an identity, address firm and paralegal concerns, and provide social and educational opportunities. This committee might also handle work requirements and salary administration for the paralegals at a firm.

Experiments in Outsourcing

In the quest to survive by staying competitive, many law firms and corporations have turned to outsourcing as an approach to cutting costs and increasing their economic efficiency. *Outsourcing* involves hiring outside specialists to perform work on an ad hoc or continuing basis. For example, an organization might hire an outside firm to do all of its tax work, or it might hire a law firm to handle a particular matter. For corporations, outsourcing might mean eliminating the legal department altogether and hiring an outside firm to do the corporation's legal work. Some organizations believe that outsourcing can save significant expenses; others believe that keeping as much work as possible in-house is the preferable way to contain expenses. It is likely, then, that firms and companies will look at various outsourcing experiments to determine if it would be beneficial for their company.

Legal professionals were among the last to turn to independent contractors and contract employment, out of fear that temporary legal help would be unprofessional and would divide client loyalties. There were also concerns about ethical issues such as conflicts of interest and breaches of confidentiality. The positive experiences many companies and law firms report concerning the use of contract personnel, combined with the economic benefits of contract labor, have allayed these fears and will result in a continuing increase in the utilization of temporary legal help.

Outsourcing also refers to the practice of hiring specialists to perform various support functions for the firm. These might include copying services, courier services, or secretarial or paralegal services. Some firms outsource computer services or accounting services rather than maintain in-house departments. The benefits of this approach include keeping personnel costs and benefit costs down and improved quality resulting from the use of specialists.

New Career Opportunities for Paralegals

An additional benefit of outsourcing is the creation of career opportunities for support personnel, paralegals, and lawyers who do not want to work within the structured setting of a firm. These individuals might prefer to work on a contract basis to fit their personal needs. To help facilitate this approach—which, it is hoped, is in the best interests of both the firm and the individual—placement organizations such as In-House Counsel of Atlanta, Georgia, and Special Counsel Inc. of New York have sprung up. Essentially, these service organizations provide law firms with experienced personnel who fit the needs of the case or situation while the firm saves expenses and bills the cost directly to the client. Attorney Susan Goodman, one of the principals of In-House Counsel, was herself attracted as an attorney to contract work because it provided a positive alternative to billing requirements and inflexible situations. She is now helping others who might prefer this alternative to the traditional full-time position.

In her guest editorial, Ms. Goodman describes this approach to work, which has great appeal for many in the contemporary workforce.

G U E S T   E D I T O R I A L

Contract Employment: How to Be a Paralegal and Have a Life, Too

Susan L. Goodman

Susan L. Goodman is a former practicing attorney and, along with Anne H. Whitaker, is a principal in In-House Counsel, of Atlanta, Georgia, which specializes in contract employment for attorneys and paralegals.

Temporary, contract employment is the wave of the future for all professions, including the legal profession. Law firms, sole practitioners, and corporate legal departments are utilizing contract paralegals and attorneys, and an increasing number of paralegals and attorneys are turning to contract work as an alternative to traditional law firm structures and inflated billing requirements. Legal professionals often turn to companies that provide paralegals on a contract basis to meet these goals and needs. In-House Counsel, Inc. is only one example of a national movement toward this less costly, more efficient form of legal services, and only one example of the companies to which clients turn for temporary legal support.

In-House Counsel, Inc. is an attorney-owned and -operated company that specializes in placing attorneys and paralegals on a contract basis. There are many such services placing paralegals nationwide. One advantage some of these companies have is that the principals have been practicing attorneys themselves. In our case, both

principals practiced law for several years before beginning the company. I practiced as a commercial litigator at large and medium firms, and then on a contract basis. Anne practiced as a commercial and residential real estate attorney at medium firms, and as an independent contractor. Such practical experience enables us to understand both the needs of the client and the experience and desires of the paralegals and attorneys seeking positions.

Placement through companies such as ours is very easy. Although the companies have different processes, the basics are very similar. Submit your résumé, with a cover letter detailing your desires. Some companies will have you come in for testing; others will bring you in for a personal interview, with no testing involved. Most will then check references before referring you to their clients. The more thorough the reference check and interview process, the more professionally oriented the company. Check your local legal publication for a listing of companies that place paralegals on a contract basis.

The practicing paralegal finds several major advantages to becoming a contract paralegal. First and foremost is flexibility. Not only is there flexibility in the hours worked, but also in the types of assignments accepted and location of jobs. We have placed paralegals in settings as diverse as a sole practitioner to a large in-house legal department. The range of experiences includes large document productions in a warehouse setting with 60-plus people, organizing and assisting a practitioner who has never utilized a paralegal, and trial preparation and assistance. In addition, freedom to take time off for family, vacation, school, or sabbaticals is greatly increased. Second, the variety of work is significantly increased by the number of assignments a temporary paralegal may take. A paralegal could assist with a document production, requiring long hours and little expertise, and then could be placed on a project where he or she is involved in a very intricate commercial transaction requiring skills honed over the years. Third, the intensity and pressure of big firm billable hours is lessened by the nature of the work. You are more willing to shrug off the pressure if you know it is for a finite period than if you believe that the same stresses will continue *ad infinitum*. Moreover, I know from personal experience that working for a person I did not like did not bother me when I knew that the assignment was of limited duration— not anywhere near the effect it had on my mood and demeanor when I was in a "permanent" job and working for someone with whom I did not always get along. A lot of the stress paralegals may feel is eliminated, allowing them to better enjoy the work and the atmosphere in which they are performing that work. A fourth advantage is the pleasure of having your own "business" and providing your services to a number of different clients. Finally, for newer paralegals in saturated markets, working on a temporary basis enables them to gain experience in some matters, making them more attractive to employers.

The *Wall Street Journal* reported, on September 23, 1994, that "some 40,000 people worked as temporary lawyers or paralegals last year, up from 10,000 people two years earlier." Law firms of every size, from sole practitioners to corporate law departments, are increasingly turning to contract paralegals to meet their needs. The advantages to clients are numerous. Using temporary professionals enables the lawyers to increase and decrease their staff as necessary, thereby eliminating a lot of the extraneous hiring and subsequent firing of paralegals that was more prominent in the 1980s. Temporaries do not receive benefits, thereby eliminating a lot of the overhead for practitioners. No false expectations exist when a client uses contract paralegals or attorneys, and there are no hard feelings when the position ends. Temporaries are hired for a variety of situations, including special projects, for a particular case or transaction, to fill in during maternity or family leave, to determine whether sufficient work flow exists to justify a permanent hire, and to provide a trial period before hiring someone permanently. The length of assignments can range from one day, a week, or a month to an indefinite period of time, and may be full-time (i.e., 5 days a week for 35 to 50 hours) or part-time.

When a paralegal works through In-House Counsel, Inc., he or she is compensated on an hourly basis. The rate of compensation varies with the complexity of the assignment, the duration of the placement, and the paralegal's experience. The paralegal is paid through In-House Counsel, with all appropriate taxes withheld. We also pay the appropriate payroll taxes for the paralegals. Attorneys working through In-House Counsel, Inc. are placed as independent contractors, with no taxes withheld.

The types of assignments our paralegals perform vary according to the clients' needs. All disciplines within the legal profession are represented by law firms and corporations seeking to utilize temporary professionals—from the very specific to the very general. Some paralegals go into attorneys' offices that have never had a paralegal, to organize and streamline operations. On the other hand, cost-conscious corporations are handing over a lot of the responsibilities previously reserved for attorneys to less expensive paralegals. The spectrum of contract paralegal assignments covers everything in between these two extremes.

The benefits of contract professionals are well recognized in the paralegal field, and are becoming widely accepted in the attorney arena. Temporaries are the wave of the future in *all* professions, and organizations that provide contract employment opportunities can help you catch that wave in the legal field. ▐▌

Law Office Design

The physical space of the law office is important as an indicator of the culture and image of the firm, as well as a factor that either inhibits or enhances the work of the firm. As a paralegal or law office manager, you might have the opportunity to work on the design or redesign of your office. Additionally, you might have responsibilities for management of the facility itself.

Because law firms are unique in character and culture, they are often more difficult to design than many other types of businesses. As a paralegal or a law office manager, you might have the opportunity to help with initial design or renovations. Additionally, law firms with different practice orientations have different needs. For example, a firm specializing in corporate work or commercial litigation might need an impressive space with amenities for business clients who expect service and attention. A criminal law practice, in contrast, might use space in a restored downtown building, and might be more oriented to the needs of the various workers in the office than to the clients' needs. A criminal practice is also far more likely to be casual than is a practice catering to corporate issues or civil work.

When considering the usage of space in a law office, functionality is key. The space must be made to meet the needs of the law office in an efficient way.

Space needs may be broken into two main groups. First, space must be allocated for all of the professionals and paraprofessionals. They are the attorneys, law clerks, legal administration team, paralegals, medical researchers, and secretaries. Second, space must be allocated for support services, such as the photocopy center, library, mailroom, supply rooms, dining, kitchen, and break room facilities, file rooms, reception and conference rooms, and the like.

Because the square footage rental cost for space is usually very high, many lawyers are finding themselves in far smaller offices than their predecessors. It is important, therefore, that all necessary spaces be designed to use the least amount of footage while gaining maximum efficiency. (See Figure 3-10.) Many law firm designers have been using an open concept for a number of years. By *open*, we mean that secretarial and often paralegal spaces are not necessarily fully enclosed and do not have doors. On the positive side, those secretaries and paralegals have a feeling of spaciousness and light. On the downside, they often complain of a lack of privacy and noisy work conditions. There now exist modified open plans, where secretarial spaces are located behind partial walls with discreet openings in lieu of doorways; paralegals may have small, fully enclosed offices.

It is now rare to find the layout of years gone by where a secretary sat directly outside an attorney's office. One reason for this is the change in the secretary/word producer (attorney, law clerk, or paralegal) ratio. Now that the ratio is no longer one to one (one secretary for one attorney), the secretarial support is most efficiently placed for optimal access by the word producers whom he or she supports (i.e., one secretary for one attorney and one paralegal). Additionally, many paralegals and attorneys generate their own completed

FIGURE 3-10   Open work spaces can be flexibly designed to accommodate paralegal work areas (shown here), secretarial stations, and the library. (Photograph by Peter Aaron. Space designed by STUDIOS architects.)

work on personal computers, thus eliminating the need for extensive secretarial support.

Another important feature of the modern law office is natural light. Years ago, the accounting, word and data processing staff, and other support personnel were tucked away in interior spaces. Today, we know how important it is to give all workers as much natural light as possible. Now interior space is used for such things as photocopy centers. supply rooms, break rooms, and so on.

Conference rooms are designed with privacy in mind. They often have extra soundproofing between the walls and above the ceilings. Additionally, if glass is used as an interior wall for aesthetic purposes (as well as light), the glass may be frosted, or drapes may be provided. (See Figure 3-11.)

Achieving Image Through Interior Design

Law firms may select their interior style based upon the personalities and taste of the partners, the geographical location of the firm, or the market they are

FIGURE 3-11 Extensive use of wood and glass provides a warm yet professional environment. (Photograph by Peter Aaron. Space designed by STUDIOS architects.)

seeking. They may range from ultracontemporary, using glass, stone, granite, and light woods, to ultraconservative, using marble, rich mahogany, wood, and brass—or anywhere in between. Not very many years ago, most law firms looked similar in space and interior design. Today, architecture has become progressive, and law firms look extraordinarily different, but a common characteristic of well-designed firms is the efficient use of space. (See Figure 3-12.)

When an architect and interior designer are hired to develop space for a law firm, it is extremely important that they understand and respond to the law firm's requirements. To achieve this understanding, they work through a process called *programming*. It is their job to recognize and solve problems and to communicate clearly the character, philosophy, and desired image of the firm. In addition, they must make the space effective, efficient, and comfortable for all who inhabit it. These professionals must be intimately aware of the latest in technology so that they allow for the proper space requirements, lighting, and electrical needs. Equally important in the programming process, the principals of the law firm must be willing to communicate directly and effectively their perceived needs and desires. All in all, a collaborative effort is needed to stay within the budget while reflecting no compromise on design—either aesthetically or functionally. (See Figure 3-13.)

FIGURE 3-12 A multipurpose room can be used for conferences or training, has movable tables and chairs, and has kitchen access. (Photograph by Peter Aaron. Space designed by STUDIOS architects.)

Recent Trends in Law Office Design

A look at recent developments in law office design reveals the following trends, which, naturally, you are most likely to see in larger law firms:

Using offices that will later house attorneys and paralegals as "war rooms"— a place where attorneys can spread out large projects that will take a fairly long period of time.

The open plan work station concept for secretaries, with the added touch of clustering these stations and allowing panels tall enough to provide some privacy.

The location of all conference rooms on one floor, making it easier to control their use and availability, as well as enabling attorneys to take clients to the conference rooms without walking throughout the busy work environment.

The addition of many more conference rooms, as attorney offices are reduced in size (see Figure 3-14).

FIGURE 3-13 A professional image is created through design of lobby and reception area. (Photograph by Peter Aaron. Space designed by STUDIOS architects.)

FIGURE 3-14 Conference rooms can be used for a variety of purposes.

Greater attention to temperature, sound, ventilation, safety, personal preferences, the needs of handicapped workers, easier access to necessary facilities, and proper lighting.

The use of investment-quality art collections, including photography and sculpture.

Public areas that may be either contemporary or traditional, while the attorney offices may be the opposite, allowing for separate and unique identities.

The use of transom doors and clerestory-type glass, which allow exterior light to reach interior spaces.

Heavier filing accommodations throughout the firm.

Nicer surroundings for all of the people, not merely the attorneys, so that they enjoy their jobs more and look forward to going to work.

Day-care facilities for children of employees.

Staff lounges, executive dining rooms, and catering kitchens.

Regardless of whether a firm has several floors of a large, modern, office building, or whether a sole practitioner works out of his in-town neighborhood home, law offices must convey a positive impression, so that clients feel that their legal and personal needs will be fulfilled. Offices must have an effective layout so that all of the partners and employees can easily reach all support areas. They must not be wasteful, but should be planned carefully for future growth and expansion. They must place those who work together on a daily basis, such as attorneys, secretaries, and paralegals, in close proximity for greater productivity. They must be an appealing environment for all, thus strengthening the feeling of comradery within the firm and presenting a professional image to society.

Ergonomics and Work Station Design

Ergonomics is the part of design science that attempts to create an environment conducive to safety, health, and productivity. Law firms can improve the health and productivity of their workers by paying attention to the ergonomics of the work space, especially the furniture and equipment. Chairs should be easily adjustable so that a person can have his feet flat on the floor when he sits at the desk. Chairs should also have lower back support and arm rests.

Computer equipment must be set up and used ergonomically. The terminal should be comfortable to look at, with the height of the terminal no higher than the user's forehead. Glare from the computer screen should be minimized through use of glare screens. Employees who constantly work at a keyboard

FIGURE 3-15
Law office moves will become more frequent in the future.

should stop for a minute every now and then and look around to reduce eye strain. It is also important for employees who sit in one position to get their blood flowing by performing another activity. Sitting in one position for a long period of time decreases the flow of blood to the muscles, causing a buildup of lactic acid and resulting in soreness.

It is also extremely important for those using keyboards to use the correct typing position. This will help prevent carpal tunnel syndrome, in which the wrist tendons and carpal tunnel are gradually injured by incorrect hand position. Some typists wear wrist supports to reduce pain in the wrists. If a person has pain, she should see a doctor; unless prescribed by a doctor, wrist supports may well weaken the muscles and thereby increase the chance of developing carpal tunnel syndrome.

One final area in which ergonomics is important to law firms is in filing. Heavy files should be lifted with the support of the legs, and they should not be lifted while the person is in a sitting position. Files should not be lifted over the head, as that increases the chances for back injury.

By being ergonomically sensitive, law firms can complement their interior design choices with work stations that are most conducive to comfortable, healthy, and therefore productive employees.

The Law Office Move

One activity that is happening with increasing frequency in today's law practice, for various reasons, is moving the law office (Figure 3-15). If your firm chooses to move its office, you may be called upon to coordinate or assist with the move. It is a huge job, and the better organized you are, the better off your firm will be. The following considerations will help you if you are faced with this task.

Before the Move: Preparing Employees

As soon as your firm has decided to move and has given permission to disseminate this information, a memo should be sent to everyone in the firm setting a firm meeting. Inform everyone as early as possible, to avoid rumors and discontent. Also remember that people resist change, even if the change is for the better, and that you can ease their anxiety by communicating information and keeping everyone informed of relevant developments and timetables. Send frequent "newsletters" within the firm keeping everyone informed of progress. Make it fun and exciting for everyone.

If decisions are being made that will greatly affect the employees, ask for their opinions. For instance, if your firm is considering a move to a location a significant distance away, take a poll of how current employees feel about it. This will allow you to anticipate the loss of employees due to the move. It could change the minds of the partners who want to move to a distant location. If you are going to purchase new furnishings, talk about color, style, etc. in your newsletter so that everyone can enjoy and learn to live with the new items. The importance of involving all people in the move cannot be stressed enough.

Planning the Move

A tremendous amount of planning and work must be done to prepare the office for its move. The following checklist describes the things that must be attended to prior to the move.

Before the Move: Practical Considerations

Conduct a complete inventory of all equipment, furnishings, and supplies. List their value.

Consider security needs and costs, such as off-duty police officers, vehicles, etc.

Interview and ask for bids from a number of reputable movers. Get one bid for furnishings, file boxes, etc. and another for computers, photocopy equipment, and other electronic devices.

Select a moving company(ies) and finalize details.

Notify the firm's insurance carrier of the impending move.

Schedule installations for the new site.

Order dedicated telephone and fax lines.

Take bids for all new furnishings and equipment; review and select vendors; finalize details.

Advise the firm's long-distance telephone service of the new address and phone numbers.

Advise the Postal Service and all existing vendors, clients, and friends of the firm of the new address, telephone number(s), and date of move.

Destroy old, outdated forms.

Days Before the Move

In the days just prior to the move, you will need to attend to the following issues.

Files/File Cabinets   Ask the staff to close as many files as possible and have those files moved off-site to your records storage area prior to the move. It will make life a lot easier when everyone starts to unpack at the new building.

Ask that all file cabinets and desks be emptied prior to 8 A.M. on the day of the move. You may want to distribute "FILES FORMS," which can be color-coded by section, floor, etc. These forms should be taped to the outside of the boxes storing the files that are being moved to the new space.

Automation/Photocopy Machines   Because this type of equipment must be serviced and packaged some time prior to the move by outside specialists, advise everyone that the equipment will not be available after a certain date and time, and make arrangements for temporary, rented equipment if necessary.

Packing Boxes   Order more boxes than you need—you probably will still not have enough. Have a source ready to bring you additional boxes immediately upon request.

Postcards to Clients   If the firm's telephone system will allow for Direct Inward Dialing (DID), order postcards and distribute them to all. (See Figure 3-16.) Ask people to take the time to complete and mail those cards to their clients and other colleagues advising them of their personal telephone numbers, which will bypass the switchboard. Allow ample time for this process.

Formal Announcements   Design and order formal announcements advising those on your mailing lists of your move, the new address, telephone, and facsimile numbers.

As you may know, we will be moving our offices to 880 West Peachtree Street, Atlanta, Georgia 30309, on March 18, 1988. Our post office box and main telephone number will remain:

P.O. Box 7600
Atlanta, Georgia 30357
(404) 885-1400

You will now be able to reach me and the others listed below on direct dial numbers — without going through our switchboard. We believe this will give our clients better, more efficient service.

Attorney Jones   **885-6289**

Best regards,

DREW, ECKL & FARNHAM

FIGURE 3-16   Postcards advise clients that the firm is moving.

Conference Room Designations   Some firms choose to call their conference rooms by names (often those of famous people), some use colors, and others use numbers. Whatever your plan, designate the conference rooms prior to the move and let everyone know those designations.

Informational Items   Be sure to plan ahead when preparing and/or ordering the following items reflecting the new location:

business cards
letterhead and envelopes
mailing labels
firm telephone directories
notepaper

Artwork   Many firms have rules about wall hangings that can and cannot be affixed to the walls of the new space. Establish guidelines and disseminate them immediately.

Smoking or Smoke-Free Office   Whatever your partners decide, let your employees know the rules right away. This has become a major issue in the workplace. If it is decided that the space will be smoke-free, let smokers know that they are free to go outside on their morning and afternoon breaks, where they may smoke if they wish.

The Actual Move

The move itself will be a combination of excitement and chaos. People will be excited, nervous, and curious. As professional movers are generally used, make it abundantly clear that, other than those employees assisting with the move, no one should go to the new building the day of the move. It only causes confusion and impedes the progress of the movers. Do arrange to have your automation, photocopy, and telephone technicians on-site as soon as it is practical so that you can be operational as soon as possible.

Tell the attorneys and staff when they may come to the office to unpack and get organized. Encourage people to come dressed comfortably; this is one time when professional attire is not necessary. Most law firms move over the weekend so that there is very little actual "down time."

Everyone will have worked very hard to make the move a smooth one. You can provide little extras to let them know that you appreciate their hard work. For instance, order food and beverages (at firm expense) to be delivered on the day that everyone is packing up boxes and preparing for the move. Some firms purchase T-shirts with an appropriate phrase for everyone to wear on packing day. It is great for team spirit and firm pride.

If your firm is located on more than one floor, you may choose to color-code your signs. For instance, the first floor might be green, the second floor blue, and so forth. If you choose to color-code, obtain packing labels that are color-coded to match the new floor of the employee. Those labels should also reflect the room number of each individual. You may assign room numbers by using your blueprints as a guide. Be sure to give everyone a chart showing exactly where they are supposed to label office furniture.

Ask that all packed boxes be numbered in sequence with heavy felt-tip marker. After doing so, an inventory sheet must be completed and turned in to someone, perhaps the receptionist. This will assure that nothing has been misplaced or, in the event that it has, you will be able to identify the lost box.

The door to each room should have a sign affixed to it showing the name of the occupant, the new room number, new telephone extension, and type of telephone. A room layout will also be attached to the sign to assist the movers in the placement of furniture at the new location. A floor-plan layout should also be sent to each person so that they will know where everything and everyone is located in the new space.

An individualized list of office moving instructions should be given to each person. Ask that they read the instructions carefully. Be sure to arrange for parking for your employees, at least for the first day or two, and explain to everyone where deliveries of goods will be accepted in the new location.

Explain who will oversee the packing and unpacking of library volumes. Each box should be labeled with a form specifically designed for the library, listing the contents of each box. To lessen the inconvenience for researchers needing access to library materials after the move, you may wish to set up temporary tables and seating until the shelves can be installed and the books replaced.

The librarian or the paralegal assigned to assist in the library should use discretion in arranging access to volumes in frequent demand. Regular library services, such as routing and ordering of opinions, should continue uninterrupted. Prior to the move, all library materials should be returned to the library. After the move, ask that books not be removed until checkout facilities are provided.

Advise the staff of the hours that the switchboards will remain open. Let them know when the system will be shut down to be moved to the new location.

After the Move

The day after the move will be confusing at best. It is a nice idea to bring in food and beverages for lunch on that first day. It is also nice to have a small box of candy or a flower placed on each employee's desk—a small token of the firm's appreciation for their hard work and support.

Also, on each employee's desk the day after the move should be a firm directory, showing the extensions for all people and commonly used rooms; business cards, if applicable; and a form for the employees to note problems, complaints, missing items, damage, and so on. A thank-you memo from the partners makes people feel that their effort is appreciated.

Legal Environments: A Summary

This chapter has introduced you to the law office: the forms it takes, the people who work there, issues that arise there, and how offices are designed and moved. Becoming knowledgeable about all of these facets of the law office will help you as a paralegal because you will be familiar with the environment in which you will be doing your work. Additionally, this knowledge will aid your career development, as it will enable you to choose the environment in which you will be happiest and most productive.

Key Terms

boutique firm	law clerk	outsourcing
contract employment	law office committees	rainmaker
ergonomics	law office design	satellite office
freelance attorney	legal team	small law firm
government attorney	of counsel	sole practitioner
in-house counsel	open work space	summer associate
large law firm		

Problems and Activities

1. Describe the ideal legal environment for you. Why do you believe that you would be best suited for this type of environment?

2. Consult *Martindale-Hubbell* to determine the characteristics of three firms in a city of your choice. Explain your classification with references to chapter examples.

3. Review the positions described in the text. Which positions might attract your future interest? What skills must you gain to prepare for that position?

4. What do you think are the advantages of being employed by a sole practitioner? Are there any disadvantages?

5. What skills can you develop if you work with a sole practitioner to ensure that you have job security?

6. Should paralegals be involved in the management committees of law firms? Why or why not?

CHAPTER 4

MANAGING LAW FIRM GROWTH: MARKETING, STRATEGIC PLANNING, AND THE LAW FIRM OF THE FUTURE

CHAPTER OUTLINE

OBJECTIVES

By the completion of this chapter, you should:

- understand the importance of marketing and planning legal services;

- understand how to develop and implement a marketing plan for legal services;

- understand strategic planning and its place in law firm business development; and

- understand the trends and realities that will characterize the law firm of the future.

ON POINT **THE FLINTSTONES DO PRACTICE DEVELOPMENT**

"Gosh, Fred, it sure was great that the new law firm in town, Bedrock and Associates, hired us to help them with their business. Those referral bonuses will sure come in handy," says Barney.

"I know, Barney. OK, let's see. I could get Wilma to go to the hospital, since she knows so many nurses there, and she could get the accident victims to sign contracts with our lawyers. And Nick and Aaron, the ambulance drivers, could give them cards as they went into the emergency room."

"That's good, Fred! And Betty could go through the newspaper and when she saw an article about an accident or an injured-person report, we could send them one of our brochures."

"Y'know, Barney, lots of those folks at unemployment were probably illegally terminated. How about if we go to the unemployment office and see if we can roust out some plaintiffs?"

"That's a good one, Fred. Hey, how about if your construction company stops work on the new school addition until the school district changes to Bedrock and Associates for its legal work?"

"Are you sure we can do all these things?" asks Fred. "They're great ideas and all, but they seem a little sleazy, if you know what I mean."

"Fred, remember: these are lawyers. And those referral bonuses will sure buy some nice brontosaurus steaks!"

"You're right, Barney," says Fred. "Let's get to work."

Marketing Legal Services: An Introduction

To develop and maintain a viable client base, law firms must develop and implement marketing plans. This is especially true of law firms in the 1990s; as competition for clients becomes more intense, and the cost of doing business increases, law firms must concentrate their efforts on attracting new business. The objective of a marketing plan, also known as *practice development,* is to retain the firm's good clients while improving hourly billing rates; to identify and obtain new clients who will pay higher rates; to expand the practice in areas in which the firm can achieve a superior level of professional competence and profitability; and to promote the firm's image and reputation.

To achieve these objectives, everyone in the firm, from the senior partner to the mailroom personnel, must be involved in the marketing process. In addition to involving all personnel in the marketing process, law firms must explore all potential marketing channels. These channels include, but are not limited to, brochures, newsletters, seminars, advertising, entertainment of clients, office routines, telephone procedures, referrals from other lawyers, ways bills are rendered—basically everything the firm does affects the public's perception of the firm. (See Figures 4-1 and 4-2.) Also, the effective law firm must develop marketing leadership that generates a commitment to marketing at all levels from all law office personnel; firm management must promote, endorse, reward, and love the marketing program or it simply will not work.

An additional—and critically important—consideration is whether the firm's marketing plan complies with relevant ethical standards. For example, the American Bar Association Code of Professional Responsibility precludes attorneys from soliciting business. Therefore, it is imperative that any marketing plan be checked to ensure that it complies with ethical restrictions placed on lawyer advertising or soliciting. Marketing is not solicitation per se; however, if the firm chooses to advertise, either on television or in print, the advertising

FIGURE 4-1 Everyone in the firm, from the receptionist ...

FIGURE 4-2   ... to the senior partners, must be involved in the marketing effort.

must comply with advertising standards enumerated by local bar associations. Thus, for any marketing plan, it is essential that someone in the firm ensures that the plan does not violate legal ethical standards put forth by the local bar association.

The general rule for lawyer advertising, as it is with most commercial speech, is that the advertising must be truthful and nondeceptive. There exist strong sentiments in many jurisdictions, however, that the rules governing attorney advertising should be made stricter. Proponents of stricter standards look to the negative public opinions and perceptions of lawyers as a direct result of advertising. Lawyers who favor unrestricted advertising believe that the First Amendment protects their position. As various states develop restrictions on advertising, it will be interesting to see how far the courts will allow the states to go in restricting attorney speech.

As this edition enters production, a Florida law requiring a 30-day waiting period before attorneys can solicit business from injured parties is being challenged. The state is arguing that victims' vulnerability right after an accident makes them prey to overreaching; the attorney challenging the regulation counters that right after an accident is the time an injured person most needs legal advice. Future court decisions will clarify these issues in lawyer advertising.

An effective marketing program also requires materials to make people aware of the law firm. These materials might include the following:

1. A brochure and a plan for distribution to both existing and new clients. The brochure can be a significant investment and should be written from a client's viewpoint. The brochure alone will not necessarily gain a new client, but it can create a good first impression that may lead to new business.

2. Lists maintained on a database, including trade associations, civic and charitable organizations, local chamber of commerce members, health care groups, environmental groups, international groups, or any organization whose orientation and interests would mesh with those of the firm. These lists can be used for multiple purposes, such as having an attorney give a speech on a particular topic, inviting people from these various groups to visit the firm when the firm has an in-house seminar, and so on. These lists can be viewed as potential clients.

3. Weekly in-house marketing newsletter.

4. Pocket folders with firm name, address, and telephone numbers on the cover, to be used at presentations.

5. Stickers that say:

> Compliments
> of
> A & M
> Attorneys at Law

Put them on gift boxes and other giveaways.

6. A distinctive announcement.

7. A distinctive letterhead.

8. Lettering and style that is carried on all publications, announcements, brochures, letterheads, cards, and the like, giving the firm a visual identity.

9. Constantly updated client profiles and attorney profiles, which can provide valuable marketing leads and information.

10. Development of practice area résumés for distribution separate from the firm's brochure, describing the various specialties of the firm and listing any important cases the firm has handled successfully. (See Figure 4-3.)

11. Development and presentation of seminars concerning topics in the law. Seminars allow for contact with the law firm and allow the firm to showcase some of its attorneys. Seminars may carry continuing education credits as well. (See Figure 4-4.)

This list should give you a start in thinking of materials that can be used effectively in a marketing program. As a paralegal, you can make a real contribution to the firm's business development effort by developing methods and sharing ideas with those in charge of marketing in your firm. The more you make contributions of this kind, the more valuable you will make yourself, and the greater your chances will be to develop your career to include new responsibilities.

One issue that many firms face concerning business development is determining the leadership for marketing efforts. In larger law firms, the trend today is toward hiring a marketing director. Although many firms have formed marketing committees, led by a partner, to develop and implement marketing

FIGURE 4-3
Practice area résumé
informs clients and
prospective clients of
attorney specialties.

ARTHUR H. GLASER

ACADEMIC BACKGROUND
Preparatory Education:
Hampden-Sydney College (B.S., 1968)
Legal Education:
University of Virginia Law School (J.D., 1973)

ADMISSION TO BAR
Georgia (1973)

AREAS OF FIRM PRACTICE
Litigation (General Liability; Products Liability; Civil Rights;
Libel & Slander)

PROFESSIONAL MEMBERSHIPS
Atlanta Bar Association
State Bar of Georgia
American Bar Association
Defense Research Institute
Atlanta Claims Association
Lawyers Club of Atlanta

PUBLICATIONS AND LECTURES
Lecturer, Georgia State Patrol Academy (1974-1981)
Co-Author, "Jones v. State Farm, An Expensive Lesson" Georgia State Bar
Journal, May, 1982.
Speaker, "Duty to Defend, Declaratory Judgments, and Extracontractual
Liability", State Bar of Georgia Insurance Law Institute, 1983.
Chairman, No Fault Insurance Seminar, Atlanta Bar Association, 1984.

OTHER AFFILIATIONS
President, Hampden-Sydney Alumni Club of Atlanta (1979-1982)
St. Anne's Episcopal Church

MILITARY SERVICE
U.S. Army Reserve

strategies, these committees often lack effectiveness because marketing and business development are truly full-time activities. A single individual, who possesses both business development skills and familiarity with law firms, can sometimes be more effective than a committee. Of course, a marketing director cannot be successful without the active support of the legal staff. If lawyers are unwilling to speak, write articles, or come to receptions, no director can market the firm successfully. Another problem can arise if the marketing director is promoted from within. On the positive side, the firm is rewarding high achievement, but, on the negative, the person may not possess the requisite skills or may never be perceived as anything other than what she was in the previous position. Therefore, larger firms are realizing that they should hire an individual to coordinate the business development program, a desirable addition to the law office management team. There is reluctance to add a person who will not achieve billable hours, and small law firms will have an even harder time affording a marketing director. Therefore, some firms will hire outside consultants or attempt to have the marketing position filled by a person already on staff, such as a paralegal or office manager. In the future, however, more and more large firms will have a marketing director on staff to lead marketing efforts.

DREW, ECKL & FARNHAM

1994 Amendments to the
Georgia Workers'
Compensation Act

A SEMINAR

MAY 11, 1994

J.W. MARRIOTT HOTEL
AT LENOX

3300 LENOX ROAD N.E.

ATLANTA, GEORGIA

*4 Hours Continuing
Education Credit*

PROGRAM

12:45	Registration
1:00	Overview and Legislative History of 1994 Amendments – *H. Michael Bagley*
1:30	Controlling Costs of Claims: Changes Affecting Medical Care Delivery under the Act – *John Bruffey, Jr.*
2:00	Trial Return to Work – *Daniel Kniffen*
2:30	Notice, Penalties and Appeal: Changes Affecting Administration of the Act – *John G. Blackmon, Jr.*
3:00	Question and Answer Session
3:15	Coffee Break

PROGRAM

3:30	Retrospective View of 1992 Amendments – *John A. Ferguson,Jr.*
4:00	Subrogation Liens – *John A. Reale*
4:20	Changes in the Statutory Employer Rule – *Ann Bishop Byars*
4:40	New Board Rules and Recent Case Law Developments – *David A. Smith*
5:00	Question and Answer Session
5:15	Cocktail Reception

4 hours continuing education credit

FIGURE 4-4   Developing and presenting seminars allows the firm to showcase its attorneys and may carry continuing education credits as well.

An effective marketing program should be oriented toward both existing and potential clients. The following sections discuss marketing strategies for each of these target groups.

Marketing to Existing Clients

The greatest opportunity for marketing legal services is to focus on existing clients. The following methods can be effectively used to expand services to existing clients.

Activities and Events

The firm should host activities, such as receptions following professional association meetings and annual seminars (see Figure 4-5). After the function, the firm should follow up with a letter telling clients that the firm is pleased they participated. This will keep the firm's name in front of them.

FIGURE 4-5
Associates plan a reception after an association meeting.

Contact Publications

The firm should develop and send clients firm newsletters, holiday cards, announcements, and other relevant material to keep clients informed and make them feel that the firm is concerned about their interests and welfare. (See Figure 4-6.) If the firm adds a new partner with a new specialty, this information could open the door for new business from existing clients. However, nothing can develop unless clients are given this valuable information through an announcement or personal letter. (See Figure 4-7.)

Personal Contacts

The firm and its people should take time to develop personal contacts that involve the client and demonstrate the firm's commitment to satisfying and retaining that client. Attorneys can send out "client advisories," not only to let them know where their affairs stand, but also containing information that may

JOURNAL
DREW ECKL & FARNHAM

Volume 7, No. 37 January 1995

NEW DEVELOPMENTS REGARDING THE GEORGIA OPEN RECORDS ACT.

by Leigh Lawson Reeves
885-6409

O.C.G.A. §50-18-70 et seq., commonly known as the Georgia Open Records Act (the "Act"), essentially requires that all public records of an agency be open for personal inspection by any citizen of the state. Those in charge of keeping such records cannot refuse this privilege to any citizen. See O.C.G.A. §50-18-70(b). There are some documents, however, which are *not* required to be produced and

the Act lists approximately nine exceptions to disclosure. The exceptions that are relevant to the employment context are: (1) records that are specified by the federal government as being confidential; and (2) medical records, veterinarian records, and/or "similar files," the disclosure of which would be an *invasion of personal privacy.* These specific types of employer documents are expressly exempt from disclosure.

There are two other exceptions
(continued on page 3)

ELEVENTH CIRCUIT FORTIFIES QUALIFIED IMMUNITY DEFENSE.

by Phil Fridus
885-6220

With three bold strokes of the pen, the Eleventh Circuit, sitting en banc in Lassitter v. Alabama A&M University, 28 F.3d 1146 (11th Cir. 1994) resoundingly fortified the qualified immunity defense.

The doctrine of qualified immunity is familiar to all of those practicing in the area of governmental liability. Where federal constitutional violations are alleged, "government officials performing discretionary functions generally are shielded from liability for civil damages insofar as their conduct does not violate clearly established statutory or constitutional rights of which a reasonable person would have known." Harlow v. Fitzgerald, 457 U.S. 800, 818, 102 S.Ct. 2727, 2738 (1982). This immunity was judicially created to protect public officials from being sued for every error in judgment, thereby diverting their attention from their public duties, preventing them from independently exercising their discretion because of the fear of damages liability, and discouraging qualified persons from seeking public office at all. In short, the doctrine was created because society wants our public officials to make the close calls.

The Supreme Court in Harlow chose an objective rather than a subjective
(continued on page 4)

FIGURE 4-6   Newsletters are an important marketing vehicle used to keep clients informed.

FIGURE 4-7 Firms should announce new members as part of their marketing efforts.

DREW ECKL & FARNHAM

IS PLEASED TO ANNOUNCE

THAT

A. BRADLEY DOZIER, JR.
B. GREG CLINE
TRICIA R. STEVENS
C. LAWRENCE MEYER
E. JANYCE DAWKINS
PHILIP G. POMPILIO
ROBERT J. MOYE III
GREGORY S. ESSLINGER
SEÁN W. CONLEY
MARY ANNE ACKOUREY
BEVERLY POWELL SISK
MARION M. HANDLEY

HAVE BECOME ASSOCIATED WITH THE FIRM

AND THAT

KEVIN P. O'MAHONY

HAS BECOME OF COUNSEL TO THE FIRM

_____

DREW ECKL & FARNHAM

880 WEST PEACHTREE STREET
P.O. BOX 7600
ATLANTA, GEORGIA 30357

(404) 885-1400

WINTER 1995

make a difference in their businesses. For example, if the firm's attorneys have a speaking engagement, and it is possible for clients to attend, let them know. Attorneys should also make more effort to entertain their clients. Entertainment need not be expensive to be appreciated, but it should take place in an environment in which attorneys and clients can talk easily, so that they can get to know one another better, which will build loyalty.

Client Review Program

Firms may choose to conduct a client review program annually. In a client review program, each partner takes the time to call on "key" clients to get feedback about the firm's services. *Key clients* does not mean only those clients who currently spend the most money with the firm, but should also include clients

FIGURE 4-7
(continued)

KEVIN P. O'MAHONY

Mr. O'Mahony has become Of Counsel for Drew, Eckl & Farnham's Healthcare, Medical Malpractice and Business Litigation Sections. Mr. O'Mahony has extensive experience representing healthcare providers, insurers and employers in negotiating managed care and other health contracts, and litigating and resolving medical malpractice and business disputes.

Mr. O'Mahony received his degrees from Montclair State College (B.S., Business Administration and Accounting), magna cum laude, and the College of William & Mary Law School (J.D.), where he was selected to the Order of Barristers, and received the American College of Trial Lawyers' Medal for Excellence in Advocacy.

Mr. O'Mahony has spoken and written extensively about the topics of physician and hospital liability, managed care contracts, and compliance with Medicare, Medicaid, healthcare antitrust, and patient self-referral laws.

Mr. O'Mahony is a member of the American Bar Association (Litigation and Antitrust Sections and Forum on Health Law), the National Health Lawyers Association, the Georgia Academy of Hospital Attorneys, and the state Bar of Georgia (Health Law Section). He is admitted to practice in the United States Supreme Court, the federal and state courts in Georgia, and has been specially admitted in numerous state and federal courts throughout the country.

with potential. A second partner should attend the meeting, to make the client feel more at ease and allow her to be more honest and open when commenting. When the client review is reported to the firm, one person might have picked up on something that the other missed.

The client should be asked in advance if she is willing to participate. Let the client know that the firm is interested in her opinion, that the program has been designed because the firm is interested in what she thinks, and that the firm is taking the time and making the effort in order to serve clients' needs better. The client should be "interviewed" informally, but direct questions should be asked. Robert W. Denney, a management consultant, developed the following points that he believes should be covered:

1. Client's opinion of our firm and services.

2. Client's opinion of members of the firm with whom she has had contact;

3. Does client feel we have been prompt? Kept her informed? Have followed up?

4. Have we helped the client in other areas besides the particular areas we are working in?

5. Does the client feel we have let her down?

6. Would the client recommend us to other people if asked? May we use the client's name as a reference?

The most revealing answer will probably be to the last question. If the client's answers are negative, it is essential to dig deeper to determine if the client can be saved.

These interviews should be handled over lunch or a cup of coffee, but never over drinks. The partners and associates should take notes, and a report should be given to the department heads and marketing director upon returning from the interview. All interview results should be loaded into a database, sorted, distributed, and discussed at a meeting of all attorneys as soon as practical.

If a negative pattern has developed, the firm must be prepared to make changes. If clients are asked for their opinions, the firm must take them seriously and act on them. If it is not prepared to do so, a client review program could—and probably would—be more harmful than helpful. When you have completed your interviews, write the clients who participated and thank them. Let them know the basic results of the survey and any changes the firm plans to make.

Although this process can and does take a great deal of nonbillable time, the rewards from a client review program can be significant. The client feels important to the firm; the attorney has probably gained a greater understanding of the client's needs and wants; and information should have been gathered that will be helpful in cross-selling. Additionally, the firm may pick up a referral or two.

Cross-Selling

Cross-selling refers to the process of marketing additional legal services to existing clients and contacts. In all law practices, contacts are made with a large number of businesses and individuals with whom the firm has a prior attorney-client relationship through the companies they service. These contacts are an extremely fertile source of additional business for the firm. Do not hesitate to ask directly for other types of work. The firm has already won the contact's trust and confidence; therefore, she will generally be happy to give the attorneys additional work. Existing contacts are the greatest resource for new business. It is less expensive to cultivate new business from existing contacts than from new contacts, because the firm does not have to spend nonbillable time researching the business or industry, and the client is already comfortable with the law firm.

You can begin an effective cross-selling program by identifying key prospects in the existing contact base. Focus your efforts on the best opportunities, determining that the contact has additional needs the firm could handle. The contact is probably not aware of all of the services your firm offers and will be impressed if you can relate your abilities to her needs.

Once you have identified key clients to cross-sell, you should complete a client profile to be given to the marketing director or person in charge of marketing efforts so that they can be sure no duplications exist. (See Figure 4-8.) Marketing must be a coordinated team effort if it is to be successful. You can establish a budget for each targeted contact, including nonbillable time and out-of-pocket expenses. The amount allocated should be carefully compared to the amount of potential new business from the existing contact. For example, if the potential exists for one new case per year, the expenses for pursuing this business should be less than for another client who can potentially send the firm one hundred new cases per year.

When the section heads have targeted existing contacts who might give the firm new business, they should:

Date Prepared _____
Date Reviewed _____
Resp. Atty. _____

CLIENT PROFILE

Name _____   Industry _____
Address _____   Phone ( ) _____
_____   No. of Employees _____
Other locations _____
_____
Subsidiaries _____
Description of business _____
_____
Sales volume last year _____   Union(s) _____
No. of shareholders _____   Public (Exchange) _____
                                          Private _____
On file: Current annual report _____
    Latest 10K _____
    Proxy statements _____
Accounting firm _____   Bank _____
Other law firms _____
Our current services to client _____
_____
Other services we could perform _____
_____
New areas where client has needs and we could develop expertise _____
_____
Key contact/Position _____
Personal and family information _____

FIGURE 4-8   Client profiles aid the marketing director in implementing cross-selling strategies.

1. Write and submit to the marketing director a marketing plan, stating action steps to be taken by themselves, their sections, and possibly other attorneys, and including the budget;
2. Compile a list of attorneys who will take each step.
3. Create a deadline for each step.
4. Articulate the anticipated benefit.

Follow-up should be handled by the marketing director and the section heads on a routine basis. A quarterly report should be published, outlining the progress of the cross-selling campaign. If, at some point, nothing has come in, and a lot of time and expenses have gone out, a determination must be made by the marketing director and the section head to stop the campaign with that particular contact. The firm must be careful not to spend more than it can reap in increased net billings.

A number of positive steps can be taken to cross-sell legal services effectively. The goal of these activities is to make the client want to give the firm more business and to develop long-term loyalty that will result in increased and stable business. These activities include having more frequent involvement; regular phone contact; meetings at lunch/dinner; introducing the client to other partners; putting the client in touch with others who might be helpful, such as accountants or business consultants; sending the contact interesting and useful articles; offering to hold seminars at her office; giving the attorney's home telephone number; including the client in social activities; remembering dates of personal importance to the contact, such as birthdays and anniversaries; and so forth.

As the attorney and the support staff cross-sell existing contacts and clients, they will want to increase their knowledge of the contact's business, both its product and its internal structure. Find out what makes the client happy and unhappy, and be sensitive to her needs, both professionally and personally. This extra effort will engender loyalty to the firm.

Summary

These methods can be used to market legal services to existing contacts and clients and are actually the application of good business practices to the legal environment. The expansion of current client services should be the top priority for marketing, but the marketing effort should also include methods and strategies for attracting new business.

Marketing Legal Services to Prospective Clients

If existing clients are your greatest resource for new business, why spend the time, energy, and money looking for new ones? For firms to be fiscally sound today, a steady flow of new clients is a must. Additionally, new clients raise the morale of the law firm. David Maister, a marketing consultant in Boston, has stated that "There is ... somewhat of a link between the volume and variety of new clients and the motivation, morale, dynamism, and enthusiasm of the professional staff." All firms need to develop the ability to handle larger, more complex matters; to serve more clients; to replace clients lost by attrition; to upgrade their client list; to provide opportunities for younger lawyers; and last, but certainly not least, to increase the partners' incomes. To accomplish this, firms can pursue a number of options and activities. These efforts might include the following:

1. Include prospective clients on seminar lists; follow up after the functions.

2. Add prospective clients to the firm's newsletter, holiday card, and announcement lists. (See Figure 4-9.)

3. Send *bullets* (brief advisory notes) stating recent court decisions, or other matters that might affect the prospective client's business. Bullets might also cover subjects such as new practice sections added to the firm. The person might like what he reads and might contact the firm to do his legal work.

4. Have the marketing director obtain a personal contacts list from each attorney—people each attorney knows from clubs, civic and professional organizations, church, and so on who are in a position to give business to the firm. People do not have to be contacted by the attorney who knows them if she is uncomfortable about doing so in a professional capacity; others can do it. (See Figure 4-10.)

5. Have the marketing director, along with the department heads and the section heads, create a list of potential new clients. Each partner, along with

FIGURE 4-9
A legal assistant prepares a firm mailing.

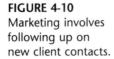

FIGURE 4-10
Marketing involves
following up on
new client contacts.

a senior associate, should be assigned to at least one potential client. Those teams should report routinely on their progress in making contact. By assigning primary responsibility to partners and having a regular reporting function, the marketing program can effectively integrate the checks and balances necessary to make it effective.

6. Using lists of CPAs, banks, and other business institutions, assign attorneys to make contacts to see how they can help each other. Present joint seminars with a public accounting firm, bank, or other business institution, thus expanding your list of participants (and contacts).

7. Require each section to have a practice development plan that includes not only cross-selling, but also plans to obtain new clients.

8. As a part of the firm's marketing awareness, put one partner or senior associate in charge of "trend-watching research," to develop new service areas and prepare to sell those services. The ideal person for this job is a creative thinker. The firm needs to be on the cutting edge while recognizing its limitations and the scope of its services and clients. Reports should be submitted to the partner in charge of marketing on a semiannual basis.

All of these methods can help a law firm increase its client base if the firm is committed to involving everyone in the process and structuring a marketing plan that fits the firm's goals and abilities. The tendency for larger law firms is to have an individual, such as a marketing director, spearhead the marketing effort. Naturally, a large firm will have a much more thorough marketing plan than a sole practitioner; it will also have greater resources and personnel to implement the plan. For the paralegal interested in marketing, therefore, the environment will dictate how to integrate marketing into your work. In a large firm, you can increase your involvement in marketing by ascertaining how the marketing effort is organized and working within established channels. This might involve communicating your interest to the attorney, marketing director, or office administrator in charge of marketing. They will tell you how you might participate. In a smaller firm, you might have the opportunity to play a greater role in marketing or even to develop a marketing plan yourself. In either situation, you will need to work with your supervisor to see how your efforts can effectively mesh with the efforts of others in your office.

Practice Development Through Firm Image and Community Involvement

Community involvement is an area where social responsibility and marketing efforts can intersect. By being involved in community projects, lawyers and paralegals can fulfill their personal interests and social responsibilities while simultaneously raising the community's awareness of the firm and perception of its competence and reputation. Because this area provides a positive opportunity for all involved, large firms are requiring community involvement, and smaller firms are recognizing its value and significance.

Training Legal Personnel in Marketing Techniques

Most attorneys and paralegals have been trained in the law, not in marketing, and firms need to develop training programs to help legal personnel understand the importance of marketing and to develop the skills necessary to perform marketing functions. Lawyers and paralegals cannot be expected to be business developers if they are not trained and encouraged, and the effective law firm needs to establish a development program in this area.

It is most important to recognize that marketing is effective only if all people in the firm are attuned to the marketing program. In-house workshops for all legal and nonlegal personnel are helpful to spread information, develop skills, and encourage participation in the marketing program. In addition to general seminars in marketing, those in charge of marketing should develop topics for training programs. (See Figure 4-11.)

There are many methods to disseminate information about marketing plans and strategies and develop marketing skills. Study groups that meet regularly can aid in training legal personnel in marketing. These groups can use videotapes and manuals focusing on a specific marketing topic each month. They should share business development experiences—a good way to motivate. These groups can then bring in speakers or experts to teach business development skills.

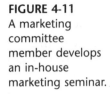

FIGURE 4-11
A marketing committee member develops an in-house marketing seminar.

A mentor program can be helpful in developing marketing skills with younger personnel. Younger attorneys or paralegals can be paired with more experienced people to learn effective communication and business development skills. This process will help young associates learn from the "rainmakers," those who bring in a lot of business, so that they can take a more active role in business development.

Every two months, all attorneys could meet for a luncheon program. At the luncheon, they could do things such as:

1. Have a high-profile CPA share how business development is done in her firm.
2. Invite clients to sit on a panel to discuss what clients like and do not like about lawyers—what they want and do not want. Similarly, invite two in-house counsel to discuss what they look for when hiring a law firm.

ON POINT *THE CASE OF ZINA THE ZEALOUS PARALEGAL*

Zina the paralegal is on her way to work, about to board the southbound train to her office. Suddenly, an elderly woman is caught in the closing doors and is hurt and shaken up. Zina, being the good citizen she is, pulls the woman out of the door, helps her to a seat, and proceeds to tell the woman that her firm specializes in personal injury cases and can get her millions in settlement. Suddenly, the woman's elbow feels a whole lot better. Zina reaches into her purse, pulls out a business card, which does not include her job designation, and says, "Keep this for your records, and I'll take you down to our office right now because you have an obvious tort claim and the sooner we get started on your case the better." Any problems with Zina's marketing efforts?

3. Invite two reporters from a local news publication to do an "interview" on a hypothetical set of circumstances with two partners.

4. Create a monthly business development newsletter (for firm use only) with tips on "how to." Also, give recognition to those who have participated in the marketing program during the month.

5. Bring in an image consultant who can tell the lawyers how important the proper image is and help them correct any negative images. You only get one chance to make a good first impression.

6. Do role-playing. One person can act as the attorney seeking new business, while the other acts as the potential client. Videotape the role-play and have others critique it.

7. Share success stories; provide an overview of progress; talk it up—get everyone excited about marketing.

8. Reproduce interesting articles in a weekly marketing newsletter (in-house).

As these activities suggest, there is no single way to create a marketing effort. In general, however, it is important for law firms to make everyone aware of the importance of marketing and to help all personnel develop the skills and attitudes necessary to a successful marketing program. This should include all people connected to the law firm; spouses and family members should not be forgotten in the process of networking for legal business.

It is also important for the firm to have a motivation and compensation program that complements the marketing strategy. A firm needs to evaluate its compensation program to see if it supports or sabotages the marketing program. If the firm rewards only for billable hours, marketing will never be successful. Bonuses are a good way to support and reward for exceptional success in business development. Award programs can also show thanks and appreciation, and daily or weekly marketing newsletters can be sent to everyone in the firm recognizing those who have made efforts. The key is to build in rewards for marketing efforts, because they generally require nonbillable hours.

For a marketing program to be successful, it should be mandatory for every lawyer to complete and give to the marketing director a personal marketing plan, on a quarterly basis. (See Figure 4-12.) Nonbillable numbers should be assigned to each attorney for the personal marketing plan. Each attorney should be expected to report time expended and a description of her activities on a timeslip so that commitment to and progress on the personal marketing plan can be evaluated. (See Figure 4-13.) Marketing efforts should also play a major role in distribution of points and salaries. If marketing is not taken as seriously as billable time, it will never be effective.

Every partner should submit a marketing plan for his or her section that contains the personal marketing plans of each attorney in that section, for approval by the marketing director and the managing partners. The marketing director and managing partners should develop a list of marketing activities ranked in order of relative value. This list must be distributed to all attorneys so that everyone knows what is expected. This will also keep the decisions on

PERSONAL MARKETING PLAN

NAME: _____ QTR./YR.: _____

Your specific area(s) of law: _____

A. Cross-Selling Targets (Existing Clients)
   Client: _____
   Primary Contact/Position: _____
   Services Provided: _____
   _____

   Additional Services: _____
   _____

   Marketing Strategies (see key): _____
   Budget: _____

B. Potential Clients (*identified during last 3 months*)
   Company: _____
   Primary Contact/Position: _____
   Services: _____
   _____

   Marketing Strategies: _____
   _____

   Budget: _____

C. Referral Sources Contact (Accountants, Bankers, Brokers, etc.)
   Company: _____
   Primary Contact/Position: _____
   Services: _____
   Marketing Strategies: _____
   Budget: _____

D. Organizational Activities (Professional, Civic, Charitable)
   Organization: _____
   Primary Contact: _____
   Duties/Commitment: _____
   _____

   Budget: _____

E. Speeches/Publications/Seminars/Programs
   Subject: _____
   Title: _____
   Date: _____ Location/Publication: _____

Total Budget Requirements for the Quarter: $_____ Hrs. _____

Marketing Strategies:

A. Luncheon or Dinner Meeting   E. Use of Firm Publications
B. Other Entertainment   F. Special Mailings
C. Formal Presentation   G. Other: _____
D. Conference   _____

(NOTE: Please use additional pages if needed.)

FIGURE 4-12 A personal marketing plan organizes marketing efforts and commits timekeepers to marketing activities.

```
┌─────────────────────────────────────────────────────────────────────────┐
│                                                                           │
│                    MARKETING ACTIVITY REPORT FORM                         │
│                                                                           │
│              ATTORNEY   401            DATE    4/1/96                      │
│                                                                           │
│    ___a) speeches/      X b) civic activ-    ___c) direct mar-    ___d) other mar- │
│    publications         ities/organizational keting contacts      keting activities, │
│                         activities partici-  i.e., lunches, din-  i.e., correspon-  │
│                         pated in             ners, breakfasts,    dence, miscella-  │
│                                              etc.                 neous communica-  │
│                                                                   tions, etc.:      │
│                                                                           │
│    DESCRIPTION:  ___Luncheon meeting of Chamber of Commerce new airport   │
│    task force._____        │
│                                                                           │
│    _____      │
│    _____      │
│    _____      │
│                                                                           │
│    TIME SPENT:   2.0              ACTUAL EXPENSE TO FIRM: $15              │
│                                                          Plus time        │
│                                                                           │
└─────────────────────────────────────────────────────────────────────────┘
```

FIGURE 4-13   A marketing activity report form tracks marketing activities.

rewards more objective. A business development project report can also be developed and distributed to assist in accountability and determining rewards for marketing efforts. (See Figure 4-14.)

Strategic Planning for Firm Growth

With competition becoming greater and costs constantly rising, law firms have found it imperative to plan for the future. When a firm plans for the short term as well as the long term, it is engaged in *strategic planning.*

Like marketing efforts, strategic planning efforts must be accepted by the partners as necessary, or it is quite unlikely that the plans will work out well. The law firm environment is changing rapidly, and it is ever more difficult to maintain the profits of the past. Costs are overwhelming, and there is not enough high-paying legal work to go around. Therefore, only the shrewdest, most prepared firm can succeed.

Strategic planning is not an overnight assignment. It takes many months of hard work and good communication before it can even begin. Each firm has its own unique personality and culture, and these factors play an important role. A great deal of thought must go into the process, and a consensus must be reached before a plan can be implemented. A firm must also realize that

GOAL: ESTABLISH A BUSINESS DEVELOPMENT PROJECT REPORT THAT CAN BE DISTRIBUTED TO ALL ATTORNEYS MONTHLY. (SEE EXAMPLE BELOW.)

BUSINESS DEVELOPMENT PROJECT REPORT

DATE

Project	Start Date	Dead-line	Status	Responsi-bility	Priority
1. Client Satisfaction Program (survey)					
2. Firm Brochure	6/95	1/1/96	Ongoing	HMB	
3. Marketing Database	2/1/95	3/31/95	Ongoing	DM	
4. Directory Listings:					
A. Amer. Bar	7/1	10/1	Complete	AC	
B. Bar List	3/1	5/1	Ongoing	AC	
C. Bar Reg.	7/1	9/26	Complete	AC	
D. Best's	5/1	7/21	Complete	AC	
E. Cas. Adj.	6/1	7/31	Complete	AC	
F. Hine's	5/1	6/1	Complete	AC	
G. M-Hubbell	6/1	8/3	Complete	AC	
H. Yellow Pgs.	5/1	7/31	Complete	AC	
I. City Dir.	6/1	9/1	Complete	AC	
5. Budget Maint.	Ongoing	Ongoing			
6. DEF Journal	2/1	3/15	Ongoing	HMB/AC	
7. Seminar	1/1	9/27	Ongoing	DM	
8. Atl. Claims	10/2	4/19	Ongoing	DM	
9. Speaker's Bureau	3/1	9/1	Ongoing	DM/AC	
10. New Assoc./ Partner Announ.	11/1	1/5	Complete	DM	
11. New Partner Press Release	12/20	1/31	Complete	DM	
12. Atty. Bus. Dev. Training Program					
13. Firm Public Relations Prog.					
14. RIMS Chapter Meeting	1/20	2/10	Complete	DM/CHF	
15. Holiday Cards	8/1	12/5	Complete	DM	
16. Layman's Law.	6/1	Ongoing	Ongoing	WWE/HMB	

FIGURE 4-14 Business development project reports summarize business development activities.

strategic planning, especially if it is a new process for the firm, must be practical and reasonable. It takes a while for attorneys and legal staff to think like business people.

The partners who are directly involved in the planning process must first determine (1) where the firm is, (2) where it wants to go, and (3) how it is going to get there.

To determine where the firm is, the firm must evaluate its current situation and make assessments. To determine where it wants to go, the firm must formulate goals for the future. Last, to determine how the firm is going to get there, an analysis of all of the firm's resources must be made. After the analysis is completed, an action plan can be written; this plan must be adopted by a majority of the partners before action is taken. Often firms hire outside consultants to help them through the process; however, it is not so difficult that a firm cannot do it on its own.

The plan must contain specific goals and an action plan. Areas often addressed in a strategic plan are:

1. *Law firm governance.* Who will manage the firm and have the ultimate authority? It might be a managing partner with almost supreme power, co-managing partners with equal power, or a management committee that works either alone or with managing or co-managing partners. This is often one of the most critical issues for a law firm.

2. *Partner compensation.* The plan may address the manner in which the partners' compensation is decided. It may further address the idea of peer review for all partners and a salary survey. A partner compensation committee may be designated to evaluate each partner and assign points (shares) each year.

3. *Marketing.* The firm must do an internal as well as an external analysis to determine current as well as desired marketing efforts. After targeting current clients from whom other types of work might be obtained, and targeting potential clients from whom work could be sought, a marketing plan with action steps must be put into place.

4. *Personnel and physical facilities.* It is important during this process to determine how many and what types of attorneys the firm wants to add during each of the next five years, and whether the firm wants to add these attorneys through lateral hires, partner hires, or new associate hires. By doing so, it can also determine space, equipment, personnel, and expense budgets. If the firm determines that it will run out of office space by adding the desired number of attorneys, the decision may be reconsidered. It will then become very important to weigh costs versus income derived by such additions.

5. *Firm size.* Other issues may be opening branch offices, effectuating mergers, or reducing size.

6. *Equipment.* New computer and telephone equipment should be discussed and planned.

7. *Billing.* A serious look at billable hours, rates, and realizations (the percentage of billed dollars collected) must be studied. Those numbers, as well as accounts receivable, work in progress, and expenses, must be forecast over the period of the long-range plan (i.e., five years).

8. *Benefits.* Benefit packages (insurance, pension plans, vacation and sabbatical policies, etc.) must be reviewed and forecast.

9. *Hours to be billed.* Expectations for all timekeepers must be reviewed, updated, and communicated.

10. *Area of practice.* The firm may decide to make a change in direction, stop working on unprofitable or less profitable matters (i.e., real estate in a down market), and expand with other types of practices that may prove more lucrative (i.e., international law). Some lawyers believe that one cannot diversify enough.

11. *Trend watching.* The firm may decide to form a committee to watch trends. That committee would become cognizant of changes that would make certain areas of the law, either new or existing, more profitable due to changes that will take place in the future (i.e., environmental law). Conversely, trend watchers may also anticipate recessions and help the firm prepare.

The bottom line is that all firms, small, medium, and large, must have vision and direction for the future or they will not survive. Through marketing efforts and strategic planning, this future direction can best be articulated and achieved.

Practice Development: A Summary

Marketing and business development within law firms have become important because of the changing environment in which law is practiced. Twenty years ago, marketing was almost unheard-of in the legal profession; today, effective business development is the key to survival and growth of law firms. Without it, firms will only stagnate. An effective marketing plan involves all members of a law firm and is oriented toward current clients and contacts as well as prospective clients. As law firms develop more businesslike practices, marketing will become an integral part of the law office management team. It therefore represents not only a necessary development for law firms, but also an exciting new direction that gives all legal personnel opportunities for involvement.

The Law Office of the Future: An Introduction

The legal profession and the practice of law have been remarkably constant over the decades. The basic aspects of representing clients and understanding the law have not changed much, and the legal profession has tended to be conservative and generally resistant to change. Compared to medicine or engineering, where technical developments and new knowledge significantly affect the professions, the law has been quite stable.

However, changes over the past decade have clearly indicated that significant changes will characterize the legal environment and law offices as they attempt to move successfully into the 21st century. These developments have included:

We have had the notion (perhaps mistaken) that larger is better.

Lawyers have become more mobile than ever and have left firms in record numbers for higher compensation and greater personal satisfaction.

Concerns over profitability, partner compensation, and a growing lack of confidence in law firm management have caused major disruption in law practices.

The mobility of lawyers and their willingness to move around have weakened many small and midsize firms.

Fewer attorneys are being made partners, and there is a much longer track to partnership.

Compensation has not necessarily met attorneys' expectations.

Clients have realized that they have a lot of choices when selecting a law firm.

Law firms have become extremely competitive.

Marketing is essential, and it comes at a significant price.

Lawyers' work hours have increased, and their lifestyles have changed because of it.

Costs have risen sharply.

Professional liability (malpractice) insurance premiums have grown rapidly.

Because of increased costs, it is far more difficult to make a profit.

Small and medium-size law firms have found it increasingly difficult to hire high-quality associates and paralegals, because they often cannot pay the salaries offered by larger firms.

It is imperative that law firms consider each of these issues carefully as they attempt to survive and succeed in the highly competitive years to come. Certainly all employees want to work "smarter, not harder," but how can this goal be achieved?

THE LAW OFFICE OF THE FUTURE

Beth Chenault, a paralegal with the law firm of Sexton, Frank, and Hart, walks into her office after her morning monorail ride from the suburbs of Baltimore. After going to the office kitchen for her morning coffee, Beth punches her identification number into her computer and looks over her appointments and priority list for the day. A flashing light appears on the bottom of her computer terminal, indicating that she has an E-mail message. Beth pulls up the message and finds that there will be an in-house training seminar at lunch for all paralegals in the environmental law section of the firm.

When Beth started at the firm 10 years ago, the environmental law section was not a separate section of the firm, but rather part of the litigation section. She and the attorney she worked with were the only two individuals who practiced "environmental law." This specialty was just a small portion of the litigation she was involved in. Now, the litigation section has been segmented into the environmental law section, the bankruptcy section, the civil rights section, the family law section, the real estate section, the personal injury section, and the commercial section. Each section has at least two partners, four associates, and four paralegals. However, Beth's section is one of the largest, with eight associates and sixteen paralegals.

Just a few years ago, the number of associates in the firm outnumbered paralegals two-to-one. Now, the situation is reversed: Paralegals outnumber associates at least two-to-one, even three-to-one in some sections of the firm. As legal costs increased over the years, the number of paralegals hired by the firm increased and the number of associates hired decreased. Another change was in recruiting to attract paralegals. It was just like the associate recruiting plan. A paralegal recruiting coordinator arranged for the senior paralegals and some of the attorneys to meet qualified candidates at the schools. After these initial interviews, some candidates were selected to come back for a second interview at the firm, where they were taken to lunch and dinner by an attorney and a paralegal. Beth was amazed at how formal the hiring process had become for paralegals.

Beth thought back to a few years ago when the legal secretaries typed documents at their memory typewriters and when all in-house communication occurred via the typed memo. Now, she works daily on a networked computer and has *Martindale-Hubbell* available at her workstation on CD-ROM. How things have changed!

One way is to eliminate "busy" work. Question policies, procedures, and forms that you consider superfluous and suggest new and better ways. Also, try not to take on more than you can reasonably accomplish. If your assignments have pushed you beyond your limits, tell your supervisor that you are already overextended—although you would be happy to take on more work, you do not feel that you could get to it until some future date. To work smarter, you need to prioritize precisely. As you consider your assignments and obligations, identify on a daily basis your top priorities and give them your first attention. Additionally, practice excellent communication skills: communicate your expectations and understandings clearly, ask for and use corrective feedback, and, if possible, delegate less important tasks. Finally, celebrate your successes; this helps reinforce your behavior and builds your self-confidence.

In response to these developments, and in recognition of the realities of operating a law firm in the future, certain trends emerge as law firms attempt to find their way into the 21st century. The four primary trends that will characterize future law office developments are:

1. Increased business orientation of law firms.
2. Increased use of technical developments and use of new technologies.
3. Changes in structure and practices of law firms.
4. Increased concerns for ethics and social responsibility.

Now let us examine each of these trends in detail, with an emphasis on their relevance to paralegals.

Increased Business Orientation of Law Firms

Law firms in the future will see themselves less as a service and more as a business. The emphasis on the economic realities of practicing law will be greater than ever before. This is a natural result of the increasingly competitive nature of law firms, increased costs, and the economic realities of running a business.

Law firms will attempt to contain costs whenever possible, which means increased use of paralegals, on both full-time and contract bases, as well as increased salaries for paraprofessionals and associates. Most firms in the future will require zero-based budgeting for income and expenses, and will tend to avoid any costs that do not have corresponding revenue returns. There will be greater emphasis on billable hours, greater control over nonbillable activities, and stricter attention paid to new matter receipts, thus eliminating the acceptance of marginal transactions. Law firms will conscientiously attempt to hold their rates down to remain competitive, and their marketing budgets will rise significantly as they increase their marketing activities. There will be a closer scrutiny of productivity of all timekeepers, an increased emphasis on rewarding productivity rather than effort, and an overall orientation to the economic realities of practicing law.

Law firms will face higher and higher professional liability insurance premiums, as well as increasing salaries of associates, paralegals, and support staff. Law firms will have a more difficult time retaining their star attorneys and paralegals, as there will be high competition for these people. The economic realities of partnerships will also change, as the buy-in price for new partners will rise, while established partners will be forced to leave more of their profits in the firm to meet capital requirements.

All of these trends represent a significantly increased awareness of and concern for the bottom line. Law firms will be run more like businesses than services, with firms using business development specialists, rather than or in addition to attorneys, to develop and direct business development efforts. Those who have skills that can be used in these expanding business functions in law firms, and those who are highly productive, will be best prepared to work successfully in the business-oriented law firm. Additionally, this cost consciousness favors paralegals and legal assistants who can perform valuable services in the legal process without costing as much as an attorney. Therefore, the future law firm will place great emphasis on reducing costs by hiring paralegals and effectively integrating them into the legal team, or by increasing the number of contract employees to work on specific cases. One firm emphasizes the importance of paralegals so much that it asserts that "a lawyer's chances for advancement in the firm are directly related to his or her ability to work with and properly utilize paralegals." Many firms, in recognition of the economic benefits of using paralegals, will use an overall ratio of one legal assistant for every one-and-a-half attorneys. Opportunities for paralegals, therefore, will continue to increase in response to these economic realities.

Increased Technical Applications and Developments

The past decade has witnessed a significant increase in the use of technology in the law office and in legal practice, and the future decades will witness a continuing explosion of technical applications to legal practice. Both the quantity of users and the quality of applications will proliferate. Most law firms, even those with a single attorney, will employ computer applications for various functions, and new, sophisticated techniques will continue to find their way into larger law practices. (See Figures 4-15 and 4-16.) Later in this book you will learn about the specific applications of computers and technology in the law office; at this point, let us examine some trends in technical developments.

As we look into the law office of the future, we see every facet of information management, from words to data to images, on computerized systems, with all of the applications integrated so that they can be used together. Far more sophisticated communications systems will continue to streamline communication procedures, and systems such as electronic mail will eliminate unnecessary paperwork in the office, as well as between branch offices.

As new technical applications are utilized, attorneys and paralegals will have to continually add to their knowledge to avoid becoming obsolete. Additionally, law firms will employ highly skilled people in the automation departments who can deal with the technical equipment, train the staff in its use, and develop and present in-house training programs. (See Figure 4-17.) Opportunities for paralegals who possess technical expertise will continue to increase; additionally, new career paths focusing on using and training others in technical developments will emerge.

FIGURE 4-15
The law office of
the future will be
increasingly
technical ...

Changes in the Practices and Structures of Law Firms

In partial response to the two developments previously discussed, law firms will be changing their practices and their structures as they move into the future. In the future, we will see only very small and very large law firms; medium-size firms will be a thing of the past. Similarly, general practice firms will decline, and more and more specialized firms will take their place. We will also witness the development of mega-firms, possibly 30 or so national firms, each with 20 or more branches throughout the world. At the same time, we will also see more law firms closing their doors than ever before.

Changes will also take place in the personnel working in law firms. There will be a greater number of paralegals, with paralegals performing more tasks and accepting more responsibility. There will be fewer secretaries, as automation and networking enable secretaries to support greater numbers of timekeepers. It will take longer for associates to become partners, and all partners will be responsible for billable hours. More attorneys will choose to remain employees rather than becoming partners in the law firm, and more attorneys will be allowed to make lifestyle choices and tailor their work obligations to their other interests.

Increasing numbers of legal professionals, including both attorneys and paralegals, will choose to perform contract work rather than being tied to traditional law firm structures and requirements, as was discussed in Susan Goodman's guest editorial in Chapter 3.

Additionally, law firms will have to deal with new sources of competition that challenge some established beliefs concerning the unauthorized practice of

FIGURE 4-16
… and legal assistants will be expected to operate technical equipment.

law—particularly competition from the unlicensed. One source of that challenge comes from independent paralegals who are attempting to perform more and more work that has previously been the exclusive territory of licensed attorneys. A number of states, most notably Florida and California, are considering proposals to allow nonattorneys such as independent paralegals to perform legal work that had previously been the exclusive province of attorneys. The future will definitely see increased attention to issues of nonlawyer practice, as individual practitioners and organizations such as the National Association of

FIGURE 4-17 An attorney instructs a new paralegal on how to handle CD-ROM updates.

Independent Paralegals fight the legal establishment's stranglehold on legal practice.

The second source of challenge to the legal establishment comes from self-representation, also known as *pro se representation*. Our society is becoming more of a do-it-yourself society than ever before, and this trend is quite apparent in the law. More consumers are turning to self-representation, and more and more publishers, such as Nolo Press of Berkeley, California, are providing self-help materials to consumers. A blossoming industry of forms, videotapes, audiotapes, and software is also fueling this movement toward self-representation. One study by the ABA, which analyzed divorce cases in Maricopa County, Arizona, confirmed this trend. The study found that in 1990, 88.2 percent of the divorces involved at least one party who was self-represented, whereas in 1980, 10 years earlier, only 24 percent of divorce cases filed involved any self-representation. This consumer movement represents a trend that law firms must understand and confront as they move into the future.

Greater Concern with Ethics and Social Responsibility

Lawyers have always had a concern for professional ethics and social responsibility, but these concerns will become even more significant in the future. One development that will affect paralegals directly is the move toward licensing and certification, with mandatory CLE requirements for legal assistants. Another is the greater scrutiny that will accompany legal work in the future; both law firms and the media, as well as the public, will closely examine the propriety of legal practitioners' actions.

Seminars and other efforts in the public interest will also increase, in part due to their effect as marketing devices. Law firms will also continue their efforts in areas such as recycling (Figures 4-18 and 4-19) and creating smoke-free environments. In fact, it seems that recycling will become mandatory in the future. In 1990, the Illinois Supreme Court faced the issue of whether to adopt a rule requiring lawyers to use paper that is at least 40 percent recycled material for all documents filed in state court. Other states are likely to consider mandatory environmental measures for the legal industry; estimates suggest that an average lawyer may generate up to 7,000 sheets of paper a year, and figures such as these make the law office a prime candidate for measures such as mandatory recycling.

Increasingly significant attention will be paid to developing and enforcing legal ethics. The legal profession must strive to achieve a public profile of high integrity and ethics. This can best be achieved by bar associations taking an even stronger hand in regulating lawyer and paralegal behavior, and by law firms training all employees in legal ethics and professional responsibilities.

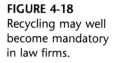

FIGURE 4-18
Recycling may well
become mandatory
in law firms.

The Law Office of the Future: A Summary

Although the basic nature of legal work will remain the same in the future, the environment in which legal practice takes place will be dramatically different. Business concerns, emphasis on productivity, increased stress due to increased competition, mandatory zero-based budgeting, pressure to achieve projected billable hours: all of these will orient the law firm to the realities of the bottom line. Technical developments will streamline the flow of information

---

From: Donna Masinter
To: NETFIRM
Subject: NEW AND OLD TELEPHONE BOOKS

PLEASE PICK UP YOUR NEW TELEPHONE BOOKS IN THE LOWER ELEVATOR LOBBY
AND PLACE YOUR OLD BOOKS IN A BIN LOCATED IN THE SAME LOBBY SO
THAT THEY CAN BE RECYCLED. IT WOULD BE GREAT TO MAKE ONE TRIP TO THE
RECYCLING PLANT, SO PLEASE HANDLE THIS BY NO LATER THAN MONDAY,
NOVEMBER 1. THANKS FOR YOUR COOPERATION.

FIGURE 4-19 Law firms are recognizing their responsibility to participate in recycling
efforts.

and communications, but they will place increased demands on the legal staff to master present applications and learn new developments. More people will be using more technology than ever before. Structures and practices will change, and ethical concerns will come to the forefront. Like the law firm of the present, the law firm of the future will be an exciting and challenging work environment.

Key Terms

client review program	marketing program	self-representation
cross-selling	practice development	social responsibility
future trends	pro se representation	strategic planning
independent paralegal	recycling programs	unethical solicitation

Problems and Activities

1. Make a list of technological advancements that you will need to learn to use prior to graduating from paralegal school. Analyze your preparedness to work productively with technical advancements.

2. The law office of the future will tend to be more specialized than it is presently. List the type of specialty you would like to be involved in and why.

3. Interview a paralegal who has worked at a firm for several years. Ask her how the practice of law has changed within the past few years. Do you see any of the trends outlined in this chapter?

4. You have been promoted to marketing director of a medium-size firm that has experienced recent growth and has not previously had a marketing director. Develop a meeting agenda for the first meeting of the marketing committee, where you identify the areas to be targeted in your efforts.

5. Acme Corporation has recently relocated its corporate offices to your city and is looking for corporate counsel. You are a paralegal on the marketing committee of a large firm. What should the firm do to get this client?

6. On your way home from work as a paralegal, you witness a motorcycle accident. The driver is injured but aware. You give him a business card and tell him that your firm specializes in personal injury litigation and has had more than a dozen million-dollar verdicts. Is this an appropriate marketing strategy?

7. You are an independent paralegal, and you advertise your services in the *National Law Journal*. In the ad you assert that you specialize in bankruptcy. Is this an ethical advertisement?

8. How has the marketing of the law profession changed in the past several years? In your opinion, are these changes advantageous for clients?

9. If you were responsible for marketing efforts in a medium-sized personal injury law firm, what would be the most cost-effective and most productive use of your marketing budget?

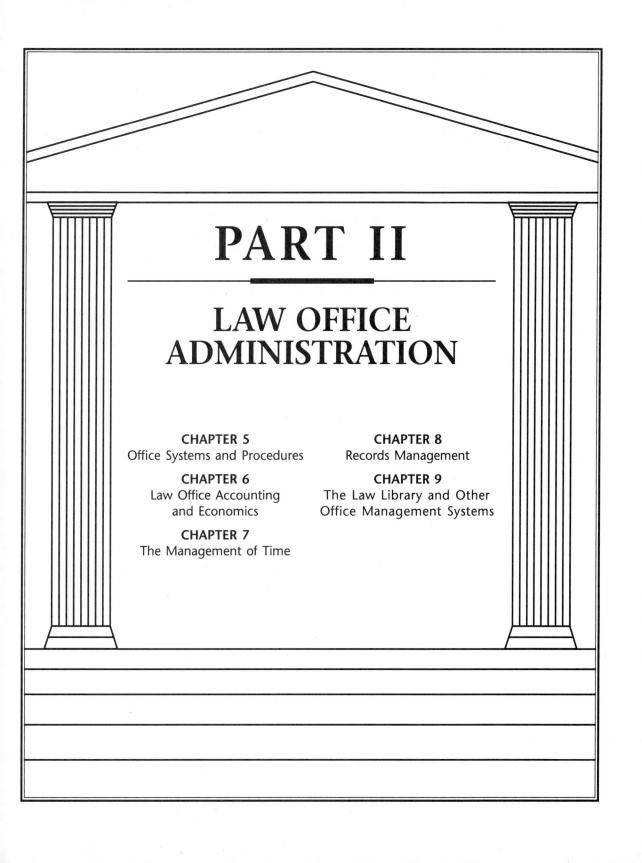

PART II

LAW OFFICE ADMINISTRATION

PART II OVERVIEW

Chapter 5: Office Systems and Procedures

An introduction to the idea of a systems approach to office management, with an emphasis on the importance of working productively and assertively within the systems in an office to achieve productivity and avoid malpractice claims.

Chapter 6: Law Office Accounting and Economics

An overview of the accounting applications found in law firms, including both manual and computerized systems. Methods of accounting for billable hours are discussed, and accounting reports and their uses are described. Zero-based budgeting is presented as a modern trend to help firms increase their profitability.

Chapter 7: The Management of Time

An introduction to timekeeping in a law office, with special emphasis on documenting and using time as productively as possible. Characteristics of good timekeepers are explored, and specific methods of docket control, such as suspense and tickler systems, are discussed.

Chapter 8: Records Management

An introduction to records management that describes the process of opening, maintaining, and closing a file. File storage methods, conflict-of-interest checks, and micrographics are also discussed.

Chapter 9: The Law Library and Other Office Management Systems

A discussion of other relevant systems found in a law office, with primary focus on the law library. Other systems, such as mail, office manuals, training programs, and vendors, are also discussed.

CHAPTER 5

OFFICE SYSTEMS AND PROCEDURES

OBJECTIVES

By the completion of this chapter, you should:

- understand the systems approach to law office administration;

- relate the systems approach to malpractice avoidance; and

- understand the necessity of approaching systems assertively.

The purpose of this section is to help you understand the importance of developing a systematic approach to organizing a law office, to help you identify the major areas of a law firm that require this systems approach, and to learn the specific applications used in a law office. The law is a highly organized and systematized field of knowledge; the processes and procedures of the law are similarly highly organized and structured. Excellent attorneys are also characterized by a highly organized and efficient approach to the process of thinking and analysis. It is of critical importance, then, that the law office, the place in which much of the work of the law is done, also be effectively organized and systematized.

ON POINT   ***BEAVIS AND BUTTHEAD DO SYSTEMS***

Beavis and Butthead arrive at their law firm at 11 A.M. It is September 13, 1997.

"We don't need any of this fancy stuff or those artificial systems," says Beavis, "we can just use our natural talents."

"Natural talents are cool," says Butthead, "and it will all work out just fine. Just like with the David Dean case. The judge hardly minded at all that we weren't in court when the case was called for trial. I told him that the file with the court date had been trashed when the commode overflowed. I don't think our client will mind paying the judgment entered against him."

"Do you have those files for Bacchus Productions? I think they have an appointment this week or next and if I remember correctly they need some contracts drawn up."

"I saw them somewhere," responds Butthead, "heck if I know where. By the way, have you tried to use WESTLAW recently? I can't get it to work at all."

"No, but I did see a notice in the mail last week saying the service was being disconnected because our check had bounced," responds Beavis.

"Funny, I could have sworn there was money in that escrow account," says Butthead. "No matter, once we get this big personal injury case filed and settled we'll be rolling in dough. Let's see," he says, "brain injury, partial paralysis, that's a big case. Who would have thought that an accident of September 10, 1995 would be so profitable for us?"

"Oh my God," shrieks Beavis. "We're too late! The statute of limitations has run! We're ruined!"

"Hey, cheer up," offers Beavis. "We've still got the MTV account ... and we've always got each other, huh, huh, huh, huh, huh."

The Systems Approach

The most effective approach to law office administration is referred to as a *systems approach.* Using a systems approach has several meanings for the administration of an office. It means that the tasks to be accomplished are each identified and systematized. This regularization of procedure assures accuracy and saves time, two major goals of a law firm. It also enables the law firm to maintain effective records over time; if a paralegal had his own system of recordkeeping, and then left the firm, no one would be able to decipher the file's meaning once he had departed. A systematized approach to file maintenance, in contrast, assures that information will be accessible no matter who the firm employs. It thereby assists in malpractice avoidance by providing a structure, complete with checks and balances, that fosters careful, effective, legal work.

The systems approach, in addition to treating each separate area as a system, also treats the whole structure—in this instance a law firm—as a system. This means that the whole system is comprised of interdependent parts, where each part understands its place within the whole. As a paralegal, you will become involved with all the parts of the law office team, from the janitor, the courier, and the word processor to the associates and the partners. You will also be a part of the legal team serving the client, and each member of the legal team—the senior lawyer, the junior lawyer, the paralegal, the legal secretary—has an important and unique role to play in providing quality services for the client. You will also learn that the law firm is comprised not only of various groups specializing in specific areas of the law, but also of the administrative section, the billing section, the word processing section, the courier/ mailroom/copying center section, the accounting section, and other specialized sections, depending on the size of the firm. By understanding the law firm as a system that demands that each part do its role in harmony with the other parts, the paralegal can make the greatest contribution to effective administration of the firm.

Avoiding Malpractice Through Systems

In the world of the law, the possibility of being sued for malpractice or being brought before the bar for ethical violations is always a reality. Lawyers and law offices open themselves to potential violations when they intentionally or negligently violate the law or legal ethics. We hope that you will never become involved with intentional violations of the law, but a negligent violation does not require bad intent: it requires merely an error, a mistake. In the world of the law, however, a mistake can be devastating, as we discussed in the chapter on malpractice avoidance. For that reason, law offices need to minimize or eliminate any behavior that falls below the standard of what a reasonable attorney would do.

The systems approach, by breaking down and organizing activities to be performed and the timetable in which they must be performed, helps a law office do its work in an efficient and organized manner, thus helping to prevent malpractice. No attorney intends to miss a court date, or to have an action barred because he failed to file a complaint before the running of the statute of limitations. But these things happen. A systems approach cannot guarantee perfection; no system can do that, because the system must be used effectively by *people* if it is to be successful. But a systems approach will create the kind of environment—organized, accurate, professional—in which the work of the law can best be done.

For example, most firms have three methods for checking court dates. First, dates are published in the local legal news organ, which is then checked by firm personnel. Second, dates are sent to attorneys by calendar clerks for the judges. Third, computer systems are set up to remind attorneys of court deadlines. Having three methods prevents the possibility that a court date will be missed, for under the systems approach the firm would have Paralegal A check the newspapers, Paralegal B open all mail for the litigation department and log court dates, and Paralegal C check the computer system. A system of having three different people checking various sources for court dates on a regular basis is more consistent and less likely to result in an error than if such a system were not in place. This example clearly shows the effectiveness of and necessity for the systems approach in law firms.

Learning the Systems in Your Office

When you first begin your career as a paralegal, whether with a private law practice, or for the district attorney's office, or within the framework of a corporation or agency, it is vital that you fully acquaint yourself with the systems and procedures of your employer. (See Figure 5-1.) Generally, an office manual and an orientation package will be given to you when you start your new job. Be sure to read it thoroughly—not to do so could cause you to make a serious mistake and might cost you your job.

Try to supplement what you learned about the firm during your job search and the preinterview process. Learn all you can about the partners and associates—where they went to school, their specialties, their clients, and how you can play an important role in their practice. On your first day, ask for a copy of the firm résumé, or simply spend a few minutes in the law library researching the firm by consulting *Martindale-Hubbell,* a paid directory that gives extensive information about the law firm and its practice. Find out if the firm is operated as a professional corporation or as a partnership; if they have a board of directors or a management committee; if there is a managing partner; if you are directly accountable to the director of administration or your supervising attorney. Is there a paralegal coordinator? If so, what is his function? All of these questions

FIGURE 5-1 It is important to learn the systems and procedures that your firm uses.

are worth asking, but be sure to ask them in a professional manner so that you do not appear overly aggressive or pushy.

By knowing what systems your firm utilizes, you can alleviate an often-cited problem with employees—failure to work within the system. Understanding and working within the framework of the systems put in place by your firm is essential to your continued success as a paralegal.

Asserting Yourself in the Law Office

Although systems are necessary to the effective functioning of a law firm, the systems cannot run effectively without people. The people who perform the work of the law office must be willing and able to learn existing systems, contribute to the development of new systems where none or ineffective ones exist, and assert themselves in order to make a contribution. Being a paralegal is an opportunity; it is not a guarantee of success. You will need to learn when to speak and when to listen, when to object and when to follow. You will encounter attorneys who are experienced at integrating paralegals into the legal team, and you will run into those who are unwilling to delegate work to paralegals. It will be a challenge for you to be adaptable enough to determine how best to contribute to the legal work in your office, but in all circumstances you must remember that the successful paralegal is appropriately assertive in requesting work assignments, developing opportunities, and asking for clarification.

The following case studies describe two different approaches to being a paralegal as the characters encounter the training systems on their jobs. The assertiveness that characterizes the successful paralegal applies not just to training systems but to all aspects of paralegal work in the law office. (See Figure 5-2.)

FIGURE 5-2
The effective paralegal must be appropriately assertive.

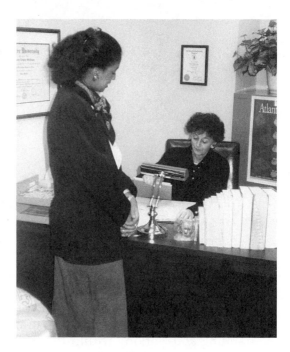

CASE STUDY   **ASSERTIVENESS IN APPROACHING SYSTEMS**

When Ann Jones received her degree in political science from a small, midwestern, liberal arts school, she decided to enter paralegal school with the hopes of establishing a career in the field of law.

Ann was a good student and worked hard in school. After finishing her paralegal training, she landed a job with a large firm in Chicago. Ann was immediately assigned to work with the attorneys in the corporate department. That department consisted of 15 attorneys and 4 paralegals.

Unfortunately for Ann, the firm she joined did not understand the need to train paralegals who were fresh out of school in the ways of the law firm. She was never told specifically what was expected of her. Additionally, it seemed that all of the lawyers to whom she was assigned were too busy to tell her. Sadly, she spent her days reorganizing her office and reading various publications that were of interest to her. She was frequently treated more like a courier or a photocopying operator than a highly trained legal assistant. It seemed that the paralegals who did well in this firm were those who came to it with experience, or those who were new at the job but who made it known that they needed support. Ultimately, the firm became unhappy with Ann and terminated her employment.

What could Ann have done differently?

1. At the time of employment, Ann could have asked questions regarding the firm's paralegal training program, their expectations, and whether they had a mentor program.
2. Ann could have sought the help and advice of the firm's management.
3. In the absence of enough work from the attorneys in her department, she could have sought work through aiding other paralegals.
4. Ann should have made it known to the attorneys in her department, if only through written communication, that she was ready, willing, and able to do whatever it took to be a successful paralegal.

Consider now the approach of Bob O'Brien, who attended a large state university in the South at which a paralegal degree was offered. He successfully obtained his degree and was determined to find a challenging opportunity.

CASE STUDY   **ASSERTIVENESS IN APPROACHING SYSTEMS**

After spending one month in search of the best job, Bob found that the paralegal market was flooded in his area. He decided that it was worth a move to find a good job. Bob sent his résumé to law firms in other areas where he was interested in living and immediately received several positive responses. After several interviews, Bob accepted a position with a medium-size law firm.

Bob knew that his new employer offered great benefits; among them were continuing legal education and a mentor program. His first day on the job was spent going through an extensive orientation program and computer training. Alice Diaz, a paralegal who had been with the firm for two years, was assigned as Bob's mentor. She worked in the same department to which he was assigned and was on hand to answer his questions on a day-to-day basis. Bob was a good communicator and was pleased to learn that most of those with whom he worked also possessed good communication skills. When he didn't have enough billable work to keep him busy, he knew that he was expected to seek work from others, and he did so readily. He thought ahead and tried to always be prepared. Bob went the extra mile and was rewarded for having done so.

Bob was a hard worker and performed tasks that were not required but which were of benefit to his department, the firm, and the clients. When volunteers were solicited, Bob was always willing to lend a hand; when faced with a crisis, he remained calm and tried to see the opportunity hidden in the problem. He took advantage of many learning opportunities, and, because he was willing to accept new challenges, his career potential grew.

He had made the systems work for him.

One may say that it was easier for Bob than it was for Ann because his firm seemed to be in tune with the needs of paralegals. That is true, but it is important to point out that we must all be diligent in our efforts; in the face of adversity, we must develop the assertiveness and the creativity to find effective solutions to our problems.

Systems Regarding Substance Abuse, Sexual Harassment, and HIV/AIDS

Substance abuse, sexual harassment, and HIV/AIDS are three of the most important contemporary areas of concern relative to law office management. Not only might these issues suggest a problem with the individual involved, but they also make the organization vulnerable to lawsuits arising from the behavior of individuals who are abusing drugs or alcohol or who are guilty of sexual harassment. Additionally, workplace laws now mandate employer actions in these areas.

Substance Abuse

Substance abuse becomes a real possibility in a pressure-filled environment such as legal practice, and it is a leading cause of malpractice. To combat substance abuse in the workforce, firms must not only identify abusers but must also educate the entire workforce—both abusers and nonabusers—to manage the problem most effectively. Programs generally begin with a testing program, providing rehabilitation for those in need. Ideally, the program would extend to educating all employees to prevent substance abuse.

The substance abuse and drug testing policy in Figure 5-3 comes from the Atlanta, Georgia, firm of Drew, Eckl & Farnham. It is a good example of a firm's policy in this area.

**EMPLOYEE ACKNOWLEDGMENT OF RECEIPT
OF SUBSTANCE-ABUSE AND DRUG TESTING POLICY
AND EMPLOYEE RESPONSIBILITIES UNDER THAT POLICY**

I acknowledge that I have received a copy of the Firm's Substance Abuse and Drug Testing Policy and have had the Drug-Free Workplace Program explained to me. I understand that it is my responsibility to become thoroughly familiar with, and comply with, the terms and conditions of this Policy, and understand that my failure to comply with any provision of this Policy may result in my being subject to disciplinary action, up to and including discharge.

I also understand that if I am convicted of any criminal drug offense involving the use, possession, transportation, sale or other activities related in any way to drugs or other controlled substances during working hours, I will notify the Executive Director in writing, within five (5) days after any such conviction occurs.

_____
Name (please print)

_____
Employee's Signature

_____
Date

FIGURE 5-3   A substance abuse and drug testing policy

SUBSTANCE ABUSE AND DRUG-TESTING POLICY

I. PURPOSE AND SCOPE

The Firm does not condone any form of substance abuse. It is the policy of the Firm, to the extent practical, to provide its employees with a working environment that is free of the problems associated with the abuse of controlled substances (including narcotics). The use of controlled substances is inconsistent with the behavior expected of employees and subjects the Firm and employees to unacceptable risks of workplace accidents and other events which undermine the Firm's ability to operate effectively and safely. Such activities by employees also have the potential to adversely affect the quality of our product and the service we provide to our clients. Therefore, the Firm has established the following policy:

(1) It is a violation of Firm policy for any employee to use, possess, sell, trade, offer for sale, or offer to buy illegal drugs or otherwise engage in the illegal use of drugs on the job.

(2) It is a violation of Firm policy for anyone to report to work under the influence of illegal drugs or alcohol.

(3) It is a violation of the Firm policy for anyone to use prescription drugs illegally. (However, nothing in this policy precludes the appropriate use of legally prescribed medications.)

(4) Violations of this policy are subject to disciplinary action up to and including termination.

All Firm partners and employees are required to comply with this Substance Abuse Policy as set forth herein. The Firm's drug-free workplace program complies with the Georgia Drug-Free Workplace Act in accordance with Title 34, Chapter 9, Article 11 of the Official Code of Georgia Annotated.

II. PROHIBITED SUBSTANCES AND CONDUCT

The non-prescriptive use, sale, possession, distribution, dispensation, manufacture, or transfer of drugs or drug-related paraphernalia at any time is strictly prohibited.

For purposes of this Policy, the term drug includes substances listed in O.C.G.A. 34-9-411. The term also includes otherwise legal but illicitly used substances. An otherwise legal but illicitly used substance includes prescription drugs and over-the-counter drugs not being used for their intended purposes or in accord with the terms of the prescription.

An employee using a drug pursuant to a valid prescription must report such use to the Executive Director prior to performing any work after beginning use of the prescribed drug where the employee is informed or has reason to believe that his/her physical or mental condition may be impaired during working hours by use of the drug. If an employee performs work without first making such a report, he/she will be considered in violation of this Policy. If, in the judgment of management, use of the prescribed drug would affect the employee's ability to safely and efficiently perform his/her normal job, the employee may be temporarily assigned other duties or placed on an unpaid leave of absence, at the Firm's option, during use of the prescribed drug.

FIGURE 5-3 *(continued)*

Upon request, the employee shall furnish the Firm with the physician's statement regarding the effects of the medication.

An employee who is under the influence of alcoholic beverages at any time while on Firm business shall be guilty of misconduct and is subject to discipline including discharge or suspension without pay from employment, even for the first offense.

III. PROSPECTIVE EMPLOYEE TESTING

All job applicants at this Firm will undergo testing for the presence of illegal drugs as a condition of employment. Any applicant with a confirmed positive test will be denied employment.

Applicants will be required to submit voluntarily to a urinalysis test at a laboratory chosen by this Firm, and by signing a consent agreement will release this Firm from liability.

If the physician, official or lab personnel has reasonable suspicion to believe that the job-applicant has tampered with the specimen, the applicant will not be considered for employment.

Individuals who have failed a pre-employment test may initiate another inquiry with the Firm after a period of not shorter than six (6) months; but they must present themselves drug-free as demonstrated by urinalysis or other test selected by this Firm.

IV. EMPLOYEE TESTING

This Firm has adopted testing practices to identify employees who use illegal drugs on or off the job. It shall be a condition of employment for all employees to submit to drug testing under the following circumstances:

1. When there is reasonable suspicion to believe that an employee is using illegal drugs. The following circumstances could cause reasonable suspicion:
   a. Observed drug abuse.
   b. Apparent physical state of impairment.
   c. Incoherent mental state.
   d. Marked changes in personal behavior that are otherwise unexplainable.
   e. Deteriorating work performance that is not attributable to other factors.
   f. Accidents or other actions that provide reasonable cause to believe the employee may be under the influence of drugs.

2. a. When employees have caused or contributed to an on-the-job injury that resulted in a loss of work time, which means any period of time during which an employee stops performing the normal duties of employment and leaves the place of employment to seek care from a licensed medical provider.
   b. When employees are involved in on-the-job accidents where personal injury or damage to Firm property occurs.

3. As part of a follow-up program to treatment for drug abuse.

4. When a substance abuse test is conducted as part of a routinely scheduled employee fitness-for-duty medical examination that is part of the employer's established policy or that is scheduled routinely for all members of an employment classification or group.

FIGURE 5-3 *(continued)*

5. In addition to grounds 1–4 above, the Firm may, from time to time, conduct unannounced substance abuse tests to ensure compliance with this Policy.

Employees with a confirmed positive test result may, at their option and expense, have a second confirmation test made on the same specimen. An employee will not be allowed to submit another specimen for testing.

Employees and job applicants who have a positive confirmed test result may explain or contest the result to the employer within five (5) working days, after the employer contacts the employee and shows him or her the positive test result as it was received from the laboratory in writing.

V. CONFIDENTIALITY

The confidentiality of any information received by the Firm through the substance abuse testing program shall be maintained as provided for by the Georgia Drug-Free Workplace Act.

VI. EMPLOYEE ASSISTANCE

The Firm will attempt to assist employees with substance abuse problems in finding effective treatment. For more detailed information regarding providers of employee assistance, including drug and alcohol abuse, mental health providers and other persons, entities or organizations available to assist employees confidentially with personal or behavioral problems, any employee may contact the Executive Director.

VII. DISCIPLINE AND TERMINATION

(1) Employees who are found to be in violation of this Policy are subject to disciplinary action up to and including termination.

(2) Any employee in violation of this Policy who is offered an opportunity and refuses to participate in a recognized rehabilitation program or who fails to successfully complete such a program as required by the Firm will be subject to termination.

(3) Any employee refusing to submit to a test required under this Policy or to execute documents related to this Policy as required by the Firm or to comply with other requirements of this Policy will be subject to termination.

VIII. MEDICAL BENEFITS FOR SUBSTANCE ABUSE REHABILITATION

Qualified employees who are eligible for assistance under the Firm medical plan may elect to seek treatment for substance abuse that may be available under the medical plan. An employee's participation in the medical plan's substance abuse treatment program does not ensure continued employment with the Firm, where this Policy allows for the employee's termination.

IX. NOTIFICATION OF CONVICTION FOR DRUG OR ALCOHOL-RELATED OFFENSE

Employees who are convicted of drug or alcohol-related violations under either state or federal law which occurred on Firm property or during working hours, or who have pleaded guilty to any such violation, must, in writing, notify the Executive Director within five (5) days of such conviction or guilty plea. Any employee who fails to give such written notice within the five (5) day period will be terminated.

FIGURE 5-3 *(continued)*

X. <u>TESTING FACILITIES</u>

Testing will be done at the expense of the Firm. All testing incident to this Policy will be conducted by licensed, professional laboratories and clinics. Individuals tested for drugs will be required to sign a consent and release form.

XI. <u>SEARCHES</u>

Based on reasonable suspicion or evidence of sale, possession or use of any substance in violation of this Policy, an employee may be required to:

(1) Submit to a search of his/her person/articles brought on Firm premises. Failure to submit to a search may result in termination.

(2) Submit to seizure of any controlled substances.

FIGURE 5-3   *(continued)*

DREW, ECKL & FARNHAM
880 West Peachtree Street
Atlanta, Georgia 30309
(404) 885-1400

<u>ACKNOWLEDGMENT OF OFFER OF EMPLOYMENT</u>

The undersigned acknowledges that he/she has been offered a position of employment with the Firm. The undersigned has agreed to accept this offer of employment and to proceed with required postoffer testing.

The undersigned further acknowledges that the offer of employment is revocable in the event of the following: (1) the undersigned cannot perform the essential functions of the job with or without reasonable accommodation; (2) the undersigned presents a direct threat to himself/herself or others; (3) the provision of a reasonable accommodation would result in an undue hardship.

_____   _____
Date   Prospective Employee

FIGURE 5-3   *(continued)*

Sexual Harassment

Although the legal community certainly became aware of the problem of sexual harassment during the confirmation hearings of Supreme Court Justice Clarence Thomas, the alarm rang loud and clear on September 1, 1994, when a San Francisco jury awarded a $7.1 million verdict against the Chicago-based law firm of Baker & McKenzie and its former partner Martin R. Greenstein in a sexual

---

CONSENT AND RELEASE FOR DRUG TEST

I hereby acknowledge that I have been informed of Drew Eckl & Farnham's (hereinafter "Firm") Substance Abuse Program and have agreed to be bound by this Program thereby for purposes of applying for, accepting, or continuing employment with the Firm. I also hereby state that I am not a user of controlled substances except as I reveal in connection with this drug test.

I understand and consent freely and voluntarily to the Firm's request for a urine or other specimen or sample. I hereby release and hold harmless the Firm, the laboratory, their employees, agents and contractors from any and all liability arising from this request to furnish this or any specimen or sample, the testing of the specimen or sample, and any decision made concerning my application for employment or my continued employment, based upon the results of the test.

I consent to allow any Firm employee, designated physician, laboratory, hospital or medical professional to perform appropriate tests for the presence of drugs or other controlled substances. I give my permission to any Firm employee, designated physician, laboratory, hospital or medical professional to release the results of the test to the Firm and I release any such designated institution or person from any liability whatsoever arising from the release of this information.

Employee or Prospective
Employee Signature

Date

FIGURE 5-3 *(continued)*

harassment case. Plaintiff Rena Weeks asserted, and the jury believed, that the firm did not make a serious attempt to curtail the crude behavior of Greenstein, even though the firm had instituted a sexual harassment policy in 1990.

Additional scrutiny is also being given to the issue of sexual harassment because of the tremendous increase of women in the legal community. Not very long ago, the law was a man's world. Today, women occupy some of the highest positions in the law and work in all levels of the law; half of the class in most law schools is female. In a field that has produced two female Supreme Court Justices (Sandra Day O'Connor and Ruth Bader Ginsburg) and a female U.S. Attorney General (Janet Reno), not to mention the thousands of female attorneys and judges who work at every level in every jurisdiction in the country, it is singularly inappropriate to reduce women to a sexual stereotype. We hope that the legal community will take a leadership role in helping to eliminate sexual discrimination and harassment in the workplace.

To take this leadership role, as well as to avoid financial liability, firms will need to develop and implement policies and training programs informing employees about sexual harassment. In a sexual harassment case, both the individual and the organization might incur legal liability resulting in financial damages.

The harasser might be liable, on a theory of direct liability, in that he committed the allegedly harassing acts; the firm might also be liable, on the theory that it did not provide proper training or did not have an effective hiring process, a theory known as *vicarious liability*. Sexual harassment may come from within the firm, as it did in the Baker & McKenzie case, or it might exist between lawyer and client.

Additionally, sexual harassment might exist in a third-party situation. Many employers do not realize that they have potential liability when one of their employees is harassed by a nonemployee, such as a customer or client. Because the law requires that employers provide a workplace free of harassment, the employer might be liable if it knew or should have known that harassment of its employee was occurring and took no action to stop it.

An example of this type of third-party harassment is the suit by six former waitresses of the Hooters restaurant chain against the company. They claim that the company should be liable for the harassment they experienced because the company created and fostered an environment where they were likely to be subjected to sexual comments and advances by customers. This ability of employees to sue for third-party harassment certainly extends the possible liability of organizations, and it puts the organizations on notice that they cannot remain indifferent to sexual harassment in any form or situation.

To avoid this liability, law firms (and other organizations as well) must take active steps—both preventive and remedial, if necessary—to educate their employees about sexual harassment and its prevention. If the organization is sued, it will have to show that it did everything it could to prevent the harassment from occurring.

The sexual harassment policy in Figure 5-4, which is an aspect of the firm's equal employment opportunity policy, also comes from Drew, Eckl & Farnham.

HIV/AIDS Issues

In addition to issues related to substance abuse and discrimination, law firms as employers must deal with a variety of issues in response to HIV and AIDS. HIV and AIDS affect every segment of society, including the workplace. To help organizations deal with HIV and AIDS, the Centers for Disease Control (CDC), in conjunction with other agencies and organizations, has developed the Business Responds to AIDS (BRTA) program. This program helps organizations develop policies and educational programs for employees and their families. It also attempts to foster community service and volunteer activity to respond to this crisis.

Law firms will, we hope, take a leadership position relative to HIV and AIDS. This begins with the development of firm policies to address:

- Compliance with federal and state laws, including the ADA, the Federal Rehabilitation Act of 1973 and OSHA guidelines

EQUAL EMPLOYMENT OPPORTUNITY

1. <u>EEO Policy</u>. The Firm is committed to maintaining a work environment that is free of unlawful conduct. In keeping with this commitment, we will not tolerate harassment, discrimination or the unlawful treatment of employees by anyone, including any supervisor, co-worker, vendor, client or customer of the Firm.

2. <u>Definition</u>. Harassment, discrimination and/or improper conduct consists of misconduct that includes unwelcome conduct, whether verbal, physical, or visual, that is based upon a person's protected status, such as sex, color, race, religion, national origin, age, disability or other protected group status as provided for by law. The Firm will not tolerate conduct that affects tangible job benefits, that interferes unreasonably with an individual's work performance, or that creates an intimidating, hostile, or offensive working environment.

3. <u>Sexual Harassment</u>. Sexual harassment deserves special mention. Unwelcome sexual advances, requests for sexual favors, and other physical, verbal, or visual conduct based on sex constitute sexual harassment when (1) submission to the conduct is an explicit or implicit term or condition of employment; (2) submission to or rejection of the conduct is used as the basis for an employment decision; or (3) the conduct has the purpose or effect of unreasonably interfering with an individual's work performance or creating an intimidating, hostile, or offensive working environment. Sexual harassment may include explicit sexual propositions, sexual innuendo, suggestive comments, sexually oriented "kidding" or "teasing," "practical jokes," jokes about gender-specific traits, foul or obscene language or gestures, displays of foul or obscene printed or visual material, and physical contact, such as patting, pinching, or brushing against another's body.

4. <u>Complaint Procedure</u>. All employees are responsible for helping to assure that we avoid any form of unlawful treatment. If you feel that you have experienced or witnessed harassment, discrimination or unlawful treatment, you are to notify immediately (preferably within 24 hours) the Director of Administration or one of the Managing Partners. The Firm forbids retaliation against anyone who has made a complaint.

If the allegations warrant, the Firm's policy is to investigate all such complaints. To the extent practicable and appropriate, the Firm will keep complaints and the terms of their resolution confidential. If an investigation confirms that misconduct has occurred, the Firm will take corrective action, including such discipline up to and including immediate termination of employment, as is appropriate.

The Firm recognizes that intentional or malicious false accusations of misconduct can have a serious effect on innocent men and women. Individuals falsely accusing another of misconduct will be disciplined in accordance with the nature and extent of his or her false accusation. The Firm encourages any employee to raise questions he or she may have regarding misconduct or this policy, with his or her immediate supervisor, a higher level manager or the appropriate human resources representative.

FIGURE 5-4   A sexual harassment policy

- Hiring, promotion, and dismissal policies with regard to employees with HIV and AIDS

- Issues of confidentiality relating to medical records and information

- Benefit programs available for infected employees

- Workplace discrimination against persons with HIV or AIDS

- Promoting prevention and understanding through educational programs and information dissemination.

Once an effective policy is in place, the leaders of the organization must take an active role in making sure that all employees understand the importance of the HIV and AIDS policies. Additionally, law firms can take a leadership position in the challenge of dealing with the HIV/AIDS crisis by encouraging their employees to become involved in community service and to volunteer for HIV- and AIDS-related projects. The law firm itself should set a good example by providing financial suppport and/or legal services to appropriate organizations and their programs.

Total Quality Management (TQM): Creating Quality Systems

The earlier section on the law office of the future described how law firms would be adopting the means and methods of business management in their quest to stay competitive in the marketplace. One approach, Total Quality Management (TQM), based on the ideas of W. Edwards Deming and Joseph J. Juran, proliferated in corporate America in the 1980s and has been adopted by more than a few law firms. Surveys have shown that more than 40 percent of the nation's largest law firms are already implementing TQM programs, with a far greater percentage indicating that they will be implementing TQM in the future. In corporate law departments, an estimated 80 percent have already implemented TQM. It seems, therefore, that if you are planning on working in a law office or in a corporate legal department, you had better be prepared to become involved in TQM.

Although there are many different applications and manifestations of TQM—there are even different names, such as TQP (Total Quality Processes) or TQG (Total Quality Groups)—TQM essentially involves the entire organization working together as partners to assess areas that need improvement and to devise strategies, oftentimes with the input of clients, to improve those areas. TQM is client-focused, and uses client surveys and audits to learn from and respond to client perceptions. TQM advocates building quality into everything by looking into the processes and systems within a company and making them more efficient. Ultimately, TQM encourages an organization to continually examine everything about itself and transform and improve itself in response to that analysis. To achieve this self-examination and transformation, TQM advocates several key concepts:

- Managing by teamwork and committees

- Listening to and creating partnerships with clients

- Empowering employees to make decisions

- Getting things right the first time

- Removing barriers to communication

- Using statistical measurement to evaluate progress

- Systematizing work processes

- Having a continual commitment to quality.

Not all lawyers or law firms are enthusiastic about TQM. Naturally, some resist change simply because it means examining and perhaps abandoning what is already being done. Some cite the difficulty of training or the time spent in meetings. Still others feel that most of their clients are already satisfied with their services. Nonetheless, TQM seems to be a part of the office systems landscape. As you prepare yourself to work effectively in an office environment, consider it highly likely that you will at some point become involved with TQM. At the very least, this means that your organization is committed to its own development and improvement, a sign that your firm is attempting to move forward with excellence into the future.

The achievement of quality at all levels is perhaps the major goal of all business organizations, including law firms. Many commentators believe that quality is the difference between success and failure for the contemporary law firm. The following guest editorial, although oriented to business in general, is highly applicable to law firms. It will give you a good overview of the elements of a quality-oriented organization and some ideas on how to apply the principles of quality to your job.

Quality is one of the key concepts as business organizations attempt to be successful and profitable in the future. The guest editorial emphasizes the actions and behaviors that can help an organization assimilate quality into everything it does. However, it is important to understand that quality is not merely an external set of actions; it is also, and perhaps most importantly, a matter of individual choice, an individual commitment. For quality to be complete, it requires that quality and excellence permeate not only what you do, but also who you are. If the organization and the employee are each committed to quality as a total concept, success and fulfillment will surely follow.

G U E S T   E D I T O R I A L

Quality: It's the Name of the Game

Gary B. Roberts, Ph.D.; Carlotta D. Roberts, J.D.;
and William B. White

*This article was reprinted courtesy of the National Small
Business Journal.*

Raise the subject of quality and you'll soon
hear a confusion of three-letter acronyms (TLAs).
Some common ones are:

- TQM—Total Quality Management
- SPC—Statistical Process Control
- TQI—Total Quality Improvement
- MDQ—Market Driven Quality
- TCI—Total Continuous Improvement

Renowned quality authority W. Edwards Deming died late last year. Since then the quality
movement in the United States appears to be
holding its collective breath. Businesses are waiting for either a new, charismatic successor or a
definitive statement about what the right "quality" vocabulary should be.

The disadvantage of focusing on vocabulary
is that it distorts business priorities. The first
quality-related priority of a business must be the
implementation of an integrated, systematic,
organization-wide strategy for improving products and services. Neither the right guru, the
right acronym, nor the right vocabulary alone
will help most managers.

The quality movement embraces a vast spectrum of topics and perspectives. Nevertheless,
certain elements are both common and key to
most approaches to quality. These elements
serve as useful tools for small business owners
and managers to self-analyze progress in their
quest for quality.

David Waldman of Concordia University in
Montreal outline[d] eight elements common to
all major quality approaches in a July 1994 article in the *Academy of Management Review*. These
elements should be part of your business' quest
for quality. They capture the spirit of Deming

and other quality leaders, such as Juran, Crosby,
Tom Peters and Taguchi.

1. *Upper management commitment to place quality as a top priority.* There is strong evidence to
suggest that most successful quality efforts have
broad support from senior management. Quality—in reality customer satisfaction—becomes
the driver for all management strategies and in-
itiatives. "Whatever it takes!" should be the
company mantra. The phrase "Walking the
Talk" should typify management's actions. Employees quickly sense a lack of commitment.

2. *A broad definition of quality as meeting customers' expectations at the least cost,* which encompasses all phases of the design, production,
and delivery of a product or service. A quality-
oriented business provides products and services
with the highest value. In addition, such a business works at being hassle-free for its customers.
Our interviews with hundreds of customers
have confirmed that they want three results:

- Reasonable prices.
- Products and/or services that work (meet
  their needs).
- Hassle-free interactions (including ordering,
  billing, and delivery).

Do you systematically and regularly ask
your customers how well you provide these three
results?

3. *The institution of leadership practices that
are oriented toward quality, values and visions.*
Leaders in the organization recognize that truth,
knowledge, and improvements can come from
the bottom as well as the top of the organization. These leaders also recognize that all of us
working together are smarter than any one of
us. We've worked with small businesses that use
self-directed work teams to extend the responsibility for quality throughout the organization.

4. *The development of a quality culture.* Culture represents the values of an organization.

Certain values are common in quality-focused businesses:

- Do it right the first time.
- When in doubt please the customer.
- We do not punish well-intentioned failures.
- Never lose a good customer.
- Never lose a good employee.
- Teamwork dominates.

Real business quality comes about only when all employees buy into values such as these.

5. *Involvement and empowerment of all organizational members in cooperative efforts to achieve quality improvements.* Only decisions made at levels close to the customer can reflect true customer needs. All employees must look for ways to continuously improve the business' systems to meet those needs. Improving everything becomes an important part of everyone's job.

6. *An orientation toward managing-by-facts, including the prolific use of scientific and problem-solving techniques such as statistical process control.* Opinions are important and should be welcomed. But at a certain point reliance upon a scientific method for problem solving and decision making becomes essential. All members of the organization need training to use these techniques. Brainstorming, list building and flowcharting are helpful in even the smallest businesses.

7. *The commitment to continually improve employees' capabilities and work processes through training and benchmarking, respectively.* People grow both personally and professionally in a quality-focused environment. Business processes and procedures continuously improve. World-class examples are found, studied, and then improved upon. Small businesses that do not train their employees and that do not benchmark against their competition quickly fall behind.

8. *Attempts to get external suppliers and customers involved in quality efforts.* Stakeholders are a valued part of a business improvement system. Customers and suppliers participate in problem finding and problem solving activities. Have you involved your customers and suppliers in your quality improvement efforts?

These eight elements serve as a useful tool for small businesses to self-analyze where they are in their quest for quality. Use them to assess your own quality efforts. They stand on a good, scientific understanding of people and organizations.

Quality Question of the Month

Q. I'm a middle manager in a medium-size family owned business. I am a firm believer that our business needs to develop systems that support continuous improvement in practically everything we do. The problem is that the top managers appear to have learned the quality vocabulary, but they're certainly not "walking the talk!" I don't feel that I really have senior management's commitment to improve quality in our company. What should I do? ...

A. You raise a difficult problem faced by many middle managers—what to do when top management does not adequately support a quality focus.

We've interviewed hundreds of managers who are in your predicament. Although many TQM purists would consider it heresy, we think the answer is simple. In these circumstances, most people go ahead and improve services and products through guerrilla quality programs. They role model appropriate quality-oriented behavior for their boss, whether or not they're rewarded or recognized for it!

Most good in the world comes from good men and women doing the right thing at the right time for the right reason. They want to do a good job. You do not need permission to do your job better. You need to operate by the two well-known slogans that make things happen:

- If it's not forbidden, it's allowed.
- It is better to ask for forgiveness than to ask for permission.

Bucking the system is going to be difficult at times. But you've got to follow your precepts of quality in your work, or a part of your spirit will die. Improve service for at least one customer today, and you'll feel better about yourself and your job. Who knows, maybe even your boss will learn from your successes.

Step One: Identify a specific customer to help. Ask that customer, "How can I help you better?" Then listen to what that customer tells you. Show empathy and be open minded. Don't assume that you already know what your customer really wants.

Step Two: Find a process for improvement that will benefit the customer. Ask questions. "What do you need from me?" "What do you do with what I give you?" "Are there any gaps between what you need and what I give you?"

Step Three: Involve other members of your organization. Ask for help and advice from your boss, your peers, and those who work for you. Listen.

Step Four: Design an improvement. Act on your ideas. Coordinate the change with your customer. Pick something likely to succeed quickly—you need visible successes and early results. Tell those who need to know abut the improvement to make them aware that changes are underway.

Step Five: Take some risks. You don't need permission to make improvements—this is part of your job. Don't be afraid to fail. We learn from successes and failures.

Step Six: Measure, measure, measure!!! Management by facts is better than management by opinion. Use some statistics and charts. As Vince Lombardi said: "If you're not keeping score, you're only practicing."

Step Seven: Publicize. If you improve service for a customer, tell others. The best cure for opposition, cynicism, hostility, doubt, hesitation, and resistance is visible, measurable success. Use the bulletin board, newsletter, and department meetings to share these results. Celebrate.

Now, go improve service for at least one customer today. ▥

Office Systems: A Summary

The key to effective law office administration is the development and maintenance of effective systems. As a paralegal, you should endeavor to become proficient in the use of all of the systems in your law office. If your office is not effectively organized and systematized, one of your first tasks should be the implementation of a systems approach to your legal work. As you learn or develop the systems used in the office, remember that it is up to you to make those systems work or develop better ones. By taking an assertive and systematic approach to your work, not only will you make your work easier, but you will also have developed additional skills and thereby advanced your career.

The following chapters cover the major systems used by law firms. There you will see not only the importance of this systems orientation, but also the specific applications used in the law.

Key Terms

assertiveness	sexual harassment	systems approach
drug testing	substance abuse	TQM

Problems and Activities

You are a paralegal in charge of office systems in a medium-size law firm. In the following chapters, you will be learning the specific systems used in law office administration, and, in the problems and activities that follow each section, you will have the opportunity to apply what you have learned. The activities in the chapters in this section concern the following clients, who are described for you now.

1. Your firm has a large manufacturing client that regularly purchases real estate in the area. For several years your firm has handled the closings for all of these real estate purchases. The client's corporate name is Yard Manufacturing, Inc., and the president and the firm's primary contact at Yard is Peggy Rickles. Cindy Bush is the attorney at the firm who usually handles matters on behalf of Yard. The following matters are being handled by your firm on behalf of Yard:

   a. Purchase of vacant lot at 123 McKenzie.
   b. Lease of 100-story office building at 1118 November Blvd.

2. Your firm is also handling personal injury litigation on behalf of Joe and Irene Turner against Blowtorch Manufacturing Company. Mr. Turner was injured when a torch manufactured by Blowtorch blew up in his face. The case is quite voluminous. The firm has done a great deal of discovery in the case and expended a great deal of time and energy. The attorney in charge of the case is Reginald Hothead.

3. The firm handles a criminal defense case on a pro bono basis. The client is Tom Johnson, who is accused of armed robbery. Dudley DoRight is the attorney representing Tom in his criminal case.

4. Your firm routinely handles Chapter 7 bankruptcies for individuals. Presently you are involved with the case of Mr. and Mrs. Overlimit, whose bankruptcy problems are a result of their excessive spending habits during the 1980s. Colleen Hallaran is the attorney handling the case.

Refer to these clients as you prepare the activities in the other chapters in this section.

CHAPTER 6

LAW OFFICE ACCOUNTING AND ECONOMICS

CHAPTER OUTLINE

OBJECTIVES

By the completion of this chapter, you should:

- understand and apply basic accounting procedures to legal applications;

- understand general procedures used with automated and manual billing systems; and

- understand zero-based budgeting and how it affects law firm economics.

How a Law Firm Generates and Distributes Income

A law firm is a business, and as such it must earn income. Therefore, to understand the law firm environment, it is essential to understand how a law firm generates income.

Legal personnel earn money for their services, which are rendered in time. Many lawyers, law clerks, and paralegals earn income for their work by recording billable hours. That means that they account for their time in writing, and the client is charged for services based on the hourly rates of the people working on the project. For instance, a paralegal arrives at the office and is prepared to begin work at 8:30 A.M., takes a one-hour lunch break, and leaves for the day at 5 P.M. The paralegal has spent 7½ hours, excluding the lunch break, on work. He or she must account for those hours, generally in tenths of the hour, for everything that has been done. All time spent on behalf of a client is considered billable time, or billable hours. All time spent on nonclient-related matters, such as participation on a firm committee, a work break, or office organization, is considered nonbillable time, or nonbillable hours. The time cannot be charged to a client and, therefore, is time that the firm must absorb in its overhead.

Some situations, however, do not require billable hours. Under a contingency fee arrangement, the client pays a percentage of what is won. In a fixed fee arrangement, a set fee for the entire project is established at the outset. In these situations, billable hours do not apply.

For the law firm to be economically viable, lawyers and paralegals must work in an organized fashion in order to record as many billable hours as possible during each workday. Time wasted is money wasted when you work by the hour. Depending upon geographic location, lawyers are expected to work between 1,800 and 2,200 billable hours per year; paralegals are expected to bill between 1,600 and 1,800 hours per year. The number of billable hours usually increases in direct proportion to the size of the firm. Salaries and points (in the case of equity partners) are directly related to the billable hours worked and billed.

It is very important for all lawyers and paralegals to remember that they should never reduce their own time for timekeeping purposes. In other words, if you work on a project with which you are unfamiliar or slow, and it takes you four hours to finish the project when you know it should only have taken two hours, you must record the four hours—not the two that you feel it should have taken. This is the sole responsibility of the billing attorney, and it is the only way that you can successfully account for your time on the job. It is possible that you are incorrect in your expectation and that the four-hour time period was perfectly acceptable.

Just as you earn income for the firm by recording and billing billable hours, the firm pays you for your work. As a paralegal, you will be paid a salary, as are all of the lawyers other than equity partners. The salary is negotiated at the time of your hiring and is adjusted at the time of your reviews, either annually or semiannually.

At the time of your hiring, a benefit package should also be discussed. The benefit package may be made up of a number of parts, such as:

- medical, dental, and life insurance

- pension plan

- parking

- sick/personal leave

- vacation.

You may or may not be required to contribute to the purchase of your medical, dental, and life insurance, but it most likely will be on a voluntary basis.

In addition to distributing income through the compensation package, law firms use some other methods to distribute income. Partners share in a points system for their compensation. Point distribution is a division of 100 percent of the shares of the profits of the partnership. For instance, a senior partner may have 5 percent of the points, which contrasts greatly with a new partner, who may have only 0.5 percent of the points. All of this varies by law firm, depending upon the size and structure of the organization.

Some firms give bonuses to those who do extraordinary work on specific tasks or overall good work during the year. They may give across-the-board bonuses, meaning that all share in additional monies in an exceptionally profitable year. When you are making a decision to accept a position, it may be a good idea to ask if the firm has a bonus plan and if you would be eligible to participate.

The Basics of Billing

The age-old saying, "time is money," could not be truer than in the law office environment. Because time is an intangible, it is often elusive and hard to sell. Think of it this way: If you were a shopkeeper selling clocks, you would have a full range of styles, sizes, colors, manufacturers, and, of course, prices. A customer could come into your shop, look at the clock, touch it, and maybe even hear it chime. She could then determine how much the clock is worth to her.

In the law office, the professional staff (of which you are an integral part) sells ideas, expertise, and services in general for an hourly rate. One cannot see or touch the ideas, expertise, or service, so the item for sale is an intangible. It is, therefore, much more difficult for the average client to determine the worth of the purchase.

Lawyers have traditionally billed for their services by the hour. This approach requires agreement on the hourly fees to be charged by the lawyer and any other timekeepers. The attorney tries to keep careful, accurate records as to the time expended on the client's case and bills the client in the agreed-upon way, which may be monthly, quarterly, or at the end of the case.

Hourly rates differ among legal personnel, depending on experience, area of expertise, and so on. Also, rates differ significantly in different parts of the country. Paralegals may bill in the $65–$80/hour range; associates in the $85–$125/hour range; and partners in the $125–$300/hour range. When you submit or input your new matter report and any ancillary forms, you include the billing for that client in that information. As time is expended on the matter, that information is correlated with the billing for that client. If there are exceptions for a particular client or matter, you will want to communicate those changes to the appropriate person so that the bill accurately reflects the client's understanding and expectations. (See Figure 6-1.)

In addition to the hourly rate, lawyers use other methods to charge the client for legal services. One approach is the *contingency fee,* where the client pays a percentage, usually a third, of what he collects in a lawsuit or by settlement to the attorney. If the client does not collect anything in the lawsuit, she does not pay any legal fees, although the client must pay expenses such as court costs, filing fees, or court reporting fees. This type of fee arrangement is most frequently used in tort cases, especially personal injury situations. Essentially, in a contingency fee arrangement, the attorney agrees to represent a client in litigation without the client having to pay any legal fees unless the attorney is successful in obtaining a monetary recovery.

Another type of charge is the *fixed fee,* which is most frequently used for standardized procedures such as real estate closings or bankruptcies. Standardized fees are used by attorneys for performing legal tasks that are routine and should take a predetermined amount of time. For example, the preparation of a basic will without any trust documents may cost $100; however, if the client wants a more specialized will, with trusts and so on, the fees will probably not be covered by a fixed fee. Another example of a fixed-fee service is an uncontested divorce for a couple with no children. The preparation of the paperwork for such a divorce, as well as the court time, is minimal; therefore, attorneys can still make a profit by charging fixed fees.

By thinking of the "sale" of legal services as an intangible rather than tangible thing, you can see how important it is to give the client quality service for

---

BILLING EXCEPTIONS

Client Name: American Ins. Agency

Client Number: 9006   Matter Number: 60009   Atty Number: 789

Exceptions affect:
-   ✓   All matters for this client.
- _____ All matters for this client for this billing attorney only.
- _____ Specific matter.

Please check the appropriate line if your client demands a billing procedure other than the standards set forth below.

1. Standard billing format is 42 (Date, timeslip, hrs.).
   - _____ 52   Date, timeslip, attyinit.
   - ✓ 62   Date, timeslip, attyinit, hrs.

2. Standard billing frequency is quarterly from the date file received.
   - _____ Monthly
   - _____ Semi-Annual
   - _____ Annual
   - _____ Bi-Annually
   - _____ End of Case (hrly matters)
   - _____ End of Case (contingent)

3. Minimum billing rates are:

Senior Partner	$110.00	Lower Rate:	_____
Junior Partner	$110.00	Lower Rate:	_____
Senior Associate	$100.00	Lower Rate:	85.00
Junior Associate	$100.00	Lower Rate:	95.00
Medical Researcher	$ 60.00	Lower Rate:	_____
Paralegal	$ 60.00	Lower Rate:	55.00
Law Clerk	$ 60.00	Lower Rate:	_____

4. Bills are mailed directly to the client by Data Processing. The original bill will be sent back to the attorney only if the client mandates a letter or other special procedure attached to the bill. Please note: Mark the BSR with "return original bill to attorney".
   - ✓ Send original bill to attorney to forward to client.

5. Bills display at the bottom of the bill: Total Hours x Rate
   Breakdown of attorney hours at the end of the bill is an exception.
   - Ex: Hrs. at Rate = Total (Atty - Class)
   - Ex: Hrs. at Rate = Total (Atty - Class of P/L only)
   - _____ Breakdown of attorney hours and class.
   - _____ Breakdown of attorney hours and P/L class only.

6. _____ Grid breakdown of hours by services performed is an exception. The original bill and BSR are sent back to the secretary for grid preparation. The secretary mails the bill and returns the BSR to Data Processing.

7. Postage is added to each bill.
   - ✓ No Postage.

FIGURE 6-1 Billing exceptions are noted to accurately reflect the client's understanding and expectations.

---

8. Mileage charge is $ .35 per mile
   Exception: $_____

9. Photocopy charges are $ .25 per page.
   Exception: $_____

10. Computer document preparation is $25.00 per hour.
    _____ Charge cannot appear on bills.

11. Westlaw and Information America are billed as an attorney.
    _____ Transfer to working attorney number.

Billing Attorney's Approval: _James B Hunt_____

Managing Partner's Approval: _____

Date: _4/13/95_

FIGURE 6-1   *(continued)*

a fair price. To do so, all timekeepers (attorneys, paralegals, and law clerks) must be efficient and effective and keep good time records. (See Figure 6-2.)

Alternative Billing

Although hourly billing remains the most widely used approach in most law firms, changes in the economy, changes in client expectations, and concerns about the practice of hourly billing have led some lawyers to adopt new approaches to client billing. Taken together, these new approaches represent alternative approaches to billing.

What limitations of and concerns about hourly billing have caused alternative billing options to proliferate in recent years? One problem is that in an hourly billing situation, the client does not really know how much the legal services will cost; the client merely knows what the hourly fee will be. This might cause uncertainty or anxiety on the part of the client about her expenditures on a matter.

Another problem is that hourly fee accounting causes attorneys and paralegals to work "on the clock." It takes a great deal of work to keep up with time; also, some people find it demeaning in a professional relationship to "put up the meter" whenever they interact with a client. It is hard to be personable, warm, and caring with a client when that meter is clicking. If a lawyer does spend extra time with a client and bills for it, the client may feel the attorney is running up the fees; if the lawyer gets down to business to avoid running up expenses, the client may feel that the lawyer is too abrupt. Also, the client who receives an hourly bill might feel that certain actions are unnecessary or excessive, leading to fee disputes and conflicts between attorney and client about bills and choices of activities.

```
┌──────────────────────────────────────────────────────────────────┐
│                    Juris, Samples and Samples                       │
│                         151 Athens Way                              │
│                       Nashville, TN 37228                           │
│                                                                     │
│                        January 31, 1999                             │
│                                                                     │
│                      Billed through 01/31/99                        │
│                 Bill number    2050-00000-001 GCT                   │
│                                                                     │
│  Mr. & Mrs. Robert Philips                                          │
│  4819 West Meade Court                                              │
│  Fairfax, VA 22030                                                  │
│  Prepaid balance brought forward                      $1,000.00 CR  │
│  Estate planning for Philips' family                                │
│  FOR PROFESSIONAL SERVICES RENDERED                                 │
└──────────────────────────────────────────────────────────────────┘
```

Date	Atty	Description	Hours/Rate	Amount
01/01/99	EMB	Fees Balance Brought Forward	2.00 hrs 95/hr	190.00
01/01/99	MJR	Fees Balance Brought Forward	4.50 hrs 80/hr	360.00
01/15/99	JAM	Meeting with Jerry Bass	1.75 hrs 95/hr	166.25
01/15/99	GCT	Library research on tax laws and control guidelines in Virginia	3.50 hrs 90/hr	315.00
		Total fees for this matter		$1,031.25

BILLING SUMMARY

Name	Hours/Rate	Amount
Esther M. Bradberry	2.00 hrs 95/hr	190.00
James A. Martin	1.75 hrs 95/hr	166.25
Michael J. Ryan	4.50 hrs 80/hr	360.00
Grant C. Tyler	3.50 hrs 90/hr	315.00
TOTAL FEES	11.75 hrs	$1,031.25
Metro Tax		$ 61.88
TN State Tax		$ 41.25
TOTAL CHARGES FOR THIS BILL		$1,134.38

FIGURE 6-2   A sample bill for legal services. (Courtesy of Juris, Incorporated.)

These concerns have led to the development of alternatives to hourly billing. The following alternatives are some of the most widely used by contemporary law firms.

Fixed Fee/Flat Rate/Project Billing   As discussed earlier, flat-fee billing involves giving a single fee for work or a project to be done. For example, in a criminal case, an attorney might charge $2,500 for running a preliminary hearing and negotiating a plea agreement; or she might charge $7,500 to try a case. Once the fee is decided upon and accepted, the attorney and her team are free to do the work the way they feel it should be done. This approach eliminates client uncertainty about billing and fee disputes over bills; however, the attorney quoting the fee needs to be able to predict accurately the amount of work and time involved in order to charge an appropriate amount.

Capped Fee   *Capped fee* refers to an hourly billing situation in which the client is promised that the total bill or total hours will not exceed a certain amount. Although this approach still requires timekeeping, it assures the client of the maximum expense for a particular matter.

Discounted or Blended Fees   These approaches modify the traditional hourly fee. A *discounted fee* is a reduced fee for certain clients or situations; a *blended fee* averages the billing rates for lawyers, paralegals, and support staff and gives the client a single hourly fee, rather than a different hourly fee for each person who works on the case.

Incentive Billing   This approach combines hourly fees with a bonus for achieving certain results. Some clients like this approach because it rewards the result, not merely the time spent; be aware, though, that ethical guidelines prohibit result-oriented billing in certain areas, such as criminal law or divorce cases.

Modified Contingency Billing   This approach combines a reduced hourly fee and compensation based on results. For example, Bud and Jonathan might work on a case for a reduced hourly rate of $60 an hour, with an additional 12 percent of the amount won as compensation for the attorneys. Another variation is charging a normal hourly fee for the work performed, but having that fee be a down payment against a future contingency fee. For example, Bud and Jonathan might charge $125 an hour for legal work; upon completion of the case, the amount already paid would be subtracted from the amount of the contingency fee and the client would pay the difference out of the settlement or jury award.

Hybrid Arrangements   Any billing approach that combines elements of two or more other approaches might be referred to as a hybrid arrangement.

All these alternative billing approaches have one thing in common. They attempt to find an approach to billing that satisfies the client in terms of communication, expectations, and fairness, and also satisfies the financial needs of the lawyers or law firm. As the legal profession moves toward the 21st century, you will see a proliferation of new approaches to billing that attempt to meet the goals of both attorney and client.

The Timeslip System

When a law firm bills by the hour, strict attention must be paid to accurate recording and billing for the actual time expended for each client and each matter. The timeslip system enables all timekeepers to keep accurate and consistent records of time expended.

The most common way of thinking about time involves dividing up an hour into tenths and billing in tenths of an hour. One hour is generally represented by 1.0, a half hour by 0.5, and so forth. That means that timekeepers must track their activities over six-minute intervals. Another option is to keep time by quarters, with the smallest unit being a quarter of an hour. All attorneys and paralegals should use the same time unit system for consistency of reporting. Most people do not generally monitor their time this carefully, so it is essential that you immediately get in the habit of looking at your watch or clock when you begin and end every task.

In a firm that bills in tenths of hours, the following equivalencies would be used by all timekeepers:

    0–12 minutes = 0.2 hours
    12–24 minutes = 0.4 hours
    24–36 minutes = 0.6 hours
    36–48 minutes = 0.8 hours
    48–60 minutes = 1.0 hours

A daily time diary (Figure 6-3) is the most commonly used method to record time. It contains the original data and is the source document for the preparation of the final timeslips, so naturally the recorded information must be clear and legible in order to facilitate the transfer of this data to the final document. It is most effective to record your time on a daily time diary as each task is performed. Record each task when you start, giving a description of the work and the time you began. Immediately upon finishing, record the time. If you keep track of your time this way, you will be surprised at the end of the day that you can account for almost all of it. Your supervising attorney may also review your timesheets and offer valuable suggestions for managing and recording your time effectively. Accounting for the majority of your time increases your productivity. In addition, keeping good, accurate time records permits the firm to collect for the majority of the time you bill. Increasing productivity and recovering for most of the time worked are two important factors that keep the law firm in business.

The daily time diary is complemented by the computerized timeslip system. This system uses the processing capabilities and efficiency of the computer to record and analyze time use. This system is used when the timekeeper, such as a paralegal or the attorney, either directly inputs his information into the computer or gives it to a clerk for inputting. The data entry person takes the handwritten sheets and types them either directly into the computer or on the word processor so that the time information can be fed into the computer for accounting purposes. When computerized timeslips are read or scanned into the computer, they can be recorded and analyzed to give the firm accurate profiles for each timekeeper. This system also aids in the preparation of bills for clients because, when the bills are prepared, the timekeeper's time does not have to be retyped—it is already on the system.

| DREW, ECKL & FARNHAM | | | | DAILY TIME DIARY | |

DATE 2/3/95   ATTY. 401

CLIENT # MATTER #	DATE	TIME	ATTY.	CODE	SUB CODE
1053 . 10276	2/3	.5	401	A	ii

Telephone conference w/ S. Selfridge re
prenuptial agreement

CLIENT # MATTER #	DATE	TIME	ATTY.	CODE	SUB CODE
4062 . 51324	2/3	1.2	401	—	—

Initial Draft of Lease Agreement
for "I Love Ice Cream, Inc."

CLIENT # MATTER #	DATE	TIME	ATTY.	CODE	SUB CODE
2372 . 10001	2/3	.8	401	B	—

Intra-office conference w/ R. Means
re dispute

CLIENT # MATTER #	DATE	TIME	ATTY.	CODE	SUB CODE
0001 . 10001	2/3	2.2	401		

Management committee meeting

CLIENT # MATTER #	DATE	TIME	ATTY.	CODE	SUB CODE
8062 . 54231	2/3	1.3	401	F	i

Library Research

CLIENT # MATTER #	DATE	TIME	ATTY.	CODE	SUB CODE
7241 . 00246	2/3	2.2	401		

Meeting w/ co-counsel re trial

CLIENT # MATTER #	DATE	TIME	ATTY.	CODE	SUB CODE
0001 . 02401	2/3	.3	401		

Office organization

CLIENT # MATTER #	DATE	TIME	ATTY.	CODE	SUB CODE
2376 . 21094	2/3	.4			

Telephone conference w/ Nicholson Masinter

TOTAL TIME   8.9

FIGURE 6-3 A daily time diary enables attorneys and paralegals to track their time effectively.

ON POINT   *LITTLE JOHN'S SLACK ACCOUNTING*

It is the end of a long day for Robin Hood and Friar Tuck, principals in the law firm of Hood and Tuck, P.C. As they are sitting around the fire roasting a leg of lamb, Little John, their new associate, approaches.

"Good to see you, Little John," says Robin. "Come and sit by the fire, and tell us about your activities on the Nottingham case so that we can pay you accurately."

"Well, Robin, that is kind of difficult. I went to town in the morning, spent some time asking questions, got ambushed by some road warriors, then—let's see, gosh, I went to the Equity Court at some point, I guess about 3:00. I met up with Friar Tuck at some point just before dusk, I think—you know, it's hard to remember exactly what I did and when I did it, now that you ask."

"I know, Little John, and let this be a lesson to you. You must learn to keep up with your time accurately. Lucky for you I charged a fixed fee on the Nottingham case. Here's your share. Just be thankful I didn't charge them on an hourly basis. If I did, and you couldn't prove what you had done, I don't know how I would have been able to submit an accurate bill or get paid for the time that you did devote to the case."

"You're right, Robin. Just because we want to achieve justice doesn't mean that we should neglect our accounting responsibilities. That could lead to trouble for everyone."

"You are a wise associate, Little John. If you can just improve your billing practices, I am confident that you will have a long career with our firm."

Some firms may use other timekeeping systems. One that is popular among smaller firms is the slip system. Slips are printed on perforated paper or on pads, and attorneys and paralegals complete one slip for each activity they perform. The slip is then filed in a billing folder or envelope for each client. At the end of the billing period (i.e., monthly, quarterly, etc.), slips are pulled from the folders or envelopes and tallied. From that information, bills are prepared and sent to the clients.

Another method, also used primarily in smaller firms, involves using a ledger sheet. This form enables the individual timekeeper to record, usually by hand, the activities she performed during the day, the time spent, and the amount to be billed. These ledgers may then be accumulated and used for billing at the appropriate time.

Good timekeeping habits not only allow the firm to bill effectively, but they also let you know what you have accomplished, the value of those accomplishments, and the tasks left to be done.

Management Reports Based on Time

The management team in a law firm frequently uses time data as a basis for various management reports. These reports can be used for a variety of functions, as the firm attempts to understand and improve its productivity and profitability. The following time-based reports are frequently compiled in a law office.

With the tremendous computing power now available to law firms through their computer systems, an infinite variety of management reports and information can be generated. The following examples are only some of the most common applications for law firms. Once the information has been input into the system, the firm's management can manipulate the data in many ways to get the information needed to help the firm remain profitable.

File Status Report

A file status report may display unbilled time, unbilled disbursements, and fee and disbursement receivable totals, as well as other status amounts used in calculating the investment in a client/matter. The report is generally sorted by billing attorney, but would show all timekeepers who were active on the matter for a given period. (See Figure 6-4.)

Attorney Detail Report and Timekeeper Analysis

A detail report displays all billed and unbilled time for each client/matter for each attorney. The firm may decide to show hour and dollar amounts, or hours only. This report may also reflect current month and year-to-date numbers. (See Figure 6-5.)

Attorney Realization Report

The realization report may well be one of the most important of all reports. It shows, for all timekeepers, the hours and dollars relieved (billed and/or written off) and the percentage of the timekeeper's time that was billed. Suppose, for instance, that you work long hours, but, because your work is inadequate or untimely, only a portion of the time can be billed and the balance must be written off. Your realization rate will be low.

Timeslip Delinquency Report

A delinquency report shows timekeepers who have not turned in timeslips for any given date. As you might guess, one would not want one's name on this list. Such delinquency causes a dramatic slowdown in the firm's billing practice.

REPORT DATE   03/02/91
REPORT NUMBER JP061- 000023
SORTED BY CLIENT - DETAIL
RANGE SELECTED: BEG OF FILE TO END OF FILE

Bachman, Wilson & Juris
ACCOUNT ANALYSIS

PAGE   1

CLIENT MATTER NAME	BILL TMKP	LAST BILL DATE	UNBILLED EXP/FEES	YEAR TO DATE BILLED EXP/FEES	RECEIVED EXP/FEES	BALANCE DUE	PPD BALANCE
000100 00000 Abbey Industries Incorporated	ABC	02/03/91	242.12	270.00	1,045.00	.00	.00
			.00	17,500.00	54,500.00		
00001 Abbey Industries Acquisition	ABC	02/12/91	561.37	975.00	975.00	1,706.25	.00
			2,626.25	5,806.25	4,100.00		
00002 Abbey Industry Pension Plan	ABC	02/03/91	561.37	630.00	955.00	.00	.00
			3,531.25	.00	2,000.00		
00003 Abbey Industries EEOC Matter	ABC	02/03/91	17.40	686.25	966.25	.00	.00
			3,990.00	.00	1,400.00		
00004 Abbey Industries 1988 IRS	ABC	02/12/91	125.40	598.00	598.00	2,589.25	.00
			960.00	4,688.75	2,099.50		
00005 Abbey Industries Logo	EFG	02/03/91	.00	482.50	482.50	.00	.00
			.00	.00	2,750.00		
CLIENT TOTAL			1,507.66	3,641.75	5,021.75	4,295.50	.00
			11,107.50	27,995.00	66,849.50		
000150 00000 American Insurance Company	CDE	02/03/91	.00	.00	.00	265.00	.00
			1,040.00	565.00	300.00		
00001 Johnson, Elliott vs.	CDE	02/03/91	152.75	.00	.00	1,240.00	.00
			620.00	1,240.00	.00		
00002 Northern, Polston vs.	CDE	02/03/91	580.12	383.75	.00	2,073.75	.00
			5,370.00	1,690.00	.00		
00003 Fischer, Schrebenski vs.	CDE	02/03/91	84.15	465.00	.00	2,195.00	.00
			4,375.00	1,730.00	.00		
CLIENT TOTAL			817.02	848.75	.00	5,773.75	.00
			11,405.00	5,225.00	300.00		
000200 00000 Anderson Printing Company	CDE	02/05/91	.00	205.00	.00	8,431.25	.00
			.00	4,800.00	.00		

FIGURE 6-4 A file status report details the work expended on each case file. (Courtesy of Juris, Incorporated.)

```
REPORT DATE   03/02/91                        Bachman, Wilson & Juris                              PAGE   1
REPORT NUMBER JP062-000018                      TIMEKEEPER ANALYSIS
SORTED BY TIMEKEEPER                                                                        PRINTED BY  TDD
RANGE SELECTED: BEG OF FILE TO END OF FILE
```

TIMEKEEPER	PERIOD	TOTAL HOURS	N.B. HOURS	BILLABLE HOURS	BILLABLE AMOUNT	BILLED AMOUNT	BILLED RATE	FEES RECEIVED	UNBILLED HOURS	UNBILLED AMOUNT
Allen B. Colby	MTD	156.50	.00	156.50	19,167.50	16,418.88		23,336.70		
	YTD	314.00	.00	314.00	39,442.50	50,995.66	123	51,331.32	187.00	22,682.50
Carolyn D. Elkins	MTD	165.25	.00	165.25	17,907.50	15,615.91		19,830.61		
	YTD	343.75	.00	343.75	38,357.50	42,991.11	113	43,455.54	207.50	22,555.00
E. Franklin Garrison, III	MTD	165.75	.00	165.75	14,752.50	13,448.44		19,532.25		
	YTD	342.75	.00	342.75	32,670.00	40,964.18	96	41,918.25	214.00	19,095.00
Harold I. Juris, Jr.	MTD	152.50	.00	152.50	14,157.50	13,339.96		19,023.94		
	YTD	333.75	.00	333.75	32,150.00	41,650.20	95	42,130.29	203.25	18,560.00
Karen Langley Morris	MTD	174.00	.00	174.00	15,292.50	11,908.14		24,094.81		
	YTD	358.50	.00	358.50	33,191.25	39,640.05	93	46,164.60	242.35	21,049.75
Anne Rollins Stewart	MTD	158.75	.00	158.75	13,245.00	11,716.20		19,637.40		
	YTD	345.75	.00	345.75	29,635.00	40,265.58	87	43,137.47	218.75	18,045.00
Linda H. Talbert	MTD	164.50	.00	164.50	5,833.75	6,113.26		10,332.69		
	YTD	363.95	.00	363.95	13,424.50	19,203.26	39	21,582.69	204.05	7,218.00
James David Williams	MTD	163.00	.00	163.00	6,500.00	5,974.21		8,880.10		
	YTD	349.90	.00	349.90	14,601.00	18,832.46	40	19,284.34	213.35	8,514.00
FINAL TOTALS	MTD	1,300.25	.00	1,300.25	106,856.25	94,535.00		144,668.50		
	MTD								1,690.25	
	YTD	2,752.35	.00	2,752.35	233,471.75	294,542.50	84	309,004.50		137,719.25

FIGURE 6-5 A timekeeper analysis report tracks each attorney's time and billing. (Courtesy of Juris, Incorporated.)

Billable versus Firm Hours

Most firms have annual hourly time goals—but they are really more than goals. They are "musts." These goals are the firm's attempt to project and maintain its objectives by making sure that each contributor is appropriately productive. These time requirements are referred to as *billable hour requirements. Billable hours,* as the name denotes, are those hours of your work that you can directly bill to the client. Billable hours include any activity, from interviewing the client, to making phone calls, to doing legal research, that is necessary for the case on which you are working. Nonbillable hours are called *firm hours,* as the firm must absorb their cost in overhead because there is no corresponding revenue. When you are in a committee meeting, or when you are organizing your office, your hours are nonbillable. In many firms, attorneys are expected to bill a minimum of 2,000 hours per year, and paralegals are expected to bill between 1,600 and 1,800 hours per year. If you divide these yearly goals to determine how many billable hours you must have every day, you will see just how important it is to do your work correctly and efficiently—and to record every billable minute of your time.

The following sections describe manual and computerized approaches to billing.

Billing: Manual Systems

In smaller law firms, time is often kept on timeslips similar to the daily time record. Each client/matter is given a separate file labeled "Billing." Those timeslips are dropped into the billing file until the attorney is ready to send a bill. As a paralegal, it may be your responsibility to prepare and send the bills for attorneys.

Manual bills may be typed on a typewriter or into a computer. They may display for the client a variety of information, such as (1) timekeeper's name; (2) task performed; (3) date(s) tasks were performed; (4) length of time spent on the task(s); (5) dollar value for each task. Some attorneys prefer to give the client a lot of information, whereas others prefer to use the words "For Legal Services Rendered . . . . $xxxxx." Today, clients generally seek more information about their bills, and it is a good idea to provide as complete and thorough an accounting as possible, for both professional and economic reasons. An example of a general bill is shown in Figure 6-6.

A detailed bill, which is probably a more effective method for billing the client for the same matter, is shown in Figure 6-7.

After the bill is prepared, the attorney may wish to send a cover letter, or she may simply want you to send it directly to the client. Keep a copy of the final

---

Tlaine, Bagby & Reynolds
Attorneys at Law
111 North Avenue
Buena Vista, Florida 23094
Telephone: (912) 555-1213

To: Acme Manufacturing Company
3736 Pine Oak Circle
Doraville, Florida 23096

Attention: Mr. Jim Jones
President, Acme Manufacturing Company

Incorporation of Acme Manufacturing Company, Inc.

Legal services:	$1,050.00
Expenses:	660.00
TOTAL:	$1,710.00

Remittance due within thirty (30) days of receipt or balance is subject to finance charges at the legal rate of 12% per annum.

FIGURE 6-6   An example of a general bill

bill in your billing file for that particular client/matter and "suspense" a copy in case it is not paid timely. *Suspensing a document* means putting it in a place where you will automatically be reminded of it within a particular period of time. For example, you could note in your tickler system (which will be discussed shortly) to check and see if the bill was paid. You would probably put in a follow-up or suspend the bill 33 days from sending it to permit time for mailing. If you have a bookkeeper, send a copy of the bill to her; it is generally her responsibility to follow up or, at the very least, advise the attorney that the client has not paid the bill on time. If you are keeping the books, you will learn later in this chapter how to post a receipt using a one-write system.

Automated Timeslip Systems

Another system that is now widely used is the direct input of timeslips by the timekeeper or a secretary into the computer. This system uses the processing capabilities and efficiency of the computer to record and analyze the use of time. These systems generally work as follows. The timekeeper manually records time and gives hard copies to the secretary or other designated person, who inputs the time into the billing system. The information put into the system usually includes the client name, the file number, the timekeeper's name

Tlaine, Bagby & Reynolds
Attorneys at Law
111 North Avenue
Buena Vista, Florida 23094
Telephone: (912) 555-1213

To: Acme Manufacturing Company
3736 Pine Oak Circle
Doraville, Florida 23096

Attention: Mr. Jim Jones
President, Acme Manufacturing Company

Date	Timekeeper	Task	Time	Amount	Total
11/18	RJR	Interviewing client	1.5	$150	$225
11/19	TMT	Draft Articles of Incorporation	3.0	$75	$225
11/20	RJR	Review & Revise Articles of Incorporation	1.0	$150	$150
11/20	TMT	Draft By-Laws Draft Stock Certificates Order Corporate Book Telephone conference with Secretary of State re: filing fees; obtain and file name registration Conference w/RJR	4.0	$75	$300
11/20	RJR	Conference w/TMT Review and revise stock certificates; review name registration	1.0	$150	$150

TOTAL: $1,050.00

Expenses:

11/20	Filing Fee for Secretary of State	$ 500.00
11/20	Costs for Corporate Book	$ 150.00
11/20	Copies of Documents	$ 10.00

TOTAL: $ 660.00

TOTAL AMOUNT DUE: $1,710.00

Remittance due within thirty (30) days of receipt of bill; or interest will be added at the legal rate of 12% per annum.

FIGURE 6-7 An example of a detailed bill

and billing rate, the designation of the timekeeper (i.e., attorney, law clerk, or paralegal), the time spent on the specific task, the date the task was performed, and a narrative of what task was performed. From this data, the computer system can compile the complete bill for the client, as well as various reports for the firm.

It is important to note that most firms set a time deadline each afternoon (i.e., 3:30 P.M.) to close the time entry files and transfer data to the main billing database. You should not enter any timeslip data after the deadline, as there is a good possibility that the data would be lost. Most firms also set a deadline for when timekeepers must have all of their time entered into the system. Some firms even fine timekeepers if their time is not in by the designated time. For example, time for each week may be due the following Monday at 12:00 P.M. If the timekeepers do not have their time in by Monday at 12:00 P.M., they are fined $5.00 for every day their time is not logged into the system.

Even from this general description, you should realize that timekeeping is a somewhat complex process that requires accuracy and thorough attention to detail. Also remember that the level of professionalism of your billing work directly affects the firm's income and image. You can contribute to your firm's professionalism, as well as your own professional development, if your timeslips are neat, accurate, and timely.

Timeslip Verification Forms

A timeslip verification form (see Figure 6-8) is used to keep track of the attorneys'/paralegals' time that has been input on the system. The form generally asks the following questions:

Name:	Attorney's/paralegal's name
Month:	Month during which the time was worked
Date:	Actual date of work—not the date you actually entered the time
Time submitted:	Total hours submitted for each date
Time confirmed by data processing:	When you receive a copy of your timesheet, confirm total hours input for each date
Date submitted:	Date time was entered on the system
Batch total:	Total hours for each batch
Total hours:	This number should equal the total hours listed on the month-end report (i.e.. a report generated at the end of each month that reflects the billable hours and value of each timekeeper).

TIME SHEET VERIFICATION

NAME:_____   MONTH:_____

DATE	TIME SUBMITTED	TIME CONFIRMED BY DATA PROCESSING	DATE SUBMITTED	BATCH TOTAL
1				
2				
3				
4				
5				
6				
7				
8				
9				
10				
11				
12				
13				
14				
15				
16				
17				
18				
19				
20				
21				
22				
23				
24				
25				
26				
27				
28				
29				
30				
31				

FIGURE 6-8   A timeslip verification form assures that computer information is accurate.

Timeslip verification forms are a quality control mechanism that assure the proper maintenance of time and billing records. Each firm has its own method of cross-checking time slips, and it is highly important that your firm have an effective system of checks and balances to assure accurate and professional billing practices. (See Figure 6-9.)

```
                        Bachman, Wilson & Juris
    REPORT DATE 02/12/91           TIMEKEEPER DIARY              PAGE    1
    REPORT NUMBER JP076-000020
    SORTED BY TIMEKEEPER BY DATE                        PRINTED BY  TDD
    RANGE SELECTED:  02/11/91 to 02/11/91

                             Allen B. Colby
                          02/11/91 - 02/11/91

      DATE    CLIENT MATTER                            HRS   RATE    FEE

    02/11/91  000100  00001  Abbey Industries Acquisition  0.25  125   31.25
              Telephone conference with Anne McNaron Clayton of
              Better Deals Real Estate, Inc.

              000150  00001  Johnson, Elliott vs.         4.00   80   320.00
              Travel to Franklin and meet with Leonard Johnson.

              000150  00002  Northern, Polston vs.        1.50   80   120.00
              Receipt and review of deposition of Lawrence
              Alperstein.

              000150  00003  Fischer, Schrebenski vs.     1.00   80    80.00
              Office conference with Harley Fischer.

              000400  00000  Carroll, Linda Sue           0.50  125    62.50
              Draft letter to Ms. Carroll.

                             DAILY TOTAL                  7.25        613.75

                             TIMEKEEPER TOTAL             7.25        613.75
```

FIGURE 6-9 Using the Timekeeper Diary, your timekeepers can verify that all of their time was entered correctly. (Courtesy of Juris, Incorporated.)

Automated Billing Summary Reports

Billing summary reports (BSRs) summarize and document a client's billing status for a particular period of time. (See Figure 6-10.) In general, they are automatically processed during the first few days of each month if the billing frequency code that was selected at the time the file was opened falls within that month.

You will generally be able to choose the frequency with which you receive BSRs. If, when you completed the file record, you requested that your BSR for that particular file be given to you on a monthly basis, then you should receive a BSR for that file every month until the file is closed. If, when you completed the file record, you requested that your BSR for that particular file be given to you on a quarterly, semiannual, or annual basis, then you will receive your BSRs accordingly.

BILLING SUMMARY REPORT

Juris, Samples & Samples

BILLING SUMMARY

REPORT DATE   01/01/99
REPORT NUMBER JP067-000017
SORTED BY CLIENT/MATTER
RANGE SELECTED: BEG OF FILE TO END OF FILE

PRINTED BY SMGR

PAGE 1

CLIENT NUMBER	MATTER NUMBER	REPORTING NAME	BILL TMKP	LAST BILL	TOTAL AMOUNT	FEES AMOUNT	EXPENSE AMOUNT	INTEREST AMOUNT	SALES TAX AMOUNT
0617	00000	Emma's Florist	MJR	01/31/99	1,970.14	1,612.00	187.47	9.47	161.20
0920	00000	Reed Products, Inc.	EMB	01/31/99	4,329.20	3,365.11	604.06	23.52	336.51
1613	00000	Theatre District Association	JAM	01/31/99	1,688.16	1,511.25	20.40	5.38	151.13
	00001	Redevelopment Project	JAM	01/31/99	582.05	.00	582.05	.00	.00
		CLIENT TOTAL			2,270.21	1,511.25	602.45	5.38	151.13
1710	00000	Mercantile Trust Bank	CLC	01/31/99	3,005.34	2,610.70	130.76	2.80	261.08
	00001	Clayton County Bank	CLC	01/31/99	570.59	496.00	17.95	7.04	49.60
		CLIENT TOTAL			3,575.93	3,106.70	148.71	9.84	310.68
2050	00000	Philips, Mr. & Mrs. Robert	GCT	01/31/99	1,143.18	1,039.25	.00	.00	103.93
		FINAL TOTAL			13,288.66	10,634.31	1,542.69	48.21	1,063.45
		TOTAL SALES TAX Metro Tax							638.08
		TOTAL SALES TAX In State Tax							425.37

***Report includes only those transactions since your last period end dated 00/00/00

FIGURE 6-10 A BSR recaps client bills. (Courtesy of Juris, Incorporated.)

When you receive your BSRs, decide which files you want to (1) bill or (2) hold and bill at another time. Review each one carefully. This is your only opportunity to make corrections. Write legibly and be sure all original time amounts can be read. (Do not write over the original time entries.) Then send the information to the data processing department so that a clerk can prepare the actual bill, which will be sent to the client.

Profitability, Realization, Utilization: The Bottom Line

The index of *profitability* is the difference between the billing and the cost to the firm of doing the work. The cost of doing the work takes into account all firm overhead. Many costs are fixed (i.e., rent, utilities, etc.). Other areas, such as salaries, benefits, goods, and other services are somewhat negotiable.

Salaries and benefits should be competitive with firms of similar size in the community. It is one of the most important ways to obtain and retain valuable employees. The cost-of-living index should be reviewed every six months, and merit should play a major role in deciding salary increases and bonuses.

Costs for goods and services must be watched carefully. Law firm managers are responsible for obtaining the best possible quality goods and services and the fairest prices. Bids for goods and services should be taken at least one time per year from other vendors.

Outsourcing is often extremely cost-effective. There are a number of major companies in the United States that offer facilities management. Those companies offer teams of their employees to go to companies with which they contract to perform services such as photocopying, mailroom, and fax center tasks.

Many law firms also outsource the care of their law libraries. Qualified law librarians can be utilized by contracting with a library outsourcing company. Their schedules can be arranged so that they are flexible and meet the needs of the law firm.

Other outsourcing companies that are popular with law firms are records management firms, which store closed records offsite and offer destruction services; and courier firms that take documents to clients, courthouses, and so on. Additionally, firms are finding it very useful to contract with a mail sort house, which picks up the firm's mail, sorts it by zip code, posts the mail, and then delivers it to the Post Office. The mail is sent first class, but it is mailed at a discount, bulk rate. This can amount to a considerable savings for firms with large quantities of outgoing mail. One of the best bonuses of using outsourcing firms is that when one of the employees is sick or on vacation, the spot is always immediately filled by the outsourcing company, thereby reducing down time.

It is important for a law office manager to keep a close eye on utilization (the number of profit contributors (associates, paralegals, law clerks) per partner). Most law firms now enjoy a 2:1 ratio of work producers to secretary—some are able to accomplish an even better ratio through the use of the latest technology.

To improve the bottom line, consideration should be given to the following.

1. Improve hiring and retention of lawyers. All employees (lawyers and staff) should be treated as investments for the long term, and the firm should strive to retain happy and healthy employees. They will be more productive and thus more profitable. If firms develop a pattern of losing lawyers and paralegals (either voluntarily or involuntarily) and then adding new employees in their place—without developing better systems for more effective workload distribution, training, and quality control—utilization and realization will continue to drop as firms are forced to write off more and more lawyer and paralegal hours. To curtail such problems, law firms need:

    ■ To institute better, more effective in-house training programs (paying particular attention to legal writing, client relations, and people skills) to help younger lawyers improve their ability and become more profitable

    ■ To work toward better supervision and improved short- and long-range planning within practice groups

    ■ To consider the implementation of mentor groups

    ■ To stress flexibility to personal needs

    ■ To allow vacation time *without guilt*

    ■ To constantly work on maintaining a high level of morale

    ■ To promote institutional stability and loyalty.

    With emphasis on billable hours as a measure of success, firms are placing the focus almost entirely on transportable skills, rather than other factors such as training and mentoring that could help retain employees and thereby save untold amounts of money.

2. Firms should begin experimenting with various forms of alternative billing (i.e., volume discounts, flat rates for particular jobs, blended rates, etc.). To do so makes it imperative that management know what it *really* costs to produce a product. Effective alternative billing should help reduce the cost to produce and, at the same time, address some of the lifestyle issues noted previously.

3. Management should become more aggressive in determining less profitable areas and work out of them while simultaneously filling the void with better-paying clients.

4. Management also needs to be aggressive in collecting outstanding payables. The firm needs to promote the desire of its attorneys to get involved when all other efforts have failed.

5. If firms determine that overhead is not a problem, management should then focus on:

- Optimizing utilization and realization. Cost-of-chair reports can be a step in the right direction. Some attorneys do not meet their billable hour goals because they do not have enough work available. At the same time, there are usually a number of partners who are very vocal about needing help. This is a situation in which management should be very involved and ultimately very effective. It should aggressively deal with these situations and make every effort to maximize the return.

- Leverage. Routine legal services are clearly a commodity, and clients can and do shop for the best bargains. Therefore, leverage is key for increased profits. Firms need to look for the opportunity to provide unique or higher-level services. Otherwise, they will find it increasingly difficult to raise their billable hour rates enough to exceed inflation.

- Attorneys and paralegals often attend scores of lengthy meetings—some with agendas of considerable significance and others that are relatively unimportant or unnecessary for group participation. The use of word producer hours discussing insignificant issues severely affects utilization.

- Law firms might now look for ways to expand client services into other areas, as accounting and consulting firms have done for years.

Law firms must carefully determine when it is in their best interests to reduce staff and consolidate positions. A cavalier reduction in force will cause morale to drop to a dangerous level; it could lead to errors that could potentially cost the firm considerable amounts of money (i.e., penalties due to late human resources or accounting filings, late billing cycles, etc.), as well as the loss of top-notch employees.

In the 1990s, law firms are experiencing a tightening of profit due to the cost of labor and a flattening of billing rates and the overall cost structure of running the firm. New lawyers do not return profits immediately, so firms must find ways to hire good ones and keep them for the long term in order to become profitable.

Management must also remember that all billable hours are not equal. If hiring efforts are maximized, effective training programs are provided, and file/case distribution is managed so that the right people work on the right work, then each hour will be worth more (i.e., fewer hours written off; fewer hours to produce a quality product, etc.).

The firm must set a definite billable hour goal for all attorneys and paralegals. Those who make it should be rewarded; those who do not should be counseled and given less of a salary increase.

Accounting Systems Used in Law Firms

Law firms, depending upon size and type, use a variety of accounting systems. You, as a paralegal, may be assisting with the accounting process. This section will familiarize you with accounting processes most commonly used in law firms.

Accounts Receivable: One-Write System (Manual)

The one-write method may be used by the smaller law firm, and can be purchased from an office supply store. Each client/matter is assigned an individual ledger card. By using a special pegboard and various carbonized forms, information such as amount charged to client, date of charge, amount paid by client, date paid by client, and balance due may be easily reflected by recording information with a ballpoint pen onto the necessary forms. You record the information all at one time—hence the name *one-write system.* It is a very simplified system of bookkeeping, but, for the smaller firm, can be very effective. It does not, however, allow for any complex recordation, and it requires storage space such as file drawers to maintain the ledger cards.

Similar to the one-write system, a general manual system for accounts payable and receivable can be used by very small law firms, generally those with no more than five attorneys with a low volume of monthly transactions. Using this method, the bookkeeper or person responsible for the accounting process issues checks for general office operations and client disbursements from the firm checking account. At the end of each month, all disbursements and receipts are posted in a general journal and allocated to the various income and expense account numbers. From that, balances are posted in a general ledger; a trial balance is run, and a financial statement is prepared. (See Figure 6-11.)

Accounts Receivable: Computerized Systems

In the larger, more automated law firm, a bookkeeper is generally in charge of recording all accounts receivable. We have already discussed automated timekeeping and billing, which is complemented by automated bookkeeping. (See Figure 6-12.)

After the computerized bill has been sent to the client, it is logged into the system. The bookkeeper maintains copies of all statements to clients generated on the system, as well as copies of statements paid and the payment checks made within the calendar year. Any checks received in payment for services and reimbursement for uncommon expenses relating to a client, as well as honoraria and refunds, must be forwarded to the bookkeeper for credit to the proper account.

On a monthly basis, all billing attorneys are provided with an aged work in progress report (Figure 6-13) and a schedule of past due accounts, which will

FIGURE 6-11   A paralegal performs manual accounting.

provide them with information regarding the current status of each of their files. At any time during the month, updated information may be requested from the bookkeeper detailing the status of unpaid or delinquent statements. If an account is delinquent, the billing attorney may wish to send a reminder to the client. If so, a copy of the statement in question should be obtained from the bookkeeper.

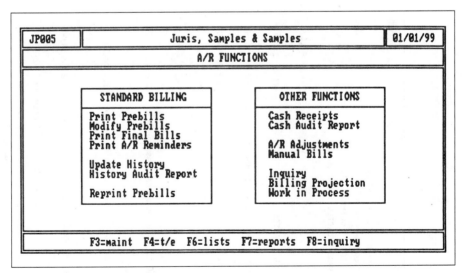

FIGURE 6-12   A menu shows computerized accounting functions. (Courtesy of Juris, Incorporated.)

```
REPORT DATE    03/02/91                   Bachman, Wilson & Juris                          PAGE    1
REPORT NUMBER JP064-000040               AGED ACCOUNTS RECEIVABLE
SORTED BY CLIENT - DETAIL             BILLING TIMEKEEPER  Carolyn D. Elkins              PRINTED BY  TDD
RANGE SELECTED : CDE to CDE
```

		BILL/ PYMT	TOTAL	FEES/		------------ PAST DUE ------------			
CLIENT MATTER	BILL	DATE	AMOUNT	EXPENSES	CURRENT	30 DAYS	60 DAYS	90 DAYS	120 DAYS
000100 00000 Abbey Industries Acquis	001	02/19/91	4,180.00	3,800.00	4,180.00	.00	.00	.00	.00
				.00					
	002	02/31/91	702.00	602.00	702.00	.00	.00	.00	.00
				.00					
MATTER TOTAL			4,882.00	4,402.00	4,882.00	.00	.00	.00	.00
				.00					
000150 00000 American Insurance Co.	002	02/31/91	1,165.25	947.50	1,165.25	.00	.00	.00	.00
				123.00					
000200 00000 Anderson Printing Co.	001	02/20/91	2,640.00	2,400.00	2,640.00	.00	.00	.00	.00
				.00					
000300 00000 Brentwood Tree Surgery	002	02/31/91	769.88	676.25	769.88	.00	.00	.00	.00
				26.00					
00001 IRS vs. Brentwood Tree	002	02/31/91	585.00	.00	585.00				
				585.00					
CLIENT TOTAL			1,354.88	676.25	1,354.88	.00	.00	.00	.00
				611.00					

FIGURE 6-13 Computerized accounts receivable reports enable firms to have instantaneous information on the status of accounts. (Courtesy of Juris, Incorporated.)

It is becoming more and more common for firms to actively pursue past due accounts. The reason for this is that once accounts are past due more than six months it is often difficult to collect on them. By keeping in constant contact with clients who have past due accounts, the probability of collecting these accounts dramatically improves. Failing to collect on past due accounts causes the firm to lose money, because it has spent time on an unprofitable file when the time could have been spent on a client whose accounts are current. The tax benefits given for uncollectible accounts at both the state and federal levels rarely adequately compensate the firms for monies lost through uncollectibles.

To improve collection, many firms send letters to clients with past due accounts in a front-line attempt to collect these monies. By staying on top of accounts and keeping in constant contact with clients, monies are less likely to become uncollectible. Figures 6-14, 6-15, and 6-16 show sample letters sent to

---

MOBLEY, PRIE, SUTTLE & HIU
Attorneys at Law
12978 Morgan Street
Rhodes, Delaware 45678
(302) 687-2390

March 28, 1996

Mr. George Bertshaon
East Ridge Tire Company
4958 Scottsdale Boulevard
East Wisconsin, Michigan 45920

RE: East Ridge Tire Company v. Birdsong

Dear Mr. Bertshaon:

Our records currently show the following statement to be outstanding with regard to the above-referenced file:

Statement No. 2367-980, December 22, 1995, $23,456.78

In the event you did not receive our original statement, I have enclosed a copy for your reference. If you have any questions or disagreement with the above, please contact Mr. Prie or me; otherwise, we will anticipate the prompt receipt of your payment.

Please disregard this notice if your payment has been mailed.

Sincerely,

MOBLEY, PRIE, SUTTLE & HIU

Daniel Garcia

Daniel Garcia, Bookkeeper

cc. Mr. Jonathan Prie
Enclosure

FIGURE 6-14   A first letter is rather gentle ...

MOBLEY, PRIE, SUTTLE & HIU
Attorneys at Law
12978 Morgan Street
Rhodes, Delaware 45678
(302) 687-2390

April 12, 1996

Mr. George Bertshaon
East Ridge Tire Company
4958 Scottsdale Boulevard
East Wisconsin, Michigan 45920

RE: East Ridge Tire Company v. Birdsong

Dear Mr. Bertshaon:

I wrote to you on March 28, 1996, informing you that Statement No. 2367-980 dated December 22, 1995, in the amount of $23,456.78 remained outstanding. To date, I have heard nothing from you.

In order to avoid penalty, it is of utmost importance that you (a) either send payment in full by return mail or (b) contact me to work out a mutually agreed upon payment schedule.

I look forward to hearing from you.

Sincerely,

MOBLEY, PRIE, SUTTLE & HIU

Daniel Garcia

Daniel Garcia, Bookkeeper

cc. Mr. Jonathan Prie
CERTIFIED MAIL - RETURN RECEIPT REQUESTED

FIGURE 6-15   ... a second is more serious ...

clients whose bills are overdue. You can see from these examples that the letters become more and more firm as the delinquency increases.

Accounts Payable

In the smaller law firm, generally one person is designated to pay bills. These bills might include rent, equipment leases, stationery, office supplies, utilities, salaries, and so forth. (See Figure 6-17.) If you are the person in charge, invest first in a good adding machine with both a digital display and a tape. Time-stamp your bills as they arrive and pay careful attention to their terms, meaning the conditions under which you may repay the debt. For example, the bill might be due upon receipt, or it might be due within 30 days. Meet all deadlines so that the firm does not create a poor credit rating. Your banker will

MOBLEY, PRIE, SUTTLE & HIU
Attorneys at Law
12978 Morgan Street
Rhodes, Delaware 45678
(302) 687-2390

May 12, 1996

Mr. George Bertshaon
East Ridge Tire Company
4958 Scottsdale Boulevard
East Wisconsin, Michigan 45920

RE: East Ridge Tire Company v. Birdsong

Dear Mr. Bertshaon:

My letters to you of March 28, 1996, and April 12, 1996, regarding your outstanding statement remain unanswered. Please send your check immediately in the amount of $23,456.78. If we do not receive it within the next ten (10) days, we feel that we have no recourse but to take legal action.

Sincerely,

MOBLEY, PRIE, SUTTLE & HIU

Daniel Garcia

Daniel Garcia, Bookkeeper

cc. Mr. Jonathan Prie

CERTIFIED MAIL - RETURN RECEIPT REQUESTED

FIGURE 6-16 ... and a third threatens legal action.

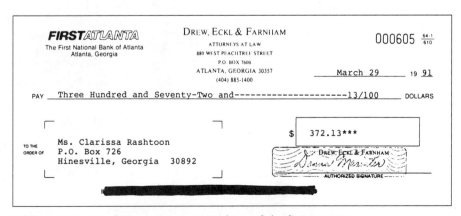

FIGURE 6-17 Law firm expenses are paid out of the firm account.

be pleased to establish a corporate checking account for the firm, and you may wish to select a system with duplicate copies of all checks so that you can have a detailed reference on hand.

You may also be asked by various attorneys to write checks for expenses that the firm is willing to pay on behalf of a client. As these bills are incurred, they must be charged to the client's file so that the client can repay the debt to you.

In larger firms, accounts payable are generally handled on the computer system. Information is entered into the computer on a screen that looks much like a check. Continuous-form checks may then be printed on laser printers. In either case, timeliness is highly important. Bills must be kept current so that the firm's credit reputation is not tarnished. Frequently. these checks for client expenses are sent to the same vendors (i.e., courts, court reporters, or investigators), and it is important to keep the accounts current so that you can maintain a positive working relationship with these services.

If a check is written on behalf of a client, that information must be fed into the database as well as entered on the check. Generally, checks written for expenses for which the client reimburses the firm will have information about the client number and name, the matter number, the amount, the date, the person being reimbursed, and an explanation of why the expense was incurred. Copies of these checks or computer printouts from inputting the information will then be forwarded to the billing department so that the expenses can be billed to clients. (See Figure 6-18.)

Payroll

In small law firms, payroll checks can be prepared by the bookkeeper or the individual chosen to perform the accounting process. Checks are usually issued

FIGURE 6-18
A legal assistant performs accounts payable functions.

either on a biweekly or semimonthly basis. Employee payroll deductions are calculated from federal, state, and, in some cases, city withholding charts by using the employees' withholding allowance certificates. It is very important when preparing any payroll that all tax deposits and all quarterly and annual reportings be made in a timely manner, as serious penalties are levied for failure to comply.

For the larger law firm, a payroll service is recommended because it will cut the time spent by the payroll processor. This is an example of outsourcing a support service, as discussed earlier. Today payroll services can be found that match exactly the firm's needs at a relatively inexpensive cost. A small firm may choose to use a teledata service or a phone-in procedure to transmit payroll data. Larger, more automated firms may choose a personal computer payroll system that transmits data to the payroll service by modem. One of the major assets of a payroll service is that the firm is notified of all forthcoming payroll deposits and reportings. Additionally, payroll services will, in most cases, prepare quarterly and annual reports, including W-2 forms, and, if prearranged, will make tax deposits, thus alleviating any worry about failure to make timely filings.

Check Requests

In order to safeguard and control the flow of firm checks, one person is assigned the responsibility of writing (but not signing) checks and balancing accounts. In the smaller firm, you, the paralegal, may be assigned this task, and in the larger firm a bookkeeper would be in charge. Check requests are used so that all necessary information can be captured. Each item listed on the check request should be completed. (See Figure 6-19.) If the payee is not a corporation (i.e., Inc., Corp.) or a professional corporation (P.C.), but rather an individual, it is necessary to include the payee's address and federal identification number or social security number. Typically, the only exceptions to this rule are for witness fees. Any check found not to be needed or returned for duplication of payment must be marked *void* and returned to the responsible person.

The Safe

Many firms have safes for important documents or checks that require safekeeping for a period of time. Evidence, stocks, bonds, and original wills and trust documents are other important papers which may be kept in a firm's safe. (See Figure 6-20.) These items should be kept in envelopes with notations on the outside indicating the client/matter number, the attorney/paralegal placing the package in the safe, the attorney/paralegal number, and a brief description of the contents. The package should then be logged. Removal of items from the safe must require the signature of the responsible paralegal or attorney and the date of removal.

FIGURE 6-19
A check request
form

```
┌─────────────────────────────────────────────────────────┐
│                    CHECK REQUEST                          │
│                                                           │
│  CIRCLE ONE:      (REGULAR)     TRUST     REAL ESTATE     │
│                                                           │
│  PLEASE DRAW CHECK TO THE ORDER OF:                       │
│     Atlanta Law Committee for the Homeless                │
│                                                           │
│  CHECK TO BE CHARGED TO:                                  │
│                                                           │
│  FIRM EXPENSE (EXPLAIN) Charitable Gift                   │
│                                                           │
│  CLIENT NAME    n/a                                       │
│                                                           │
│  PURPOSE--                                                │
│                                                           │
│  CLIENT NUMBER  n/a        MATTER NUMBER n/a              │
│                                                           │
│  DATE  4/18/91             AMOUNT $ 2,000.00              │
│                                                           │
│  ATTORNEY:  NUMBER  401    NAME Masinter                  │
│                                                           │
│  APPROVED BY  TF                                          │
│                                                           │
│                                                           │
│                                                           │
│                                                           │
│  ACCOUNTING DEPARTMENT USE ONLY:                          │
│                                                           │
│  CODE____SUB-CODE____CHECK NUMBER_____               │
│                                                           │
│  VENDOR NUMBER_____VOUCHER NUMBER_____              │
│                                                           │
│  GENERAL LEDGER:  DR._____CR._____                │
└─────────────────────────────────────────────────────────┘
```

Postage and Change

In most firms, you may obtain postage stamps and/or change from the bookkeeper. You may, in fact, find yourself in charge. Should the responsible party be out of postage stamps, personal mail may generally be posted by the firm's mail machine if the postage expense is immediately reimbursed to the firm. However, it is unwise to post your personal mail on the firm's postage machine without prior permission. Such an action could result in your immediate dismissal.

Trust Accounts

You, a bookkeeper, or another responsible person in the firm may be in charge of the firm's trust accounts. These are separate bank accounts established for

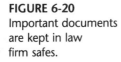

FIGURE 6-20
Important documents
are kept in law
firm safes.

deposit of funds delivered to the firm in a fiduciary capacity. For example, in some cases the firm is given money to hold in escrow until a case is finally completed or settled, or the firm receives money to hold to disburse at the request of the client; in another situation, the firm might receive funds on prior written instructions from one party and disburse them to other parties when the funds clear.

Funds received by the firm in its fiduciary capacity are deposited in the firm's trust account when the attorney receiving the funds instructs the person responsible to do so. The firm will establish a trust account file for each client using the client's regular client/matter number. Copies of the deposit, the withdrawals, and any instructions are kept in this file.

Withdrawals from the trust account are made through a check request signed by the responsible attorney. This request must clearly identify the client and indicate that the funds are to be withdrawn from the trust account. Even funds to be paid directly to the firm from the trust account must be requested through a check request. The reasons for the particularities of trust accounts are that the funds in these accounts belong to clients, not to the firm. Therefore, every safeguard must be taken to ensure that there can be no question that the funds were used only for the benefit of the client and not the firm. (See Figure 6-21.)

The policy of all firms should be that funds deposited into the trust accounts cannot be disbursed until they have cleared the issuing bank and are credited to the firm's trust account. The procedure takes a minimum of two days, but can take a substantially longer period of time.

REPORT DATE 02/29/91   PAGE 1
REPORT NUMBER TA160-000054
SORTED BY CLIENT   PRINTED BY TDD
RANGE SELECTED: 000150 00003 TO 000150 00003

Bachman, Wilson & Juris

TRUST ACCOUNT LEDGER HISTORY

CLIENT MATTER REPORTING NAME TRANSACTION DESCRIPTION	BANK CODE	TRANS DATE	CHECK NUMBER	ACCOUNT BALANCE	RECEIPTS AMOUNT	DISBURSEMENT AMOUNT	ADJUSTMENT AMOUNT
000150 00003 Fischer, Schrebenski vs.							
Received from client	TAB	02/11/91		.00			
				20,000.00	20,000.00		
Patient # 45925-87 Invoice 4601 Medical Bills for Mr. Schrebinski Methodist Hospital 2201 Church Street Nashville, TN 37210		02/12/91	010026	18,468.00		1,532.00	
Police Report #87-12884 Metropolitan Police Department P.O. Box 9999 Franklin, TN 37064-9999		02/12/91	010027	18,428.00		40.00	
Disbursed to plaintiff Harold R. Schrebenski c/o Ardman, Phillips & Clay, P.C. 600 Lewisburg Pike, Suite 600 Franklin, TN 37064		02/12/91	010028	.00		18,428.00	
MATTER TOTALS				.00	20,000.00	20,000.00	.00

FIGURE 6-21 Trust account funds must be kept in a separate escrow account and accounted for accurately.

In some states, trust accounts must be held in interest-bearing accounts; the interest obtained on these accounts is forwarded to the bar association for indigent defense or other bar activities. If this is the case in your state, contact the local or state bar association to make sure that your trust account complies with its requirements. These states often require a ledger with complete records of trust monies received and disbursed by each client. However, some states may require the banks in which the trust accounts are held to do this accounting.

Reimbursable Expenses

A number of expenses incurred by paralegals and attorneys are reimbursed by the firm. Such expenses might include automobile mileage; travel expenses, including hotel accommodations, airfare, taxis, long-distance telephone, food, and entertainment; continuing education expenses, licensing fees, bar dues, and similar expenses; or car phone charges. The list varies depending upon the law firm and its rules on reimbursement. Before you spend your money on behalf of the firm, make sure you know what will be reimbursed and what will not.

Be sure to keep all supporting data concerning reimbursable expenses. The Internal Revenue Service requires special, detailed reporting of all business meals, client entertainment, out-of-town travel, and business gift expenses taken as deductions on a firm's tax return. The aggregate amount of these deductions must be shown separately on the tax return, which calls for care in charging only the appropriate items to these accounts. The reimbursement request forms for such expenses are detailed and require adequate substantiating information.

For business meals and client entertainment deductions, records must be kept of the person or persons involved, the amount of the expense, the date and place where the expense was incurred, the business purpose or discussion, and the business relationship of the person. Receipts for such amounts must be attached to the expense reimbursement request. If the credit card receipt does not show the date and place the expense was incurred, this information should be written on the receipt. If the entertainment was expended for prospective clients, the receipt should indicate the names of the persons entertained, their occupations or businesses, and that the purpose of the entertainment was business development.

Receipts for out-of-town travel and amounts expended for approved business gifts and event tickets should indicate the amount, date, place where the expense was incurred, and business purpose. (See Figure 6-22.) For example, if the firm purchases tickets for the Super Bowl for clients, the amount of the tickets, the recipients, and the fact that the funds were expended for client development should be indicated on the proper form so that the expenses can be properly treated on the firm's tax returns. It is important to note that not all business expenses are 100 percent deductible, so you will need to make sure that your records adhere to federal tax requirements.

OBTAIN RECEIPTS AND ATTACH TO THIS REPORT

DREW, ECKL & FARNHAM

EXPENSE REPORT

NAME _Caroline Kushner_ LOCATION _San Fran., CA._ WEEK ENDING _4/15_, 19 _95_

FROM _Atlanta_
TO _San Fran._
TO _Atlanta_

NO.	EXPENSE DESCRIPTION	SUN. 4/9/95	MON. 4/10/95	TUES. 4/11/95	WED. 4/12/95	THURS. 4/13/95	FRI. 4/14/95	SAT. 4/15/95	TOTALS	
1	ROOM	145.	145.	145	145	145	145	0	870	00
2	BREAKFAST	12	10	15	8	12	10	10	77	00
3	LUNCH	15	9	11	20	14	15	0	84	00
4	DINNER	45	32	28	52	30	51	0	238	00
5	TRANSPORTATION	520	0	0	0	0	0	20	540	00
6	TAXI & LIMO.	5	8	6	4	10	8	0	4	00
7	AUTO EXPENSE	0	0	0	0	0	0	0	0	
8	TELEPHONE	18.	5.92	6.45	17.20	14.	6.	5.40	72	97
9	TIPS	18.	16.00	15.	21.	18	24	6.	118	00
10	PARKING	5.	5.	5.	5.	5.	5.	5.	35	00
11	ENTERTAINMENT	210				82.	36		328	00
12	MILEAGE									
	DAILY TOTALS INCLUDE ITEMS CHARGED TO FIRM FOR PLANE & AUTO RENTALS	993.00	230.92	231.45	272.20	330.00	300.00	46.40	2403	97

DATE	NO.	DETAILS OF ITEMS LISTED ABOVE BUT NOT CHARGED TO THE FIRM	AMOUNT	
4/9	11	Metropolitan - San Fran. Opera	210	00
/				
/				
/				
/				
/				

	ITEM DINNER ETC.	PLACE	AMOUNT	BUSINESS Purpose	Name of Company	NAMES OF PERSONS OR GROUP ENTERTAINED
4/12	Dinner	The Grill	52.00	Bus. Enter.	Masinter Co.	Mark Masinter
4/13	Theatre	Rialto	82.00	Bus. Enter.	Kartt & Co.	Jonathan & Matthew Kartt
4/14	Cocktails	Brasserie	36.00	Bus. Enter.	SMS, Ltd.	Shannon Selfridge

DETAILS OF ITEMS CHARGED TO THE FIRM

/	All items Noted Above, Except Item 11 on 4/9/95,
/	Are Charged to the Firm
/	
/	
/	
/	
/	
/	

PURPOSE OF TRIP: _Educational Conference; Speaking Engagements; Client Development_

CLIENT NAME: _Firm_
CLIENT NUMBER: _0001._
MATTER NUMBER: _10001_

TOTAL EXPENSES:	2403	97
TOTAL ITEMS CHARGED TO FIRM:	210	00
BALANCE:	2193	97
ADVANCE:	500	00
DUE ATTY. OR EMPLOYEE:	1693	97
DUE FIRM:	0	

SIGNATURE: _Caroline Kushner_
APPROVED: _Am_
DATE _4/18/95_

FIGURE 6-22 It is important to note all expenses on an expense report, even ones not reimbursed by the firm, so that expenses can be properly treated on the firm's tax returns.

Items Typically Charged Back to Clients

A number of items are typically charged to the client. These items are not attorney fees, but are expenses of litigation or other legal representation that the client has agreed to pay. In this case the client's bill would reflect the enumerated charges, and you would use the billing system discussed earlier. The following items are frequently charged to the firm's clients.

File Storage/Retrieval

Rental space is very expensive; therefore, it is of utmost importance that records (files) be closed and sent to off-site storage as soon as practical. To retrieve a box from storage, a records request form should be completed and sent to the person in charge of closed records. There are generally routine times when stored records can be delivered to you. The records company charges the firm a flat rate for routine deliveries. If you need closed records quickly, you may request priority service, and an additional charge will attach to that request. Those costs are ultimately passed back to the client.

Telephone

Telephone charges include long-distance calls made from the office, and credit card, cellular phone, and collect calls. The cost for all these calls is charged back to the client, and each firm has specific ways of recapturing necessary information. The following examples will give you an idea of a typical procedure.

Credit Card Calls   When the phone bill is received, the responsible person within the firm makes copies of the bill and sends them to the attorneys/paralegals whose credit card number appears, requesting that they be returned by a certain deadline reflecting the correct client/matter numbers for chargeback purposes.

Long-Distance Calls Made in the Office   There are scores of telephone systems. Two common ways to recapture this information are: (1) recordation of the long-distance telephone number, date, party making the call, party to whom the call was made, client/matter number, time, and charges; or (2) a computer system attached to the telephone so that the caller may enter billing information on his or her touch-tone set when making the call. This information then "dumps" into the computer and is listed on BSRs.

Cellular Calls   Those who use cellular telephones for business purposes are responsible for indicating the correct client/matter numbers on a car phone daily time diary (see Figure 6-23). Itemized bills are also available from the phone company. When the attorney/paralegal is reimbursed by the firm for legitimate, business-related charges, the charges are passed on to the client.

DREW, ECKL, & FARNHAM			CAR PHONE DAILY TIME DIARY				

DATE | 1-15-95 | ATTY. | TF |

CLIENT #	MATTER #	DATE	TIME	ATTY.	CODE	SUB CODE
1234	98765	1-14	.2	789	165	165
	t/c Fred Friendly					

CLIENT #	MATTER #	DATE	TIME	ATTY.	CODE	SUB CODE
5687	04009	1-14	.1	789	165	165
	t/c Frank Fife					

CLIENT #	MATTER #	DATE	TIME	ATTY.	CODE	SUB CODE
					165	165

CLIENT #	MATTER #	DATE	TIME	ATTY.	CODE	SUB CODE
					165	165

BATCH NAME | CP | TOTAL TIME | 3 |

FIGURE 6-23 Client/matter numbers are logged on a car phone daily time diary.

Collect Calls The only way that collect calls can be charged to the client is if the attorney, paralegal, or secretary who receives the call and accepts the charges notes immediately the city from which the call is originating, the approximate time and day received, and, if possible, the telephone number and area code from which the call was made. This information should immediately be passed on to the bookkeeper for billing purposes. It should also reflect the client/matter number to which it can be billed.

Computer Research Databases

When a paralegal or attorney accesses a computer research database, she should complete a log sheet indicating the client/matter number, date, and amount of time spent. (The researcher will be informed by the database. See Figure 6-24.) Most of these computer-generated research systems have an online system that provides a printout so that the firm can bill clients for the time logged on these systems. However, many firms also require that a log sheet be completed so that it can be compared with the computer-generated timesheet. The type of research should also be indicated. This type of research is generally passed back to the client on a time basis. For example, a paralegal does a research request on

FIGURE 6-24 Computer research is generally charged back to the client on a time basis.

LEXIS for 10 minutes; the firm is charged $60 per hour for LEXIS. The client for whom the paralegal is doing the research will be billed $10 for the time used and may sometimes be billed an additional percentage predetermined by the firm in order to recoup the costs of the terminal, paper, and so on.

Photocopying

A smaller firm may use a log-sheet system that is usually located on or near the photocopy machine. The log requires that the person making the copies record the date; their name, initials, or personal billing number; the client/matter number; number of copies made; and, optionally, a description of the information copied. The bookkeeper then takes that information and includes it in the billing system to charge back to the client. In larger firms, copy control devices, such as the Lex System's "The Count," Equitrac, or a variety of others, are attached to the photocopier. Required data such as the client file number must be input before the photocopy machine will activate. The machine will then keep track of the number of copies made, and that information ultimately appears on the client's BSR. (See Figure 6-25.)

In-House Courier Charges

If a firm has people on staff who act as couriers for dissemination of information outside the firm, courier service orders must be completed and given to those persons in a timely manner so that delivery or pickup can be made. At

FIGURE 6-25 Copying expenses can be charged to the client.

the end of each day, the orders are assigned a charge for the client/matter numbers listed, based upon the zip code and priority of the run. The client is ultimately charged for this service. The same holds true if the firm engages the services of a professional courier service.

Overtime Expenses

Many firms charge their clients for any overtime that a secretary or paralegal must work on their behalf. The person who has worked the overtime must write the appropriate client/matter number and the number of hours worked on his or her payroll time sheet. The client is generally charged the exact value of the secretary's/paralegal's time based upon his hourly earnings.

Facsimile Charges

If a client is to be charged for a facsimile (fax) message, a facsimile transmittal form must be completed, showing the client/matter number, the attorney (personal billing) number, and the name of the case. A copy of the transmittal is sent to the bookkeeper for recordation on the client's account.

Postage

Some firms, but not all, charge for postage used to send information to their clients. It is handled in a variety of ways. In small firms, a log may be kept. In others, a 1 percent charge may be added to the fee bill. In still others, cost-control devices are attached to the postage meters for recapture of the information. Additionally, special mail, such as U.S. Express Mail, Federal Express, UPS, and other delivery services, may be charged to the client. In that case, the client/matter number must be given to the vendor at the time the call is made, and it must be recorded on the vendor's form in the appropriate space. Other postage expenses that might be incurred include certified mail or return receipt fees.

Petty Cash

A nominal amount of money, as well as rapid transit tokens, is usually available for business use as petty cash. In contrast to check request forms, petty cash forms are usually provided for an immediate need when a check would not be timely or otherwise used. As with any distribution of funds, a client/matter number is needed in order to withdraw the funds or tokens from petty cash. You will generally need to see the person in charge and complete the necessary petty cash voucher.

Law Firm Economics and Zero-Based Budgeting

The preceding portion of this chapter focused on the specific accounting systems used in law firms, and on the importance of accurate, timely timekeeping

---

ON POINT   *THE CASE OF VERBAL VICTORIA*

Victoria the paralegal is alone in her office, her supervising attorney having left to attend a day-long deposition. Early in the morning, Gail Golddigger throws open the door of the office, asking to see the supervising attorney, who is well known as a prominent divorce attorney. Because the attorney is not available, Vicki takes Gail into the attorney's office. Gail then proceeds to tell Vicki about her horrible marriage and how she needs legal assistance desperately.

Vicki knows that this is exactly the kind of case the attorney wants to handle, and tells Gail that the attorney will not even speak to her unless she gives Vicki a $5,000 retainer. Vicki came up with that figure because the rent was due that day and she knew the attorney did not have the money. Vicki tells Gail that she will be charged $250 an hour for attorney time and $100 an hour for Vicki's time, which will be charged against her retainer. Gail, confident that she is well represented, leaves the office, and Vicki immediately deposits the $5,000 check into the firm's general operating account. Any problems with Vicki's actions?

for the operation of an ethical and profitable law firm. In this section, you will learn about an approach to law firm accounting and economics based on the idea of zero-based budgeting. Generally, zero-based budgeting requires a justification of all expenditures and develops a budget based on merit rather than the former year's allocations.

Zero-based budgeting has been applied over recent years to law firm accounting because of the reality that the practice of law has changed greatly. Because of the competitive business environment in which law firms exist today, law firms must exhibit great fiscal control if they are to be successful. Because it has gotten so costly to run a law firm in a competitive way, it is mandatory that everyone, from the bottom up, be aware of the economics of the practice and contribute to the firm's economic goals.

Zero-based budgeting is a very specific budgeting process designed to maximize the firm's productivity by making all relevant employees accountable to an overall structure. Each person is accountable for his or her bottom line—that is, income versus expense. With zero-based budgeting, every word producer plays a role to some degree with regard to his or her overhead and income. It is therefore imperative that all attorneys, paralegals, and other affected employees understand their own realization rates (work effort versus dollars earned). It is equally important that billing partners recognize the effective rates that their billing practices create.

In the zero-based budgeting process, word producers commit to how many billable hours they believe they will work in the forthcoming year and the quality of that work (proposed realization rate). *Realization rate* means the amount of time that is billed versus the amount of income the firm has received from that billed time. For example, an attorney may bill 3.0 hours on her timesheet for the drafting of a complaint, but the billing partner may bill only 1.5 hours to the client. Thus, the firm will only receive profits from 1.5 hours rather than 3.0 hours, which would make the attorney's realization rate on that particular task 50 percent. A good realization rate is 80 percent or more. Those are the same commitments asked of the partners. This procedure gives the firm a potential gross revenue figure that all partners have the responsibility to bill and collect in a timely fashion. After the budgeting process is completed, someone with a firm grasp on reality must review the completed proposals to identify unrealistic estimates and confront the authors of those proposals.

A typical zero-based budget form, given to paralegals to complete, may look something like Figure 6-26. You will generally be asked to list all of the attorneys for whom you work and to state that they agree with your proposed realization rate.

After all word producers have completed this form, and with the input of additional information from the partners in charge of departments, the information is fed into a computer (although a smaller firm may choose to do this work manually). The output may be on a report for each word producer, similar to Figure 6-27.

Now we discuss this form in more detail.

```
                         1994 INCOME BUDGET


   NAME:_____    ATTORNEY NO._____

        (A)   PROPOSED WORK EFFORT
              (BILLABLE HOURS)               _____

        (B)   JAN - SEPT. '94 AVG.
              HOURLY RATE                    $_____

        (C)   VALUE AT 100%
              REALIZATION
              (A X B = C)                    $_____

        (D)   EXPECTED REALIZATION
              RATE                           $_____

        (E)   EXPECTED GROSS
              BILLING
              (A X B X D = E)                $_____

   9/30/94 UNBILLED TIME/
   DOLLARS INVENTORY              _____/$_____

   =================================================================
   I work for the following Attorneys who acknowledge and agree to the
   proposed realization rate shown above:

        SIGNATURE(S) OF SUPERVISING PARTNER(S):


   _____      _____

   _____      _____


   NOTE:   PLEASE COMPLETE NO LATER THAN 11/15/94 AND RETURN TO YOUR
   DEPARTMENT CHAIRPERSON.   THANK YOU.

                         _____
```

FIGURE 6-26 Zero-based budget form

Revenue

This means the actual dollars billed and collected—not just billable hours. There is a huge difference. For example, you may work 1,600 hours at a rate of $60 per hour. If you could bill and collect at 100 percent realization, you would bring $96,000 to the firm. If, however, you worked 1,600 hours at a rate of $60, but, because of writeoffs, you only billed and collected 80 percent, then the revenue figure attributed to you would be $76,800. This is only one of many reasons why you must be efficient, concise, and on point the majority of the time.

PARALEGAL ZERO-BASED BUDGET

	12/31/97	1998
REVENUE:	_____	_____
COSTS:		
1. SALARY		
A. BASE PAY	_____	_____
B. PAYROLL TAXES	_____	_____
C. BENEFITS	_____	_____
2. RENTAL EXPENSES	_____	_____
3. GENERAL OVERHEAD	_____	_____
4. ADMINISTRATIVE OVERHEAD	_____	_____
5. SECRETARIAL SUPPORT		
A. SECRETARIAL SALARY (INCLUDING TEMPS)	_____	_____
B. SECRETARIAL RENT	_____	_____
C. PENSION PLAN	_____	_____
TOTAL EXPENSES	_____	_____
NET	_____	_____

FIGURE 6-27   Zero-based budget report

Costs

The following costs are balanced against expected revenue.

1. Rental expenses. This figure is allocated to each word producer depending upon the amount of space she physically occupies. It is typically allocated by shares, which are units to measure space allocations. For instance, a partner-sized office may be worth five shares; an associate-sized office four shares; and a paralegal office two shares.

2. General overhead. This is your share of expenses, such as electricity, equipment, water, maintenance, security, and so on.

3. Administrative overhead. This is your share of services rendered by receptionists, couriers, word and data processing, accounting—administration in general.

4. Secretarial support.
   a. Secretarial salary, word processing staff, including temporary secretaries. An attorney/paralegal sharing a secretary may use a 75 percent/25 percent allocation. Obviously, if you need more secretarial help and for that

reason are paired with another paralegal, you would share the expense 50-50. The salary of the secretary includes the benefit package. If you request temporary secretarial assistance, that cost is also added to your budget.

b. Secretarial rent. This is figured much the same as yours. The secretaries are all allocated a certain portion of overall rent.

5. Personal expenses.

a. Dues and licenses. Dues paid for by the firm to professional or civic associations are included in this category. These might include ABA or local bar membership fees, paralegal association fees, and other relevant fees.

b. Retirement. This reflects the contribution made on your behalf by the firm to your retirement plan. These include pensions, profit-sharing plans, 401k distributions, and matching fund allocations.

You can see, when you add up all the expenses, that one must make a significant contribution through revenue to come out with a profit. The general rule of thumb is that paralegals may expect to earn approximately one-third of their gross (not net) revenue figure. It has never been as important as it is now for paralegals to understand that the practice of law is a business and must be operated as one. Clients are acutely aware of the costs of legal services and no longer hesitate to shop around for the best service at the best price. Many corporate clients are broadening their in-house legal departments, thus reducing the need for outside counsel. Law firms must cut out the "fat" and become keenly aware of the competition. You as the paralegal can and will play an extremely important role in the 1990s. Many firms are hiring large numbers of paralegals and reducing the numbers of young associate attorneys. It is easy to understand—paralegals work for good but reasonable salaries compared to those of attorneys; they will never have to be considered for partnership; they are well-trained professionals who can do a wide variety of tasks, including research, writing, interviewing of clients—the list goes on endlessly for the motivated, self-directed, efficient paralegal.

Cost of Chair

Some firms feel that it is too much trouble to do a zero-based budget; others have conflicts with the percentages used to charge back various costs. Rather than use a zero-based budget, these firms may use the *cost-of-chair approach*, which attempts to identify expenses on a per-person basis. This approach is far simpler than zero-based budgeting and also gives the management of the firm a good estimate of its costs.

The sample cost-of-chair report in Figure 6-28 compares the expenses of a paralegal and a senior partner. The secretarial costs that are reflected include base salary, overtime, taxes, benefits, credit for overtime chargebacks, and temporary and overflow secretarial costs.

```
                         COST OF CHAIR

    FOR THE PERIOD 1/1/96–6/30/96
         A. B. MONAHAN, PARTNER
         SECRETARIAL COSTS              $22,777.64
         BUSINESS DEV.                     $268.65
         CLE                               $16.50
         DUES, LICENSE & FEES           $1,190.00
         PUBLICATIONS                     $760.60
         TOTAL                         $25,013.39
                         COST OF CHAIR

    FOR THE PERIOD 1/1/96–6/30/96
         CAROLINE KUSHNER, PARALEGAL
         SECRETARIAL COSTS               $5,310.64
         DUES, LICENSE & FEES              $50.00
         TOTAL                          $5,360.64
```

FIGURE 6-28   A cost-of-chair report compares the expenses of a paralegal and a senior partner.

Accounting Systems: A Summary

In this chapter you were introduced to the major billing and accounting systems used in the practice of law. Lawyers have accounting needs similar to those in other businesses; they also have particular needs emanating from the nature of legal work. As a paralegal, you might be exposed to a range of different involvements with accounting systems, from using them to actually designing and maintaining the system. Whatever the level of your involvement, doing quality work will demand that you do your accounting precisely and punctually.

Key Terms

accounting systems	contingency fee	time-based management
billable hours	cost of chair	reports
billing summary reports	daily time diary	timeslip system
computerized timeslip	firm hours	trust accounts
system	reimbursable expenses	zero-based budgeting

Problems and Activities

1. Create a bill for the following clients based upon the following work done by the following individuals:

   a. Client: Yard Manufacturing. File: Vacant Lot 123 McKenzie.

   Attorney Bush: Review and revise warranty deed, security deed, and other closing documents. 3 hours.

   Paralegal Mick: Draft warranty deed, security deed, and other closing documents. 5 hours.

   Bush bills at $100 per hour, and Mick bills at $50.

   b. Client: Joe and Irene Turner. File: Turner v. Blowtorch.

   Attorney Hothead: Review and revise answers to defendant's 10th interrogatories and request for production of documents; take deposition of the president of Blowtorch.

   Paralegal Mick: Draft answers to defendant's 10th interrogatories and request for production of documents; summarize deposition of Mr. Turner.

   Hothead spent 15 hours and bills at the rate of $150.

   Mick spent 8 hours and bills at the rate of $75.

   c. Client: Tom Johnson. File: Armed Robbery.

   Attorney DoRight: Attend plea and arraignment hearing.

   Paralegal Mick: Interview police officer.

   DoRight spent 2.5 hours and bills at $110 per hour.

   Mick spent 3.0 hours and bills at $55 per hour.

   d. Client: Mr. and Mrs. Overlimit. File: Chapter 7 bankruptcy.

   Attorney Hallaran: Prepare debtors' Petition and List of Creditors.

   Paralegal Frances: Attend § 341 hearing with debtors.

   Hallaran spent 0.5 hours at $250/hour.

   Frances spent 3.0 hours at $95/hour.

2. Prepare a time sheet based upon the preceding information for paralegal Frances for the day, December 8, 1997. Frances also spent one hour preparing a memo on the Overlimit bankruptcy hearing and did three hours of research on various bankruptcy questions.

CHAPTER 7

THE MANAGEMENT OF TIME

OBJECTIVES

By the completion of this chapter, you should:

- understand the importance of time and its special importance in a law firm;

- understand and apply the principles behind personal time management;

- understand and apply the principles behind professional time management;

- understand specific time-management methods used in law firms, such as suspense, diary, and docket systems; and

- understand how time management interrelates with other aspects of law office administration.

Time Management: An Introduction

The effective management of time is one of the most critical goals of any individual or organization. Time is perhaps our most precious commodity—everyone always seems to want more of it—as well as our most limited resource—there never seems to be enough of it. The effective organization, and the effective individual within that organization, is the one that can maximize productivity by organizing and managing its time in the best possible manner. (See Figure 7-1.)

Although time management is important to all organizations, it is especially significant in a law firm. The major commodity a lawyer or a paralegal has to offer is his or her time, and from the standpoint not only of effective

FIGURE 7-1 It is important to utilize time effectively in the law office.

lawyering but also of law office management, effective time management is of the greatest significance and importance. Because of the special importance of time management in a law office environment, we shall consider both personal time management and professional time management.

Personal Time Management

There are numerous books and articles available that present methods of effectively managing your time. A number of general principles emerge from the literature on effective time management:

1. Effectively categorizing tasks to be accomplished; decide upon (a) importance, (b) urgency, (c) importance versus urgency, (d) busy work, and (e) wasted time.

2. Breaking down tasks into manageable units; use "To Do" lists to help prioritize tasks so that you can determine what must be done now and what can wait until another time. In doing so, the tasks as a whole will be far more manageable.

3. Planning to avoid procrastination; if you plan your time carefully, you will avoid the obvious traps that frequently lead to procrastination ("I can't get organized"; "I'm constantly interrupted"; "I'll wait until I have more time").

4. Setting goals for yourself; daily, weekly, monthly, annual, five year, ten-year goals—articulate what you want to accomplish in each time frame.

In addition to these general considerations, several important considerations for personal time management in the law office merit further discussion.

Categorizing Time Effectively

Categorizing time effectively will help you reach your personal and professional goals for the day, week, month, year, and, ultimately, your lifetime. Law offices can be, and often are, hubbubs of activity, with many tasks and activities going on simultaneously. If you do not control and organize your time, time will control and overtake you.

As a paralegal, you will learn timekeeping methods used in law firms so that clients can be appropriately charged. You will soon find that your workday is comprised of dozens of different activities, all of which must be categorized if you are to handle them efficiently and effectively. In only one work hour, you may find yourself:

- placing telephone calls;

- answering telephone calls;

- giving instructions to your secretary;

- typing information into your computer;

- discussing a case with your supervising attorney;

- making photocopies that are urgently needed;

- meeting with a vendor;

- reviewing a client's account;

- preparing to leave for the courthouse.

The list is endless, and you can easily see that, without good time management, you will be unable to accomplish your goals for the day. Learn early in your career how to plan and effectively run a meeting and how to bring it to a timely conclusion; learn how to effectively use the telephone and avoid playing "telephone tag"; learn how to efficiently communicate on all levels; and, most important of all, learn the value of your time.

For example, from the preceding list of tasks that you may have to accomplish in an hour, you should start by doing the one job that must be completed in the allotted time. Instead of focusing on the task that you wanted to do during that time, focus on the most urgent job. From the list, it seems that making copies is the task that must be completed within the hour; therefore, making copies should be the task you attack first. Follow this procedure for all of the jobs in the list, and soon those tasks that are priorities will have been accomplished. The other lower-priority tasks can be completed at another time, such as returning nonurgent telephone calls.

As mentioned earlier, time can best be divided into four categories: (a) wasted, (b) busy work, (c) important, and (d) urgent. Be sure you know the difference between these categories, and as you get work assignments, determine the time category appropriate for the work. Sometimes activities fall into the gray area between time categories. For example, you may think of time spent in the break room talking with a co-worker about your busy schedule as wasted time. However, this time could be construed as important if the person is someone you need to know better in order to work together more pleasantly and efficiently. Time spent cleaning out your desk and reorganizing your files could be busy work, or it could be important because you really needed to get organized. A research memo that is due next week might be important, but, because of the time frame, it is not particularly urgent. Last, *urgent* could mean anything that you feel compelled to handle right away, but it is not always considered important. The bottom line of this exercise is that only you can make these decisions, but, if you use good judgment and common sense, you will be able to categorize the work pending into these categories so that you can set goals for your day, week, and year. (See Figure 7-2.)

The following hypothetical situation should help you categorize your tasks.

Halley is a paralegal at a large New York law firm. Her "To-Do" list for Tuesday looks like this:

Draft interrogatories for Jones v. Daly. Discovery ends in three months.

Summarize deposition in Acme v. Hayes. Trial specially set next May.

Interview and subpoena witness for trial Thursday.

Clean up litigation section's form files.

Halley starts with the project that absolutely must be done today—interviewing the witness. This is an urgent matter because it can under no circumstances be delayed. Her next task will be drafting the interrogatories for the discovery period in the case that ends in three months. (The laws in her state

FIGURE 7-2 A "To Do" list organizes and prioritizes tasks to be accomplished.

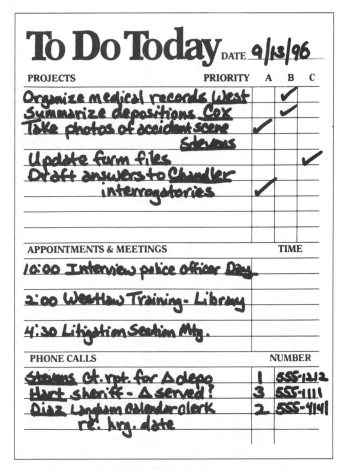

give respondents 30 days in which to answer interrogatories.) Clearly the form file organization is less important than summarizing the deposition, for the deposition summary may be used in subsequent depositions in the case. By assigning each task a priority number, Halley is able to complete all of the required tasks, thus avoiding undue stress and reaping the rewards of effective time management.

Setting and Achieving Goals

Goal setting is extremely important if you want to accomplish the tasks you set out to do. Establishing goals also works hand-in-hand with time management, for the purpose of the effective management of time is the achievement of the goals you have established.

NOT-TO-DO LIST

1. All low-priority items, unless the high-priority items have been completed.

2. Any task whose completion is of little or no consequence. (Ask: "What is the worst that can happen if this isn't done?" If the answer isn't too bad, don't do it.)

3. Anything I can give to someone else to do. (There are three ways to get something done: do it myself, hire someone else to do it, or forbid my kids to do it.)

4. Anything just to please others because I fear their condemnation or want to put them in my debt.

5. Thoughtless or inappropriate requests for my time and effort.

6. Anything others should be doing for themselves.

Goal setting is obviously important for the effective accomplishment of your legal work, but it really starts with your general attitude and approach to life. The people who are most successful in life are thoughtful about their life plans and what they want to accomplish, personally and professionally, for both the short and long term. One helpful way to get started is to make a list of your goals on separate pieces of paper with headings such as MY GOALS—TODAY; MY GOALS—THIS WEEK; MY GOALS—THIS MONTH. (All of these are basically "To Do" lists that are more immediate.) Next, consider recording your goals (i.e., things you want to accomplish, earn, own, etc.) over a longer period of time—MY GOALS THIS YEAR; MY FIVE-YEAR GOALS; MY TEN-YEAR GOALS; MY LIFETIME GOALS. You will find that after you have recorded your goals, you can try to determine the best ways to reach them. For instance, you may want to own a home in 10 years that you believe will cost $150,000. Now is the time to try to analyze your income, currently as well as projected for the next 10 years, versus your savings and ability to borrow the balance (and pay off the mortgage without too much stress).

It may be easier for us to focus on a goal of smaller proportion and a shorter time frame. Let us pretend that in one year I want to purchase a new car costing $15,000. I currently earn $25,000 annually, and, after all of the monthly bills are paid, I am able to put $100 in the bank per month. I currently have $2,500 in savings, own a used car that is worth approximately $3,000, and trust that value will not drop markedly during the next year since the car has already depreciated sharply.

ANALYSIS

Cost of New Car	$15,000	
Current Savings	$ 2,500	
Anticipated Savings at the End of One Year	$ 1,200	
Cash Value of Used Car	$ 3,000	
TOTAL $ TOWARD NEW CAR	$ 6,700	
$ Needed for "Cash" Purchase of New Car		$ 8,300

By setting my goal and looking at it realistically, I can now decide if (1) I should plan to increase my savings, continue to save for another year, and plan to purchase a similarly priced car for cash or (2) I can afford a car payment stretched over a reasonable period of time to pay the difference, plus interest, for the car of my dreams.

Although this was a simple example, the principles behind effective goal setting also apply to more complex situations that are important to you and that you will encounter as a paralegal. An example in the context of a paralegal position would be when you are given a big project on a particular case. Assume that you are the paralegal assigned to a huge patent and trademark infringement suit. Fifty depositions have been taken, and you are solely responsible for summarizing them. The trial is not set for five months, and the summaries will not be needed until then. However, you must continue to keep up with your workload. If you have five months in which to summarize the depositions, review them, and put them in final form, ten depositions must be completed per month, or a little more than two depositions per week. By breaking the task into its fundamental time elements, you can ensure that the task is completed in a timely and efficient manner.

Let us consider an example for the criminal law context which has multiple tasks. The same thinking—breaking down a large task into component parts and prioritizing them—applies here. Imagine that you are working on an aggravated assault case which is heading for a jury trial. Your work involves interviewing witnesses, writing motions and writing proposed jury instructions, along with receiving and accounting for the $250 a month that is being paid until the fee is completely paid. Each of these activities exists within time; for example, motions must be filed at a certain time (say, 10 days after arraignment), unless there are special circumstances. That gives you your time deadline. You must then work backward to give yourself time to research, write, receive feeedback from the attorney, rewrite, and submit. Motions, with supporting briefs, will take a significant amount of time, you realize. To interview a witness, you must think of the appropriate approach to and forum for the interview, prepare the necessary questions, conduct the interview, write your notes, and begin thinking about questions to ask during examination of the witness in court. Jury instructions, according to court rules, must be filed at the beginning of trial; because you have jury instructions on disk that can simply be checked and printed out, that can be attended to as trial nears.

As you can see, work in the legal field is extraordinarily time-sensitive, and those in the legal field must become excellent at organizing time and prioritizing tasks in order to provide effective representation.

Too often we find ourselves setting unrealistic goals, both professionally and personally, and then wondering why we never reach them. By setting effective goals for yourself personally, you will have established an approach that will also help you be successful at work. In your work you will become involved in many different tasks. Goal setting will help you prioritize your activities and avoid becoming overwhelmed by what you need to do. The same analysis described earlier can be done on a daily, weekly, or monthly "To Do" list at your office. Categorize the projects by importance, using the principles discussed in this section. If you take on more than you can do, you will disappoint not only yourself, but also your employer. Sometimes the problem is that you really are given too much to do; in this situation, you should contact your supervisor and explain the situation—you have been assigned x, y, and z, all of which must be completed today, and each requires at least six hours to complete. Either your supervisor will make the priority decision for you and reassign the other tasks to another paralegal, or he will determine which tasks are really urgent. It is im-portant to handle this type of situation immediately. Do not whine and complain for three hours and then ask for relief. As soon as you determine that you cannot complete your assigned tasks, get help. Waiting could be a fundamental mistake, for some important task may not get completed.

A Day in the Life

It is important to understand personal time management before one can understand time management from the law firm perspective. The old saying "time is money" could not be more true than when applied to a work producer in a law firm. You are selling your time as well as your expertise, but billing is based on the use and value of your time. Learn to make the most of every min-ute—time cannot be recovered if it is lost.

There are many ways to save time each day and to apply that time to mean-ingful tasks, which, translated, means money. Now we will walk through an av-erage day at the office and think of the many ways we can save a few minutes here and there.

A typical work day lasts from 9 A.M. to 5:30 P.M.

1. Arrive at the office at 8:50 A.M. Announce your arrival to the receptionist; pick up that irresistible cup of coffee on the way past the break room.

2. Enter your personal office or work space and check your messages; answer them in order of importance immediately. Do not put off the one that you think will be too involved, too painful, or just too boring. Deal with each one. If you have an electronic mail system, which enables you to use your computer to receive and send messages within your office, you can easily respond to messages and requests without playing "telephone tag." (See Figure 7-3.)

3. Next, as soon as your mail is delivered, quickly evaluate it, opening the "real" mail first. If a reply is required, prepare your reply immediately if you have all of the information to do so. If not, put the letter in a file folder marked "RESPONSE NECESSARY—TODAY." If the mail requires no action, either mark it for file and place it in a folder marked "FILE-TODAY," or throw it away. If the mail should have been sent to another person in the

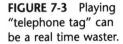

FIGURE 7-3 Playing "telephone tag" can be a real time waster.

firm or if you want to share the information and do not need to retain a copy, mark it immediately for intraoffice mail and put it in your out box. You should time stamp your mail and keep a log of mail received and redistributed. Quickly make decisions about catalogs, notices, seminar invitations, and "junk mail" in general. If you really do not need it, throw it away. File space is precious and expensive.

If you receive an informal request for information through intraoffice mail, write the answer on the bottom of the request and return it. There is no need to be formal at all times. Most firms encourage quick, handwritten responses to intraoffice requests, unless, of course, you are being asked for a report or lengthy research memo for a client's file.

It has been said that an efficient businessperson tries never to handle the same piece of paper twice—meaning, do not read it, put it aside on the desk, lose it in a stack, look through the stacks on a number of occasions, and eventually get to that piece of mail. It is a great feeling to stay in control.

4. Now you've successfully answered your mail and are just about to begin a project. Your friend whose office is just down the hall stops by to chat with you about the party she attended the night before. You need not be unfriendly, but, remember, time is money, and it is up to you to control the amount of time/money you want to spend.

Put it in perspective. If you earn $25,000 annually and work 40 hours per week, you are paid $12.02 for every hour and $.20 for every minute. Therefore, if you spend 20 minutes chatting with your friend about the party, you have spent the equivalent of $4. By figuring out the cost of your time, you can determine the actual cost of a five-minute, nonbillable telephone call or a 10-minute interruption. It will be up to you to determine if it is worthwhile.

There are many ways to reduce interruptions and save time. Close your door when you really want to concentrate. If you deal with salespeople, ask them to call your secretary for an appointment—be sure they know that they should never drop in unexpectedly. When meeting with a client or visitor, pay absolute attention to that person and remain focused on the issues. When the meeting is over, rise and extend your hand, letting the individual know that you have concluded. Try to find time every day, no matter how brief, to be quiet and regroup—ask the receptionist to hold your calls during that period. If you are working on a project with an impending deadline and cannot seem to concentrate in your office due to distractions, take your work to the law library. It is always quiet there, and often a change of scene helps one to concentrate. (See Figure 7-4.)

It is time to get back to our schedule. You have answered the telephone messages that were waiting for you when you arrived at work; the mail has been answered, filed, or suspensed. You have sorted through your reading material and have determined what must be read now and what can be filed for

FIGURE 7-4 It is hard—but necessary—to make time to concentrate without distractions.

another time—perhaps on an airplane, in a doctor's waiting room, or on a rainy Saturday. It is 11:05 A.M., and your supervising attorney phones and asks you to report to her office. Always take a notepad and pen with you. When you arrive, she wants to discuss a project. Ask for specific instructions; if you are unclear about any of the instructions or if you need more detailed information, ask her now for that information. Don't plan to return later for clarification. That is a waste of the attorney's time and yours.

By the time you return to your office with the project, you have just enough time to answer a couple of quick telephone calls or return messages, and then you are off to lunch. Leave your desk—everyone needs a break, a change of scene, and a breath of fresh air. By doing so, you will find that you will return refreshed and ready to do your best during the afternoon hours.

It is now 1:00 P.M., and you have the best part of the day ahead. Study your "To Do" list, and plan your strategy. Remember the categories of time management discussed previously, and apply those guidelines. Your afternoon will be at least as busy as your morning. Often emergencies arise that must be handled before the day is concluded. There are always last-minute rushes preparing documents for filing deadlines at the courthouse, and there are always situations that fall into every busy person's day that are totally unexpected but nonetheless expensive in terms of your time budget. When your workday has ended, you should feel fulfilled and pleased that you reached your goals for the day.

Professional Time Management

The law firm's income is primarily generated by charging clients for time spent on their behalf by the firm's professionals. For that reason, prompt and accurate completion of daily time records is imperative. Without accurate and complete information, the firm is unable to prepare timely and accurate invoices for its clients. (See Figure 7-5.)

Preparation of Timekeeping Records

As discussed earlier, it is essential that your professional time be recorded efficiently and accurately. Your time should be recorded throughout the day and summarized at the end of each day. This process of tracking your time carefully is a professional habit that you must develop quickly. You will learn how your office handles time units; that is, whether you are to account for your time in hours, quarter-hours, tenths of an hour, or minutes. All systems are used; the key is that a law office be consistent among all people working on cases.

```
REPORT DATE    03/02/91                                                                                      PAGE    1
REPORT NUMBER  JP065-000044
SORTED BY ORIGINATING TIMEKEEPER - DETAIL
RANGE SELECTED: CDE to CDE

                          Bachman, Wilson & Juris
                  ORIGINATING TIMEKEEPER ACTIVITY REPORT
                           Carolyn D. Elkins
                                                                                                       PRINTED BY   TDD
```

CLIENT MATTER NAME	BILL TMKP	UNBILLED EXP/FEES	CURRENT FEES BILLED	CURRENT WR-OFF	CURRENT MK-UP/DN	YTD FEES BILLED	YTD WR-OFF	YTD MK-UP/DN	YTD FEES RECEIVED	BALANCE DUE
000100 00003 Abbey Industries EEOC Matter	ABC	561.37 / 3,990.00	.00	.00	.00	.00	.00	.00	1,400.00	.00
00004 Abbey Industries 1988 IRS	ABC	17.40 / 960.00	2,688.75	.00	.00	4,688.75	.00	550.00-	2,099.50	2,589.25
00005 Abbey Industries Logo (50%)	EFG	62.70 / .00	.00	.00	.00	.00	.00	.00	1,375.00	.00
CLIENT TOTAL		1,444.96 / 11,107.50	7,395.00	.00	340.00	27,995.00	.00	1,810.00	65,474.50	4,295.50
000400 00000 Carroll, Linda Sue	EFG	.00 / 62.50	4,000.00	.00	360.00-	4,000.00	.00	360.00	1,100.00	4,921.25
00001 Carroll, Linda Sue Estate	EFG	3.75 / 2,505.00	4,375.00	.00	476.25-	7,052.50	.00	476.25-	7,052.50	.00
00002 Carroll, Linda Sue Admin.	EFG	448.87 / 4,103.75	4,800.00	.00	.00	4,800.00	.00	122.50-	7,300.00	.00
00003 Carroll, Linda Sue 1990 Taxes	EFG	541.52 / 4,922.50	7,400.00	2,500.00	260.75-	29,400.00	2,500.00	2,345.75-	25,000.00	49,895.00
00004 Carroll, Linda Sue 1991 Taxes	EFG	151.65 / 4,830.00	5,000.00	.00	300.00-	6,100.00	.00	337.50-	6,100.00	.00
00005 Carroll, Howard E. Estate	EFG	245.15 / .00	.00	.00	.00	.00	.00	.00	1,340.00	.00
CLIENT TOTAL		1,390.94 / 16,423.75	25,575.00	2,500.00	1,519.50-	51,352.50	2,500.00	3,642.00-	47,892.50	54,816.25
TIMEKEEPER TOTAL		2,835.90 / 27,531.25	32,970.00	2,500.00	1,179.50-	79,347.50	2,500.00	1,832.00-	113,367.00	59,111.75

FIGURE 7-5 Without accurate time records, law firms would not be able to prepare acceptable invoices. (Courtesy of Juris, Incorporated.)

The following chart, showing the conversion of time into decimals, represents the most widely used way to record time. Note how precise you must be with tracking and recording your time.

6 minutes = 0.1 hour	36 minutes = 0.6 hour
12 minutes = 0.2 hour	42 minutes = 0.7 hour
15 minutes = 0.25 hour	45 minutes = 0.75 hour
18 minutes = 0.3 hour	48 minutes = 0.8 hour
24 minutes = 0.4 hour	54 minutes = 0.9 hour
30 minutes = 0.5 hour	60 minutes = 1.0 hour

Whether you use a simple time planner bought from an office supply store, a more complex time planner made for legal use, or a computerized system with sophisticated capabilities, keeping time accurately and efficiently is a key skill required in the law office. If you become an ethical, accurate, efficient, and productive timekeeper, you will surely add to your value in the law office.

One practice to avoid is reducing or cutting your own time because you believe you spent too much time on a project. This decision should be made only by the billing attorney. Sometimes, a billing attorney's decisions can be frustrating for a paralegal; for example, a paralegal may bill for 50 hours, and the attorney may cut it in half, thus causing the paralegal to lose the credit on production. If you are faced with this kind of situation, discuss it professionally with the appropriate person, perhaps the paralegal coordinator or the attorney. Your purpose in such a discussion should be to understand why the reduction was made and to remediate the situation by establishing more realistic expectations or increasing skills.

In addition to the 1,600–1,800-hour annual requirements, paralegals are expected to have a small number of nonbillable hours. This is different from the expectations for lawyers, who are expected to have a greater number of both billable and nonbillable hours.

In a well-organized law firm, the general billing procedure, regardless of the specific application used, is based on the preparation of daily timesheet records, which document attorney and paralegal activities during the workday. Whatever the system, the timekeeper must get into the habit of recording work as it is done by keeping a daily time diary on the desk where it will be easy to record each and every item as it is done. It is almost impossible to recreate your day at the end of it. Because time is money, you must be accurate. If you keep a rough log during the day, and then make a final one at the end of the day, you will help yourself maintain the level of accuracy expected of you. (See Figure 7-6.)

Timesheets and timekeeping systems vary, but you must follow your firm's procedure to the letter. As you might imagine, some people are excellent timekeepers, whereas others seem never to learn the techniques that are so important in this area. A good timekeeper is one who keeps an eye on the clock all day, every day; who records on a daily time diary every single thing he does when it is done; who learns telephone do's and don'ts as they relate to timekeeping; who learns how to deal with interruptions and tactful ways to shorten

DREW, ECKL, & FARNHAM				CAR PHONE DAILY TIME DIARY		

DATE 7/2/90   ATTY. 999

CLIENT #	MATTER #	DATE	TIME	ATTY.	CODE	SUB CODE
0001	10004	7/2	.4	999	165	165

Discussion with parties concerning most convenient time to schedule depositions.

CLIENT #	MATTER #	DATE	TIME	ATTY.	CODE	SUB CODE
0284	11006	7/2	.2	999	165	165

Discussion concerning whether feasible to set up conference calls between client and opposing counsel for 7/3.

CLIENT #	MATTER #	DATE	TIME	ATTY.	CODE	SUB CODE
					165	165

CLIENT #	MATTER #	DATE	TIME	ATTY.	CODE	SUB CODE
					165	165

BATCH NAME   CP   TOTAL TIME   .6

FIGURE 7-6 A car phone diary demonstrates how time-efficient and time-conscious legal professionals must be.

conversations; who learns how to successfully bring meetings to a close; who practices timesaving dictation and reading techniques; who learns how to delegate and, at the same time, get good results; who learns how to set and meet goals; and, ultimately, who knows the value of time. A poor timekeeper is one who, at the end of the day, or worse, at the end of the week, tries to "remember" how he spent time; who loves to chat on the telephone—unable to quickly say goodbye; who never closes a door or asks that calls be held, thus lessening the numbers of interruptions; who calls a meeting but cannot end it in a timely way; who reads everything that lands on the desk, whether or not it applies to his position or interests; who never learns the proper use of dictation equipment or, even worse, who dictates directly to a secretary; who wants to do everything himself in the belief that it is embarrassing to ask others for help or that he can do it better than anyone else; who is not interested in learning to set goals; and, finally, who has no idea how much time is worth. Other time wasters might be spending time tracking down an attorney, when an appointment might save valuable time; spending excessive time on clerical chores; or repeating tasks because they were not done properly the first time.

One approach to increasing the productivity of paralegals, who may not be accustomed to the world of billable hours, is to have the paralegal manager or paralegal review committee take responsibility for increasing paralegal productivity.

This approach frees the attorney to focus on practicing law and increases the professionalism and satisfaction of the paralegals by teaching paralegals how to effectively delegate clerical tasks while concentrating on billable hours. It also reflects a growing belief in many law firms that professional managers, rather than lawyers, might be more effective at handling some of the business aspects of a law firm.

As we said earlier, time is money, and, as a paralegal, you will be selling your time to clients. Those clients must be satisfied not only with your work product, but also with the cost of your services. If you take an extraordinary amount of time to complete a project—no matter how good the results may be—the client will be unwilling to pay the extraordinary cost; the client may, if this abuse continues, become so dissatisfied that he selects another law firm.

Suspense and Diary Systems

The Suspense and Tickler System

There are a number of good ways to have a personal suspense (often called a tickler) system. A *suspense,* or *tickler, system* is a reminder system whose essential purpose is docket control. It is a means to keep track of follow-up dates for various activities or procedures. For example, if you served opposing counsel with interrogatories today, and her responses are due 30 days later, you should make a note 30 days from today that the responses are due so that you can follow up.

As its name suggests, a tickler system "tickles" your memory so that you can keep track of your work effectively. One of the best methods is to purchase a legal-size, expandable envelope with individual pockets marked 1–31, or an index card holder with dividers marked 1–31 (see Figure 7-7). That gives you a pocket or divider for each day of the month. As you work through the day, there will be a number of items that will require follow-up. Mark the follow-up date of your choice in the top right-hand corner of the file or file copy, and insert it in the correct pocket. Every morning, first thing, be sure to look in the pocket corresponding with the date to see what must be done. Obviously, in pocket #1 you may have items suspensed for January 1, March 1, and December 1, but at a glance you will know what must be done on any given day. A suspense system is only as good as you make it. If you forget to check daily, your system will fail.

This is a simple system, but it is also a powerful one. By simply inserting information or files into the correct dates in an expandable folder and retrieving that information regularly, you will never again forget deadlines. (See Figure 7-8.) You may also use this system for personal deadlines, such as birthdays, social engagements, civic and charitable obligations, and personal appointments.

FIGURE 7-7
Expandable
envelopes can
house your tickler
system.

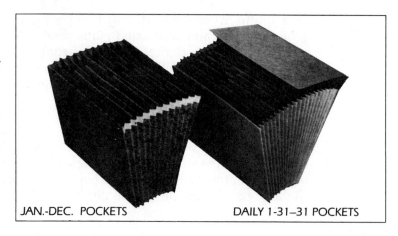

JAN.-DEC. POCKETS   DAILY 1-31–31 POCKETS

The Diary System and Docket Control

A diary system is used to keep track of court dates and other important dates relative to a case. Its form can range from a date board to a computerized calendar. Life in a law firm is extremely busy and often hectic. Without the use of excellent control systems, important events could easily be forgotten. This, of course, could lead to malpractice, the prevention of which is a major goal of the timekeeping systems used by a firm. In fact, very specific questions regarding docket control are asked on malpractice insurance applications. The answers might make a difference in the firm's ability to obtain malpractice insurance, and they will certainly affect the premium paid.

TICKLER RECORD

DREW, ECKL & FARNHAM

Client/
Case ___Rodriguez v. Janeski_____ File No. _2356.78945___

Event ___Deposition of Witness Jones_____

Date of Event ____April 22, 1991_____

Reminder Date(s) _April 6, 1991___   _April 13, 1991___   _April 21, 1991_

Attorney Responsible _Barrow_____

Notes: ___Arrange for court reporter_____

☐ **Done**

(DEF 4/83)

FIGURE 7-8   A tickler system reminds you when tasks must be accomplished.

Naturally, it is critical that the legal team working on a case be accurately apprised of the deadlines relative to that case. This is generally done in two ways: through paralegal research or backup services.

Paralegal Research A paralegal is assigned the task of reading all local legal publications (newspapers and journals) containing calendar information for various courts. The paralegal reviews court calendars on a daily basis for appearances by the firm's lawyers and notifies the attorneys as they appear. The attorneys are provided with a copy of the calendar one or two days before it is noticed. Docket control is prepared for the attorney by providing her with tickler records (notices) on the three Mondays preceding the court date.

Some firms may use a computerized tickler system, also known as a *computerized calendar,* to achieve docket control. In a computerized system, the responsible person enters all necessary information, including that found on the tickler record and additional information, into the computer. The computer then sorts the information, arranging it in date order. The responsible person calls up the information each day and notifies the attorneys and paralegals of their obligations. Additionally, this system allows the person in charge of docket control to send all docket information for that day to the timekeeper.

Diarymaster II, a product of Litigation Technologies, Inc., is an example of docket control software that can also be integrated with case information management. Products such as Diarymaster II give law firms the tools to manage tremendous amounts of information and helps them attract clients because work is performed promptly and efficiently. Diarymaster II provides the following information fields:

- File number
- Matter name
- Attorney 1 assigned
- Attorney 2 assigned
- Court
- Docket number
- Attorney responsible for case
- Team or area of practice
- Date of event
- Time
- Event code
- Description
- Adjourned (yes or no)
- New date (if adjourned)

- Appearance necessary (yes or no)
- Calendar number
- Client name
- Location of event
- Result
- Previous date (if previously adjourned)
- Continuous reminder (yes or no)

Additionally, reports based on time are easily provided; they can be produced on a daily, weekly, monthly, or any other time period basis. The following are examples of reports that can be generated through computerized docket control:

- Attorney activity
- Activity in a particular court
- Activity in a particular location (i.e., county)
- Adjournments
- Appearance necessary list
- Appointments
- Attorney assignments
- Chronology of activity in a case
- Closing dates
- Correspondence reminders
- Court file date reminders
- Critical reminders
- Daily activity reminders
- Depositions
- Discovery deadlines
- File review reminders
- Interrogatories
- Prepare list of files to be pulled
- Meetings
- Motions
- Persons to notify (i.e., court reporters, clients)

- Personal reminders
- Research deadlines
- Statute of limitations
- Telephone call reminders
- Trial lists

On the other end of the spectrum from computerized systems is the date board, which can be used to remind timekeepers of upcoming events. One person is generally assigned to accept the information, post it, send written reminders to the people affected, and then erase the information when the event has passed. For various reasons, this system is not one of the better ways to handle docket control, and it is not recommended.

Backup Services Law firms often use backup services, frequently provided by court reporting firms (see Figure 7-9). These computerized services send the attorney a card showing the following information:

1. The name, address, and telephone number of the service
2. The date the card is printed and mailed
3. The date the information was published in the newspaper
4. The style of the case

```
L. LEE LAWSON & ASSOCIATES, INC. (Court Reporters)
Estab. 1958        PHONE: 296-6063
Post Office Drawer 4298, ATLANTA GA 30302-4298
 ======= Your Complete Backup Service =======
PRINTED: 08/14/90    PLACE #  15
PUB'D DATE:  8/13/90
233227 NORTON & RITTER INC
         -VS-
W B MCCLANAHAN & ASSOC INC WALLACE C MCCLANAHAN J
R & KINGSBERRY HOMES INC
PLFF MTN TO ADD ADDITIONAL DFT
MTION & BRIEF IN SUPPORT OF MTN TO COMPEL

                                               TO Jim Poe

FULTON  STATE JUDGE CARNES          ROOM 218   DREW ECKL & FARNHAM  LAW OFFC
Julia Couch          CLNDR CLERK INFO? 730-4358 ATTN: ALLISON COUVILLION
COURT DATE: TUESDAY,  SEPTEMBER 4, 1990, 9:30 AM  P O BOX 7600
MOTIONS CALENDAR                                 ATLANTA GA 30357
TUESDAY,  SEPTEMBER 4, 1990, 9:30 AM, ROOM 218
***SEE REVERSE SIDE FOR REST OF INSTRUCTION    5
No atty's lines
Thanks for being a SUBSCRIBER
SOURCE: DREW ECKL & FARNHAM          8851400   S
```

FIGURE 7-9 A backup service reminds attorneys of court dates and deadlines.

5. The description of the action

6. The specific name of the court

7. The name of the judge

8. The court date and time

9. The name(s) of the attorneys who are to appear

10. Specific instructions (i.e., It will be necessary to be in court for oral argument on all motions unless specifically excused. Movant will notify respondent with a notice of motion, not less than five (5) days prior to the hearing date of the motions. Please direct all inquires to this calendar to Julia Smith (333-0000), Calendar Clerk for Judge Charles P. Jones.)

11. Filing deadlines

12. Deposition dates

13. Discovery deadlines

14. Statute of limitations.

Once you receive the instructions listed on these computerized cards, which have been copied from either the legal publication (newspaper), source documents, or the court's records, you should pay careful attention to any special instructions that the court may publish in these notices. For example, many times court calendars will list 30 cases for a particular calendar, but only require that the parties and attorneys for the first 10 cases appear. Another example is when the court requires all settlements to be finalized by a specific date or the case will be tried. Failure to follow these instructions could result in sanctions against the parties and/or their attorneys. Some services use the telephone to advise the firm of calendar dates, to determine readiness, and to ask for adjournment, but most people prefer a hard copy of this important information.

Even though law firms have the types of systems discussed here, docket control is ultimately the obligation of the attorney and the paralegal. If the person in the firm who is responsible for reading the legal publication overlooks a

---

ON POINT

DEBBIE DOES TIME

Debbie is finishing her work on a file when she realizes that there is an extra $200 left from the retainer. Because the money seems ripe for taking and she has not met her monthly billing requirement, she goes back to her time sheets and inflates her totals for that file. As she opens her mail for that day, she finds a motion for entry of default judgment in the Blankenship case. She checks her tickler system, which indicates she has another five days to file the answer. Confused, she pulls the file and is suddenly horrified, because she realizes that the case had been filed in federal, not state, court, and that the answer was due in 20 days, instead of the 30 days that state court would have given. Has Debbie kept her time effectively?

hearing and does not notify the appropriate attorney and/or paralegal, or if the card from the backup service never reaches your office, it remains the inescapable obligation and duty of the attorney and the paralegal.

Time Management: A Summary

Because of the complex and important nature of the paralegal's work, it is essential that the paralegal learn to manage time in the most effective way possible. Setting priorities, establishing goals, maximizing productivity, and using specialized systems can all help in the effective management of time. In the world of the law, your time is what you have to offer. Your ability to manage it productively will in large part determine how successful you will be.

Key Terms

diary system	suspense system	time categorization
docket control	tickler record	time reports
docket control software	tickler system	to-do list

Problems and Activities

1. Prepare a timesheet for paralegal Mick based upon the information contained in the Chapter 6 Problems and Activities. The timesheet will be for the date December 8, 1997.

2. You have the following tasks to complete on December 9, the next day. How would you prioritize and attack these projects?
   a. Prepare for closing to be held on December 11 on McKenzie property for Yard.
   b. Draft lease documents for closing to take place on December 18.
   c. Interview witness who saw that Mr. Turner was using the blowtorch correctly when it blew up in his face. The witness's deposition will be taken December 10.
   d. Interview character witness for Tom Johnson, whose trial is scheduled for December 13.
   e. Prepare timesheet for December 8.
   f. Clean up personal form files.
   g. Draft biography for firm's resume due December 12.
   h. File bankruptcy petition for the Overlimit case.
   i. Meet with John Morgan regarding his proposed living will.

3. What information should be put on a tickler system for the cases of *Yard Manufacturing; Turner v. Blowtorch; State v. Johnson;* and Overlimit bankruptcy?

CHAPTER 8

RECORDS MANAGEMENT

CHAPTER OUTLINE

OBJECTIVES

By the completion of this chapter, you should:

- understand the role of records management in a law firm;

- understand how legal filing systems work;

- learn how to open, maintain, and close files; and

- understand file checking for conflict of interest.

Records Management: An Introduction

The operation of a law firm, and the effective representation of a legal client, generates a tremendous amount of written material. Legal paperwork can take many forms, from client correspondence to formal court documents. These records may also be stored in a variety of ways. Computers enable information to be stored on data diskettes, compact discs, or magnetic tape. Other information may be stored on microfiche or microfilm; computer-generated reports may be stored in special, oversized cabinets; and, of course, we still store millions of pieces of paper in file folders and file cabinets. Records management refers to the entire spectrum of activities necessary to generate, maintain, and close files.

In a large law firm, and in some medium-size ones, one individual is in charge of records management. This individual may be called the *records manager* (see Figure 8-1) and might handle the following tasks:

1. Assign file numbers (which may, in a centralized filing system, be different from the client/matter numbers).

2. Send either the file numbers or the actual labeled files to the person requesting them.

3. Store and maintain all open records in a central file room; microfilm materials and destroy duplicates.

4. Oversee the closing of records:
   a. Assign box numbers for files being sent to off-site storage.
   b. Maintain a computerized database of all closed records.
   c. Coordinate transport of boxes from secretarial, paralegal, or attorney work areas to the records management area and then to storage.
   d. Retrieve files from storage as requested. Return files to storage and maintain records on file retrieval activity.
   e. Send appropriate information to the bookkeeper regarding file storage and retrieval so that the clients may be billed appropriately.

FIGURE 8-1   A records manager is responsible for maintaining accurate and organized records.

f. Monitor review/destruction dates for closed files that are in storage and arrange for stripping and destruction of files after receiving written approval from the attorney.

In large records rooms, the records manager is often assisted by a records clerk who sorts, indexes, stores, retrieves, and disposes of records, as well as a records center supervisor, who handles the day-to-day operation of the center and directs the clerks. This leaves the records manager free to develop and implement new policies and procedures.

In smaller firms, records management might be done by a variety of people, or by a paralegal or other legal assistants. One of your most important responsibilities as a paralegal is to keep accurate files and maintain them in an organized, systematic manner. Remember also that many cases take years to complete, and that other people as well as you must be able to retrieve and use the records you have filed. Therefore, your recording system must be logical so that others can use it effectively.

Filing Systems in General

Each client file is given both a client and a matter number, both of which are collectively called the "client/matter" or "file" number. This is done only after a conflict-of-interest check has been performed. The conflict-of-interest check assures that representation of the client, or use of certain people on

---

**ON
POINT**   *BARNEY DOES RECORDS*

The Law Firm of Barney & Speedracer is on retainer from the Power Rangers to perform their legal work. Unfortunately for the Power Rangers, Barney & Speedracer does not have an effective records management system. When it comes to records and other office management practices, Barney, it seems, is way too slow, while Speedracer is way too fast; as a result, it is easy for things to get in a muddle.

Trini has called the firm to file a contempt action, as her ex-husband is four months delinquent on his child support payments. Barney remembers seeing her final divorce in a stack of files somewhere. "I'll find it soon," he tells Trini.

Tommy calls the firm looking for a copy of his will. "I think that was mistakenly destroyed because it was put in the wrong file," Speedracer confesses to Barney. "I guess I need to slow down and be more careful."

Jason and Billy are in the middle of asbestos litigation against their training school, The Young Ninja. "Y'know, we never did a conflict check on that case; do you remember that I used to represent The Young Ninja?" Speedracer asks.

"No, I didn't remember that. My goodness, our practice is sure in a mess! There are two things I'm glad about, though," says Barney. "First, we got our retainer already. Second, our malpractice insurance premiums are all paid up! Now, where was that file with the information on defending malpractice claims?"

---

the case, will not violate ethical guidelines. (See Figure 8-2.) Once the conflict check is performed, the firm will know whether it can begin representation of the client. (Conflict-of-interest checking is discussed in detail later in this chapter.)

Client numbers are used to identify the specific client. That number may be strictly numeric (generally four or five digits), or it may be alphanumeric. For instance, in the first case, the client number could appear as 9586. In the latter, it could appear S2345, with the S denoting attorney Stevens. The data processing or accounting departments are generally in charge of assigning numbers after they have received a fully completed file record. Of course, in a smaller law firm, you might have this responsibility.

Matter numbers are added to the client number, following a period or dash. They are generally four to six digits. The matter number is assigned to separate the many different items of business a law firm handles for any one client. As an example, XYZ Corporation has been assigned 9586 as its client number. The first case it sends is *Stone Electric v. Kartt,* and that matter is given the number 56349, which, of course, makes the client/matter number 9586.56349. The next work XYZ sends to the firm regards an employment contract for its chief executive officer. The file number would reflect the same client number, 9586, but would be given a different matter number—perhaps 23897. These numbers are especially important for several reasons. First, it is easy to identify all of the files pertaining to a particular client. Second, obtaining records for a particular case or matter is easier once the file is closed. Third, it assists the firm in

DREW, ECKL & FARNHAM

REQUEST FOR CONFLICT SEARCH

THIS FORM MUST BE TYPED

TO: RECORDS CENTER | DATE/TIME NEEDED: 1/16/91 - 10:00 a.m.

FROM: Jane Johnson Ext. 3100 (Attorney Name) | DATE/TIME SUBMITTED: 1/15/91 - 10:00 a.m.

REQUEST IS IN REGARD TO: [XX] Proposed Client–Matter [ ] Existing Client–Matter

File I.D. Number: No number - a proposed client

Client Name: Friendly Insurance Company

Matter Name: Wendell Pate

SEARCH FOR THE FOLLOWING INDIVIDUALS OR ENTITIES: Pick-A-Pair and Wendell Pate

WHITE COPY: RECORDS CENTER, YELLOW COPY: SEE CONFLICTS REPORT

FIGURE 8-2 A lawyer requests conflict search on a prospective client.

marketing by automatically being able to determine how much business and what type of matters a particular client is sending the firm.

Client numbers and matter numbers must always be used together. Numeric or alphanumeric lists of client/matter numbers are always used together. Numerical lists of client/matter numbers are generally available to you, as are alphabetical lists identified by the client or the matter name.

In addition to client/matter numbers used specifically for clients, all firms use firm client/matter numbers. These numbers are used to record nonbillable time spent on behalf of the firm. An example of a numeric firm client/matter numbering system, which keeps track of firm (nonbillable) hour categories, is as follows:

0001.10001	OFFICE ADMINISTRATION
0001.10002	PERSONAL TIME
0001.10003	RECRUITING AND INTERVIEWING
0001.10004	CONTINUING EDUCATION
0001.10005	BUSINESS DEVELOPMENT
0001.10006	PROFESSIONAL ACTIVITIES
0001.10007	MEMO BANK
0001.10008	PRO BONO
0001.10009	WRITING OF ARTICLES
0001.10010	COMPUTER FORMS
0001.10011	FIRM NEWSLETTER
0001.10012	CLIENT SEMINARS
0001.10013	MANAGING PARTNER'S TIME

You can see from this detailed listing the importance law firms place on non-billable activity, as well as the meticulous approach to timekeeping that law firms take.

We have discussed client/matter numbers in some detail. Some law firms use client/matter numbers for their file system. This is called a *numeric system.* It means that files are placed in the drawers of the file cabinet in order, beginning with the client portion of the number. If the following files were being placed in a drawer, and they were the only files in the drawer, you would arrange them in this order:

2345.68907	FIFTH
2345.56892	FOURTH
1456.78942	SECOND
1326.94837	FIRST
2345.18764	THIRD
7954.90786	SIXTH

Although many firms use a numeric filing system, others use an alphabetic system (see Figure 8-3). Under this system, commonly referred to as a *direct access system,* files are placed in A through Z order. Unless standard filing procedures are followed by all, the system will not work. Standard procedures are published by the Association of Records Managers and Administrators (ARMA).

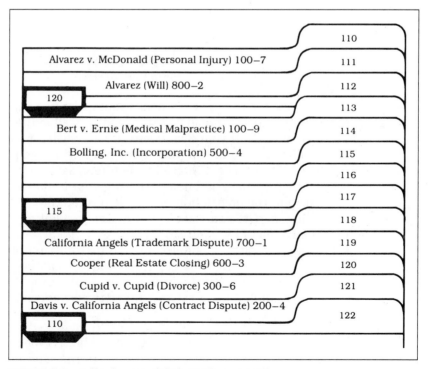

FIGURE 8-3 A file drawer, alphabetically arranged.

File folders may or may not be color-coded according to letter, where each letter is assigned its own color.

The three subsystems of the alphabetic system are name, subject, and geographic location.

Name   Names may be organizations, businesses, or individuals. Individuals should be indexed by last name. The first name and middle initial follow. The name E. Michael Masinter would be indexed as Masinter, E. Michael, under this system.

Businesses and organizations are indexed in the proper order. For example, Atlanta Legal Copies is filed under the complete name. If the name of the company was Donna Stone's Copy Service, it would again be filed in the proper name order.

Subject   The second subsection of the alphabetic system categorizes files by subject, or content of the document. Examples are gasoline, hotels, insurance, law, music, and so forth. Information within the subject folders are generally alphabetically arranged by a method agreed upon by all.

Geographic   This is the third subsection. Within the United States, one would normally file according to state, county, and city. Other topics might be added for countries outside the United States, such as province, region, and so on.

Opening a New File

When a new file has to be opened, a multipart form called a "File Record" or "New Matter Report" should be completed with all of the necessary information. (See Figure 8-4.) If your firm does not have such a form, you must nonetheless get all of the required information. You might then purchase or create a form to facilitate new client intake in the future, as a method of both improving records management and demonstrating your initiative. Considerable care must be taken in the preparation of the file record, as this is the only source of data regarding matters undertaken by the firm. In addition, this information is used for the conflict-of-interest search.

When you complete the file record, be sure to fill in every space. If the file is a new matter for an existing client who has already been assigned a client number, write the established client number in the proper space. If the file is for a new client, note that fact. Other questions are asked, such as:

1. *Date:* Enter the date the file was received.
2. *Responsible attorney:* This is the attorney who has the primary responsibility for the file. (Typically, initials of the attorney and his personal number are used.)

FILE RECORD — NEW MATTER REPORT

FORM COMPLETED BY: *Sally Smart*   DREW, ECKL & FARNHAM
ATTORNEYS AT LAW

DATE: *01 / 15 / 95*

CLIENT # *1 2 3 4*   MATTER # *9 8 7 6 5*

1. When was filed received? *01/14/95*   2. Which attorney will have primary responsibility for this file? *TF* atty. int. *669* atty. #

3. Which attorney will have responsibility for billing this file? *TF* .... _____ atty. int. _____ atty. #

4. What type of case is this? (Supply One) *20*

THIRD PARTY INSURANCE DEFENSE LITIGATION:	FIRST PARTY INSURANCE DEFENSE:	OTHERS:	LABOR:
11 Products or Aviation Litigation	31 Accident & Health Claims	50 Local Counsel	71 Labor General
12 Automobile or Trucking Accidents	32 Arson Claims	51 Divorce	72 Labor & Employment Law
13 Medical Malpractice	33 Property-(Non-arson) Claims	52 Deposition for Out of State Counsel	73 Creditor's Rights
14 Other Prof. Malpractice	34 Surety	53 Sports Law	**FIRM:**
15 Homeowners Liability	35 Coverage Questions-Auto	54 Releases	81 Employee
16 Business Liability or Patent, Trademark & Copyright	36 Coverage Questions-Other	55 Minor Settlements	82 Client Rate
17 Civil Rights Litigation	37 Environmental Matters	56 Criminal Matters	83 ID Change
18 Libel & Slander / Malicious Prosecution & Personal Injury Torts	38 Trucking/Cargo		84 Firm
19 Municipal/County Liability (Non-Civil Rights)	39 Fidelity	**CONTRACTS:**	
20 Municipal Liability (Non-Civil Rights Litigation)	**PLAINTIFF'S CLAIMS:**	61 Contract Claim — Plaintiff	**CORPORATE:**
	41 Personal Injury	62 Contract Claim — Defendant	90 Commercial Litigation
WORKERS' COMPENSATION:	42 Major Subrogation-Property-(over $10,000)	63 Lien Claim — Plaintiff	91 Corporations/Business Transactions
21 Defendants-Self-Insureds	43 Major Subrogation-Property-(under $10,000)	64 Lien Claim — Defendant	92 Real Estate
22 Defendants-Insurers	44 Major Subrogation-Other-(over $10,000)	65 Government Contract	93 Trust & Estates
23 Claimants Cases	45 Minor Subrogation-Other-(under $10,000)	66 General / Miscellaneous	94 Bankruptcy
24 Stipulations	46 Premium Collection	67 Labor (OSHA, Wage and Hour)	
25 Defendants-Uninsured Employers	47 Collections	68 Contract Documents	

5. When should this file be billed?

(Supply One) *16*

BILLING FREQUENCY CODES:

01 Annually-January	13 Every month	21 Semi-annually for matters opened in Mar., Sept.
02 Annually-February	14 End of Case-(Hourly matters only)	22 Semi-annually for matters opened in April, Oct.
03 Annually-March	15 End of Case-(Contingent matters only)	23 Semi-annually for matters opened in May, Nov.
04 Annually-April	**16 Quarterly for matters opened:**	24 Semi-annually for matters opened in June, Dec.
05 Annually-May	**Jan., April, July & Oct.**	25 Bi-annually (every two years)
06 Annually-June	**17 Quarterly for matters opened:**	
07 Annually-July	**Feb., May, Aug. & Nov.**	
08 Annually-August	**18 Quarterly for matters opened:**	
09 Annually-September	**Mar., June, Sept. & Dec.**	
10 Annually-October	19 Semi-annually for matters opened in Jan., July	
11 Annually-November	20 Semi-annually for matters opened in Feb., Aug.	
12 Annually-December		

6. To which attorney did this matter come? *TF* atty. int. *669* atty. #   8. Interest charged _____ (If applicable) 2 = 1% 3 = 1½%

7. In which format should this bill be printed? (Supply One) *42*

FORMAT PROVIDES:

32 Date Svcs.	42 Date Svcs., Hrs., Item Disb.	52 Date, Atty., Svcs., Item Disb.	62 Date, Atty, Svcs., Hrs., Item Disb.
33 Date Svcs., Collapsed Disb.	43 Date Svcs., Hrs., Item Disb., Collapsed Disb.	53 Date, Atty., Svcs., Item Disb., Collapsed Disb.	63 Date, Atty., Svcs., Hrs., Item Disb., Collapsed Disb.

(36 Max.)

9. Client Name: *Friendly Insurance Co.*

(36 Max.)

10. How should we identify this matter? *Gumpo vs. Fair Foods*
(ex: Jones vs. State Farm or in re:)

11. Where do we send bills?   (30 Max.)

Friendly Ins. Co.
Attn. Line or Street Address: *Fred Friendly*

P.O. Box 10286
P.O. Box or Street Address:

Dallas, TX 75043-1323
City, State, Zip

12. What was the client's reference # or I.D. for this file?

D.H.690430

13. Telephone #:

(214) 996-0440

14. If we need a special client rate for this client, what rates should be entered?
A RATE MUST BE SUPPLIED FOR EACH CLASSIFICATION.

1) *125.00* sr. ptr. 2) *110.00* jr. ptr. 3) *90.00* sr. assoc. 4) *90.00* jr. assoc. 5) *60.00* med. res. 6) *———* law clerk 7) *60.00* pll

For conflict purposes, please list complete names of all parties involved:

Plaintiff(s)
Gary Gumpo
Martha Gumpo

Their Attorney(s)
Haffine + Huey
100 Bank Plaza
203 Apache St.
Dallas, TX 75040

Defendant(s)
Fair Foods Corp.
600 Technology Park
Suite 1400
Norcross, GA 30001

Their Attorney(s)

Court *USDC*
Civil Action No: *CHD 00654*   Judge: *Campbell*
15. Who referred the Client to DEF? _____

DATA PROCESSING

FIGURE 8-4 New matter reports, also called *file records,* give all sections of the firm the information required when a new case is opened.

3. *Billing attorney:* This is the attorney who will be in charge of the billings to the client. To clarify, the responsible and billing attorneys may be the same. Often, however, the billing attorney is senior to the working attorney.

4. *Referral:* This space is specifically for the name of the person or company who referred the case to the firm.

5. *Case type:* This reflects the type of case (i.e., will, liability, surety, etc.); there may be codes for these case types also.

6. *Bill code:* This code determines the frequency with which the file will be billed (i.e., monthly, quarterly, annually, etc.).

7. *Referring attorney:* In this space, the name of the attorney who received the file is completed. That attorney may elect either to keep the file or to refer it to another attorney in the firm.

8. *Bill format:* This determines the manner in which the invoice will be prepared for presentation to the client. Firms differ in the format that is used. For example, a firm may display the time entries that include the time-sheet date, the text, and the hours spent, as well as itemized disbursements. Another possibility lists all of those items plus the attorneys' names or initials.

9. *Client name:* The name of the client represented is written in this space. You are usually limited to a specific number of characters, so you need to use abbreviations appropriately.

10. *Matter name:* The matter, or the style of the case, should be written in this space.

11. *Name and address:* Again, enter the name of the client, as well as the address. Space is limited, so use abbreviations wisely. Be accurate—it is from this entry that the address for the invoice is taken.

12. *Client reference number:* Upon occasion, clients require that reference be made to a specific number—one they use internally, such as their file number or the court case number, or perhaps the claim number or policy number.

13. *Client rates:* If you open a file for a new client, you will be expected to supply the rates. Most firms classify their legal staff for rate purposes. Those classifications are:

Senior Partner
Junior Partner
Senior Associate
Junior Associate
Medical Researcher
Law Clerk
Paralegal

There are usually high-low rates for each category of legal work, such as litigation, corporate work, or estate work, and the billing attorney who has asked you to open the file must supply you with all necessary information.

It is critical that you correctly complete the file record. Be specific and give all the information you can. For example:

1. The file record asks, "Which attorney will have primary responsibility for this file?" If two or three attorneys will have equal responsibility, you should give all three names.

2. When the client's name is requested, be sure that you give the client's name. You may be working with Don Brown of the ABC Corporation. Don Brown is not the client—ABC Corporation is, although they both should be checked for conflicts of interest.

3. The question, "How should we identify this matter?" can be tricky. Generally, the answer to the question would be "In Re:" or "plaintiff v. defendant." Sometimes a brief explanation may be necessary—for example, you may show "Jones v. Smith," but in the space provided for "plaintiff" you show "John Jones," and under "defendant" you show "Trump Trucking." Explaining that Trump Trucking is the defendant and that Mr. Smith was the driver of Trump's truck will aid in finding a potential conflict. Be sure about the spelling of names—don't show "Bill Burne v. Atlanta" if it is really "Bill Burn v. Atlantic."

4. Clearly identify the plaintiff and the defendant. Show the firm's relationship and position in the case. Even if a case is not yet a lawsuit, for conflict purposes be clear as to who would be the plaintiff and the defendant—identify all parties involved.

5. When using an apostrophe in a name, place it correctly (i.e., Bill's Barn or Bills' Barn).

Once the new matter report is completed, any other initial forms must be completed as well. An address list, for example, directs the person sending out firm mailings to send certain items to this client at a certain address. This form can be input directly into the computer, if the firm's system can integrate the information; or by hand, to be input into the computer later.

Once these initial record reports have been completed, the firm will have the foundational information about the client it is considering representing. As work for the client continues, the file will expand, sometimes to multiple boxes, to accommodate the materials and information accumulated in the course of client representation.

Active Files

The term *active files* refers to cases or matters that have not yet been resolved, and which require additional actions or activity. Depending upon the type of law practice, active files may be stored in a central file room, or, in the case of many litigation practices, they may be stored in the file cabinets within each department—

often lining the hallways. Of course, some files that are used frequently will be kept at the attorney's, paralegal's, and secretary's offices or workspace.

Each person who removes a file is expected to complete an "out card." The name of the working attorney and the location of the file must be given. The out card is then placed in the corresponding alpha or numeric sequence. (See Figure 8-5.) If a central file room is used, indices will be available so that files can be easily located. They will be filed numerically, alphabetically, or by a combination of the two.

Naturally, appropriate file security measures must be taken to protect your firm's records, whether they are in individual offices, in file cabinets, in electronic media, or in central storage. The firm must protect against theft, water, or fire damage, or decomposition resulting from atmospheric conditions in the storage room. Additionally, the firm must develop policies and procedures to assure the integrity and confidentiality of file contents.

DREW, ECKL & FARNHAM
RECORDS REQUEST

TO: RECORDS CENTER

DATE: __1/3/91__   FILE NAME: __Pick-A-Pair v. Wendell Pate__

REQUESTING ATTY: __Attorney Jones__   # __999__ EXT: __1000__

SEND TO: __Attorney Jones__   BOX NO. __000.101__

HOW LONG DO YOU EXPECT TO KEEP THIS FILE? __1 Day__

CLIENT/MATTER: __0002.20004__

[PORTION BELOW TO BE COMPLETED BY RECORDS CENTER]

> OPEN CLIENT/MATTER TO BE CHARGED
> 0004.40008

SEARCHED BY: __Ms. Find__   TIME SPENT: __10 minutes__

DATE DUE: __1/4/91__   DATE RETURNED: __Has not been returned__

REFILED BY: __Has not been refiled__   TIME SPENT: _____

AMOUNT CHARGED: _____

REMARKS: __This file still in Attorney Jones' office. Not sent back for storage.__

COPY 1 / TICKLER FILE   COPY 2 / RECORD
COPY 3 / OUT CARD   COPY 4 / DATA PROCESSING

FIGURE 8-5   Record request forms document file movement to assure security.

Internal File Organization

The manner of organization and filing of material with each separately numbered client file should be discussed shortly after the commencement of your employment with your supervising attorney, the paralegals within your department, or the person responsible for your training and orientation. Naturally, each firm will have particular ways it does things. Make sure you learn the filing system thoroughly so that you can help your firm manage its records effectively.

Examples of the various components of litigation files include:

- Correspondence
- Legal research
- Pleadings file
- Discovery file
- Billing file
- Attorneys' notes
- Deposition file
- Witness file
- Client documents
- Memos

Paralegal Index Card System

It is a good idea to keep a card index in your office of all files being handled within your department. Those cards should reflect pertinent information, as shown in Figure 8-6. This will enable you to access the files and maintain appropriate security precautions.

FIGURE 8-6
An example of a paralegal index card

```
01-04-91              JMP              0001.10001

EASTERN MANUFACTURING, INC. vs. GENERIC OFFICES

Fulton Superior Court D-80001

Joan Smithson                        404-555-1213
Claims Adjuster                      fax:_____
Insurance World        claim #  _____
P.O. Box 7600          policy # _____
Atlanta, GA  30357                   D/L: _____

¶ counsel:
James H. Morris                      404-296-5555
Morris & Morris                      fax:_____
715 W. Ponce de Leon Ave.
Post Office Box 7600
Decatur, Georgia  30030
```

File Storage

When a matter has been completed and "final billed," it is a good idea to prepare it for storage, making room in the file drawers for new matters. To do so, a file storage inventory form should be completed (see Figure 8-7). Files should never be closed without up-to-date conflict-of-interest information. This means that the name of the client and all pertinent participants in the matter should be placed on the conflict-of-interest checklist so that the firm can ensure that the firm does not represent opposing parties when other cases are accepted.

When the file storage inventory form has been completed, it is submitted to the person in charge of records management and assigned an identifying number. The same number will be written in large print on the box itself. (See Figure 8-8.)

All legal pads should be removed from the files, thereby decreasing the bulk. You will also want to remove duplicate copies of documents, and sometimes pleadings are removed since they are on file at the courthouse. Additionally, all papers should be hole-punched and inserted into the file on prongs so that no papers can be lost. Original documents such as wills or trust documents should be copied, and the copies placed in the box. The originals should be returned to the client. This same principle holds true for any documents a client may have given the firm when she brought the matter to the firm.

The firm may have its own space designated for closed files, or the firm may use an outside storage company to store closed files. It is imperative that firms be able to quickly and efficiently retrieve closed matters. Often clients have other matters for which information in the closed files can be helpful. (See Figure 8-9.)

Micrographics

Technical advances have seen the development of several forms of document storage and retrieval systems that can aid law firms in maximizing access to records and minimizing storage space requirements for records and documents. One commonly used method is microfilming documents. In this method, information is stored on *microfilm,* a piece of film that is a photographic record of printed or graphic information on a reduced scale, or on *microfiche,* which is a sheet of film containing printed or graphic information on a reduced scale. A microfilm or microfiche *reader* is the electronic equipment through which one may view the film or the fiche. (See Figure 8-10.) Firms may microfilm their own materials if they have the proper equipment, or they may engage an outside service to perform the microfilming.

FILE STORAGE INVENTORY

ATTORNEY: NICHOLSON,M.   •Box No. _029685_

DATE SENT TO STORAGE: REVIEW/DESTROY DATE: (Add 7 yrs
  10/13/95   10/13/2002

(X) This storage box contains more than one file.
( ) This storage box contains only one file in its entirety. (LIST SUBFILES).
( ) This storage box is ___ of ___ containing a single file. (COMPLETE A FILE STORAGE INVENTORY SHEET
                                           FOR EACH BOX, AND LIST SUBFILES IN EACH BOX).

CLIENT/ MATTER NO. (0222.12345)	FILE IDENTIFICATION (Style & client name: e.g. Lewis, Left v. Wright, Ron) (Friendly Insurance Company)	IS CONFLICT OF INTEREST DATA CURRENT? Check One YES /NO / SUPPLEMENT ATTACHED
4769.02428	Penn vs. Temple Depositions - 6/1/95-9/30/95	
4769.05749	Penn vs. Temple Correspondence - 1/1-9/30/95	

FORM COMPLETED BY:

                                   Signature _Gail Gordon_

I hereby authorize the destruction of the files listed above.

Date: _____   _____
                    Signature of Attorney
  * To be completed by
    Records Manager

FIGURE 8-7 A file storage inventory form prepares files to be stored.

Both open and closed records may be microfilmed and available for ready reference. Even though the cost of microfilming can be substantial, it is often offset by space savings, such as the cost of the square footage leased space, additional cabinets, and/or off-site storage. It is also a very quick reference to

FIGURE 8-8 Box numbers facilitate the retrieval of closed files.

materials. Files can become very bulky, and looking through them to find the desired information often takes considerable time. With the use of electronic filing with microfilm, the desired information can be found quickly. Microfilming may also lend the advantage of increased security. Duplicate copies of materials may be microfilmed and stored off-site.

Microfilm or microfiche is also valuable in the library. Shelving space is often limited, and endless volumes of books can be stored and quickly retrieved by the use of microfilm or microfiche. Many volumes can be purchased on film or fiche—the law firm does not have to go to the trouble and expense of filming them on its own document camera. As a matter of fact, in some instances older reporter volumes are no longer available in hard cover and may be available only on microfiche.

FIGURE 8-9
A records attendant retrieves stored files from in-house file storage.

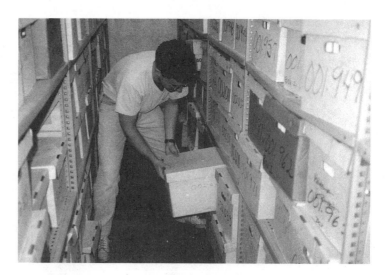

FIGURE 8-10
A paralegal uses microfiche to retrieve a closed file.

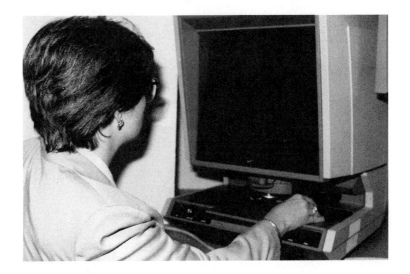

Micrographics technology has improved greatly over the past few years, making it a more affordable and desirable alternative to paper storage. It is no longer considered viable for passive storage only.

In addition to micrographics, there exist technologies such as electronic document retrieval systems involving optical scanning and imaging, which promise to revolutionize file storage by eliminating as much paper as possible. The imaging process involves the reproduction of images (electronic pictures) onto an optical disk or CD-ROM. This provides for compact storage as well as easy retrieval and viewing. It also decreases storage costs and litigation costs to the client. The chart in Figure 8-11 gives you a good overview of the imaging process. You will learn more about these new technologies in Chapter 13.

Document Destruction

One additional issue that arises when files are closed concerns the retention or destruction of documents. On the one hand, document storage is an expensive proposition, and law firms do not want extra expenses if they can be avoided. On the other hand, some documents are critically important and must be retained. These might include property records, audit reports, minute books of corporations, or payroll records.

There are two main sources for document retention guidelines. The first is the law itself, which specifies retention rules and regulations for documents such as employer records or tax records. The state or federal code may contain specific record retention policies or guidelines. As an example of a state law specifying records retention, see Ga. Code Ann. § 48-7-111:

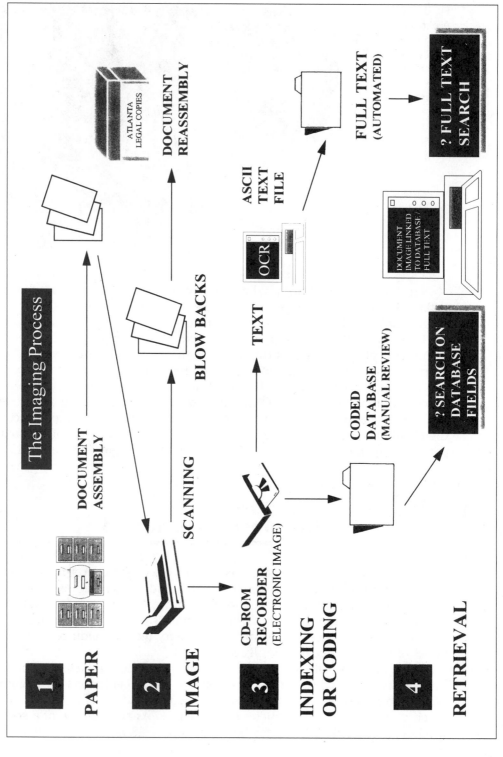

FIGURE 8-11 Overview of the imaging process

48-7-111 Employer's records; contents; period of preservation.

—————— IIII ——————

(a) Each employer required to deduct and withhold taxes under this article shall keep accurate records of all remuneration paid to his employees, including, but not limited to, remuneration paid in forms other than cash. The records shall contain the information required by rules issued by the commissioner.

(b) The records required to be kept pursuant to subsection (a) of this Code section and records relating to refunds shall be preserved and maintained for a period of at least four years after the date the tax to which they relate becomes due or the date the tax is paid, whichever is later.

Complementing records requirements specified by law are the policies and practices that the firm, through experience and discretion, has developed. Legal guidelines combined with practical experience, therefore, give the parameters for an effective retention system.

To develop and administer a legally acceptable records retention program, many firms follow the retention recommendations of the Association of Legal Administrators. Their guidelines concerning retention and destruction of various types of documents can be found in Appendix A, following the standardized filing rules.

Generally, files are reviewed for destruction when they are a minimum of seven years old. An important exception to this is original wills, trust documents, final divorce decrees and settlement papers, and the like. However, firms usually keep these documents in their safes. The records manager checks for files with a review/destroy date eligible for consideration. The printout of these files, along with a memo, is sent to the responsible attorney. The memo encourages careful yet timely scrutiny of each file, allowing an average two-week review of the list. It is then sent back to the records manager with the proper instruction. The attorney may wish to see the actual file in storage before making a decision. In that case, a records request form must be completed and sent to the records manager.

When it is decided to destroy a file, your firm's file destruction procedures must be followed. You will want to shred or pulp files to be destroyed, rather than dumping them, for security reasons. Legal documents may contain information that is subject to the attorney-client privilege, and to dump the documents would be a breach of this duty. Although no one may think to look in the dumpster at old files, one can never be certain.

For confidential documents, document destruction assures the client that proper security measures are taken with his information. For other documents, paper recycling is appropriate. It has never been more important for all of us to participate in recycling projects. Many law firms are leading the way in this effort since they use ream after ream of computer, bond, photocopy, and assorted other paper. Recycling one ton of paper saves 29 trees, 410 gallons of fuel, and 8 cubic yards of landfill. Law firms can definitely play a leadership role in recycling efforts and fulfill their social responsibility to the environment.

Conflict of Interest

All new matters must be searched for potential conflicts of interest. Conflicts of interest arise when there is a personal or financial connection among the lawyer, the law firm, the client, and other clients, and there exist ethical guidelines that explain how conflicts should be handled.

Potential conflicts of interest arise in many different forms and situations. Some of the more common conflict situations include when the firm has sued a person or corporation who wishes to become a new client; when an attorney was an attorney in another firm when that firm represented the opposing party; and when the firm incorporated the defendant corporation, an employee of the firm is on the board of directors or is a majority stockholder of the corporation to be sued. The situations in which conflicts of interest arise are many and varied. The specific situations amounting to conflicts are discussed in paralegal courses on ethics.

To alert everyone to a possible conflict, firms may either:

- Send a daily memo to all attorneys and paralegals

- Send a daily newsletter, including this memo

- Send an electronic message.

The memo should list all new matters received the previous day. (See Figure 8-12.) The firm's client may be underlined for easy reference. If a conflict or any question exists, the person in charge of conflict searches, as well as the responsible attorney, should be contacted immediately. If you know of a file or matter that you have been involved with that sounds or looks even remotely similar to the names listed in the memo, you should alert the responsible person to pull the file to ensure that a conflict does not in fact exist. Being overly cautious when checking for conflicts is the best practice.

Some firms still use manual systems for searching for conflicts, but the majority now use sophisticated computer databases. If the firm is automated, certain information from the file record or a separate "Conflict Information" form will be entered into the computer database to check it against possible conflicts. It will check (1) the name of the client, (2) all plaintiffs, (3) all plaintiffs' attorneys, (4) all defendants, (5) all defendants' attorneys, (6) the name of each parent or subsidiary corporation, corporation's chief executive officer, partnership's general partners, and other assorted information. A new file may not be opened if the conflict search discloses any potential conflict with any past or present client or adverse party. Any conflict must be immediately reported to the attorney who requested the new file number. It is of great importance that, as information becomes available on all client files, such information be sent to the data processing department and the person in charge of conflict searches. This may be accomplished by completing and submitting a "file maintenance"

```
REPORT DATE 03/15/91                      Bachman, Wilson & Juris                    PAGE    1
REPORT NUMBER CC330-000077
SORTED BY REFERENCE NAME               CONFLICT LIST BY REFERENCE NAME            PRINTED BY TDD
RANGE SELECTED: BEG OF FILE TO END OF FILE

REFERENCE NAME              CLIENT MATTER  REPORTING NAME                TYPE A/O  OPENED   CLOSED

Davidson County Bank       000500 00000   Davidson County Bank            C    A   06/26/90

   Ackerman, Marion A., President
   Bankers, Frederick, Board Member
   Bradford, Timothy R., Board Member
   Frierson, Jeanelle, Board Member
   Gray, Steven A., Board Member
   Thompson, Joan L., Chairman


Endicott Insurance Company 000600 00000   Endicott Insurance Company      C    A   10/01/90

   Ackerman, Louise, Board Member
   Endico Services, Inc.
   Endicott Marilyn, Board Member
   Endicott Properties
   Feilweil Supplies
   Foxworth, James, Board Member
   Freeland, Ronald, Board Member
   Lackey, Arnold, President


Fischer, Schrebenski vs.   000150 00003   Fischer, Schrebenski vs.        C    A   01/12/91
   Adams, Eric E., MD
   Fischer, Harley R.
   Schrebenski, Harold I


Herbert / Brentwood Tree Surg 000300 00004  Herbert / Brentwood Tree Surg C    A   08/31/90
   Herbert, Jane Levore


Herbert Materials, Inc.    000850 00000   Herbert Materials, Inc.         C    A   01/15/86 02/28/90
```

FIGURE 8-12 A conflict list shows possible conflicts of interest by alphabetic listing of all clients. (Courtesy of Juris, Incorporated.)

form with the new information clearly marked. The computer system is then updated, and the conflict system is kept up-to-date. (See Figure 8-13.)

If the firm is not automated, it is often the responsibility of a paralegal to handle all conflict checks manually. (See Figure 8-14.) The same items are checked—it just takes a bit longer.

Conflict of interest is of extreme importance and must be checked to avoid the possibility that the firm may be engaged by a new client whose problems

---

FILE MAINTENANCE

TO: DATA PROCESSING/RECORDS MANAGER

DATE: 4/18/96   ATTY NO.:   401

- -

CLIENT NO.:   3425   MATTER NO.:   67859
FILE IDENTIFICATION: A567.8900

- -

PLEASE ADD THE FOLLOWING INFORMATION TO THE COMPUTER FILE FOR THE MATTER LISTED ABOVE:

( ) Civil Action No. _____
( ) Court _____
(X) Judge   Nicholson Masinter

( ) PLAINTIFF(S)	( ) THEIR ATTORNEY(S)
Mark Lewis a/k/a The Boy Wonder	J. Harberg and R. Golden

(X) DEFENDANT(S) or ( ) ____-PARTY DEFENDANT(S)	( ) THEIR ATTORNEY(S)
Edwin's Family Tree	Allison Daniel and Shannon Selfridge and Marcy Masinter

- -

PLEASE MAKE THESE OTHER CHANGES OR ADDITIONS:

OLD INFORMATION	NEW INFORMATION

FIGURE 8-13   File maintenance forms are used to update client files.

CONFLICT OF INTEREST
INVENTORY FOR CASES NOT ON COMPUTER

Please fill out this form when closing files that are not on the computer and attach it to the grey Files Storage Inventory sheet.

Client/Matter Number: 4562.09876

File Identification: Lynton Paving Co. Re: Gravel

Client Name: Lynton Paving Co.

Attorney Responsible (Number):   123

Date File Opened: 2/4/83

Case Type: 03

Client Reference Number: n/a

Court: DeKalb Superior

Civil Action Number: A45274-0987-4

Judge: Beans

Plaintiff:	**Plaintiff's Attorney:**
Dubraski Gravel Distributors	Smyth & Smyth

Defendant:	**Defendant's Attorney:**
A & B Trucking Co.	Jazy & Smoozer

Other Information: _____

FIGURE 8-14   Conflict-of-interest inventory form captures relevant information that is not in the computer database.

ON POINT   *THE CASE OF THE RECKLESS RECORDKEEPER*

Billy James is getting ready to dispose of the drafts of his client's final patent application for a new car waxing technique, which are in the trunk of his car. Rather than following the regular procedure of taking the documents to be shredded at his office, Billy dumps them in the car wash trash bin next to the car wash owner's office, while his car is drying. As he drives away, the owner, whose curiosity was aroused when he saw the official seals on the documents, retrieved them from the trash and somehow knew that he had found himself a treasure.

As Billy arrives at his office in his newly cleaned car, he finds a memo checking for conflicts of interest for Fathers & Sons, Inc. Billy checks his file list and sees Fathers & Sons Company. Since it has a different name, he indicates on the memo that he has no conflict of interest. A month later, as he is drafting interrogatories in the Fathers & Sons Company case, he realizes that the company is really called Fathers and Sons, Inc.

What problems do you see with Billy's recordkeeping?

could in some way adversely affect a current or former client. Conflicts can be checked a number of ways, and conflict checking must be viewed as a critical assignment. The system within each firm varies, but it is vital that you as a paralegal understand the seriousness of the task. A fundamental principle of ethical behavior is the avoidance of conflicts of interest. All parties in the law firm must work together to ensure that a present or former client's interests are not adversely affected by the representation of a new client.

Records Management: A Summary

Proper records management is one of the major goals of an effectively operating law office, and the paralegal has an important role to play in their maintenance. In larger law firms, you will have to understand the proper procedures to use, and you will interact, personally or through correspondence, with others responsible for records management. In a smaller firm, you might be involved with a greater range of activities concerning file maintenance because there will be less specialization. Whatever environment you are in, systematized file maintenance is an absolutely essential part of your work. It is virtually impossible for a lawyer to provide quality services to clients if she cannot rely on an organized, well-maintained system of records. The systems and procedures discussed in this chapter will help you achieve that goal.

Key Terms

alphanumeric system	document retention	numeric system
client/matter number	file storage	optical imaging
conflict of interest	micrographics	records management
direct access system	new matter report	records manager

Problems and Activities

1. Open a file and create the proper subfiles for the matters involving Yard Manufacturing, Turner v. Blowtorch, State v. Tom Johnson, and Overlimit bankruptcy.

2. Close the files for the matters involving Yard Manufacturing, Turner v. Blowtorch, State v. Tom Johnson, and Overlimit bankruptcy. What names should be added to the firm's conflict-of-interest database?

CHAPTER 9

THE LAW LIBRARY AND OTHER OFFICE MANAGEMENT SYSTEMS

OBJECTIVES

By the completion of this chapter, you should:

- understand the law library and its role in the law firm; and

- understand additional administrative systems that are necessary to the effective functioning of a law firm.

Office Management Systems: An Introduction

The systems and procedures of law office administration discussed in the previous chapters represent the most significant areas for the effective administration of a legal practice. You will also need to understand and use a number of other systems within a law office. The purpose of this chapter is to acquaint you with those other systems.

The Library

Paralegals typically spend many hours in the law firm library, and certainly one of the characteristics of a good paralegal is the ability to do effective research and to use legal resources efficiently. You should therefore become intimately acquainted with your firm's library at the outset of your employment with the firm. (See Figure 9-1.)

Law firm libraries differ widely in size and scope of their resources. In most medium to large firms, the library will be maintained by professional librarians and their staffs. In a very small firm, you may be the librarian! If there is no formal library orientation for paralegals, meet with the librarian as soon as is practical. Scan the card catalog if there is one; look over the shelves and make notes of what resources are available. This is especially important if there is no library staff; it is your responsibility to determine what is available to you in-house and what additional sources you may need to identify elsewhere. If you require books or materials not available in the library and not provided by the firm, send a written request to the library committee or the attorney in charge of the library.

In smaller firms where librarians are not on staff, paralegals often do their share of library maintenance. If you happen to be assigned library tasks such as the filing of supplements or looseleaf services, be sure to do them in a timely fashion. Neglected, out-of-date publications are not only a research inconvenience but may also result in a serious error at trial, in briefs submitted to the court, or in advice given to clients.

FIGURE 9-1 A paralegal will spend many hours in a law library.

No matter how large or small your firm's library and its staff may be, it is a good idea to become familiar with all local and area libraries. Courthouse and law school libraries are obvious sources for case law, law review, and journal articles and treatises. Public libraries can supply a wealth of information—city directories, out-of-state telephone directories, general periodicals, newspapers, and much more. There is often a telephone reference service. Some large public and university libraries are depositories for government documents such as federal agency publications, census statistics, and legislative materials. There may be specialized libraries in your area maintained by state and federal government agencies, professional societies or associations, and large corporations. Many of these will provide research assistance to the general public. Attorneys routinely require information on a wide variety of subjects; a notebook (or well-annotated Rolodex!) with phone numbers, names, and sources will be invaluable.

The Modern Library: Books Without Pages

When most people think of a library, they generally think of a place where books line the shelves. Although it is unlikely that books will ever be totally replaced, it is certainly true that CD-ROM and online computer services have totally revolutionized the way in which information may be transmitted.

The contemporary law library must account for both books and bytes. Shelves of books are now being complemented with rows of computer terminals. Online reference services such as LEXIS or WESTLAW provide immediate access to a virtually limitless amount of information. The LEXIS service, which is accessed through the telephone lines, provides continuously updated federal and state case law, state and federal codes, and more than 45 specialized libraries for various areas of practice. Most legal publishers now have material available both in traditional book format and in compact disc format. A single CD-ROM disc can hold more than 400,000 pages of text and thereby save the firm a great deal of space. For example, the *Official Code of Georgia* comprises nearly 40 big, hefty print volumes, and each volume is supplemented by a pocket part each year. By contrast, *Georgia Law on CD-ROM* takes less than four inches of shelf space, and the discs provided are updated three times a year via replacement discs. Additionally, CD-ROM allows the user to interact with the material; you can print out sections or retrieve related information.

Both traditional texts and electronic media have their place in the modern law library. As you learn about the library in your firm and are introduced to its contents and capabilities, you will learn how to use both books and bytes to accomplish your goals. For now, it is important to realize how thoroughly advanced electronics systems have integrated themselves into the library environment. Later in this book you will be introduced to some of the specific technical applications used in legal work.

Finally, recognize that the proliferation of electronic and print materials requires each library to balance the need for quality resources with the economic reality that the cost of resources is high. Law books, online services, and electronic media are very expensive, and choices must be made concerning which materials or services to purchase. In the future, you will see firms carefully scrutinize their libraries and their additional purchases in order to maintain quality for a reasonable price.

Library Resources

Most law firm libraries, regardless of size, will have at least some resources in the following categories. Most of these resources are available in both traditional book form and electronic media.

Case Law

A library may contain published opinions of trial and appeals courts, state and federal. Large firms may have, either in book form or microform, all reported decisions of the federal district courts, the circuit court of appeals, and the Supreme Court. In addition, the collection may contain all or part of West's National Reporter System, which publishes many of the opinions of the appellate courts in every state.

Specialized reporters featuring decisions in specific fields are common in many libraries. These range from titles such as *West's Bankruptcy Reporter* and

Callaghan's *Federal Rules Service* to CCH's *Federal Securities Law Reporter* and BNA's *Labor Relations Reporter;* which ones your firm's library has reflects the nature of the firm's practice.

Published opinions are a primary source of the law, and, as such, are one of the focal points of any law library. Familiarize yourself with those in your library and learn which ones have advance sheets and how to use them.

Statutes and Regulations

Federal statutes, another primary source of law, are collected in the official U.S. Code and in two unofficial, annotated versions—West's *United States Code Annotated* and Lawyers Cooperative's *United States Code Service.* Most firms own one of the two annotated versions.

State statutes are published in much the same way, and a firm will certainly own a set of its own state's codes, and perhaps the codes of other states as well. There may also be local government statutes or ordinances.

Regulations of state and federal agencies are similar to statutes, but are usually much more detailed. A multivolume set entitled the Code of Federal Regulations (or C.F.R.) is found in some collections. State regulations are sometimes published in a set, but may be issued independently by various agencies.

Finding Tools

Finding tools are sources that help to locate relevant case law or statutes. Some typical finding tools include the following.

Digests   The various federal and state reporters all have multivolume digests that offer a subject reference to published opinions. West's *Federal Practice Digest* digests reported decisions of the federal courts. There are digests for regional reporters of state decisions—e.g., *Southern 2d Digest*—and individual state digests as well. Generally, if the library contains the reporter, it will often have the appropriate digest also.

Annotations   Another case finder and research aid is the *annotation,* which is an analysis of opinions relating to a particular point of law. The best known collection of annotations is the system published by Lawyers Cooperative, *American Law Reports* (ALR), now in its fourth series. There is also a current ALR series devoted to federal issues.

Citators   These sources are both case finders and a means of verifying the authority and current status of an opinion. The Shepard's Citator System notes, in abbreviated style, each instance in which one case has been cited by another case. There are different sets of Shepard's citators for different courts and jurisdictions. Most firms will own some Shepard's citators, and perhaps other, topical citators as well. "Shepardizing"—determining the treatment afforded a particular case by the courts—is a skill required of many paralegals. Your librarian can assist you in the accurate use of citators.

Treatises, Texts, and Looseleaf Publications

Treatises, texts, and looseleaf publications are another major component of the law firm library. These are considered secondary sources of law and vary from multivolume sets to single monographs. Their purpose is to explain or amplify a single topic or area of the law (e.g., *Attorneys' Textbook of Medicine, Georgia Automobile Insurance Law, Employee Non-Competition Law*). Most are supplemented through regular, periodic filing of updating material, pocket parts, or supplementary pamphlets. Some titles simply publish revised editions every few years.

Court Rules, Form Books, and Jury Instructions

Court rules, form books, and jury instructions are publications found on most library shelves. These can be limited to a few volumes containing local court rules or might include entire banks of shelves with sets of books devoted to standardized forms for many legal purposes, all depending on the scope of the firm's practice.

Periodicals

Periodicals are another important secondary legal source and may occupy a prominent part of the collection. These range from serious, in-depth, academic law review articles to bar journals and publications, newspapers, and newsletters—thanks to desktop publishing—on every imaginable topic. Some periodicals may be bound at the end of every year or so; others are kept in looseleaf notebooks or in file boxes. Most legal periodicals have annual indexes, and many may be accessed through general indexes (such as *Index to Legal Periodicals* or *Current Law Index*, available in subscription form or through an on-line database).

Encyclopedias, Dictionaries, and Directories

These are other legal resources basic to most libraries. There are two well-known legal encyclopedias—*Corpus Juris Secundum* (or CJS) and *American Jurisprudence 2d* (or Am. Jur.). Like regular encyclopedias, they offer a general overview of a subject and are frequently a starting point for research. There are some state-specific encyclopedias as well. Virtually every law library has either Black's or Ballentine's law dictionary, and there may be other, topical ones. Look in the reference section. The most prevalent directory of lawyers is the multivolume set by Martindale-Hubbell. There are sixteen volumes at present covering the United States (plus four volumes dealing with international law-yers and a digest of laws), and several states are covered in each. For every state, there are two listings, one alphabetical and one by city. The first gives basic in-formation in coded abbreviations about individual lawyers and law firms—date of birth, bar admission date, college and law school attended. The second, and much larger section, is advertising by law firms, with in-depth biographical information about their lawyers and the areas of law in which they specialize.

Nonlegal Resources

Nonlegal resources can be found to some extent in every library. Some of these may be familiar from your school or public library experience. Dictionar-ies, almanacs, atlases, directories of all types, and bibliographies are usually found in the reference section. There may be a selection of local and national telephone and city directories. In addition, there may be a good many nonlegal, industry-related materials concerning the type of clients that the firm services, such as annual reports of companies or medical texts.

The Law Librarian

It is important to understand the role of the law firm librarian, because his knowledge and expertise will be invaluable to you. Remember, they are the ex-perts! Most law firm librarians have, at a minimum, an M.L.S. (Master of Li-brary Science) degree, and some have a law degree as well. (See Figure 9-2.) Some of the responsibilities of a librarian or his staff are:

1. To provide research assistance, including online computer database searches.
2. To recommend and purchase library materials required by the firm and to see that the collection is up-to-date and grows with the practice.
3. To perform daily and weekly library maintenance functions, such as filing supplements and looseleaf services, routing periodicals and other library materials, shelving, and binding periodicals.
4. To catalog and process new acquisitions and maintain a catalog of the col-lection.
5. To handle interlibrary loans with other law firms or area libraries.
6. To organize and index the firm's internal work product in its various forms, such as legal memoranda, expert witnesses and other deposition files, microforms, brief banks, and any other documents the firm deems useful.
7. To provide library orientation for new attorneys and paralegals.

FIGURE 9-2 A law librarian can be a tremendous help to paralegals in performing effective and efficient research.

8. To keep attorneys and paralegals informed of recent acquisitions, new sources of information, and other developments.

9. To plan space requirements that take into consideration future expansion of the library collection.

10. To perform library bookkeeping/accounting chores, including approving and paying invoices and statements.

11. To create bibliographies and other library utilization aids.

The importance of having a good working relationship with the librarian and his staff cannot be overemphasized. Here are a few things to remember:

Be a considerate library patron. Do not remove reference materials from the library. Follow checkout procedures. (See Figure 9-3.) Return items promptly. Reshelve your books and leave a clean workspace when you leave the library.

Do not ask the librarian to do your work for you. Learn what services your library and its staff customarily provide. In general, a librarian will help you find the information you seek or the specific resource that contains it. If extensive research is required to extract the needed information, that is probably your job. In addition, because of staff limitations, most libraries cannot be expected to act as a copy service for documents or cases. Sometimes, in some firms, the line between the duties of a paralegal and a librarian is a little blurred. To avoid conflict, communicate with your library staff before making broad assumptions.

FIGURE 9-3 Checkout procedures keep track of law books at all times.

The Law Office Manager as Office Librarian

Some smaller firms do not have the funds to hire a full-time or even part-time librarian to maintain and update the library. This task, as one can imagine, is imperative to support the proper practice of law. One cannot rely on outdated statutes or regulations when practicing law. Without effective library administration, valuable time is wasted, and the firm potentially exposes itself to malpractice liability as well as professional embarrassment.

In smaller firms, the task of updating a library often falls to the office administrator or a paralegal. To effectively administer the library, the office administrator or paralegal needs to have at least a working knowledge of the law and the particular publications needed for practicing the type of law in which the firm specializes. For example, most firms would want to have a copy of the statutes for the state in which the firm is located, as well as the case law for that jurisdiction. If the firm specializes in tax law, bankruptcy, or some other exclusively federal topic, copies of the United States Code and relevant reports are probably essential. For litigation practices, the Federal Rules of Civil Procedure and the Federal Rules of Criminal Procedure, as well as local court rules, are also required.

If you are delegated the responsibility of maintaining the library, use the following guidelines:

1. Send a memorandum to the managing partner outlining the types of references you believe are essential for the practice area, or, alternatively, ask for her suggestions. Elicit suggestions from others in the firm as well.

2. Call the vendor/publisher of the books to determine the price of updates and when updates are provided.

3. Compare the cost of using a computer-assisted legal research system, such as WESTLAW, LEXIS, or CD-ROM, with the cost of obtaining new hard-copy print material.

4. Learn how the update volumes work. When new volumes or supplements are forwarded, detailed instructions on how to update the material is always provided. Read the instructions before attempting to update the material. If you are unsure about what you are doing, contact the publisher, who can often walk you through the process. (After all, they want to keep you as a customer!)

5. Reserve time to organize materials. One of the problems you will often encounter is that people using the library will not reshelve books. You can rant, rave, and threaten murder, most often with no response. Therefore, you should set aside some time each week, or better yet daily, to have someone reshelve materials. Make sure if someone is still using materials that a note is left not to reshelve those items.

6. Take pride in the library. Create and maintain a clean, comfortable, well-organized space to aid the attorneys and paralegals in their work.

Computer Research

Computer-assisted legal and nonlegal research is rapidly becoming indispensable in many law firms. LEXIS or WESTLAW, or both, are services commonly found even in small firms. In addition to these leaders, there are a growing number of other online database services available to law firms. Some are legal in nature, such as Veralex, Information American, or ABA Net; others are nonlegal, such as Dialog, Vu-Text, Dow-Jones News Retrieval, or CompuServe. These databases may contain online versions of sources available in print. The firm may decide it is more practical or efficient to access an online service than to own the actual volumes. Various vendors offer databases that are indexing and abstracting tools only; others are full-text. Search techniques vary widely, and assistance from a reference librarian is advisable.

Library Organization

Typically, law library materials are classified and catalogued according to the classification scheme used by the Library of Congress. In many instances, however, the small- to medium-sized collection will be grouped by general subject area—bankruptcy, real estate, tax. The familiar card catalog is rapidly being

---

ON POINT

REM, 90210

Michael Stipe, lead singer for the band REM, is writing a new song based on an injustice he has read about. Michael's friend Mitch is a partner at the law firm of Later, Fer & Sure, and Mitch has given Michael access to the law library so he can do his research.

As Michael enters the library at the law firm, he sees several associates and asks for help to save him time. Luke and Kelly tell Michael that their approach to research is to "just kinda look around and hope you find something helpful. It's nice to just hang in this cool library," they tell him. Brenda is listening to Pearl Jam on the CD-ROM: "You mean you can use this computer to find cases, too?" she exclaims. Brandon tells Michael that the law librarian can really help with research, "but since I've only been here for eight months, I haven't had a chance to meet her yet."

Exasperated at this lack of intellectual intensity, Michael calls his friend, attorney Moon Zappa, at Zappa, Zappa & Zappa. "C'mon over here," Moon tells him. "Dweezil and I have set up this killer library and you'll be able to find whatever you want easily and quickly. It's really a drag when your resources aren't organized."

Michael hangs up and prepares to go to the Zappa firm. "Frank would be proud," he thinks, and heads out the door.

---

replaced by a computer-generated system, and you may find an online version at your firm. With a little practice, you will be able to search by title, author, or subject with no difficulty.

Other Law Office Systems

The foregoing sections discussed the office system of greatest importance to the paralegal, the law library. Naturally, there exist many systems in each office, which structure that organization and, presumably, propel it toward its goals. The following sections describe some additional systems that are used in law firms and are relevant to the paralegal.

Committees

In most firms, depending upon the size, there are a number of committees, such as business development, summer associate program, associate orientation, forms, newsletter, CLE, library, and so on. The recruitment committee, for example, reviews résumés and recommends people for interviews, whereas the forms committee reviews and standardizes forms for firm use. You may be asked to assist committee members from time to time. Acquaint yourself fully with the overall goals of the committees, respond promptly, and offer to "go the extra mile." Committee work is a great way to make a real contribution to the firm, even though it is nonbillable. It is also a way to increase your own knowledge and exposure. If you want to gain more challenge and responsibility in your work, you will want to show your employer that you have the skills, ability, and drive to warrant those added responsibilities.

Pro Bono Work

One approach to fulfilling the social responsibility of the legal profession is to implement an effective pro bono policy. *Pro bono* refers to legal work that is performed for free or for a substantially reduced fee. Many commentators on the legal profession believe that the law has not fulfilled its commitment to the economically disadvantaged, and has shunned those who are most in need of yet most alienated from the legal system. Performing pro bono work is one way in which legal professionals can fulfill this moral imperative. Developing and implementing an effective pro bono policy enables the law firm to meet this need while still maintaining a focus on its own business and economic survival.

One trend that might be on the horizon is mandatory reporting of pro bono work. Although most states encourage pro bono work, Florida took a bold step in 1993 by coupling a mandatory reporting provision with a requirement that lawyers provide at least 20 hours of pro bono work per year to the poor or contribute $350 to a legal aid program. Though few have problems with the aspirational goals underlying pro bono work, some believe that the public reporting requirement is unnecessarily coercive. The majority of commentators, however, believe that the Florida rule will withstand the test of time and will become the blueprint for other states as they attempt to make legal services more accessible to the poor.

The pro bono policy in Figure 9-4 is an example of a private firm's approach to providing legal services to those who are least able to afford them.

Firm-Sponsored Seminars

Many law firms sponsor client-development seminars several times per year. These seminars serve a valuable marketing function, in that they advertise the law firm, and they might also be a source of continuing legal education (CLE) credits, which are required for attorneys and recommended for paralegals. The paralegal is often asked to assist in producing program materials.

PRO BONO POLICY

In 1975, the American Bar Association House of Delegates stated that, "The basic responsibility of each lawyer engaged in the practice of law [is] to provide public interest legal services" without fee, or at a substantially reduced fee, in one or more of the following areas: property law, civil rights, public rights law, charitable organization representation, and administration of justice. This resolution was later formalized into 6.1 of the ABA Model Rules of Professional Conduct, which states as follows:

> A lawyer should render public interest legal service. A lawyer may discharge this responsibility by providing professional services at no fee or a reduced fee to persons of limited means or to public service or to charitable groups or organizations by service and activities improving the law, the legal system or the legal profession, and by financial support for organizations that provide legal services to persons of limited means.

In 1988, the American Bar Association House of Delegates passed a resolution calling for all attorneys to devote 50 hours per year of legal services and other public service activities that serve those in need or improve the law, the legal service system, or the legal profession.

The Georgia Supreme Court's Commission on Professionalism also emphasizes the importance of public service. As part of the "Lawyers' Creed" drafted by this commission, all lawyers on the Georgia Bar are asked to affirm that:

> To the public and our system of justice, I offer service. I will strive to improve the law and our legal system, to make the law and our legal system available to all, and to seek the common good with the representation of my clients.

This same commission also proposed a specific aspirational ideal as follows:

> As to the public and our systems of justice, I will aspire:
> ... to provide the pro bono representation that is necessary to make our system of justice available to all.

Drew Eckl and Farnham recognizes this commitment as identified by both the ABA and the Georgia Bar Association and hereby formalizes this commitment.

Definition of Pro Bono

Drew Eckl & Farnham encourages its attorneys to meet the obligations as identified in the ABA and Georgia guidelines as stated above. In meeting this commitment, Drew Eckl & Farnham defines "pro bono" in the same terms as the ABA. Specifically:

> ... providing professional services at no fee or a reduced fee to persons of limited means or to public service or charitable activities improving the law, the legal system, or the legal profession, and by financial support for organizations that provide legal services to persons of limited means.

The Firm recognizes the following organizations within the state of Georgia as potential sources of pro bono work. They are:

—The Atlanta Volunteer Lawyers Foundation
—The Saturday Morning Lawyers Program
—Legal Clinic for the Homeless
—The Truancy Project
—One Thousand Lawyers for Justice

FIGURE 9-4 An example of a firm's pro bono policy

This list may be amended at any time upon approval of the managing partners or by the Pro Bono Coordinator (to be defined below).

Recognition

This Firm hereby adopts the aspirational goals as stated by the ABA that each attorney dedicate 50 hours per year of its time to pro bono work as defined above. Recognizing that the commitment of such time may call for services above and beyond a lawyer's already burdensome work load, the Firm acknowledges that specific recognition should be given of this contribution. The Firm proposes to acknowledge this recognition in two ways.

First, and foremost, the Firm encourages the continued use of the separate pro bono billable code (0001.10008) for the recording of all pro bono work. The Firm further commits to acknowledge pro bono contribution in an associate's evaluation. This will be treated as a separate category from the current general discussion of "non-billable" contribution.

Second, in recognition of the competing time demand upon an attorney, 25 hours each year will be allowed as an off-set of an attorney's billable hour goal.

Coordination of Pro Bono

The supervising partner(s) will act as pro bono coordinator and will be responsible for the following duties:

1. to monitor generally the acceptance of pro bono engagements;

2. to serve as a contact in the Firm for various public interest organizations, such as those set out above;

3. to seek attorneys and paralegals who are willing to handle specific pro bono matters;

4. to identify and evaluate projects which are opportunities to use the special legal skills of the Firm;

5. to provide encouragement to, and recognition of, the pro bono efforts of individual attorneys in the Firm;

6. to evaluate the extent to which the Firm is meeting its pro bono goals;

7. to develop and implement administrative policies with regard to the opening, staffing and supervision of pro bono assignments within the Firm; and,

8. to report on a quarterly basis to the Managing Partners with regard to the above seven listed duties.

PLEASE NOTE: Continued work on a pro bono matter(s) <u>must</u> be approved by the Supervising Partner(s) <u>and</u> the Co-Managing Partners as soon as it appears that this work will result in the inability to meet the billable hour goal.

FIGURE 9-4 *(continued)*

Additionally, paralegals often act as firm representatives at the seminars, allowing considerable client contact. It is important to dress and act professionally any time you are representing your firm. (See Figure 9-5.)

DREW, ECKL & FARNHAM

LEGAL
90
FORUM

September 27, 1990
Sheraton Century Center Hotel
Atlanta

IV. PROPERTY SECTION

▲ 1:05-1:30 p.m.
"Who You Gonna Call When they Send the Bill to You?"
Pollution/Contamination and Property Insurance.
Clayton H. Farnham

▲ 1:30-1:55 p.m.
"Building Codes in the Rebuilding Process: The 'Original' or the 'Improved' Model?"
Kenneth A. Hindman

▲ 1:55-2:20 p.m.
"Oh, Mr. Wilson, Vito is Here and He Wants His Money Now!" Or, Dealing With Claims of Third Party Lienholders.
John P. Reale

▲ 2:20-2:45 p.m.
"We Have Ways to Make You Talk." The Insured's Duty to Cooperate.
Daniel C. Kniffen

▲ Break – 2:45-3:00 p.m.

▲ 3:00-3:25 p.m.
"When the Economy Burns Your Insured" Business Interruption Claim in a Recessionary Economy
H. Michael Bagley

▲ 3:25-3:50 p.m.
"The Hijacked Insurer: Direct Claims on Cargo Losses."
Paul W. Burke

▲ 3:50-4:15 p.m.
"Finding Fraud During Your Investigation: Do You Fight It, Ignore It, or Just Despair"
Barbara Jo Call

▲ 4:15-4:50 p.m.
"The Surge of Claims After the Storm: Hugo Revisited."
Charles R. Beans

V. WORKERS' COMPENSATION SECTION

▲ 1:05-1:30 p.m.
"Allergic to Work: Occupational Disease."
David A. Smith

▲ 1:30-1:55 p.m.
"Malignant Claims: The Accidental Disease."
H. Michael Bagley

▲ 1:55-2:20 p.m.
"Recent Appellate Decisions and Other Tales From Beyond"
John G. Blackmon, Jr.

▲ 2:20-2:45 p.m.
"Pigeonholing – A Communicable and Frequently Fatal Disease of Lawyers and the Insurance Industry – Four Illustrative Examples."
Charles L. Drew

▲ Break – 2:45-3:00 p.m.

▲ 3:00-3:25 p.m.
"What's New Pussycat? The 1990 Legislation"
John A. Ferguson, Jr.

▲ 3:25-3:50 p.m.
"Posted Panel . . . Use It or Lose It." Retaining Control of Medical.
John C. Bruffey, Jr.

▲ 3:50-4:15 p.m.
"But Your Honor, I Never Saw the Guy Before in My Life!" Or, Liability as a Statutory Employer.
John P. Reale

▲ 4:15-4:50 p.m.
"The Newest Form of Civil Rights – The Americans with Disabilities Act."
Benton J. Mathis, Jr.

▲ 4:20-4:50 p.m.
"Papa Was a Rolling Stone. . .And When He Died, All He Left Us Was a Mess of Dependancy Claims." Death Benefits and Dependancy Under the Workers' Compensation Act.
Daniel C. Kniffen

ADDITIONAL PARKING IS AVAILABLE AT THE **2300 BUILDING** LOCATED DIRECTLY ACROSS THE STREET FROM THE SHERATON. SHUTTLE SERVICE WILL BE PROVIDED.

FIGURE 9-5 A program from a firm-sponsored seminar

Personnel Management

Personnel management encompasses all of the processes, policies, and attitudes that an organization has toward its employees. Each law office has its own character and culture, embodied in the policies and procedures the firm develops and uses, and the way in which the employees are treated is an integral part of the firm's culture.

Personnel management is important for paralegals for two reasons. First, as employees, paralegals must work within the firm's overall approach to personnel management. This approach in many ways determines the prevailing work environment, so it is important to understand the approach toward people that a particular firm takes, to see if it matches your needs as a prospective employee. Second, in many cases paralegals are asked to perform activities that fall into the realm of personnel management. This is most likely to occur in a small or medium-sized firm, because paralegals in those situations might well perform a variety of activities; in larger firms, those tasks would be handled separately by personnel specialists. (See Figure 9-6.)

A paralegal might take on some of the following responsibilities usually associated with personnel management:

- Compliance with federal or state legislation

- Development of personnel policies and job description

- Compensation and benefit management

- Hiring of new personnel

- Continuing education benefits and requirements

- Employee evaluation

- Analysis and implementation of new work approaches

As you assess your own interests, abilities, and career goals, you will learn whether you are attracted to this type of work. If you are, you will want to find a situation where paralegals perform personnel management functions, or you might consider complementing your paralegal skills with more formal training or education in personnel management.

Office Manuals and Handbooks

We have already discussed the necessity of carefully reading your office manual at the commencement of your employment with your firm. A good office manual will include a wide range of information, from employee benefits to working hours to vacations. It will also set forth the various procedures

REQUEST FOR LEAVE OF ABSENCE
UNDER THE FAMILY AND MEDICAL LEAVE ACT

TO BE COMPLETED BY EMPLOYEE:

Employee Name: _Allison Daniel_

Date: _5-1-95_

Date Requested That Leave Commence: _5-15-95_

Duration of Requested Leave: _3 mos._

Purpose of Leave:
_✓_ birth of a child
_____ adoption of a child
_____ placement of a child in foster care
_____ care for the serious health condition of
   _____ parent
   _____ spouse
   _____ child
_____ serious health condition of the employee

Date: _5-1-95_   _Allison Daniel_
                                            Employee Signature

---

TO BE COMPLETED BY EMPLOYER:

CERTIFICATION

   First - Doctor _Peter Jones_   Date _4-16-95_

   Second - Doctor _____   Date _____

   Third - Doctor _____   Date _____

Request for Intermittent or Reduced Leave
   _____ Yes   _✓_ No

   Describe Periods of Requested Intermittent or Reduced Leave __—__
   _____
   _____

Leave Approved: _✓_ Yes   _____ No

Period of FMLA Leave: Dates _5-15_ to _8-15-95_

Description of Leave: _FMLA_

Paid Leave Remaining in Account _60_ Days
Remaining Leave, Unpaid _30_ Days

Date: _5-1-95_   _Deana Masinter_
0941124940.FM   Employer Signature

FIGURE 9-6 A personnel manager processes various leave requests, such as this FMLA form.

utilized by your firm, such as mailing procedures, file closing procedures, and billing procedures. Make sure you read your office manual carefully, as it contains the general rules and parameters that govern your working environment.

In some cases you may be called upon to assist in the writing of an office manual. This is a major project, which takes considerable time, thought, and work. It is also important to get advice relating to any issues that may be construed to be discriminatory.

Appendix B shows a sample table of contents from a law office manual. By reading through this table of contents, you will gain some insight into the kinds of things that may be included in an office manual.

In addition to an office handbook or manual, many firms write and distribute a variety of specialized manuals. Orientation manuals for law clerks and paralegals may include information on local area judges, docket control, special mail procedures, court filing procedures, and rules on obtaining court opinions. Manuals for legal secretaries cover areas such as dealing with clients, general responsibilities, confidentiality, timekeeping, and reading files. The content of these manuals may vary considerably from law firm to law firm, but, regardless of their differences, they are essential in a well-organized, efficient law firm.

Because these manuals contain private, confidential information and are the property of the firm, you should expect to be required to turn in your office manual upon ending your employment, for whatever reason, with the firm. While you are in possession of the office manual, make sure that it does not fall into any unauthorized hands. (See Figure 9-7.)

Paralegal Training Programs

The training procedures a firm uses to orient new paralegals to the firm's policies and procedures represent another system. The completion of paralegal training is not the end of education for the effective legal assistant. Law firms, corporations, and the government all realize that continuing legal education must exist for paralegals as well as attorneys. Firms that make a commitment to their paralegal programs, and to continued paralegal training and development, can expect increased satisfaction and productivity from their paralegals.

There is great variation in the extent of training offered to paralegals by firms. You might get very little guidance, or there may be an elaborate orientation and training effort by the firm. If there is an effective system in place, your goal should be to learn and use that system as expertly as you can. In the absence of a well-organized training program, you may have an opportunity to establish your own training system. This involves organizing all of the procedures you are expected to know, ranging from office procedures to forms to court information to billing information, and learning the procedures for each process. Even if your firm has a thorough training program to help you get acclimated to your position and working environment, you will still want to

```
                      OFFICE HANDBOOK

                    CHECK-OUT REQUEST


       ON  April 26        , 199 2,  I CHECKED OUT A COPY OF THE
DREW, ECKL & FARNHAM HANDBOOK, NO. 747 .  I UNDERSTAND THAT IT IS
MY RESPONSIBILITY TO READ THIS HANDBOOK THOROUGHLY IN ORDER TO
BECOME BETTER INFORMED OF THE FIRM'S POLICIES AND PROCEDURES.

       I ALSO UNDERSTAND THAT THE INFORMATION CONTAINED IN THE
HANDBOOK IS STRICTLY CONFIDENTIAL AND THAT THE HANDBOOK MUST BE
RETURNED TO ADMINISTRATION ON MY LAST WORKING DAY AT THE FIRM.



                      _____
                              SIGNATURE


- - - - - - - - - - - - - - - - - - - - - - - - - - - - - - - -


       ON  April 10        , 199 5,  I RETURNED MY COPY OF THE DREW,
ECKL & FARNHAM HANDBOOK, NO. 747 ,  SINCE I WILL NO LONGER BE
EMPLOYED BY THE FIRM.



                      _____
                              SIGNATURE


RECEIVED BY:

       _____
       ADMINISTRATION
```

FIGURE 9-7   A firm tracks office manuals for security purposes.

actively pursue guidance and responsibilities, rather than passively wait for others to tell you what to do.

One training system that is highly successful is the mentor program. When a new paralegal, whether experienced or just out of school, joins a firm, a mentor is assigned to help that new employee through the first few weeks on the job. The new paralegal may ask a variety of questions, some of which may pertain to legal research, library rules, personality of the firm, and so on. It is the mentor's responsibility to be a friend and a helpmate. (See Figure 9-8.)

Complementing the mentor might be formal or informal training sessions on the use of WESTLAW, LEXIS, or other research tools. Weekly or monthly

FIGURE 9-8 A paralegal receives training on legal research terminal.

newsletters distributed to all paralegals also keep communication open and provide relevant information, such as cases that have been won or settled, or seminars that are available.

Most firms have paralegal manuals that detail the paralegal's responsibilities and the firm's procedures and expectations. These manuals are generally written by experienced paralegals in various departments in the firm and cover a wide range of information, which will help both new and experienced paralegals.

Another effective training activity for paralegals uses monthly luncheon meetings for the entire paralegal staff. At those luncheons, paralegals, attorneys, or hired speakers may discuss a number of areas relevant to the everyday responsibilities of the paralegal. Some topics that might be discussed are:

Document production
New software
Trial preparation techniques
The court system
Cite checking and legal research
Work-product confidentiality

A firm may agree to pay for paralegal seminar programs if the attendees will agree to make a presentation to the paralegal staff as a whole to pass on the information. Others host annual, day-long seminars off premises at which specific topics are discussed by a variety of speakers. Workshops can be held during which study groups work on projects. Paralegals who are trained in a specific area, such as environmental law, may be asked to lead training programs for others within the firm.

Firms now know the importance of cross-training their paralegals and are working hard to develop and provide excellent educational programs on an ongoing basis. This training is not merely helpful for the firm, but also helps the paralegal by equipping him with additional skills and expertise.

The Mailroom

The mailroom is an important law office system because it controls the flow of important legal documents. Law firm mailroom procedures vary. The size of the mailroom and the number of employees depend largely upon the size of the firm. Typically, a room is set aside in a central area specifically for receipt, sorting, and distribution of mail. Each attorney, paralegal, and administrative employee is given a mailbox.

Schedules for mail pickup at the post office, intraoffice deliveries, and pickups and mail runs outside the office are posted and strictly adhered to. The following schedule is typical for a law office mailroom:

8:00 A.M.	Mail pickup from post office
9:00 A.M.	Intraoffice delivery
10:00 A.M.	Intraoffice pickup
10:30 A.M.	Second mail pickup from post office
12:00 NOON	Intraoffice pickup and delivery
3:00 P.M.	Intraoffice pickup and delivery
5:15 P.M.	Last intraoffice pickup

Mailroom personnel deliver and pick up intraoffice mail by use of an "In Box/Out Box" system at each secretary's and paralegal's desk, at the receptionist's work area, or at central mailrooms located on each floor. They might also be responsible for fax pickups, which need to be done often.

Unless the law firm is quite small, mail is generally metered. A mail meter automatically puts in the amount of postage necessary for mailing a particular letter or parcel. This is often more efficient than putting stamps on every piece of mail. If postage stamps are required, the bookkeeping department usually keeps a supply on hand. Sophisticated mail equipment incorporates scales connected electronically to the meter. The mailroom employees can place an envelope on the scale, which then automatically calculates the postage and activates the meter for the correct amount. If the mail equipment is not that sophisticated, a freestanding scale will calculate the amount of postage after taking into consideration the weight, class, zones, and special services. The mailroom attendant then enters that amount into the meter and posts the mail. (See Figures 9-9 and 9-10.)

Another convenient feature on many mail meters is the ability to add postage by telephone, thus avoiding the need to physically take the meter to the post office. If the meter has this feature, the firm must keep money on deposit

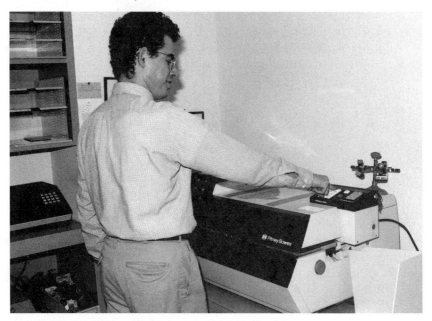

FIGURE 9-9 Mailroom personnel meter outgoing mail ...

with a postage data center. When the meter reflects that the postage is running low, the operator can dial the data center and use phone lines to resupply the meter with postage, thus enabling the mail process to continue without interruption.

The mailroom is also responsible, in most cases, for administering air freight and express mail services. In a law firm, those services are frequently

FIGURE 9-10
... and distribute documents.

required, and requests for those services should be coordinated with the mail-room attendants. A client/matter number should be included on the air freight bill or the express mail form so that a proper charge can be made to the client. Many law firms have their own courier services to deliver and pick up documents, or runners to deliver local mail to other offices or to the courthouse.

Courier Services

In addition to mail systems, law firms often use couriers to deliver materials to clients, courthouses, and other law firms. Many law firms have their own courier services to pick up and deliver their documents. (See Figure 9-11.) Some have runners to deliver local mail or other documents to other offices or to the courthouse. A small firm might use couriers only occasionally; for those situations it probably uses a local courier that charges on a per-trip basis. Larger firms that generate a lot of activity will have a regular courier service to make regular runs to certain locations, such as courthouses in adjoining counties, as well as special-need deliveries. Some firms also use couriers to serve subpoenas for depositions or witness appearances.

Dealing with Vendors

As a business, a law firm uses many materials that are supplied by outside vendors. *Vendors* are companies that make products you use, and their sales representatives naturally want your firm to use their products. The most common vendors you will encounter are law book publisher representatives, but you will also encounter vendors who sell legal forms, copiers, stationery, telephone systems, fax machines, computers, legal software, and so forth. In a large company, a paralegal would probably not order supplies, but in a smaller firm, the task of comparing and ordering supplies and materials might well fall to a paralegal. (See Figure 9-12.)

In today's highly competitive environment, when firms are trying to gain the greatest value for their dollars, it is not unusual for a firm to send a request for proposal (RFP) to a number of different vendors in order to get the most competitive price. This practice is especially common when purchasing expensive items such as computers, computer components, and telephone systems.

Effectively managing the sales representatives who call on your firm will not only make your task easier, by saving time and avoiding hassles, but will also enable you to contribute to the economic bottom line of the firm. By choosing materials effectively, you will be able to maintain the quality of research materials and references (if you have library responsibilities) and of office supplies in

```
┌─────────────────────────────────────────────────────────────────────┐
│                                                                       │
│      DREW ECKL & FARNHAM          Insurance Run (10:00am)    ___     │
│                                   Cobb County Run (12:30pm)          │
│              MLQ                  DeKalb County Run (1:30pm)   X      │
│         COURIER REQUEST           Downtown Run (2:15pm)      ___     │
│                                   Special Request            ___     │
│                                                                       │
│   Requesting Attorney/Legal Assistant #: ___409___   Date: _1/15/95_ │
│                                                                       │
│   Secretary: ___S. Smart___         Court File No. _D-090075_        │
│                                                                       │
│   Client Matter Number: _6890-00945_    Bill Note: _____    │
│                                                                       │
│                                                                       │
│   ___ Pick-up From  Company Name: __Swertz, Fig & Flander__          │
│   ___ Deliver To        Address: ____1000 BankSouth Bldg.____        │
│    X  Round Trip        Suite Number: _1015_____                     │
│                         City: ___Decatur___  Zip Code: _30033_       │
│                         Phone Number: __378-6000__                   │
│            Person(s) To Be Contacted: _Francis Flander_              │
│                                                                       │
│                                                                       │
│   Complete By: _____3:00_____ AM/PM   Date: _1/15/95_             │
│                                                                       │
│   Level of Service Requested: __ 60 Min.  __ 90 Min.  __ 2 Hr. x 3 Hr.│
│                                                                       │
│   ____ Have Document Filed or Recorded                               │
│    X   Have Copies Stamped "Filed", "Received", or "Recorded", and Return Same Day. │
│   ____ Have Copies Stamped "Filed", "Received", or "Recorded", Return to DEF by Mail. │
│   ____ Obtain Copies From Clerk -- Description: _____ │
│                                                                       │
│                                                                       │
│                          INSTRUCTIONS                                │
│   _____  │
│   _____  │
│   _____  │
│   _____  │
│   _____  │
│   _____  │
│   _____  │
│   _____  │
│                                                                       │
│   To Inquire About the Status of a Request, Please Call Your Courier  │
│   Coordinator at 885-6276.                                            │
│                AFTER HOURS CALL 984-7000                              │
│                                                                       │
└─────────────────────────────────────────────────────────────────────┘
```

FIGURE 9-11   An example of an in-house courier request form

general. It is also helpful to develop a positive relationship with suppliers so that your firm is informed of discounts and special deals.

The rapidly growing National Association of Legal Vendors (NALV) is an organization of more than 300 members who engage in publishing, technology, and other services and products for the legal industry. NALV members market

Date 03/02/91   Time 23:35:49

Bachman, Wilson & Juris

Report #0104   Page 0001

A L P H A B E T I C   V E N D O R   L I S T

Starting vendor name: "First"

Ending vendor name: "Last"

Vendor status: Blank = normal   A = always take discount   H = hold payment   N = not to be purchased from

Ven-#	Name Address	Phone-# Contact(s) 1099 data	Type Status	---- Terms ---- Due Disc Disc days days pct	Last purchase Dflt-acct-#	Purchases-YTD Discounts-YTD	Purchased-1st-yr Discounts-1st-yr
2	Court Reporters, Inc. 200 2nd Avenue North Nashville TN 37201	615/244-1306 Susan Marshall 1099 ID: 76-3214568		30 0 .00	01/15/91 6700	.00 .00	1,235.00 .00
1	Federal Express P.O. Box 3461 Memphis, TN 38201-3461	901/344-2222 Jim Arnold		30 0 .00	01/31/91 6010	.00 .00	.00 .00
15	Juris, Inc. 151 Athens Way Nashville, TN 37228	615/242-2870 Molly Boyte Tina Abbey		15 0 .00	02/25/91 6090	200.00 .00	4,600.00 .00
22	Matthew Bender 4051 Winding Way Drive P.O. Box 308 Jersey City, NJ 07231	201/459-3620 Ronald Gergins		30 0 .00	02/11/91 6070	.00 .00	5,900.00 .00
3	Morrison Management Corp Suite 1600 L & C Building Nashville TN 37219	615/741-2000 Jim Ledyard 1099 ID: 86-5632106		30 0 .00	02/25/91 6300	.00 .00	17,000.00 .00

FIGURE 9-12 Vendor list shows information on vendors used by the firm. (Courtesy of Juris, Incorporated.)

to law firms and corporate legal departments and are guided by a high sense of professionalism and ethical standards. The organization also works with groups to plan and organize exhibits and publishes information on trends and developments in the industry.

Office Management Systems: A Summary

A law office is comprised of a number of small systems (in addition to larger systems such as timekeeping or billing) that help the firm run smoothly and help you do your job effectively. When effective systems are in place, you should strive to gain expertise in each of those systems, because they will help you organize and effectively complete your work. If some areas need systemization, you might become involved in reorganizing an area or process. By thus gaining expertise in all of the systems used in your firm, your work will be professional, and your firm's clients will be highly satisfied with the quality of their legal representation.

Key Terms

courier service	mail systems	office manual
firm seminars	mandatory reporting	paralegal training programs
law librarian	requirement	personnel management
law library	mentor program	pro bono work
law library resources	NALV	

Problems and Activities

1. You are in charge of the firm's manual. What matters must you be sure to cover in this manual?

2. List questions that you will need to ask the law librarian before you can use the law library effectively.

3. What firm committees would you like to serve on, and why?

4. Are there any ethical issues involved in a paralegal's relationship with a legal vendor? If so, what are these issues and how would you resolve them?

5. You are a paralegal at a large metropolitan law firm, and you have a personality conflict with the law office administrator who is responsible for all of the management decisions of the firm. What is the most professional way to handle this conflict?

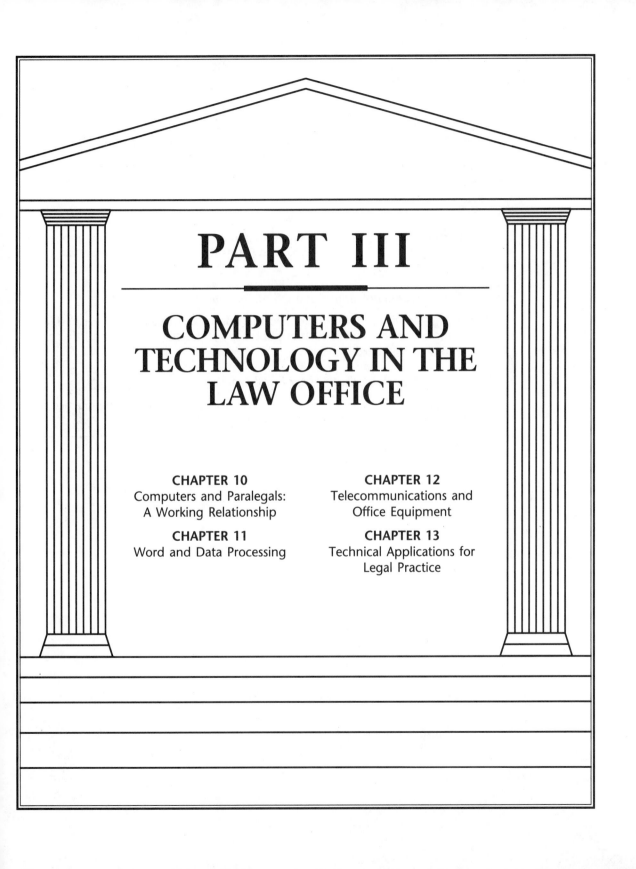

PART III

COMPUTERS AND TECHNOLOGY IN THE LAW OFFICE

PART III OVERVIEW

Chapter 10: Computers and Paralegals: A Working Relationship

An introduction to computer systems, their components, and their capabilities, with an emphasis on the extreme importance to the contemporary paralegal of becoming proficient in using technical applications. An introduction to computer security is also included.

Chapter 11: Word and Data Processing

A comprehensive overview of the purposes and benefits of word and data processing, with an examination of ways in which law firms use word and data processing in their work.

Chapter 12: Telecommunications and Office Equipment

A thorough discussion of telecommunications devices, such as telephones and fax machines, and office equipment, such as photocopy and dictation machines, that are commonly used in legal work.

Chapter 13: Technical Applications for Legal Practice

An overview of technical applications that are geared specifically to the practice of the law. Special features include litigation support and optical imaging.

CHAPTER 10

COMPUTERS AND PARALEGALS: A WORKING RELATIONSHIP

OBJECTIVES

By the completion of this chapter, you should:

- understand the importance of technology to the legal process;

- understand the basic components and abilities of a computer system;

- understand how integral computer skills are to the work and professional development of the paralegal; and

- understand some of the major issues that relate to computer work in general.

Technology in the Law Office: An Introduction

When you decided to begin your paralegal studies, you were probably attracted by the lure of the law: tense courtroom battles, the quest for justice, the search for truth. All of those things happened in the O.J. Simpson trial, and they are certainly appealing aspects of the legal process. In terms of the real work of the law, however, computers and technological applications in the law office will demand much more of your time and interest than the romanticized ideas you see in movies and on television. In fact, the successful paralegal must become highly proficient with the technological innovations that shape the modern law office. To be sure, computers cannot replace humans or the analytical skills that paralegals bring to their work, but computers and technology provide such a significant and powerful tool to improve legal work that the successful legal assistant must learn to use modern technology as an integral part of her work. For the modern paralegal, therefore, a productive working relationship with modern technology is a necessity. Technology provides the tools through which the work of the law proceeds: it is up to you to develop the skills that will enable you to use technical innovations to your advantage. (See Figure 10-1.)

Overcoming Technophobia

If you have not had previous exposure to computers or modern telecommunications, you can easily be baffled. Even if you have had previous exposure, technology is a complex and sometimes intimidating phenomenon, and it is easy to become fearful and frustrated. This frustration can sometimes lead to

FIGURE 10-1
Paralegals must
work productively
with technology.

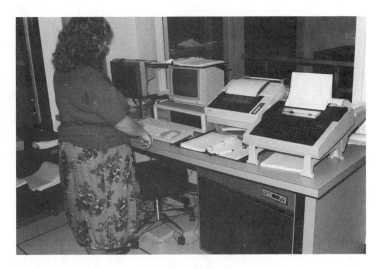

technophobia, a fear of technology, that can cause people to shun technical advances that could help them perform their jobs more efficiently and effectively.

You can overcome technophobia by realizing that, although technology is complicated, it is nonetheless a logical system that can be learned through work and perseverance. Most people find, in using technical advances, that practice and use make for comfort and fluency. (See Figure 10-2.) Therefore, do not let yourself get intimidated by modern technology, but rather make a commitment to spend the time to become technically fluent with the tools of your work. This commitment also entails a recognition that technology is a continually developing and evolving field, and that technical fluency demands continual learning and practice.

FIGURE 10-2
Practice will help
you become
fluent on technical
equipment.

In this chapter you will learn about the basic components of a computer system, and you will learn about some of the issues that arise in the course of using technology. In the following chapters, you will learn about specific applications of computers and technology in the law firm. By the end of this part of the book, you will have been exposed to the major technical applications used in law firms, and you should be confident in your ability to use technology as a working partner in the course of your work.

Computer Systems: An Introduction

A basic computer system consists of hardware and software. *Hardware* refers to the actual physical components; *software* refers to the written instructions or programs that make the hardware perform an intended task. Later in this Part III, you will learn about software packages and applications. Before you can use software, however, you must be familiar with the hardware components of the system. (See Figure 10-3.)

FIGURE 10-3
A typical computer system includes a keyboard, disk drives, monitor, and printer.

Typically, the hardware of a system includes:

- A keyboard and a mouse, to input information

- A monitor, to display information on the screen

- A processing unit, to perform instructions

- Internal storage devices, which give the computer its memory

- Online storage devices, such as hard or floppy disk drives, tape, or CD-ROM

- A printer, to print your documents (hard copy).

A sophisticated system may also include more advanced features and functions, including:

- A modem, which allows the computer to use the telephone lines

- A fax card, which transforms the computer into a fax machine

- A scanner, which allows for the direct input of data from any printed source

- Electronic mail, which allows you to send and receive mail through your computer

- a PC pen or digitizer, which are input devices that allow you to input material without keying it.

There are different levels of hardware systems with different sizes and capabilities. Smaller computers are called *microcomputers;* the IBM Personal Computer (PC) is a typical example of a microcomputer. PCs are widely available and are capable of a tremendous number of functions, and many smaller firms will not have systems larger than the PC (see Figure 10-4). For a larger firm with many users, or for complex litigation involving many documents, the PC may not have the features to be as effective as a larger system.

FIGURE 10-4 A typical PC setup

Mini-computers, which comprise medium-sized computer systems, can be found at many medium- and larger-size law firms. Usually a firm with more than 15 attorneys will have a mini-computer, which allows for simultaneous users and has far greater storage capabilities than PCs. Mini-computers make multiple applications available to a broad range of users; they thereby provide law firms with greater flexibility as well as more computing power. (See Figure 10-5.)

A larger computer system is the *mainframe computer.* The mainframe will be found only in the largest law firms because they are very expensive and require

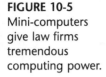

FIGURE 10-5
Mini-computers
give law firms
tremendous
computing power.

extensive overhead to maintain. As you can imagine, their capabilities are tremendous, but so are the costs associated with their upkeep.

Once you are situated in your work, you will learn the technical capabilities of the system used in your office. Traditionally, larger firms have the most sophisticated and advanced features, whereas smaller firms, or the government, will have more basic systems. Because the system you use, and its capabilities, will depend on the environment in which you work, it does not make sense for you to learn every system in case your future employer uses it. Rather, it is important that you learn the basic aspects of working with a computer system, for all systems have basic similarities, and it is important that you familiarize yourself with the range of features available. Complementing this awareness should be your own positive attitude toward technology and your commitment to learn and use technological advances in your work. Thus equipped, you will best be able to develop an effective working relationship with modern technology.

Portable Computers

More and more *portable computers* are being utilized by legal professionals. Portable computers permit legal professionals to have their offices at their fingertips, and transform formerly low-billable or totally unbillable time, such as travelling or waiting in court, into new billable hours. (See Figure 10-6.) This is

FIGURE 10-6 Notebook and laptop computers enable associates to turn an airport waiting lounge into a temporary office.

a result of the increased flexibility, convenience, and productivity that the "laptop" computer affords. Obtaining the best portable computer for your needs is the best way to maximize formerly unbillable time, as well as to give you increased flexibility as to where your work is performed.

Computer technology is rapidly expanding, and the system you use today may be outdated next month. This problem can be minimized with portable computers if the user first determines how she will use the portable technology. By deciding what you want to do with your portable computer, you can determine what software is needed to satisfy those needs. By determining what software is necessary, it is much easier to decide on the appropriate hardware to purchase. For example, if you merely draft documents, you can use almost any portable computer. However, if you need to communicate with your office via e-mail, or to fax from your portable machine, you will need a portable computer with those capabilities. One should also look at battery life, processing speed, and size and quality of screen, as well as something as simple as the size of the keyboard.

There are several types of portable computers. They range from laptops the size of a small briefcase to notebooks and super-notebooks that are literally the size of a notebook. The most impressive new development is the docking station for a notebook computer. After a day on the road, the portable computer can be connected to the desktop computer so valuable data can be transferred. One legal professional may work exclusively from a portable computer, whereas another will have a portable that is compatible with her desktop machine.

In the law, as with other fields, portable computers open the door to the "virtual workplace." Whether laptops and notebook computers remain merely useful tools, or become vehicles of radical changes in the structure of the legal environment, is something that only the future will tell.

Computer Security in the Workplace

Working with computers and technology introduces a new factor into effective office management, that of computer security. *Computer security* refers to physical access to the hardware and telecommunications lines, and to the access of specific data by specific users. This is especially important in legal work because a large amount of confidential information is recorded, and, as discussed earlier, the abuse of confidentiality might be grounds for a malpractice claim.

Computer-related fraud and abuse can take a number of forms. It ranges from theft of the actual equipment, to theft of programs or data, to manipulating input data, to using the computer for nonwork purposes. The first federal crime involving computer use occurred in 1966 when a computer programmer modified a bank's auditing program so that it ignored his personal checking account when checking for overdrafts. Since that time, the types of computer abuse and fraud have multiplied many times—perhaps because computer abuse perpetrators are frequently bright, young, energetic, and motivated people who have the access and skills to defraud the computer. Therefore, firms with computer equipment need to secure their equipment as effectively as possible to neutralize threats to their computer security.

Although total computer security can never be 100 percent guaranteed, a number of safeguards can be implemented to help reduce the risks of loss of privacy and intentional sabotage. The equipment itself should be replete with technical safeguards, such as password requirements and particularized program design. The vendor who supplies the firm's equipment will frequently provide training so that users can effectively implement their security systems. The question of what training is available should always be asked. But the main problem is people. When you work with computers, data, and confidential information, you have an obligation of ethics, honesty, and professionalism that will prevent you from aiding or committing computer abuse or fraud.

Your office will probably have established procedures concerning security, and of course you should become fully aware of your office's procedures and conform fully to them. (See Figure 10-7.) If your office does not have security procedures in place, it is a real opportunity to establish them in order to safeguard your firm's assets. At your workstation, you should always sign off before leaving the area, and conform to the practice established in your environment relative to shutdown procedures at the end of the day. If there are no

FIGURE 10-7
Computer users
should take
precautions to
secure their data.

procedures in place, you may simply power off your workstation and its peripherals, but only after closing up in an orderly manner: closing files properly, updating your backup files, storing disks in appropriate, secure places and actually logging off on the computer.

Choosing Computer Equipment

One function in which you may become involved is choosing computer equipment. You might be in a situation where your firm has virtually no technological capabilities and is trying to convert to computer technology, or you might be in a larger firm that is looking for additional hardware capability or a specialized software package. If you become involved in choosing technical equipment, the following approach will help you:

1. Assess your needs and budget; define what you want and what you are able to spend. Rank and prioritize your needs.
2. Learn about what is available.
3. Contact vendors to get information and demonstration disks so that you can see how the product works.
4. Develop an evaluation procedure involving all relevant people.
5. Make a recommendation based on fulfilling your needs and anticipating future needs and developments.

Getting Organized with Technology

As you can see, the process of integrating the capabilities of technology into the modern law firm is an extremely complex one. However, there is no doubt that technology has revolutionized the way in which lawyers and paralegals go about their work. New changes and developments will further alter the technological landscape as it continues its evolving partnership with the law firm.

The following guest editorial, although focusing on case management systems, provides an excellent overview of the thinking processes that must precede use of technology in the law firm. Mr. Keane also refers to the vast array of products available, as well as to the range of capabilities these products possess. His discussion certainly embraces the notion that lawyers and paralegals must become proficient in using technology if they are to remain valuable and productive in the modern law office.

G U E S T   E D I T O R I A L

It's a "Matter" of Getting Litigation Organized

James Keane

James Keane, an independent consultant in litigation and case management systems, is president of James Keane Company in North Potomac, Maryland. He, along with Ronald Staudt, also authored Litigation Support Systems: An Attorney's Guide, 2nd Edition (*Clark, Boardman & Callaghan, 1992 and updates). He can be reached on the Internet at keanej@attmail.com.*

Larger corporate law departments have been automating for years. They are now building networks for their entire staff, perhaps as part of a larger corporate network. For the corporate counsel who is un-automated, or who has a rag-tag collection of PCs, printers, word processors and fax machines—piled up via piecemeal budget requests and endless politicking—it's time to develop a systematic strategy for automation. It will take several months just to assess your automation needs, learn about the data processing environment in your corporation and develop a strategic plan and budget.

Implementation may take several years, particularly by proceeding in several phases. Start with a core program, such as word processing and calendaring, to get lawyers and staff over the hump in the learning curve. While the most popular legal programs are for word processing and legal research, the common factor in a lawyer's work is text. Many so-called "data base" programs were designed for address lists and inventories, which have relatively uniform entries and simple text.

Legal data bases have lots of unruly text and some demanding requirements. Text handling requires Lexis-like search tools and the ability to create very professional-looking reports with features such as text columns and word-wrapping for paragraphs. For corporate counsel, the paradigm report is a list of outstanding litigation matters and contingent liabilities for the Board of Directors. The list will contain free-form case descriptions, numerical ranges, sub-totals and totals.

A case management system covers a broad range of information. It has to strike a balance between demographics, tracking and planning on one hand, while the other hand assesses risks and manages case finances. The following charts list the range of information and reports needed to drive an effective case management effort.

Case Management Systems—Information Categories (1 of 2)

CASE PROFILES
- case name
- filing date
- people (lawyers, judge, client contact)
- jurisdiction and venue
- product or business line
- case description

STATUS AND PLANNING
- current status
- key upcoming events
- outstanding tasks/assignments
- past activities
- closing date
- win-loss-settled results

ASSESSMENTS

MANAGEMENT

While these categories cover basic tracking and mere bean-counting, the next set of categories assesses the case risks and the management of case finances. The ad damnum clause or the damage claim may be for a sum certain in a commercial transaction or a vague million dollar shot-in-the-dark for product liability claims. But the lawyer is asked to do more than provide dollar guesses for potential settlements, downside risks projections and insurance reserves. The concept of contingent liability calls on the lawyer to determine the probability of a negative outcome and advise the client on how to proceed.

Several programs handle a mix of textual paragraphs (status and assessment), short items (lawyers assigned) and numbers (damages/settlement/expenses). These functions are typically combined in custom programs or data-base management systems used as application generators.

Case Management Systems—Information Categories (2 of 2)

CASE PROFILES

STATUS AND PLANNING

ASSESSMENT/BUDGET DATA
- lawyer's impressions and evaluations
- ad damnum clause
- potential for settlement
- downside risk
- reserves/insurance
- contingent liability assessment

MANAGEMENT REPORTS
- budgets
- plan vs. actual
- counsel hours and fees
  - current and projected
  - cumulative and trends
- expenses
- ratios
  - expenses as % of fees
  - cost vs. risk (recovery)
  - partner : associate : paralegal
  - to comparable cases
  - inside to outside

Data-Base Management Systems

Programs such as dBASE IV, R:BASE, Paradox, Revelation, SyBASE, and ORACLE can handle much more complex files than INMAGIC, Q&A and AskSam. Instead of repeating each lawyer's name, law firm address and phone number in each case record, these programs let you create and link separate lists or tables. Thus, 20 case profiles might refer to a lawyer by name, but the full data on the firm is only listed once in a separate table of lawyers and firms. The two tables "relate" to each other and can behave as separate data bases. Systems that can handle multiple data bases and relationships between tables are called Database Management Systems (DBMS) or relational systems.

Because they handle inherently more complex operations, these are not packages you can pull out of the box and operate in a day. They are really best used by trained personnel, if not qualified programmers, to create unique applications, such as an inventory and check-out system for a video store, or a system to manage a more complex skein of data and relationships encountered in a corporate law department.

In the corporate world, ORACLE and SyBASE dominate the mainframe and minicomputer market. But it does not follow that private law firms or corporate counsel use these programs. Indeed, among the 500 top law firms these corporate favorites barely make the list. The dominant relational DBMS programs (in 127 responses to the Chicago-Kent Annual Legal Software Survey) are:

- Paradox (27.8%)
- dBASE (21.2%)
- R:BASE (11.9%)
- FoxPro (9.0%)
- Revelation (5.3%)
- SyBASE (2.6%)
- Oracle (2.0%)

Typically paralegals with modest training in INMAGIC or Q&A can set up a straightforward but simple data base of matters and cases, or lawyers' schedules, or deposition digests. Unless they have significant computer training or consulting assistance, it is asking too much to ask them to create complex data bases or applications using a DBMS.

By the same token, a trained DBMS specialist cannot just waltz into a general counsel's office and set up a comprehensive system using a DBMS or a higher level programming language. They need senior lawyers' and paralegals' collective knowledge of what the corporate law department does. It takes several months to a year for a law school or paralegal graduate to figure out his or her job; it is presumptuous to expect a programmer without legal experience to program functions from everyone's job in several months.

Developing a complex application is a marriage of system design and substantive skills, frequently involving a multidisciplinary team. Insist on knowing the background of any corporate programmer assigned to set up a system. Find out if he or she has worked with other legal organizations

and his or her experience, particularly with text-oriented applications rather than DBMS programs. If they say they can set up a system in few weeks—run—don't walk to nearest exit. Vendors of the legal speciality systems have spent years trying to program serviceable systems, tested on real matters, with suitable documentation and help screens.

Litigation Support (Documents and Transcripts)

The Chicago-Kent School of Law Annual Legal Software Survey reported that more than 90 percent of the top 500 law firms now use computers for litigation.

The leading transcript packages in this group showed a different pattern:

IIT 1992 Chicago-Kent Large Law Firm Survey
Top Litigation Software % Reporting Some Use
(Transcript Databases—with Document Results)

TRANSCRIPTS	DOCUMENTS
DiscoveryZX (32.5%)	DiscoveryZX (17.2%)
ZyIndex (23.8%)	ZyIndex (19.9%)
SUMMATION (23.2%)	SUMMATION (21.9%)
DiscoveryBase (11.3%)	DiscoveryBase (6.0%)
BRS/Search (9.9%)	BRS/Search (16.6%)
INMAGIC (9.3%)	INMAGIC (26.5%)
Folio VIEWS (7.3%)	Folio VIEWS (11.9%)
CATLINKS (6.6%)	CATLINKS (2.6%)
AskSam (2.6%)	AskSam (8.6%)
Ipso Facto (2.6%)	Ipso Facto (0.7%)

"Integrated" Litigation Support Programs

Several programs handle both transcripts and document data bases together. SUMMATION allows a single search across the structured document data base and the transcript file, complete with line numbers and the complete full text. BRS/Search and Folio VIEWS permit the user to break up the lengthy transcripts programmatically into page size "chunks," which they can search in conjunction with document summaries. ZyIndex and DiscoveryZX were designed as full-text retrieval packages. They can combine the two somewhat distinct functions of managing documents and transcripts by treating the document summary as just another full text file.

DiscoveryBase has a two step design. The user first searches the document records. If the document record has a link to a transcript, the user presses a function key to view and browse the full text. Once in the full text, the user can then search any and all DiscoveryZX full-text documents or transcripts.

The two Discovery packages overlap each other. Counting the DiscoveryBase transcript package as the equivalent of DiscoveryZX, these two companion packages are reported in use at a 33.5 percent (down from 41.7 percent in 1991) of the top 500 law firms.

SUMMATION has a very broad range of tools for the litigator, but is more suitable for small to medium cases. It cannot handle cases with hundreds of thousands of documents. It has built-in tools for data entry global editing, lawyers' notes, transcript cleanup, true full-text browsing and reports.

BRS has limited tools for data entry, true full-text browsing, annotations and reporting. Its microcomputer UNIX version has extraordinary search tools and capacity for very large cases on powerful microcomputers with up to five concurrent users. BRS also has a NOVELL LAN version. Because of its mainframe and UNIX roots, BRS is already a multiuser system that runs on mini- and larger computers. BASIS and INQUIRE are well-respected litigation support programs for larger computers, but they do not run on microcomputers. SUMMATION and DiscoveryBase only run on microcomputers.

DiscoveryBase is a more recent market entrant. Its core underlying product is the venerable DiscoveryZX, for a long time the most popular transcript management program. Authorized "Discovery" court reporters promote the ZX package heavily by offering it for free with a disk copy of their transcripts. Under the new management of Stenograph Legal Services Corp., DiscoveryZX has been joined with a document management program. This combined package is DiscoveryBase, which has data-entry facilities, but limited reporting features and only a two-step integration between documents and transcripts.

The up-and-coming trend in litigation support is the ability to see a computer image of a document in lieu of hardcopy or a microfilm image. DiscoveryBase has a very limited but easy-to-use imaging capability. Some of the major litigation support vendors provide software for imaging with BRS. SUMMATION has just released a limited image display and print capability using inVzn software on re-writable Compact Disks (CDR). The key to evaluating imaging is the ability to print images of all the search results with a single command. It can become very tedious to tag or print individual pages or documents if the search uncovers 100 or 200 items. This is important because the critical payoff of imaging is the ability to sort and print a witness book without having to handle (and misfile) multiple paper copies.

Calendar Systems (Ticklers and Due Dates)

There are more than 40 computer packages that address the problem of scheduling due dates and ticklers for lawyers. Some of these run only in conjunction with broader systems for law firm timekeeping. According to publicly listed prices, they range from $39.95 to $1,000 for single-user systems, typically (but not necessarily) with more features for higher-priced systems.

Network versions run from $299 to $2,500 for unlimited site licenses, though some systems cost even more with charges based on numbers of users. Some of these systems include timekeeping and interoffice electronic mail functions.

Volume Case Management Systems

A more interesting group of packages has come to call itself "Case Management" systems. These attempt to schedule events and create pleadings and other repetitive documents from an underlying database of information about the parties, insurance companies, investigators and insurance agents.

By and large these packages have been aimed at the personal injury lawyers (plaintiff and defense). Indeed, some of them offer generic forms for worker's compensation cases, automobile injury and the like. If you have a specialized in-house practice group that handles volumes of personal injury cases, these may be good candidates to purchase.

It is possible to adapt this software to corporate counsel's needs, but that means setting up built-in schedules and document assembly rules for each practice area you want to manage. Typical purchase-installation costs for this class of system runs from $5,000 to $10,000 and higher.

Fully integrated corporate counsel systems pull a number of disparate elements into one cohesive framework. The base cost and price differential between the systems are driven by "make or buy" competitive forces. Are they reasonable? If they work, if they are properly installed and run with care and precision, they can dramatically increase your management control and information handling capability. What is that worth to your company?

Plan, Plan, PLAN

It's critical to identify the number of users, data volumes and the type of software you need. Buying too many computers and too many packages can overwhelm your group. The reverse of this condition is probably driving the impulse to forge ahead, namely, the law department is already overwhelmed by too much data.

The solution is not computers, and more of them, but a realistic plan, that starts with manageable pieces and allows for growth at a pace commensurate with your needs. ▮

Technology in the Law Office: A Summary

Contemporary paralegal work is so entwined with computers and technology that it would not be unrealistic to see a paralegal as an information processor within the legal process. In both your work within the law office, such as timekeeping or records maintenance, and your work within the legal system, such as legal research or client development, you will be making extensive use of technology, and your use will increase as time goes on. Therefore, one of the keys to effective paralegalism is the ability of the paralegal to learn and use what technology has to offer. A positive and productive relationship with technology can be established by understanding and appreciating how paralegals and technology form a working partnership, by becoming fluent in the basics of computer technology, and by having the curiosity and interest to learn new technical applications and expand your own technical abilities and horizons. In your paralegal studies, you should take a basic computer course and learn to operate a PC and commonly used applications, such as WordPerfect 6.1. Later, you will want to expand your technical expertise. Equipped with technical skills and the desire to learn developing technologies, you will not only be able to make the most productive contribution to your law firm, but you will also be giving yourself skills that will enhance your own value and professional development.

278 PART III COMPUTERS AND TECHNOLOGY IN THE LAW OFFICE

Key Terms

computer security	mainframe	personal computer (PC)
computer system	network	portable computer
laptop	notebook computer	technophobia

Problems and Activities

1. Assess your skills and attitudes relative to the use of technology, especially computers. If you are fearful, what accounts for your fears, and how can you overcome them?

2. Determine if your program includes at least one general course in computer information systems. If it does not, investigate other ways in which you can increase your computer literacy.

3. What types of computer software would be most advantageous to your work as a paralegal?

4. How can you become more productive in your work as a paralegal if you have access to a portable computer?

5. Your law firm asks you, in your role as a law office administrator, to check out new equipment and programs that will increase the efficiency of its practice. How would you go about researching and gathering your information? What would be important areas to study?

CHAPTER 11

WORD AND DATA PROCESSING

OBJECTIVES

By the completion of this chapter, you should:

- understand basic word processing functions;
- understand the capabilities of an integrated system; and
- understand the basics of data processing and its applications in a law office.

Word Processing: An Introduction

To say that word processing has fundamentally changed the way offices manage written information would be an understatement. The significance of word processing to the office, and the law office in particular, is matched only by the pervasiveness of word processing in offices. For the paralegal, whose work involves internal and external communication to all members of the legal team and to clients, word processing is the most important way to communicate in writing. Additionally, word processing will give you additional capabilities to use in other phases of your work. Word processing is the vehicle through which your work can get done efficiently and professionally.

Word processing is a software package that, when used in conjunction with appropriate hardware, gives you certain writing and graphics capabilities. A basic system consists of a keyboard, a monitor, a processor, disk drives, and a printer. Laptop computers, which are portable yet extremely powerful, also have word processing capabilities. Sometimes the word processor will be a popular brand, such as WordPerfect, or it might be a customized program as part of an integrated system. Whatever the word processor, it will have certain features in common with most word processors, and it will also have its own method of accessing those features. For example, to save a document in one system you might press Ctrl-S, whereas in another you might use a function key. Therefore, if you understand the basic logic of word processing, you will be able to learn other systems easily, should it become necessary.

Paralegals typically use the word processor in a variety of ways (see Figure 11-1). All correspondence and memos will be done in your word processing program. You may also store name and address records, as well as various forms. Standard forms can be stored, to be customized later according to the needs of a particular client.

FIGURE 11-1   Legal assistants use word processing for a variety of tasks.

Simple and Integrated Word Processors

In a small law office that does not have the sophisticated technology of a large firm, you might find a simple word processing system, perhaps running on a single personal computer (PC). In a larger firm, you might find a totally integrated system in which word processing is linked to spreadsheets and legal research to produce presentation graphics. In either case, the physical components may be very similar; the software creates the great differences in capability. As a paralegal, you will need excellent word processing skills even if you have a secretary who inputs information into a computer for you. The more you know about and can use the capabilities of your word processing system, the more uses you will find for it.

Basic Word Processing Functions

At its most basic level, a word processor is an electronic typewriter, and it can be used for all functions associated with typewriting. All word processors enable you to write, edit, and modify the text, as well as save it so that it can be used at a future time. Another typical feature is a spell checker, which goes through your document looking for spelling errors. Grammar programs indicate places with faulty grammar throughout your document. Most word processors will also enable you to merge texts, print in various type styles (known as *fonts*), and perform some graphics functions, such as line and box drawings.

More sophisticated word processing functions can be found in larger and more powerful programs. For example, Symphony and WordPerfect are fully integrated software packages, which include the capability to incorporate spreadsheet functions, word processing capabilities, graphics integration, and intercommunication between environments.

Integrated Word Processing Systems

In an integrated word processing system, the word processing functions previously described are combined with other programs to increase the flexibility and capability of the system. In the legal world, this means that a single system could perform a wide variety of functions, from word processing, mailing lists, accounting, and desktop publishing, to docket management, litigation support, and optical scanning. A single system, therefore, might have the following features in addition to basic word processing.

Spreadsheet Programs

A spreadsheet program provides you with a worksheet with many columns and rows. It enables you to perform various calculations and also gives you editing functions to rearrange your worksheet. Spreadsheets are used in virtually all offices and perform a wide variety of functions, from cost accounting to client analyses. Commonly used spreadsheet programs are Lotus 1-2-3, Symphony, and Visicalc.

Database Management Programs (DBMA)

A database management program allows you to store, manipulate, and retrieve records. It enables you to create a logical family of related records that can be retrieved using simple commands and criteria. A DBMA can contain all your client data and enable you to retrieve it in many combinations. For example, in a client database you could access information by zip code, by attorney of record, or by unpaid bills. (See Figure 11-2.) A law firm may have a single database or multiple databases, and may also import relevant databases such as

```
                                          PAGE 1

      CITATIONS LIST       DATABASE:  IN-TP       TOTAL DOCUMENTS:  4


          1.    PLI Order No. H4-5062

      Insurance, Excess, and Reinsurance Coverage Disputes 1989
      THE DUTIES OF GOOD FAITH OWED BY A PRIMARY INSURED TO THE CARRIERS
      PROVIDING EXCESS LAYERS OF COVERAGE.  January 1, 1989  Scott Conley
       Linda Hulse Vitlin 369 PLI/lit 337

            2.   PLI Order No. H4-5039
      Insurance, Excess and Reinsurance Coverage Disputes 1988
      THE DUTIES OF GOOD FAITH OWED BY A PRIMARY INSURER TO THE CARRIERS
      PROVIDING EXCESS LAYERS OF COVERAGE  January 1, 1988   Scott Conley
      Linda Hulse Vitlin 343 PLI/Lit 635

          3.   PLI Order No. H-5010
      Insurance, Excess, and Reinsurance Coverage Disputes 1987
      THE RIGHT OF THE EXCESS INSURER TO ENFORCE THE DUTY OF THE PRIMARY
      INSURER TO CONDUCT SETTLEMENT NEGOTIATIONS IN GOOD FAITH   January
      1, 1987  Scott Conley 320 PLI/Lit 97

          4.   PLI Order No. H-4-4985

      Insurance, Excess, and Reinsurance Coverage Disputes 1986
      SPECIAL PROBLEMS INVOLVING EXCESS INSURANCE  January 1, 1986  298
      PLI/Lit 239


      END OF CITATIONS LIST

          COPR. (C) WEST 1989 NO CLAIM TO ORIG. U. S. GOVT. WORKS
```

FIGURE 11-2 A citation list is selected from a legal research database.

West's Directory, DIALOG, or Dun & Bradstreet. Law firms also use marketing databases to assist them in their business development efforts.

Multimedia

One of the more popular and powerful software systems, which gives the user a tremendous variety of presentation options, is known as *multimedia.* Multimedia integrates the ability to use word processing, graphics, desktop publishing, sound, and video so that the user can create and present interactive, lifelike images and ideas with the computer. It adds a dimension beyond flat text, so that the user can create a multidimensional image which communicates and interacts with the user.

Some of the more popular applications for multimedia include computer-based training, demonstrations, interactive learning, and litigation support. Multimedia enables an audience, or a jury, to absorb information more quickly and more completely than mere word processing, because it appeals to all of the senses.

There are both hardware and software considerations in using multimedia applications. Multimedia must be supported by top-end hardware, such as 486,

586, or 686 processors, with adequate speed and memory to manipulate the images and sound files. You will also need a CD-ROM drive and a mouse or some sort of trackball device outside of the keyboard, as well as speakers and a large monitor. Relative to software, multimedia systems require Windows or OS/2 to take full advantage of all of the powerful features that this option offers. Naturally, using multimedia requires special training, because many of the packages offered are highly complex and sophisticated.

In the future, multimedia applications will gain in popularity and increase in use because their potential is virtually limitless and they are extremely powerful and persuasive. This is especially true of the legal environment. Multimedia presentations can be used for in-house meetings or seminars, for marketing to current or prospective clients, and in litigation. It is also very useful in a fairly new genre of software know as *groupware,* which facilitates the flow of work among the various members of a project team. The paralegal who can create multimedia presentations surely possesses a valuable skill that can only increase her value to the law firm.

Desktop Publishing

Desktop publishing software enables you to produce publisher-quality text and graphics. Naturally, production of these items requires specific hardware and peripherals in conjunction with the software package. When you are properly equipped, you will be able to produce newsletters, flyers, announcements, and various documents in a completely professional manner.

Computer-Generated Demonstrative Evidence

Related to word processing and its graphics capabilities are two emerging technologies used primarily in litigation, presentation graphics and computer animation. *Presentation graphics* refers to charts, diagrams, and other methods of presenting information visually in a trial. Computer technology has significantly simplified and improved the ability to make high-quality presentation graphics. Word processing systems contain graphics capabilities, and affordable printers and plotters enable a knowledgeable user to make stunning graphics. Some firms have the equipment to make presentation graphics in-house, whereas others use outside vendors to produce graphic images. There is little question that visual images combined with words make a significantly more memorable presentation than mere words alone. (See Figure 11-3.) Litigators will continue to use visual images in the presentation of their cases, and computer graphics make the creation of powerful images possible for everyone.

Computer illustration and animation enable the viewer, such as a jury, to reconstruct an event such as a murder, a surgical procedure, or a traffic accident. This is an extremely powerful technology that will continue to be popular in high-profile cases. One example of a sophisticated software system that produces complex illustrations is ADAM, an interactive anatomical reference

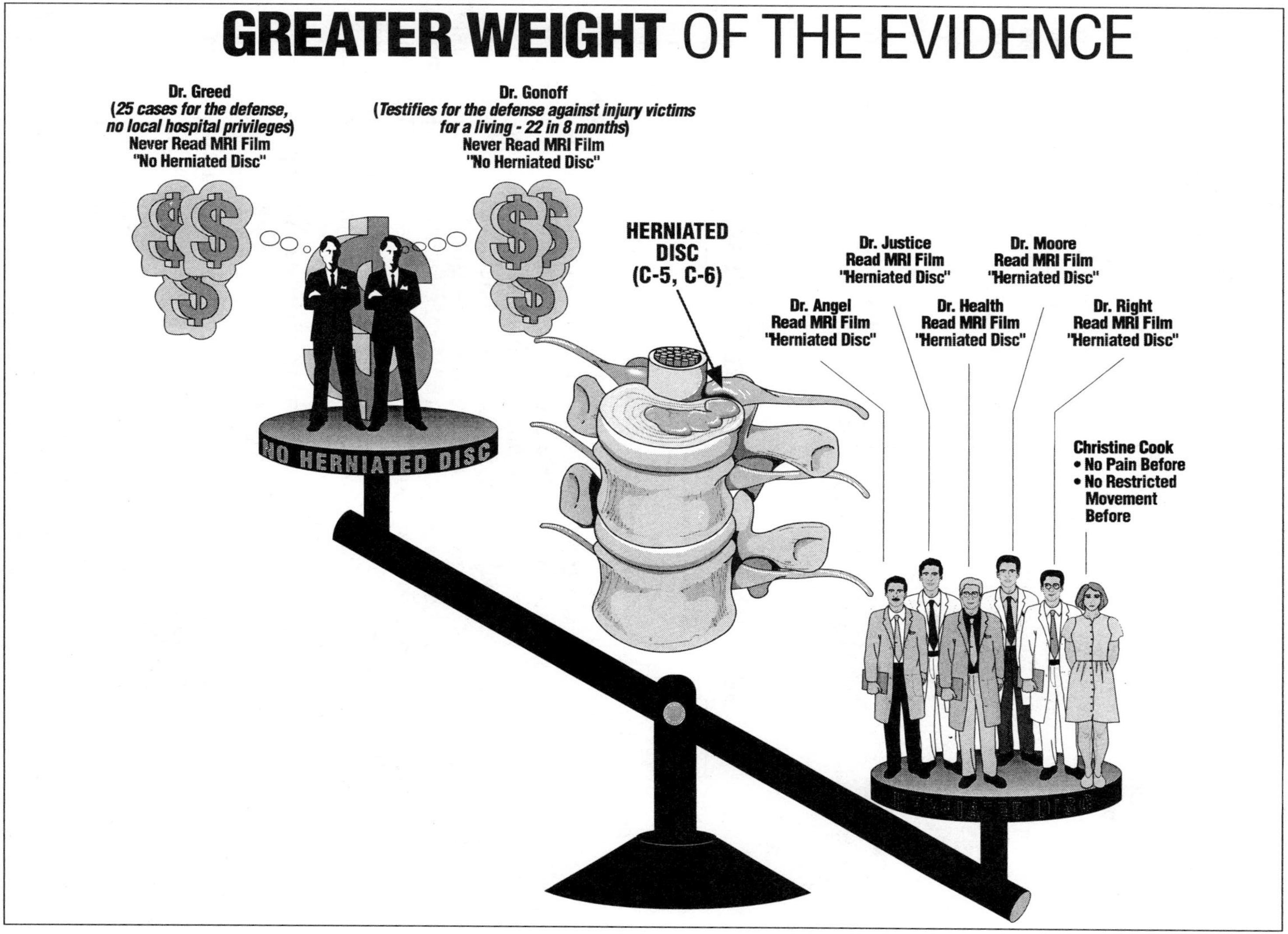

FIGURE 11-3   Computer graphics create powerful and memorable images. (Courtesy of TrialGraphix.)

program that runs on CD-ROM and produces powerful computer-generated illustrations. Using this software, the attorney can demonstrate visually the extent of his client's injuries, or he can make a compelling visual comparison between what a particular body part should have looked like after surgery and what it actually did look like after the alleged negligence.

Lawyers frequently need to convince others, such as juries and judges, about what actually happened. They must be persuasive and credible in presenting their view of the way things happened. By using computer technology to create compelling demonstrative evidence, lawyers can improve their ability to convince others that their version of the facts or the injury is the correct one. The following guest editorial tells you more about this exciting and effective application.

Legal Applications

An integrated system oriented to the legal profession, such as Juris or Barrister, includes many legal functions, as discussed in Chapter 13.

WordPerfect, DOS, and Windows

Although many companies develop and sell word processing packages, more law firms use WordPerfect than any other system. WordPerfect has reported that its product is in 74 percent of all law firms; its position of dominance is not surprising because it was the first software company to serve the legal market. WordPerfect is also a strong force in areas other than word processing, such as document assembly systems, e-mail, and presentation packages, and it is moving forward with features such as electronic document security systems and high-tech signatures. At this time, and for the foreseeable future, it seems safe to say that familiarity and experience with WordPerfect are at the least assets and at the most a necessity for those working in the modern law office.

While we are discussing WordPerfect, it is perhaps appropriate to mention the two environments in which WordPerfect, and many other computer applications, operate: DOS and Windows.

The DOS system, which preceded Windows, has been the standard operating system for PCs. DOS is typically keyboard-based and allows the user to control the environment in which the work is done. It is not as visual as Windows, and many people believe that it will be overtaken by newer graphical systems, such as Windows, in the near future. Nonetheless, many offices have and will continue to use DOS.

Windows is technically an environment rather than an operating system; it overlays DOS and provides the user with a graphical or picture-oriented view of the system. It generally uses a mouse, so access time to different applications and features is faster and more accurate than with a keyboard. Windows is a very natural, intuitive, and powerful system, which helps users be more productive

<table>
<tr><td>ON
POINT</td><td>*THE CASE OF SUZY'S SPELLING*</td></tr>
</table>

Suzy is a real estate paralegal who has been asked to draft a warranty deed. Half-way through typing the legal description of the property, Suzy receives a phone call from her new flame, Arnold Adonis. After making plans with her new hunk, she returns to her typing and finishes the document. Confident that she has made no substantive errors, Suzy spell-checks the document, prints it out, and has it executed at the closing that afternoon. Little does she know that the legal description in the document conveyed the adjoining property, rather than the correct piece of property. Is her word processor at fault?

because they are interacting directly with the system in a graphical way, rather than using the keyboard to enter commands. Without question, the contemporary paralegal must become fluent with Windows technology. It is not very difficult to learn, and it certainly represents the wave of the present and the near future in word processing.

Data Processing: An Introduction

Data processing refers to all activities that involve manipulating data electronically to give the user information. As a business carried on in an office, a law firm has many needs beyond the purely legal, and data processing helps meet many of those needs. Data processing handles functions previously done manually, and as such has the capability to perform those functions more quickly, efficiently, and accurately than before. Data processing is also part of an integrated system, so its information can be used in a multiplicity of ways for a multiplicity of purposes.

Depending on the size of your firm and the amount of specialization on the paralegal level, you might well have responsibility for functions that use data processing. You can best prepare yourself for using data processing functions effectively by being aware of data processing applications and how they are used. The following areas represent the most frequent uses of data processing by legal offices.

Automated Accounting and Timekeeping

Probably the greatest use of data processing in the contemporary law office is in the area of accounting and timekeeping. Medium-size and large law offices

GUEST EDITORIAL

New Approaches to Demonstrative Evidence Using Computer-Generated Graphics

Doug Cohen

Doug Cohen is Vice President of Marketing and Sales, as well as a founding principal, of TrialGraphix, Inc., which provides demonstrative evidence services for law firms across the country.

As the old adage goes, "a picture is worth a thousand words." Nothing could be more true in the courtroom or at the mediation table. Time and time again, experience has shown that visual presentations are an irreplaceable communication tool.

Demonstrative evidence is not limited solely to jury presentation. Bench trials, mediation, and arbitration are also excellent opportunities for using the persuasive power of visual aids. What types of demonstrative evidence are available? Enlargements of documents and photographs, mounted on foam board, continue to be standard fare for presentation purposes. However, you do an injustice to your client if you do not investigate the emerging demonstrative evidence technologies.

Computer-generated graphic exhibits, computer animation, medical illustrations, and courtroom multimedia are just a few of the options. One case that immediately comes to mind involved a multimillion-dollar securities litigation. TrialGraphix was working for the law firm representing the brokerage house. The plaintiff was passing himself off as a naive, uneducated investor with limited knowledge of his investment portfolio. He was claiming that the brokerage house had "churned" his account, making account transactions without his authorization. It was critical that the jury be left with a lasting visual image that portrayed the plaintiff as having been much more sophisticated and knowledgeable. The "Who is Dr. Smyth?" exhibit is what we came up with to portray the plaintiff as a savvy investor.

How does the process work? When a company such as TrialGraphix is called to produce custom exhibits for a case, the first step to do is a conflict check to ensure that the company is working for one side only. An InfoDesign consultant will then meet with members of the litigation team to discuss the central theme and key issues of the case and gather the necessary information to begin working on the exhibits. Mock-ups, or proofs, are provided throughout the process to keep the litigation team apprised of progress. Changes and revisions up to and even during trial are not a problem, as all work is created on computers, allowing for quick modifications.

This brings up an important point. As paralegals, often you are called upon by the attorneys you work with to secure these types of services. In many cases, you will have very little time to accomplish this. That is why it is critically important to ask certain specific questions when you call a company that provides these services. Are they available 24 hours a day, 7 days a week? Do they produce the work in-house, or do they farm it out to another location? Do they pick up and deliver, and do they rush-charge if you need it quickly? How do they maintain confidentiality? Good companies will understand the nature of the litigation process, and will do everything possible to meet your highly specialized needs.

We live in a visual society, and it has been proven scientifically that people remember a lot more of what they see than of what they hear. Demonstrative evidence is revolutionizing the way information is being presented to judges, juries, mediators, and arbitrators, and can be a powerful and effective tool in presenting your case.

Sample computer-generated trial exhibit. (Courtesy of TrialGraphix.)

will definitely have automated accounting, and even small firms or solo practitioners will probably use an automated billing and/or timekeeping system.

Many kinds of application software packages are available for accounting applications, but they all perform similar functions, with the simpler, less-expensive systems performing only the more basic ones. Accounting packages are able to perform the following functions:

- Accounts payable/receivable (see Figure 11-4)

ACCOUNT ANALYSIS REPORT

Juris, Samples & Samples

REPORT DATE 01/01/99 ACCOUNT ANALYSIS PAGE 1
REPORT NUMBER JP061-000023
SORTED BY CLIENT - DETAIL PRINTED BY SMGR
RANGE SELECTED: BEG OF FILE TO END OF FILE

						---- YEAR TO DATE -----			
			BILL	LAST BILL	UNBILLED	BILLED	RECEIVED	BALANCE	PPD
CLIENT	MATTER	NAME	TNKP	DATE	EXP/FEES	EXP/FEES	EXP/FEES	DUE	BALANCE
0617	00000	Emma's Florist	MJR	01/31/99	147.49	187.47	103.03	1,506.86	.00
					630.00	1,612.00	246.97		
0920	00000	Reed Products, Inc.	EMB	01/31/99	.00	604.06	325.56	3,834.20	.00
					.00	3,365.11	154.04		
1613	00000	Theatre District Association	JAM	01/31/99	.00	20.40	12.40	1,188.16	.00
					142.50	1,511.25	443.27		
	00001	Redevelopment Project	JAM	01/31/99	.00	582.05	.00	582.05	.00
					558.75	.00	.00		
		CLIENT TOTAL			.00	602.45	12.40	1,770.21	.00
					701.25	1,511.25	443.27		
		REPORT TOTAL			147.49		440.99		
						1,393.98		7,111.27	
					1,331.25		844.28		.00
						6,488.36			

Juris, Samples & Samples

REPORT DATE 01/01/99 ACCOUNT ANALYSIS PAGE 1
REPORT NUMBER JP061-000024
SORTED BY CLIENT - SUMMARY PRINTED BY SMGR
RANGE SELECTED: BEG OF FILE TO END OF FILE

					---- YEAR TO DATE -----			
		BILL	LAST BILL	UNBILLED	BILLED	RECEIVED	BALANCE	PPD
CLIENT	NAME	TNKP	DATE	EXP/FEES	EXP/FEES	EXP/FEES	DUE	BALANCE
0617	Emma's Florist			147.49	187.47	103.03	1,506.86	.00
				630.00	1,612.00	246.97		
0920	Reed Products, Inc.			.00	604.06	325.56	3,834.20	.00
				.00	3,365.11	154.04		
1613	Theatre District Association			.00	602.45	12.40	1,770.21	.00
				701.25	1,511.25	443.27		
	REPORT TOTAL			147.49		440.99		
					1,393.98		7,111.27	
				1,331.25		844.28		.00
					6,488.36			

FIGURE 11-4 An account analysis report assists firms in determining what accounts are past due. (Courtesy of Juris, Incorporated.)

- Timekeeping and billing (see Figure 11-5)

- General ledger

- Payroll, which concerns paying employees and keeping tax and deduction records

- Check reconciliation

- Report writer, which enables the user to write reports using generated data

- Internal auditing, which enables the firm to provide security and controls on its financial transactions.

TIMEKEEPER ANALYSIS REPORT

Juris, Samples & Samples

REPORT DATE   01/01/99
REPORT NUMBER JP062-000025
SORTED BY TIMEKEEPER
RANGE SELECTED: BEG OF FILE TO END OF FILE

TIMEKEEPER ANALYSIS

PAGE   1

PRINTED BY SMGR

TIMEKEEPER	PERIOD	TOTAL HOURS	N.B. HOURS	---- BILLABLE ----		BILLED AMOUNT	BILLED RATE	FEES RECEIVED	---- UNBILLED ----	
				HOURS	AMOUNT				HOURS	AMOUNT
Esther M. Bradberry	MTD	32.05	.00	32.05	3,044.75	3,712.63		760.01	1.50	142.50
	YTD	32.05	.00	32.05	3,044.75	3,712.63	80	760.01		
Cynthia Lee Cole	MTD	24.35	.00	24.35	1,863.75	2,671.36		471.27	8.40	630.00
	YTD	24.35	.00	24.35	1,863.75	2,671.36	89	471.27		
James A. Martin	MTD	9.75	.00	9.75	926.25	1,502.50		284.01	3.25	308.75
	YTD	9.75	.00	9.75	926.25	1,502.50	95	284.01		
Michael J. Ryan	MTD	8.60	.00	8.60	688.00	1,354.14		426.45	.00	.00
	YTD	8.60	.00	8.60	688.00	1,354.14	87	426.45		
Grant C. Tyler	MTD	6.50	.00	6.50	610.00	1,393.68		221.21	2.50	250.00
	YTD	6.50	.00	6.50	610.00	1,393.68	88	221.21		
FINAL TOTALS	MTD	81.25		81.25		10,634.31		2,162.95		1,331.25
	MTD		.00		7,132.75				15.65	
	YTD	81.25		81.25		10,634.31		2,162.95		
	YTD		.00		7,132.75		86			

FIGURE 11-5 Timekeeper information provides a database from which analytical reports can be developed. (Courtesy of Juris, Incorporated.)

Database Management

A *database* is a list of information or data that, when input into a computer with the appropriate program, can be stored efficiently and retrieved in a number of ways. For example, if you have a client database, you could get information or reports based on the referring attorney, geographic location, or date of disposition of the case. In other words, a database is an extremely efficient and flexible way of maintaining and retrieving data so that it can be used in a multiplicity of ways.

One excellent application of database principles occurs in marketing, where information of different types is distributed to selected people or organizations on your database. If your firm were offering a seminar on mortgage interest deductions, a database could easily (assuming you had input home ownership as a category) select your homeowner clients, integrate their names and addresses onto announcements, and prepare envelopes. Databases are also used for conflict-of-interest checks, where the computer looks for matches between the initiating name and the existing database.

In a larger firm, there well might be a database administrator, responsible for selecting, defining, and maintaining the database and providing reports to management. (See Figure 11-6.) In a smaller firm, these functions might fall to an office administrator, paralegal, or secretary, depending on the situation. (See Figures 11-7 and 11-8.)

FIGURE 11-6
Law office administrator uses computer setup, including LCD panel, to present information to the firm's management committee.

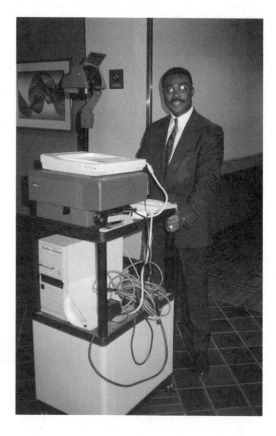

FIGURE 11-7
A legal assistant
enters
information into
a database ...

EXPERT WITNESS DEPOSITION DATABASE

NAME OF EXPERT WITNESS: Harvey Hughes, C.E.
AREA OF EXPERTISE: Road Construction/Engineer
SUBJECT OF DEPOSITION: Pavement/Rd configuration

DATE OF DEPOSITION: 6-28-94
DEF ATTORNEY: Thomas Freelance
OPPOSING COUNSEL: Sean Snodgrass
FOR LIBRARY USE ONLY:
NUMBER: TF 318

FIGURE 11-8   ... from input reports submitted by attorneys.

Management Information Systems

Management Information Systems (MIS) are computer-based systems that supply management with data, information, and reports that can be used to support management functions. In a law firm, their uses range from creating and analyzing productivity reports to analyzing zip code origins of your clients.

Management applications frequently require databases and therefore are interactive with databases and, of course, word processing. (See Figure 11-9.)

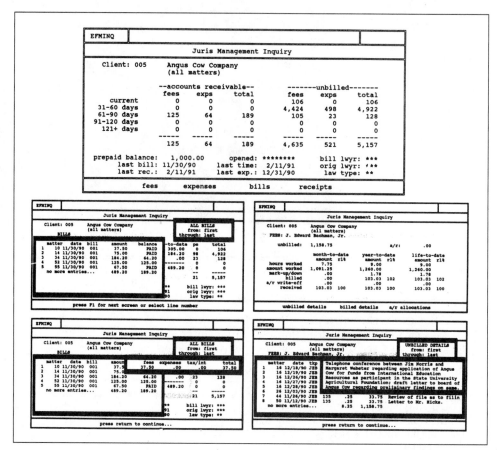

FIGURE 11-9 Management inquiry provides a top-down look into client information, allowing management to analyze relevant data. (Courtesy of Juris, Incorporated.)

Word and Data Processing: A Summary

Word processing and data processing are two of the most commonly used technical applications in a law office. For the paralegal, knowledge of both types of processing is essential. Word processing is integral to your work performance as a paralegal, as it is the primary mechanism by which you will communicate in writing. Data processing will also be used frequently in your work, through accounting, calendaring, or MIS support. Your ability to work productively with these two computer applications will play a large part in your success as a paralegal.

Key Terms

computer animation
database management
DOS
groupware

integrated systems
Management Information
   Systems (MIS)
multimedia

presentation graphics
Windows
word processing functions

Problems and Activities

1. You are the paralegal in a small firm that is considering investing in an integrated word processing system. The founding partner is concerned about the cost of such a system and has asked you to clarify for him the advantages that the system might bring to the office. What do you tell him?

CHAPTER 12

TELECOMMUNICATIONS AND OFFICE EQUIPMENT

OBJECTIVES

By the completion of this chapter, you should:

- become familiar with the major telecommunications systems and applications in a law office, including telephone systems, fax machines, electronic mail, and networks;

- learn the range of capabilities that modern telecommunications systems bring to the office environment; and

- become familiar with the major types of office equipment used in law offices.

Telecommunications Systems: An Introduction

Extremely rapid technological advances in the field of telecommunications have made telecommunications one of the most important aspects of office management. Not long ago, the telephone was the only major piece of communications equipment used in a law office, and its uses were limited. Today, the telephone has many capabilities that can be effectively used in legal work. Additionally, the integration of telecommunications with computer systems, where computer systems use the telephone lines to transmit data, has fostered an explosion of new technologies that have transformed the modern law office. In this section you will be introduced to the major telecommunications systems used in modern law offices today. As with the other technological applications we have discussed, you need not know everything about every technology; that would be impossible. Rather, you should become aware of the range of applications and capabilities that exist. Then, when you are settled in your position, you can fully learn the systems that are in use in your office; you might also become involved in upgrading the equipment as your firm's needs expand and new technologies become available.

Telephone Systems

Although firms have many different brands of telephone systems, telephone systems function very similarly: they give you options that increase your flexibility and decrease your waiting time when using the telephone. Because effective communications to multiple parties is such an important feature of paralegal work, it is essential that you become highly proficient with your phone system and its features and capabilities. Additionally, much of your contact with others will be through the phone, and it is therefore an opportunity for you to present yourself professionally and courteously.

The following features can be found in modern telephone systems:

- Call forwarding, which allows you to receive your calls at a remote extension or an entirely different number.

- Conferencing features, which enable you to speak with a number of different people at once.

- Hold features, which allow you to delay your current conversation with privacy.

- Paging, which enables the receptionist to use the telephone system to page people.

- Speaker options, which enable you to use the telephone hands-free (see Figure 12-1).

FIGURE 12-1 Speakers allow hands-free telephone use.

- Queuing, which automatically places you on a waiting list when outgoing lines are busy so you do not have to redial numbers.

- Voice mail, which enables you to send and to receive messages at your office or remotely.

- Speed calling, which enables you to save time by entering frequently called numbers into your phone's memory, then accessing those numbers by pressing a button or entering a code.

- Privacy features, which enable you to screen specific incoming calls.

- Call coverage, which enables you to arrange certain telephones in call pickup groups to answer phones that might be unattended.

- Night coverage, which causes calls that come in after the switchboard has closed to ring on night bells located throughout the firm's space.

- Cost allocation features, which capture information for billing phone charges to clients.

- Customization features, which allow the user to choose which features will be available in each of the units in the system.

- Caller ID, a function that displays the telephone numbers of incoming calls.

As you can see, modern telephone systems have numerous capabilities that can be used to save the paralegal time and effort if he or she is able to use the features effectively. Learning the capabilities of your telephone system will streamline your communications and save you time and energy as you complete your work. (See Figures 12-2, 12-3, and 12-4.)

FIGURE 12-2 Modern telephone systems have many capabilities ...

One process many firms go through in an effort to improve and streamline their telephone system is to perform a telecommunications audit. This audit involves a thorough examination and analysis of the telephone equipment and the trunking and long-distance network, as well as the cost of these services and equipment. Based on this information, it can be determined if the existing system is efficient and whether it is at capacity or if it has years more of service available. Also included in a comprehensive telecommunications audit are data communications and local area networking. Networking standards should be established and observed to ensure the firm's ability to handle future networking needs. A usage audit analyzes the way in which the system is used and evaluates the efficiency and cost of the existing system. Based on this information, the auditor can determine the adequacy and efficiency of the existing

FIGURE 12-3   ... use sophisticated telecommunications technology ...

FIGURE 12-4   ... and are not necessarily found in the office.

telecommunications system and make suggestions as to modifications or enhancements that would improve it.

Telephone Fraud

The Communications Fraud Control Association estimates that losses from telephone fraud are $1.2 billion annually. Telephone fraud prevention is clearly one aspect of an effective telephone system in an office.

Telephone fraud or misuse may come from within the organization or from without. Relative to internal misuse or fraud, there are a number of things that can be done to protect against unauthorized telephone usage. These include the use of codes that permit dialing of only certain ranges of long-distance numbers or locking the phones. However, by far the most important factor is creating an environment in which employees use tools such as the telephone for work-related purposes only; it is ultimately up to the firm to create an environment in which a professional attitude exists concerning unauthorized or unnecessary telephone usage. It is essential for a firm to inform its employees about appropriate telephone usage and train them in the proper use of its features if the firm wants to maximize its telephone communications capabilities and minimize unauthorized or nonbusiness use of the telephones.

It is also important to be aware of various scams that are commonly used in telephone fraud schemes. One telephone scam involves thieves presenting themselves as employees of the firm's telephone company. Once they get access to the telephone room, they may steal or replace expensive switches, or they may attach devices that enable them to access and use the system. To avoid this, make sure that service people are authorized representatives who have been dispatched to your office.

Telephone credit cards also present a target for con artists. One common scam involves watching callers in public places and getting their numbers by watching the digits being pressed. The thief then sells the number to the eventual users.

The best approach to limiting the risks associated with telephone fraud is to increase the awareness of all employees of the risks of telephone fraud and to train them in various approaches to telephone fraud prevention. It is most important to work together with the firm's telephone carrier to develop a cost-efficient plan for preventing fraud. The carrier can assess the organization's situation and provide services, options, and training to help the firm avoid losses due to telephone fraud.

Mobile Phones and Pagers

The use of mobile phones and pagers is increasing rapidly among legal professionals. As its name implies, a *mobile phone,* which uses cellular technology, can be taken anywhere and thereby greatly increase the flexiblity a user has in making phone calls. Additionally, mobile phones enable the user to make productive use of all time; for example, an attorney or paralegal might be able to return phone calls while driving to the courthouse. They are also extremely helpful in case of emergencies or problems; if you are stuck in traffic or in a car wreck on the way to a court date, a mobile phone enables you to call the clerk and explain your situation. Remember that cellular calls can be very expensive, so use the mobile phone with an awareness of its cost.

Pagers enable the user to be contacted at any time. Pagers may be numerical, where you can leave your phone number for a return call, or they may be voice-activated, where you can leave a voice message that will be printed out on the user's pager.

Both mobile phones and pagers can be extremely helpful communication tools for the legal professional. In all likelihood, you will not be expected to purchase a phone or pager for your work; rather, the firm will supply you with one or let you use one when the need arises. Remember that if you are using the firm's equipment, the phone or pager should be used for work purposes only. Using it for personal use would constitute the unauthorized use of firm equipment and could possibly be grounds for discipline or termination.

Fax Machines

Fax machines—the shorthand name for facsimile machines or telecopiers—are another example of a technology that has transformed office practices. (See Figure 12-5.) Fax machines enable the user to use the telephone lines to transfer

FIGURE 12-5
Fax machines
are indispensable
in the law office

documents to other fax machine users. Once you have successfully connected to a fax machine number, your fax machine sends a copy of your documents to the other location, where the information appears almost instantaneously. This enables you to send and receive information in a moment's time.

Fax systems exist in one of two forms. Most common is the stand-alone fax, which looks like another piece of office equipment on your desk. The other option is installing a fax board inside your computer. This transforms your computer into a fax machine, so that anything you have on your computer can be faxed to another fax machine.

Although fax machines perform similar functions, they do have options. Some use thermal paper, which is more expensive and harder to read than regular paper. Although most faxes operate in black and white, there are color faxes and faxes that have the ability to reproduce photographs. Faxes can also provide an accounting report, which enables the supervisor to analyze fax use. In this vein, remember that faxing can be expensive and that you should consider the costs when deciding whether to fax or use other methods.

Clients are normally billed for fax time. If the fax is local, it is usually billed at a flat rate. If it is a long-distance fax, the client is charged a flat rate plus a cost per minute.

When using a fax machine you should follow established fax protocol (see Figure 12-6). Most firms have policies regarding fax use, such as a limit on the number of pages you can fax, whether you can fax long distance, and a standardized fax cover page. Be sure that you become familiar with any policies at your firm.

Electronic Mail

Electronic mail, known simply as *e-mail,* enables users to send and receive documents on their networked computers. It provides a rapid, efficient, and paperless method of communicating. By using electronic mail, you are able to communicate with everyone in the office who has access to similar equipment, thus reducing or eliminating the need for a hardcopy interoffice memoranda. (See Figure 12-7.)

E-mail also enables receptionists and telephone operators to send all telephone and/or visitor messages instantly. If your firm has more than one office, the electronic mail system can be connected through modems, multiplexors, or other telecommunications equipment, so that all of the people in all of the offices can communicate directly. (See Figure 12-8.)

It is now commonplace for law firms to use e-mail within the firm to improve communications. A less frequent yet evolving application of e-mail involves linking up clients on e-mail. Using this technology, a lawyer who wanted to review the first draft of a document with her client, for example, would merely need to route the information into the recipient's electronic mailbox; the recipient

Drew Eckl & Farnham

ATTORNEYS AT LAW

880 WEST PEACHTREE STREET

P.O. BOX 7600

ATLANTA, GEORGIA 30357

(404) 885-1400

Facsimile Transmittal

DATE: October 18, 1995

TO: ALLISON DANIEL   FAX NO.:   404/778-9940

FIRM: CALDWELL & CO.   PHONE NO.: 404/778-0000

CITY: ATLANTA

FROM: SHANNON SELFRIDGE   ATTORNEY/PARALEGAL NO.: 401

CLIENT/MATTER NO.: 0001.10001

RE: INSURANCE RENEWAL - 1996
       (Case Name)

TOTAL NO. OF PAGES (**INCLUDING THIS COVER SHEET**): _____

IF YOU SHOULD HAVE ANY PROBLEMS RECEIVING THIS FAX, PLEASE CONTACT THE COPY CENTER AT (404) 885-6468 [FAX NO. (404) 876-0992].

REMARKS:

ALLISON: PLEASE SEND APPLICATIONS FOR ERRORS AND OMISSIONS INSURANCE RENEWAL ASAP. THANKS. SHANNON

CONFIDENTIALITY NOTE: The information contained in this facsimile message is legally privileged and confidential information intended only for the use of the individual or entity named above. If the reader of this message is not the intended recipient, you are hereby notified that any dissemination, distribution or copy of this telecopy is strictly prohibited. If you have received this telecopy in error, please immediately notify us by telephone and return the original message to us at the address above via the United States Postal Service. Thank you.

FIGURE 12-6 Proper fax protocol requires that you use a fax transmittal sheet for every document faxed.

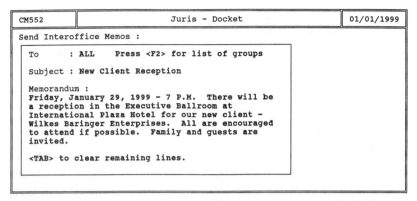

| CM552 | Juris – Docket | 01/01/1999 |

```
Send Interoffice Memos :

To       : ALL    Press <F2> for list of groups

Subject : New Client Reception

Memorandum :
Friday, January 29, 1999 - 7 P.M.  There will be
a reception in the Executive Ballroom at
International Plaza Hotel for our new client -
Wilkes Baringer Enterprises.  All are encouraged
to attend if possible.  Family and guests are
invited.

<TAB> to clear remaining lines.
```

FIGURE 12-7 Electronic mail provides a fast and paperless method of communicating.

From: Anne Landrum

To: netatty

Date: 2/20/95 9:53 A.M.

Subject: Discovery—material obtained in anticipation of litigation

In today's FCDR, there is a helpful decision explaining when material, statements, etc., can be considered to have been obtained or prepared in anticipation of litigation and non-discoverable absent a showing of substantial need. In D.O.T. v. Hardaway Co., Case No. A94A2472 (2/9/95), the Court of Appeals held that in a contract dispute, material created in response to a written claim and demand for payment outside the contract amount was prepared in anticipation of litigation. The Court cited to other cases involving tort claims in which it held that an inquiry into the existence of insurance was grounds for belief that litigation was probable, and that witness statements and notes prepared by the claims adjuster after the claimant said "you have not heard the last of this" and "you will pay" were protected. The Court also explained that in order to be protected, the material need not contain the mental impressions, etc. of the preparer, but need only have been prepared in anticipation of litigation. AML

FIGURE 12-8 E-mail enables a firm to communicate information simultaneously throughout the office.

could then respond in a paperless and highly efficient way. In addition to the speedy and clear communication channel that has been established with the client, the firm is saving money or time for secretarial and mailroom support, as well as communicating to the client that the firm is using technology productively in its quest to provide cost-effective legal services.

Naturally, any time you use electronic communication such as e-mail, issues of confidentiality arise. Because so many users might have access to e-mail, it is advisable to refrain from using e-mail if the subject material is highly confidential.

If the user has cause for concern about the disclosure of information to be communicated, it is safer and therefore better to avoid electronic media in the communication process.

Networks

Networks provide the ability to link computers together to efficiently share resources. Any size law firm that has more than one computer might have a network installed. Networks allow users to share databases, printers, and other computer peripherals. They would therefore be especially useful in a firm that has several offices because they would minimize paperwork and equipment costs as well as streamline and improve communication flows.

The Internet: A Global Network

There is much talk today about the Internet, the world's largest global computer network. It brings together millions of users and gives them access to each other as well as to all kinds of databases and information resources. This enables the user to perform a wide variety of functions, including use e-mail, research virtually any topic, access research and educational institutions, participate in open forums or discussion groups, and gain international access to other databases, software, and subject matter experts.

There are hundreds of provider services that can link a user into the Internet, usually for a cost. Some of the most popular services are America Online, Prodigy, SprintLink, AARNet, Class, and PSI. There may also be local providers in your region which provide access to the Internet as well. Each of these companies has its own market niche and its own network, and you will want to know which service best fits your needs before you sign up with one.

Use of the Internet requires an understanding of the language and etiquette of the Internet. Before you access this complex network, you will want to learn about the Internet's workings, common file types and modes, searching databases, and communication techniques, as well as policies and procedures that a firm might have concerning Internet usage. Training classes are offered in Internet use, and understanding these processes will help the user to become a good Internet "citizen."

It is also important to realize that the Internet changes daily, so the user must keep abreast of these changes and their legal, ethical, and political implications. For example, if you are shipping anything across an international boundary, export laws might come into effect. You must also consider intellectual property and license issues in the process of using other people's information.

One of the more unusual uses of the Internet was devised by Chicago attorney Brian Murphy, who used the Internet to publish the plight of his client, Girvies L. Davis, and his request for clemency in the face of his impending execution in Illinois. In the first month after Davis's home page was set up, more than 50,000 Internet users read of his plight and more than 450 sent e-mails to the governor on his behalf. Certainly this unusual campaign gives us a glimpse into the potentially infinite uses of the Internet.

The Internet is an extraordinarily powerful tool for the production and exchange of information, and it is a major component of computer systems in law firms and other legal environments. Like most tools, however, it must be used thoughtfully, purposefully, and carefully to maximize its potential and utility.

Modems

Modems are communication devices that enable computers to communicate with other computers or networks that also have modems. Some modems are stand-alone units, while others are installed within computers. These modems can be used to access WESTLAW, LEXIS, Veralex, or other commercially available computer programs. (See Figure 12-9.)

FIGURE 12-9
Modems enable computers to communicate using telephone lines.

Telex/Teletype Machines

Although telex and teletype machines have been largely replaced by the more sophisticated communications equipment previously described, some offices continue to use older forms of telecommunications, such as telex or teletype machines, particularly when commmunicating with Europe.

Telecommunications Systems: A Summary

Efficient and effective telecommunication capabilities are essential to the modern law office, and modern technology has evolved so significantly in this area that many technical applications have already found their way into the law office. Because so much of legal practice involves communications, both within the law firm and law team and outside to clients, other attorneys, and others, it is essential that paralegals become highly proficient with the means and methods of modern telecommunications. By increasing the speed and accuracy of communications, modern technology has given the legal team innumerable applications that can save both time and money. It is therefore up to legal practitioners to learn about and master modern communications applications to perform their work as professionally as possible.

Office Equipment

In addition to the communications systems previously described, law offices have a number of other types of office equipment that you will need to use in the course of performing your work. This section introduces you to the office equipment that can usually be found in a law office.

Copy Machines

Copy machines are indispensable in the legal profession. Multiple copies of legal documents must be made to supply to courts, clients, and opposing parties. Copiers have made carbon paper almost obsolete. Prior to the mass use of copy machines, law firms had to type duplicates of documents or use carbon paper; now those processes are rarely used.

Copiers come in all shapes and sizes. They have mechanisms ranging from self-feeding parts to collating and stapling documents. Every machine is different and you will need to learn the peculiarities of the machine your firm uses. (See Figure 12-10.)

FIGURE 12-10
Copy machines have many different capabilities.

Some larger firms have copy centers where there are personnel available to do copying. The machines used in these centers are usually so complicated that individuals specially trained on the machines must operate them. These copy centers are either staffed by the firm's personnel or are run on an independent-contractor basis with third parties.

Most firms have cost-control devices for their copy machines so that clients can be billed for copies made on their cases. The system can be as simple as listing a client number, date, type of document, and number of copies made on a legal pad, or as formal as a computerized file system that requires a file number to be input before the copy machine can even be operated. As with other types of office automation, each firm has its own system that you must learn how to use.

Dictation Machines

Dictation machines, like copiers, come in all shapes and sizes. The machine can be a compact model, no bigger than a portable radio, or could be a larger model, the size of an adding machine. The tapes used by the various types of machines also vary. They range from a one-inch size to a full-size cassette. The size of the tape usually varies proportionally to the size of the dictating machine. (See Figure 12-11.)

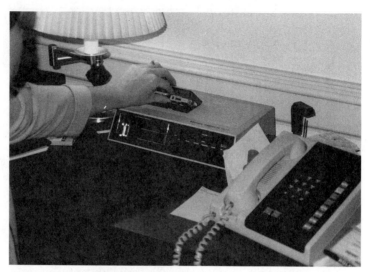

FIGURE 12-11 Dictating equipment utilizes cassette tapes to capture the dictation.

Attorneys and paralegals use dictation equipment to compose documents orally so that legal secretaries can transcribe them for the attorney's or paralegal's review. As offices become more automated, this system is becoming less common. Both attorneys and paralegals are obtaining their own computers on which to compose legal documents, with dictation rapidly becoming a thing of the past.

Although dictation is perhaps less common than in the past, it too is being revolutionized by technology. In the past, dictation almost invariably involved cassettes and tapes; today, that approach is giving way to digital dictation. In digital dictation, the voice is recorded directly onto a hard drive or other mass storage medium. This can be done in person or over any phone line. When the voice is captured in digital code, the computer can then adjust the speed of the voice to make transcription easier and reduce relistening and rewriting time. It also simplifies the editing and retrieval processes because digital technology enables you to search for information with keystrokes. Additionally, you can use the dictation much like a word processing document, inserting, deleting, or adjusting information easily and quickly. Although digital dictation requires significant storage capabilities to operate, it is, for the most part, simple and easy to use. The future will see more and more law firms making the transition to this new dictation technology.

Typewriters

Although most law firms utilize some sort of word processing equipment for transcribing and creating legal documents, most firms still have typewriters.

Typewriters can be used to address envelopes, type file labels, and fill in forms. Most typewriters have self-correcting features, and a few have memories that make them more like computers than typewriters. It is doubtful that typewriters will ever be completely replaced in the law office. (See Figure 12-12.)

FIGURE 12-12 Typewriters still have many uses in the law office.

Office Supplies

Most firms, ranging from the smallest to the largest, have supply rooms. The size of the supply room ranges from a cabinet to an office-sized room. Types of office supplies commonly used by all law firms include copying paper, legal pads, pens, pencils, various sizes and types of file folders, file labels, manila and business-sized envelopes, self-sticking notes, rubber bands, fax paper, computer disks, laser printer drums, ink cartridges, tape, staples, highlighter pens, paper clips, and indexing forms. The types of office supplies used by a firm depend upon the kind of law the firm practices. For example, real estate firms need forms required for closings by state law, whereas litigation firms need exhibit tabs to mark exhibits for trial.

Larger firms have suppliers who come into the supply room on a periodic basis and determine what supplies the firm requires. The order is then placed and subsequently delivered. (See Figure 12-13.) The office managers, legal secretaries, or paralegals in smaller firms usually determine what supplies are needed and either place orders or go to office supply stores to purchase supplies. Some firms have designated forms to be filled out whenever anything is taken from the supply room, so that they can determine when and what new supplies are necessary.

FIGURE 12-13
Supply managers are responsible for maintaining and delivering office supplies.

On Point **THE CASE OF THE OVERHEARD CONVERSATION**

Attorney Cassidy and Paralegal Sundance Kid are driving in their Mercedes down the interstate highway when they decide to call into their office for messages. Their secretary informs them that their client Billy the Kid has called five times that morning. They return the call on their car's cellular phone and Billy, frantic, tells them that he has gunned down Tammy Faye Bakker in cold blood next to the Lancome counter at Neiman-Marcus. A police car travelling in the opposite direction picks up the conversation on its communications equipment, hearing Billy identify himself. Since Billy is a well-known criminal, they know his address, and they arrest him at his home. Billy is subsequently convicted based on his confession in the telephone conversation. Was this phone conversation protected communication?

Office Equipment: A Summary

Modern communications systems have revolutionized the law office and its ability to handle and communicate information within and without the law firm. It is essential that you learn to take advantage of technical advances in the area of communications, for there are numerous applications of these advances to the work of the paralegal. Additionally, you will want to become aware of and master all the office equipment available to you in your work. Communications and office equipment are essential tools that effective paralegals must employ in the course of doing their work, as they enable paralegals to perform their tasks with efficiency and a minimum of wasted time.

Key Terms

computer network	electronic mail (e-mail)	pager
copy machine features	fax machine	telecommunications audit
dictation machine	mobile phone	telephone fraud
digital dictation	modem	telephone system features

Problems and Activities

1. What procedures should be established to prevent malpractice claims arising from the use of telecommunications equipment?

2. What information would you need to assess the long-distance carrier that your firm should use?

3. Do you think that all law firm personnel who travel, or merely attorneys, should have cellular telephones?

4. What method would you use to ensure that your cellular telephone calls are billed to the proper clients and cases?

5. How could a paralegal effectively utilize a digital pager during the course of a day spent at the courthouse?

CHAPTER 13

TECHNICAL APPLICATIONS FOR LEGAL PRACTICE

OBJECTIVES

By the completion of this chapter, you should:

- understand the different types of computer applications available for legal specialization;

- understand how technology can aid the work of the paralegal; and

- gain an in-depth understanding of computerized litigation support and optical imaging as examples of emerging technical trends in law firms.

Technical Applications: An Introduction

The previous chapters of this part made you aware of the ways in which computers are used in law offices and the most typical applications of computer technology. In this chapter you will learn about technical applications, including hardware configurations and software packages, that apply directly to specialized legal practices. Your goal at this point should be to gain a broad understanding of the range of applications of legal software. When you are on your job, you will want to become skilled in the use of all relevant technology, including hardware and software. You might also become involved with evaluating and recommending computer applications, at which time you will want to become aware of what is available in the areas you need.

The following discussion introduces you to the most frequently used computer applications and technical developments that are oriented to legal practice.

Integrated Systems

An *integrated system* for legal applications refers to a system that performs all of the functions we have discussed previously, such as word and data processing, as well as communications, accounting, calendar control, and litigation support. These integrated systems are both powerful and flexible, and can fulfill all of the needs of the law firm. Training and upgrades are continually available. Companies such as Juris produce integrated systems that are customized to the needs of the particular firm.

To give you a feel for an integrated system oriented to a law office environment, the following material walks you through a powerful yet simple-to-use integrated system, O.N.E. Ware for Lawyers. The following computer screens are reproduced with the permisssion of John T. Asselin of Windham, Connecticut, who is the sole owner of the copyright therein. The trademark O.N.E. Ware Original New England SOFTWARE Company is owned by John T. Asselin.

A Walk Through O.N.E. Ware

The first thing the user, lawyer, paralegal, or receptionist does in O.N.E. Ware is to log onto the system. Our user in this example is Attorney Annette A. Able. The user identification (id) and password protect against unauthorized entry or usage (Figure 13-1).

The main menu presents a list of choices; you begin by selecting the menu item you want. Attorney Able begins by checking her messages (Figure 13-2).

The incoming phone message screen reveals a new business inquiry from Katherine Bober. As the office had previously communicated with Ms. Bober, all of the information above the MESSAGE field has been automatically provided via the ProFILES module (Figure 13-3).

The ProFILES module is a completely integrated electronic Rolodex, in addition to providing, among other functions, contact management, marketing management, a socio-demographic database, and mailing list management (Figure 13-4).

Given that the call has been identified as a new business inquiry, Attorney Able goes to "Synopsis," the first of the New Business Inquiry screens. Note that the information in this screen was automatically entered from the incoming phone message (Figure 13-5).

Note that to this point the user has entered about 40 keystrokes, never typing the same name or information twice, and the entire new business intake process has been initiated and routed to the appropriate person—electronically. In the event that the matter is rejected or referred, the system will prompt the

FIGURE 13-1 User id and password protect against unauthorized entry.

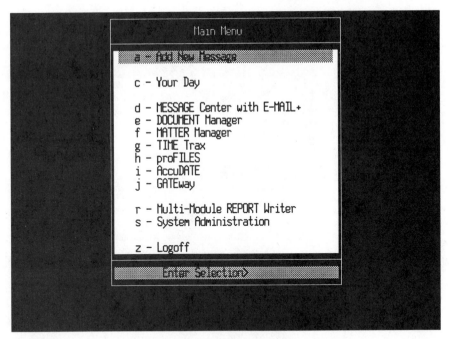

FIGURE 13-2 The main menu presents a list of choices.

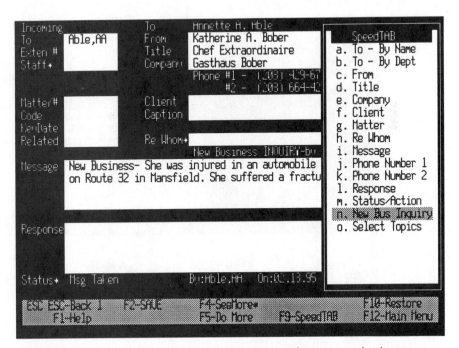

FIGURE 13-3 The incoming phone message screen shows a new business inquiry.

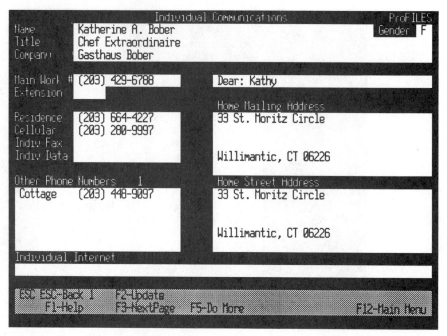

FIGURE 13-4   The ProFILES module provides a completely integrated electronic Rolodex.

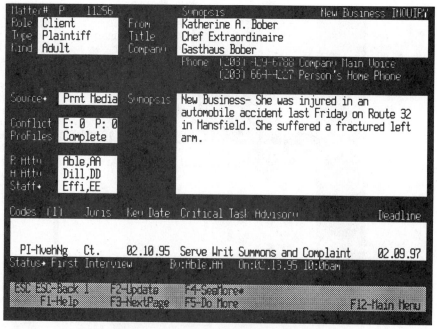

FIGURE 13-5   Information from the incoming phone message is automatically entered on the Synopsis, the first of the New Business INQUIRY screens.

user to electronically issue the appropriate confirming letter and to make any appropriate bookkeeping entries. If the matter is in suspense, it will come up electronically on the calendar every three days until a decision to accept or reject the case is made.

Attorney Able chooses to take client Bober. She opens the matter and all of the intake data is automatically put through to the Matter Manager module. The STATUS screen of the Matter Manager is shown in Figure 13-6.

Attorney Able schedules an appointment with her new client and makes the appropriate entry in the AccuDATE module. All of the data fields are filled from the data previously entered (Figure 13-7).

Attorney Able now needs to call her client. She pushes the F5 button from the previous screen in order to "Do More." All of the modules and screens are completely integrated and accessible to each other without any need to go to the main menu (Figure 13-8).

She scans through the message center, which contains the people she is most likely to call relative to the appointment (Figure 13-9). An Outgoing Call screen is then automatically created for Attorney Able's use. In a total of three keystrokes, she has created a record that serves as a foundation for confirming letters, phone log records, and billing information (Figure 13-10).

Attorney Able wants to review her time records for February 5. The system continually tracks time usage, and users can edit the entries to account for time when they are off the system, such as doing research in the library or interviewing a witness in the field (Figure 13-11).

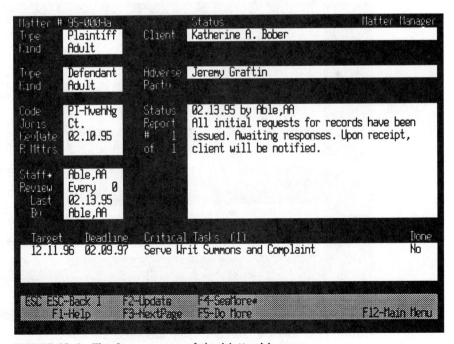

FIGURE 13-6 The Status screen of the Matter Manager

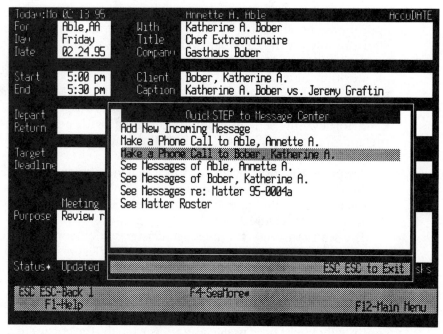

FIGURE 13-7 Data previously entered transfers to the AccuDATE module.

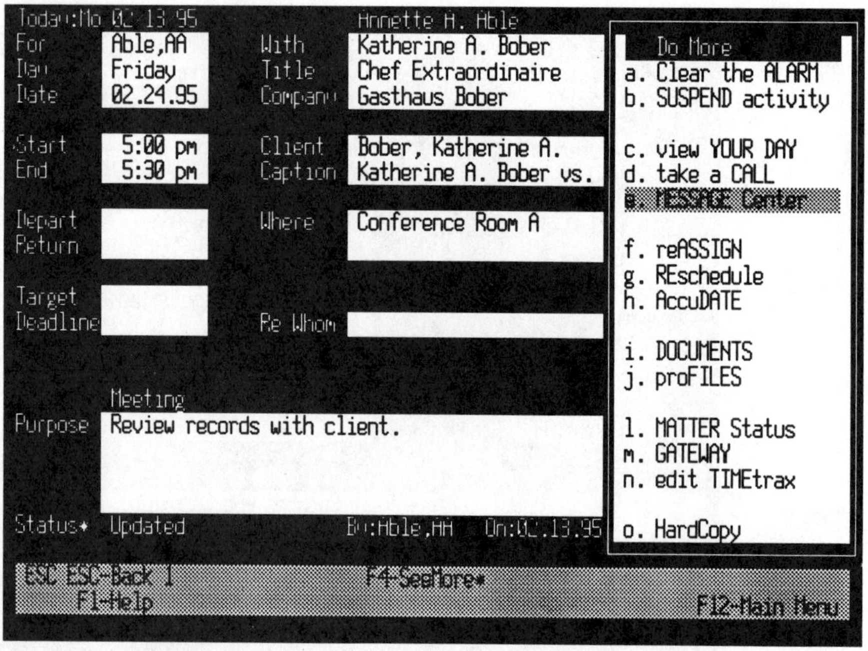

FIGURE 13-8 Modules are completely integrated and accessible without returning to the main menu.

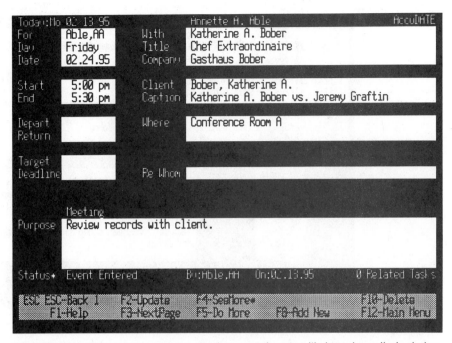

FIGURE 13-9 The message center displays people most likely to be called relative to the appointment.

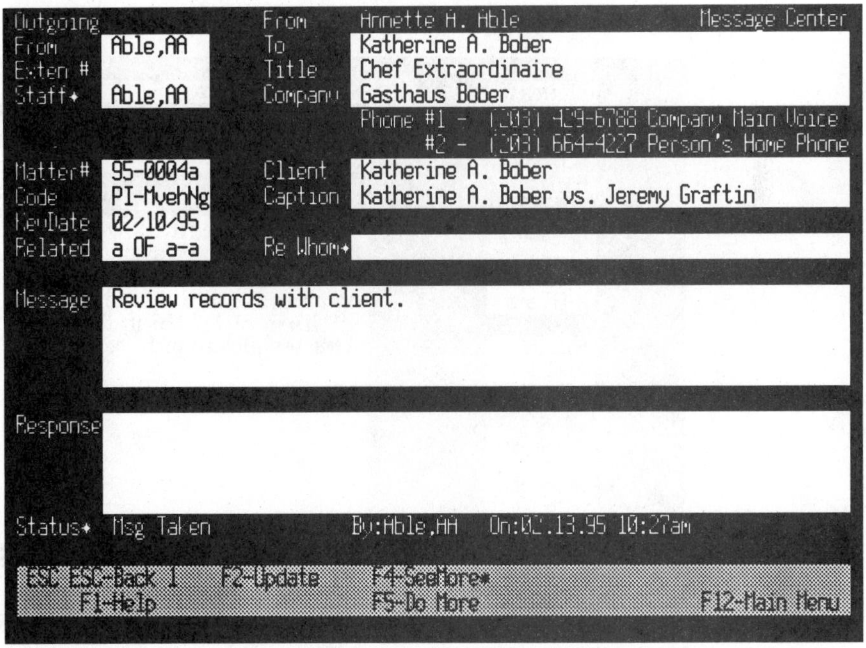

FIGURE 13-10 An Outgoing Call screen is created.

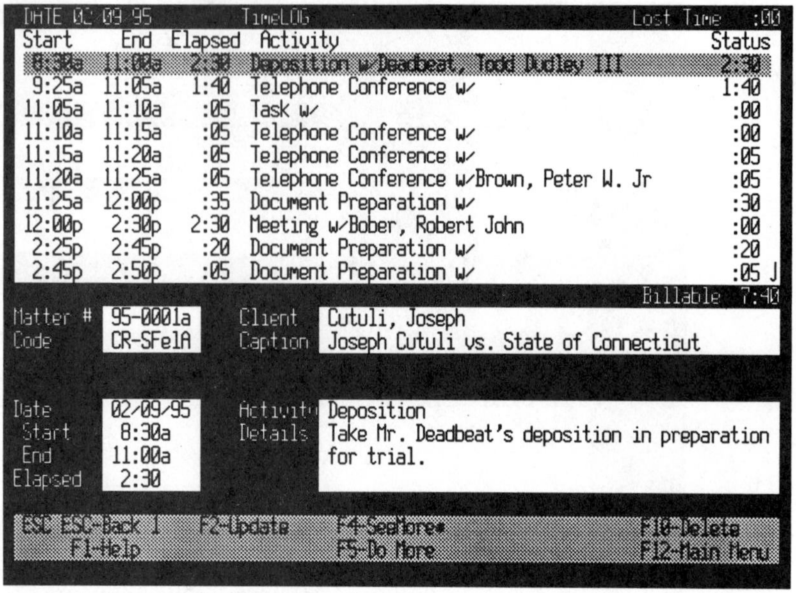

FIGURE 13-11   The TimeLOG continuously tracks time usage.

Ultimately, the case is brought to a conclusion. Attorney Able completes the Closed Matter Memo, having a thorough, accurate record of the entire matter (Figure 13-12).

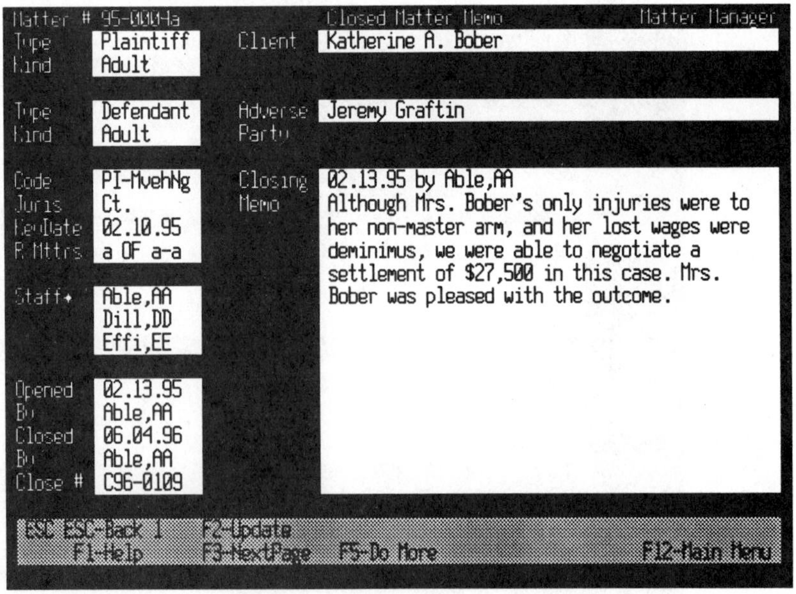

FIGURE 13-12   The Closed Matter Memo closes out the record.

As you can see, a modern, integrated system oriented to the law office is a powerful, flexible tool that can dramatically improve the way in which a law office manages its tasks and information. These systems can result in a tremendous increase in productivity and profitability for the law firm. Successful paralegals, whether working in medium-size or large law firms or for a sole practitioner, must get comfortable working with these powerful yet user-friendly systems. As John Asselin, the creator of O.N.E. Ware, said, referring to integrated systems for law office use, "This is the way you should practice law today. This is the way you will have to practice law 5–10 years from now, or you simply will not be in the business of law anymore."

Legal Research: Online Systems and CD-ROM

Using computers and telecommunications to perform legal research is, compared to other, more recent applications, a pretty traditional use of modern technology by lawyers. As we discussed in Chapter 9 on the law library, legal resources are available in both book and electronic formats. The two major forms of electronic legal research are online systems and CD-ROM.

Online systems such as LEXIS or WESTLAW use the telephone lines to provide computer access to their huge databases of federal and state case law, continuously updated statutes for all states, and state and federal regulations. In addition, LEXIS has 45 specialized libraries covering all major fields of practice. WESTLAW now offers voice-activated computer research. To access this feature, the researcher speaks into a microphone, asking, for example, "Find a case about the liability of a landlord for the negligent repair of stairs." The computer would then retrieve cases that fit the requested parameters.

Publishers such as Michie offer state and federal law on CD-ROM, updating the discs four or six times a year. Because compact discs are a product of digital technology, they store information as an undivided whole. Therefore, in addition to their huge capacity for information, compact discs allow the user to link various types of information. CD-ROM discs are also easy to store: one state code in book form takes up more shelf space than would CD-ROMs containing the state codes of all 50 states!

Computerized legal research is not a tool of the future; it is a tool of the present. You will need to be able to effectively use computerized legal research methods in your work as a paralegal.

Docket and Calendar Control

Docket and calendar control systems enable law firms to manage firm-wide critical dates. *Docket control systems,* which are an aspect of client or case management, enable firms to keep track of critical or statutory dates in a highly efficient manner. Because court dates and other significant meetings are so crucial to the practice of law, computerized docket control can greatly assist firms in controlling their schedules. A key element of the successful practice of law is keeping up with calendars, and computer systems have many advantages over manual systems, such as accuracy, power, and speed of receiving information.

Calendaring programs, like docket control programs, enable the user to maintain and report appointments and other critical dates, but these include all types of appointments, not just court dates. (See Figure 13-13.) Docket and calendar control systems can exist as self-contained software systems, or they can be integrated with other systems, such as time and billing, to provide the user with even greater capabilities and analytical tools. (See Figure 13-14.)

Litigation Support

Litigation support systems perform all of the functions necessary for complex litigation needs, and they enable the lawyer to maintain control over all the information and events relevant to the case. Litigation requires the analysis and organization of vast quantities of documents, and litigation support software enables the user to store tremendous amounts of material and retrieve relevant information in many different ways. In addition to document indexing and analysis, litigation support systems enable attorneys and paralegals to customize their own databases, control discovery products, perform micrographics and photoduplication, screen documents for relevance, review transcripts and depositions, and identify all document locations. In this era of showy litigation, where trial requires vast quantities of exhibits, summaries, and depositions, such systems become a necessity, not a luxury. It is difficult, if not impossible, to organize data from thousands of documents manually. Not only is manual organization next to impossible, the retrieval of the information in a manual system is difficult to implement. With computer systems, documents can be located in a variety of methods, such as using a computer search date or a keyword search, which save both the legal team and the client time and money.

Technology in the Courtroom

The victim, the jury is told, had her head crushed by a robotic arm that swung violently out of control while she was working at her job. The jurors are then instructed to look at the computer monitors in the front of the jury box, where a three-dimensional model of the robotic arm is shown spinning out of

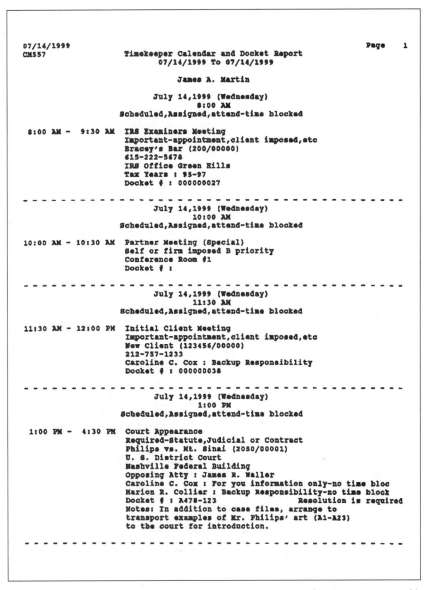

FIGURE 13-13   A calendar and docket report. (Courtesy of Juris, Incorporated.)

control and impacting a human head. The depiction shows in slow motion the exact nature of the impact.

One of the most rapidly growing areas where technology is affecting the legal system is the courtroom itself. High-tech courtrooms attempt to streamline and economize the judicial system and to improve the presentation of information and evidence. You can now see computer-graphics simulations of crimes, accidents, medical evidence, and the effects of an injury. In some jurisdictions,

FIGURE 13-14
Computer applications make time management easier. (Courtesy of Juris, Incorporated.)

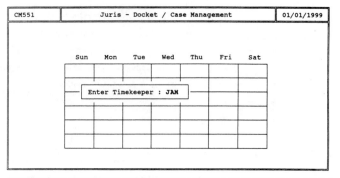

Calendar Inquiry for James A. Martin

| CM551 | Juris - Docket / Case Management | 01/01/1999 |

| | Sun | Mon | Tue | Wed | Thu | Fri | Sat |

Enter Timekeeper : JAM

| CM551 | Juris - Docket / Case Management | 01/01/1999 |

Calendar for James A. Martin

Tuesday, January 12 - 1999

Sun	Mon	Tue	Wed	Thu	Fri	Sat
					01	02
03	04	05	06	07	08	09
10	11	>12<	13	14	15	16
17	18	19	20	21	22	23
24	25	26	27	28	29	30
31						

| CM551 | Juris - Docket / Case Management | 01/01/1999 |

Appointments for James A. Martin

Tuesday, January 12 - 1999

7:00 AM		000000005,Reminder of Deposition:Emma's Flori
8:00 AM to	9:30 AM	000000001,IRS Examiners Meeting:Reed Products
1:00 PM to	3:00 PM	000000004,Court Appearance:Philips, Mr. & Mrs
5:00 PM to	6:00 PM	PM,Partners' Meeting:

<Ins>	= Add a new Event	<F1> = Display Free Time Graph
<Del>	= Delete this Event	<F2> = Reset Highlighted New Events
<Enter>	= Edit this Event	<F5> = Enter Time & Description

| CM551 | Juris - Docket / Case Management | 01/01/1999 |

Appointments for James A. Martin

Tuesday, January 12 - 1999

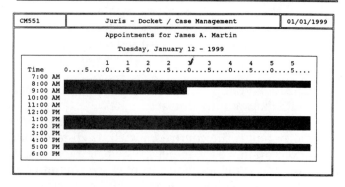

```
           1    1    2    2         3    4    4    5    5
Time   0....5....0....5....0....5....0....5....0....5....0....5....
 7:00 AM
 8:00 AM
 9:00 AM
10:00 AM
11:00 AM
12:00 PM
 1:00 PM
 2:00 PM
 3:00 PM
 4:00 PM
 5:00 PM
 6:00 PM
```

hookups exist between the courtroom and the jail, so that prisoners can have quicker access to court without having to be transported.

One interesting experiment in courtroom applications of technology is under way at the Law School at William and Mary in Williamsburg, Virginia. At that school, students have constructed a model courtroom replete with technological innovations, called Courtroom 21. Their experiments with courtroom technology strongly suggest that appropriately used computers and video technology do enable juries to better understand evidence and, it is hoped, make better decisions. Of course, *appropriate* usage is the key to successful use of technology in the courtroom. Because of technology's power, it has the potential to be used to excess, to unfairly sway a juror's emotions, for example. Projects such as Courtroom 21 must find ways to use the power of technology while assuring that its use serves but does not dominate or obfuscate the factfinding process which is the heart of the judicial system.

One issue that arises in response to the use of computer-generated simulations is whether such simulations are admissible as evidence. Computer-generated graphics are considered to be demonstrative evidence—like other charts, diagrams, drawings, and photographs—and as such tend to be admissible if the item is relevant, authenticated, and not overly prejudicial. As an example of the power of computer-generated simulations, consider *Strock v. Southern Farm Bureau Casualty Insurance Co.*, 998 F.2d 1010, 1993 WL 279069 (4th Cir. 1993), in which a property owner whose house had been damaged by Hurricane Hugo argued that his house had been blown off its foundation and then flooded. He contended that the insurance company's liability attached when the house was blown off its foundation. The insurance company claimed that the house suffered primarily from flood damage. The case went to trial twice, each time resulting in a hung jury. At the third trial, the plaintiff's attorney presented a computer-generated simulation, showing how the house had been blown off its foundation and moved by the storm surge. The simulation accounted for the roof damage and how the house came to rest where it did after the waters had receded. The jury came back with a unanimous verdict for the plaintiff, showing the power of the simulation. When the insurance company challenged the admissibility of the animation, the Fourth Circuit Court of Appeals upheld its use. However, the fact that the court issued an unpublished opinion in that case suggests that there is at least a modicum of uneasiness with this issue. Standards of admissibility related to computer simulations may well evolve in future decisions.

In addition to animation and recreation technology, video deposition technology is being used by many attorneys in the courtroom. They prefer video depositions to transcripts because they believe it is far more compelling and persuasive for the jury to see an actual image of the person than to have the words read to them from a transcript. Here is how it works. The videotaped deposition is transferred to laser disc or CD-ROM format. The information in the deposition is then assigned a specific bar code. During trial, the attorney or his staff has a laptop computer right there with them. At the proper time, the required information is accessed via bar code technology from the compact disc or laser disc and immediately presented to the jury. Imagine how damaging—and how persuasive—it would be for a jury to actually see a person telling two different stories.

Another example of the power of technology in the courtroom comes from Judge Carl Rubin of the federal District Court in Cincinnati, Ohio, whose courtroom is one of the most automated in the country. Among other things, the courtroom features 10 21-inch monitors; the bailiff controls the system. Three of those monitors are placed in front of the jury box. When the defense team in a complex civil fraud case informed the judge that they did not want to use the computer system, the judge warned them that they were making a mistake. Two months later, the jury awarded the plaintiff $15 million from the defendant accounting firm. Jurors attributed their verdict to the clarity of the computerized presentation, their comfort with video input, and their concern that the defendant's failure to use it meant the defense was hiding something. This was certainly a costly lesson to the defense, but it is also a glimpse into the future, as well as a valuable lesson to the legal community about how technology is transforming the way information and evidence are presented in a courtroom.

As you can see, technology is not merely a feature of the law office or the law firm; it has found its way into every aspect of the legal process, including the very courtrooms where judges and juries decide the law.

Document Storage and Retrieval Systems

Information management is an essential concern of the modern law firm, and it usually involves paper or magnetic storage media. Newly emerging technologies can significantly improve on these methods by using optical imaging, which enables the user to translate words and graphics into electronic images that can be stored on optical disks or CD-ROM, each of which can hold between 20,000 and 40,000 pages. Retrieval of stored documents is both flexible and lightning-fast, and optical imaging can also save the user a tremendous amount of money. One California firm estimated that it saved 54 percent of its costs on a case that involved 400,000 pages of documents, while simultaneously increasing accuracy and accessibility of documents. The upcoming case study on optical imaging will tell you more about this technology.

Computerized Document Assembly: My Paper Is Faster than Your Paper

Regardless of the area of law involved, legal work generally requires the creation of a tremendous number of documents. Wills, contracts, motions, briefs, financing agreements, covenants, and corporate charters are just a few examples of the types of documents that the lawyer or paralegal must prepare. Many users of computerized document production and assembly enthusiastically recommend this technology. Their experience is that they can save a tremendous amount of time, and thereby increase profits, without sacrificing efficiency or quality. Clients also appreciate the speed with which their work gets done.

Using a computerized document assembly program, such as Scrivener or HotDocs, a 12-page separation agreement can be prepared in less than 4 minutes. FastDraft user David Thomas uses the computer to assemble extremely complex documents. He was able to complete a two-borrower international financing deal of more than 200 pages with his system, which made more than 1,500 decisions in less than 30 seconds and printed a 200-page draft that was 95 percent correct within minutes of completing the form. He was then free to spend his time on the 5 percent that needed special consideration.

Criticisms of computerized document assembly are of two kinds. Some assert that it is not flexible enough for anything but standard agreements. Others feel it is too difficult to use. Many users would disagree. Not only can they demonstrate its effectiveness with complex documents, as described here, but new Windows-based document assembly programs are extremely user-friendly. In a world where competition for business is intense and effective use of time translates into improved bottom lines, it is likely that document assembly technology will be increasingly used in a variety of capacities, including both simple and complex document production and assembly.

Specialized Legal Applications

Because the computer is so powerful and flexible when it comes to the storage and retrieval of information, an infinite variety of applications are now available or will become available in the future to assist lawyers and paralegals with their work. Some of the areas that are presently available include applications in the following areas:

Conflict-of-interest checks
Economic damages calculations
Deed checking and plotting
Estate planning and tax applications
Computerized training
Case and client management
Patent and trademark searches (see Figures 13-15 and 13-16)
Plaintiff/defendant indices for courthouse records
Library management.

These applications use the capabilities of the computer to do exactly what their names suggest: They can calculate damages, plot deeds, or search for

FIGURE 13-15
Compact discs store
patent information ...
(Courtesy of
MicroPatent.)

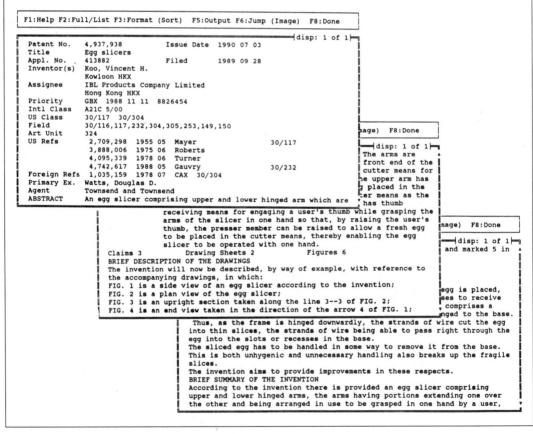

```
 F1:Help F2:Full/List F3:Format (Sort)  F5:Output F6:Jump (Image)  F8:Done

                                                 ┤disp: 1 of 1├
 Patent No.    4,937,938      Issue Date  1990 07 03
 Title         Egg slicers
 Appl. No.     413882         Filed       1989 09 28
 Inventor(s)   Koo, Vincent H.
               Kowloon HKX
 Assignee      IBL Products Company Limited
               Hong Kong HKX
 Priority      GBX  1988 11 11  8826454
 Intl Class    A21C 5/00
 US Class      30/117  30/304
 Field         30/116,117,232,304,305,253,149,150          age)  F8:Done
 Art Unit      324
 US Refs       2,709,298  1955 05  Mayer          30/117  ┤disp: 1 of 1├
               3,888,006  1975 06  Roberts                The arms are
               4,095,339  1978 06  Turner                 front end of the
               4,742,617  1988 05  Gauvry         30/232  cutter means for
 Foreign Refs  1,035,159  1978 07  CAX  30/304            he upper arm has
 Primary Ex.   Watts, Douglas D.                          g placed in the
 Agent         Townsend and Townsend                      ter means as the
 ABSTRACT      An egg slicer comprising upper and lower hinged arm which are  has thumb
               receiving means for engaging a user's thumb while grasping the
               arms of the slicer in one hand so that, by raising the user's
               thumb, the presser member can be raised to allow a fresh egg   age)  F8:Done
               to be placed in the cutter means, thereby enabling the egg
               slicer to be operated with one hand.                           ┤disp: 1 of 1├
         Claims 3           Drawing Sheets 2           Figures 6              and marked 5 in
         BRIEF DESCRIPTION OF THE DRAWINGS
         The invention will now be described, by way of example, with reference to
         the accompanying drawings, in which:
         FIG. 1 is a side view of an egg slicer according to the invention;   egg is placed,
         FIG. 2 is a plan view of the egg slicer;                             ses to receive
         FIG. 3 is an upright section taken along the line 3--3 of FIG. 2;    comprises a
         FIG. 4 is an end view taken in the direction of the arrow 4 of FIG. 1;  nged to the base.
              Thus, as the frame is hinged downwardly, the strands of wire cut the egg
              into thin slices, the strands of wire being able to pass right through the
              egg into the slots or recesses in the base.
              The sliced egg has to be handled in some way to remove it from the base.
              This is both unhygenic and unnecessary handling also breaks up the fragile
              slices.
              The invention aims to provide improvements in these respects.
              BRIEF SUMMARY OF THE INVENTION
              According to the invention there is provided an egg slicer comprising
              upper and lower hinged arms, the arms having portions extending one over
              the other and being arranged in use to be grasped in one hand by a user,
```

FIGURE 13-16   ... which can be displayed on a computer screen or on paper. (Courtesy of MicroPatent.)

patents. On your job, you will learn what legal software your firm uses. You will also want to maintain your awareness of technical applications that might be relevant to your work. In addition to publications and marketing information you might receive, a number of other sources can help you learn about new computer applications. The LawTech Center of the American Bar Association, located in Chicago, is a unique learning facility where lawyers and paralegals can learn about and use the newest law office automation equipment in an informative, nonsales setting. You can schedule a visit by calling the ABA Technology Hotline at (312) 988-5465. If you are ever in the Chicago area, a trip to this center would be well worth the time spent.

Publications exist that review available software. The Lawyers' Library publication *Legal Software Review,* for example, gives descriptions of more than 400 software titles; you can get further information from the vendors of products that interest you. Additionally, Price Waterhouse's Law Firm Services Group annually presents *Legal Tech,* which is an exhibition and conference that brings together legal personnel to discuss and view the latest in law office technology.

The following case studies introduce you to two of the most significant technical applications for law firms, litigation support and optical imaging, and give you a good idea of their features and benefits.

CASE STUDY   **TECHNICAL APPLICATIONS #1**

Is It Time to Automate Your Firm's Litigation Support?

By Anne Mehringer
Aspen Systems Corporation

For most litigating lawyers in law firms or corporations, a new case means urgency. There is seldom the luxury of excess time in preparing for litigation. Four months from today, the case goes to court. Yesterday, hundreds of Bekin's boxes of related documents were delivered to the law firm—documents that must be immediately analyzed, digested, and organized so that even a receipt can be located among reams of calendars, financial statements, and depositions.

Computerized litigation support will organize litigation documents into a system that enables lawyers and their assistants to search and retrieve case information instantly. Boxes of data become a compact, organized database. Through the use of personal computers and with the advent of laptop computers, access to case information is immediate and convenient from anywhere, even from the courtroom. (See Figure 13-17.)

Computerized litigation support (CLS) is the merging of information science and project management with specifically applied software products and hardware. In its simplest form, a litigation support system is like a library. A database, or library, is organized as a storage and retrieval center for all case documents. A lawyer can quickly review an online index to locate a document. Each document can be identified by its title, author, date or type of document, content, or relevance, depending on how the lawyer directing the litigation wants to orchestrate the case. There may be a summary of that document that the lawyer or assistant can quickly review, or, when the case demands, a document such as a transcript, deposition, or interrogatory can be viewed in full text.

FIGURE 13-17
A paralegal reviews a deposition transcript accessed at her PC through computerized litigation support.

Is It Right for Your Firm?

When should a law firm investigate a computerized litigation support system? How do you decide what system is best for your law firm or corporate legal department? Is this litigation support an individual lawyer solution or a firm-wide solution? The decision to implement computerized litigation support usually depends on the size and complexity of the cases your law firm litigates. First, review two criteria that will singularly or in concert indicate that a need for computerized litigation support or a CLS vendor exists in your law firm.

Text Retrieval

What is the volume and nature of the document collection in the case? A litigation might involve tens of thousands, even millions, of documents that must be organized so a lawyer can make critical searches and connections quickly. Specifically, computerized litigation support should be considered when a need exists to manage a case document collection of 5,000 documents or more and/or there is a need to organize the documents into a system that can be accessed at any given time by the litigating team.

Time

What are your deadlines? Do you have the staff and resources to respond in the time frames dictated by the litigation schedule? Is your need case-specific, or is it part of an overall plan to develop CLS capability for future firm-wide use?

When a tight time frame is involved, as is usually the case with litigation, computerized litigation support vendors can provide a lawyer with managers, consultants, and technical personnel trained to work whenever and wherever the litigation dictates. Effective use of a vendor can provide a quality database quickly and efficiently.

If you have the luxury of time and a trained staff to code and input a document collection, an in-house system may be what you want to pursue. The time required depends on the number of cases and documents to be organized.

Yet another approach, again depending on time frames and case demands, is a combination of in-house technology and outside resources. For example, a law firm may purchase its own computer litigation support hardware and software while using outside resources for tedious tasks such as coding a document collection.

Once the need for computerized litigation support is recognized, it is necessary to have the support and financial commitment of the entire litigation team, particularly the lead lawyer. The next step is to review the options available and decide whether to develop a system in-house or contract the services of an outside vendor to provide a variety of integrated services. Typically, outside litigation support should be considered when a case is above the 20,000-document level, particularly if the document collection must be shared among parties in a variety of locations. An in-house system is most efficient and cost-effective if a law firm's cases average between 5,000 and 20,000 documents. Again, a combination of both might be the best solution.

Regardless of the firm's decision on in-house versus outside CLS, a database—a computerized file of all evidentiary materials in a case—must be designed and built.

Building a Database

The nucleus of any automated litigation support endeavor is the database, which will be used in three basic ways:

1. Information gathering or acquisition activities
2. Information organizing or processing activities
3. Information retrieval and utilization activities.

A legal application usually involves one or both of two types of databases: full-text and surrogate. A *full-text database* contains documents in their entirety and is particularly suited for transcript management. Full-text databases can be enhanced with selective objective information to improve the user's ability to retrieve and understand the full-text data. For example, a 200-page transcript can be broken into one to ten-page units so that a lawyer can search only the information needed, rather than the entire transcript, each time the document is searched.

A *surrogate database* contains information that is extracted from documents and entered into the database. For example, selected information such as author, recipient, date, document type, title, subject matter, and attachments are keyed into the database. This type of database is particularly suited to managing large document collections that have a variety of types of documents.

Although it is usually more effective and cost-efficient to implement separate databases, full-text and surrogate databases are occasionally combined to serve certain applications. For example, where similar language is used in a series of documents, such as prospectuses, and the specific words used are critical to the litigation, a database of extracted text and bibliographic information can be most effective. Surrogate databases can also be linked with image storage systems to provide access to the full document.

Assembling a Team

Whether you're working with a vendor or building a database in-house, choosing the right person to perform information acquisition, organization, and processing in the litigation support effort is critical. The decision will depend on the needs of the lawyer, as well as timing and staffing demands imposed by the litigation. To compound these demands, evidentiary materials in need of organization can be located anywhere—on hand at the law firm or stored at warehouses around the country. It may be in the best interest of the lawyer directing the litigation to utilize a litigation support vendor, particularly if the case at hand is the litigation team's first experience with CLS. The vendor's role can range from simple consultation on the effort to implementation and management of the entire litigation support effort.

It is wise to have the lawyer in charge of the litigation establish criteria by which a document collection will be organized. Lawyer involvement in database design is critical—it will protect against discoverability and allow the lawyer to be a hands-on document manager in control of the case. Building a database, however, is a labor-intensive task. A vendor's ability to mobilize the microfilming and coding process with speed, accuracy, and objectivity can be a tremendous advantage in litigation. The vendor can also offer expertise in establishing guidelines for coding and keying information consistently.

Once a database is built, the document can be immediately and conveniently accessed by a lawyer from a terminal at her desk.

If you decide to use the service of an outside vendor, that company should fill the role of educator as well as consultant. It should provide training and be easily accessible, whether you need to ask an operational question or to supplement support capabilities as issues shift or the strategy of the case changes.

The number and complexity of litigations in the United States are increasing at a phenomenal rate each year. Law firms that take on more and more litigations must strive to maintain efficiency and productivity—litigation support is one way for firms to do that, CLS can indeed be a very profitable new partner for your law firm.

CASE STUDY

TECHNICAL APPLICATIONS #2

Optical Imaging: Paper Meets the 21st Century

By Irving Green, President
Skan Technologies, Inc.

Despite predictions of the "paperless" office, paper documents are, and will remain, the basis of business communications. But how are large numbers of paper documents to be managed? Existing solutions range from the simple filing cabinet to complex computer-aided micrographic storage systems. The weakness of these systems is in their slow retrieval times, inefficient indexing, bulkiness, and limited longevity of the storage. The chances are that in our own lifetime we will not live in a truly paperless society. But paper—the old standby—is bulky, costly to store, and easily lost or destroyed. Imaging systems are a viable alternative in a number of legal applications.

It helps to understand that 95 percent of all documents are housed in low-tech filing cabinets. These cabinets take up expensive real estate, and the storage of this paper causes many firms a great deal of distress (see Figure 13-18). Lawyers and paralegals spend an inordinate number of hours annually looking for information that is misplaced, misfiled, mislabeled, or simply cannot be found (see Figure 13-19). These nonproductive and often nonbillable hours take a toll on the firm's bottom line and tend to frustrate the user—taking an additional toll in lost productivity and initiative. Unfortunately, no relief is in sight for the paper storage problem. If anything, your firm can expect an annual increase of some 20 percent in the amount of paper it will be called upon to store. Imaging can reduce the increase and maybe take some of the bite out of the backlog.

FIGURE 13-18
Paper storage is a significant problem for law firms.

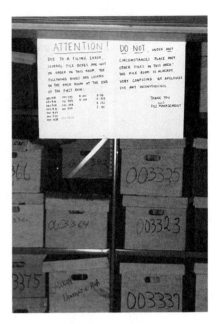

FIGURE 13-19
Misplaced files cause frustration and wasted time.

A few statistics about paper files will help you appreciate the seriousness of the situation:

- A simple misfile will cost your firm in excess of $120.
- The cost per filing inch for annual maintenance is upwards of $11—and even more if you're located in a major city.
- The cost of owning and maintaining a standard five-drawer filing cabinet is hovering at the $900 mark—annually.
- A single 5¼-inch optical disk can hold up to 25,000 business letters—the equivalent of three four-drawer file cabinets.
- A single 12-inch optical disk can hold more than 30 file drawers—the equivalent of some 200,000 cubic inches of drawer space.

A successful imaging system can generate additional revenues for the firm and greatly reduce the cost of preparing for litigation. A speaker at a recently held imaging conference claimed that one of his litigation clients spent $15 a page to locate and produce documents needed during litigation. By putting the information on optical disk, the firm reduced that figure to just $4 per page!

It is important to make certain that the time of attorneys and other staff members is put to use in an efficient and revenue-producing manner. An imaging system will allow you to profit on document production and storage and in the retrieval of information from these documents. Digital Image Management System (DIMS) applications offer a way to manage the increasing burden of paper-document storage and retrieval. In a DIMS application, rather than storing an actual document, an electronic image of the document is stored. Documents are read by a scanner, which creates a high-resolution digital image of the document. The document image is then stored on a high-capacity optical disk. These 12-inch optical disks can store in excess of 100,000 pages each. Entire cases can be stored in a single optical disk juke box containing multiple optical disk platters—replacing the use of file cabinets, complete file rooms, and the efforts of numerous file clerks. Finally, the stored image can be indexed using a Database Management System (DBMS), simultaneously viewed on network workstations, or printed on high-resolution laser printers.

How Imaging Works

An imaging system assumes that all documents will be numbered according to acceptable methodology currently employed (Bates stamp, removable labels, bar coding). The documents will be batch-scanned. Each batch bears a different number, usually the first number in the document. Once the documents are scanned and recorded on the optical disk platter, with each platter storing between 25,000 and 100,000 pages or more, the operator will be asked to enter the necessary information. In each case, the data entered will accurately reflect the requirements that you have for any particular case. The imaging system will automatically track the number of pages in each document, and it will allow you to view a document in its entirety, by specific page or by a group of pages within the document.

You can retrieve the documents in the case by any of the categories previously indexed—date, address, or any combination—author, addressee, subject, date, etc. You will then see a series of documents—a "hit list" on the screen. You then have a choice of:

- Printing out a copy of the hit list
- Viewing the documents on the screen
- Printing out all or some of the documents.

You can call up the files for all documents of a particular type, for a finite time period, or for specific particles of information, all without having to physically search the files. Your ability to search the records that you have previously scanned is virtually unlimited. What you will get out of this system is limited only by what you have put into it; it is your duty to help your staff design the database to meet and anticipate all your needs. By so doing, you will receive the following benefits:

- *Less expensive.* The handling of large numbers of paper documents and files is surprisingly expensive. Costs include the staff needed to file, retrieve, copy, and transport paper, as well as the price of storage space and copying equipment.
- *Labor saving.* In contrast, documents scanned into an imaging system can be filed, retrieved, reproduced, and distributed with a push of a button. This eliminates labor costs associated with paper handling, as well as the need for large storage facilities.
- *Multiple users.* Because scanned documents can be viewed by multiple users simultaneously, the need for copying is greatly reduced. Further, lost productivity because of critical documents being "out of file" is eliminated.
- *Reduces search time.* Although difficult to measure accurately, time spent searching for files or documents prevents attorneys and members of their staffs from applying their skills and experience to higher-value activities, such as reviewing relevant documents and making decisions that can play an important role in determining the development of the case.
- *Speeds processing.* When transactions are paper-based, processing is limited by the speed at which the paper can move through the organization. For example, documents cannot be reviewed until they have gone through the process of being received and entered into the appropriate paper file. Often you cannot proceed with a case until certain papers

are received and documented. Very often these papers have already been received, but have not been properly entered into the paper system or are residing on one of your associates' desks.

- *Immediate availability.* Document imaging lifts this constraint. Information is updated on-line and in real time, providing complete details in vital areas. Once documents are received, they can be scanned and made available immediately to all interested parties. The result is faster, more responsive service; a better handle on the material available; and a competitive edge over your opponent.

- *Reporting capabilities.* Because electronic processing can be managed with software—for example, software specifically designed to meet your litigation support requirements—sophisticated reporting capabilities are available to you. This gives you the tools needed to effectively monitor the progress of your case. For example, the system gives the users all the information needed for processing the images and accounting for them in an orderly and efficient fashion. A key feature of document imaging systems is that they can use software to control the flow of information—that is, files, documents, and data—through the firm. This feature eliminates many time-consuming tasks that staff members must perform on a paper-based information system. The software can also check to see if a file is complete (that is, if all documents have been received); retrieve relevant information; or track the status of documents and files.

Partners All

The law firm is in partnership with the information scientist of today. This partnership, though still not fully understood by both sides, is an absolute necessity. The steady growth of technology and the impact it has on our daily life have found their way into the law office. The complexity of legal practice in today's economy is such that one must use modern means and devices to deal with the complexities of legal practice.

Optical imaging provides a definite advantage for clients. The legal practitioner has a clear responsibility to give his client the greatest potential advantage by using the latest tools of litigation support available and by affording maximum value for the money the client is spending on the case. The cost savings to clients using optical-based litigation support systems can be quite substantial over older methods of document production and storage.

Optical imaging also provides a number of advantages for professionals. As a professional, you are interested in using available resources to maximize the personal objectives of your profession. Litigation support is a collection of assisting activities that helps the attorney maximize her use of time. Optical-based litigation support adds modern technology and systems to the traditional manual support methods. Many of the cases you are called upon to deal with are so large or complex that manual methods of handling the information would be impossible, or would not yield a convincing set of supporting facts in time to be effective. The facts, or data, must be combined with and processed through computer programs or sets of instructions that you have a hand in designing, so that they will select and manipulate the data, format it, and put it out in a form that is understandable and usable to the reader within the context for which it was selected.

These techniques, as well as the training necessary to operate these new systems, have been highly developed and can provide a multitude of advantages for the lawyer and legal client. They are available to you if you will take just a small amount of time to learn them and to apply a few easy concepts in your practice.

Technical Applications: A Summary

Legal software refers to computer applications that are directly oriented to the specialized needs of the lawyer and law office. Ten years ago, only a fraction of the applications that exist today were available; ten years hence, even more will exist. In addition to becoming expert on the systems used in your firm, you will want to maintain an interest in new technical developments as they find their way in increasing numbers and applications into the law office.

Key Terms

CD-ROM	LawTech Center	optical imaging
docket control	LEXIS	WESTLAW
integrated system	litigation management	

Problems and Activities

1. For one of your areas of interest, such as litigation, real estate, or bankruptcy, find out what computer applications exist. You may want to write to some companies to get detailed information about their products.

2. Find out the ways in which law firms are using and anticipate using CD-ROM technology.

3. What ethical issues arise from the use of software for legal applications?

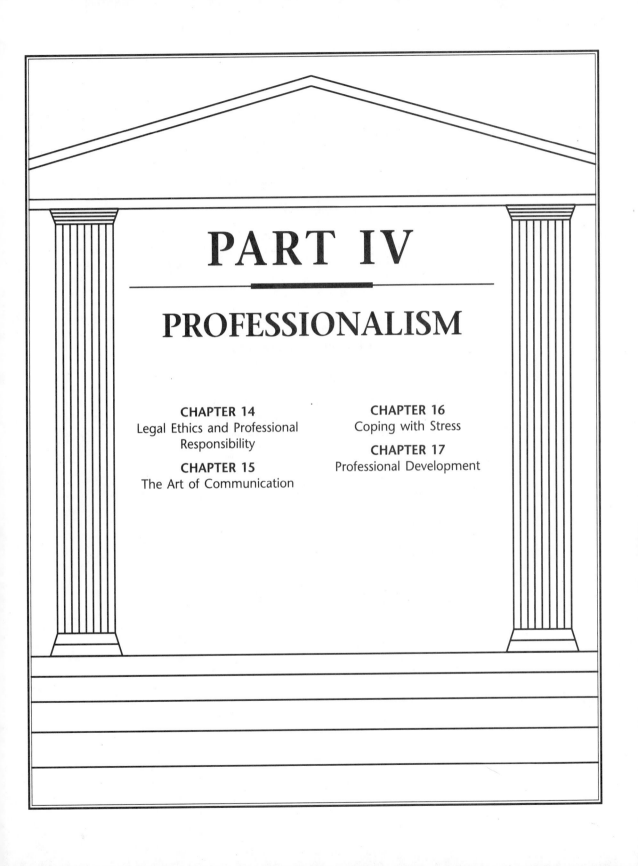

PART IV

PROFESSIONALISM

PART IV OVERVIEW

Chapter 14: Legal Ethics and Professional Responsibility

An introduction to legal ethics, with a special emphasis on those aspects of legal ethics that have the greatest relevance for the paralegal, including issues of unauthorized practice of law, confidentiality, conflict of interest, and prohibited activities. Ethical behavior is emphasized as a means of achieving client satisfaction.

Chapter 15: The Art of Communication

A primer to help paralegals achieve clear, effective communications by examining how each aspect of the communication process can be a source of miscommunication. Also included are hints about how to communicate effectively in the law office.

Chapter 16: Coping with Stress

Sources of stress in a law office are described, and strategies for handling stress are presented. The cognitive approach to handling stress, which emphasizes not external events but rather our coping strategies, is discussed.

Chapter 17: Professional Development

An introduction to the process of professional development, beginning with the paralegal job search, including sample résumés and interviewing skills, and including continuing education and preparation for growth and advancement in the legal field.

CHAPTER 14

LEGAL ETHICS AND PROFESSIONAL RESPONSIBILITY

OBJECTIVES

By the completion of this chapter, you should:

- understand the idea of professionalism in the law;
- understand the sources of professional conduct for the paralegal;
- understand and apply the major ethical provisions relevant to paralegals; and
- understand the relationship between ethical behavior and client relations.

Professionalism in the Legal Process: More than "Be Professional"

When the word *professionalism* first comes to mind, most people think it means something in terms of "act and look like you belong in the business world." Professionalism for legal professionals, such as paralegals, is much more than merely following John T. Molloy's advice in his book, *Dress for Success*. Although the paralegal needs to look and dress effectively (as does any other professional), paralegals, like attorneys, have written standards and guidelines that define professionalism for them.

Professionalism in the legal context consists of the rules by which attorneys play the game of lawyering, and it is a far more comprehensive system than you might have imagined. Like the baseball pitcher who has a killer fast ball, but cannot pitch until he learns the difference between a ball and a strike, the paralegal with the brilliant legal mind cannot effectively put her skills to use until she has learned the rules of the game of law. The rules of the law game are *ethics*. Such fundamental principles as confidentiality, conflict of interest, and the appearance of impropriety must be mastered before the paralegal can put practical skills to use. By equating ethics and professionalism with the do's and don'ts of practicing law, the definition of ethics becomes rather simple. A paralegal cannot become successful if the paralegal is not willing to learn and follow ethical standards imposed on the profession. (See Figure 14-1.)

The standards for the ethical conduct of attorneys is set forth in the American Bar Association (ABA) Model Code of Professional Responsibility and the ABA Model Rules of Professional Conduct. Many state bars have used these model rules to create their own codes of professional responsibility. Paralegals, like attorneys, have rules; theirs appear in the Affirmation of Responsibility of the National Federation of Paralegal Associations (NFPA) and the Code of Ethics and Professional Responsibility of the National Association of Legal Assistants (NALA), although portions of the ABA and state standards may affect paralegal conduct.

FIGURE 14-1 Attorneys and their assistants must conform to high ethical standards.

The Sources of Professionalism for the Paralegal

Four principal sources define professionalism in the paralegal context. First, there are the ABA standards, detailed in the Model Code of Professional Responsibility and the Model Rules of Professional Conduct. Second, paralegal behavior is regulated by state codes of ethics, which are usually modeled on the ABA model codes. Third, the NFPA sets forth standards for paralegal conduct in its Affirmation of Responsibility. Fourth, NALA has established a code of professional behavior for paralegals. The importance of ethics to the legal profession is evident from the work of the ABA, NFPA, and NALA in creating ethical guidelines. Let us examine each of these standards.

ABA Standards

The American Bar Association (ABA) is a voluntary organization of attorneys; it is the largest single national organization for attorneys. One of its important roles is the development of ethical guidelines for the legal profession. These guidelines are then adopted, perhaps with modifications, by each of the states, which retain jurisdiction to license and discipline attorneys.

The ABA has developed two sets of ethical rules. The Model Code of Professional Responsibility, called "the Code," was initially published in 1969 and was the earliest version of ethical rules. Many felt that the Code was not as effective as it should be and in 1982 the ABA published a second set of guidelines, the

---

On
Point   *THE BUNDYS VISIT NORTHERN EXPOSURE*

Al and Peg Bundy have just graduated from law school and passed the bar in two states. They attended the part-time night program in law school so that Al could continue to support the family through his shoe sales career. Because they weren't doing anything else at night, Al and Peg decided that a change of career wouldn't be a bad idea. To help their parents, Kelly and Bud went to paralegal school during that time.

To bolster their client base, the Bundys decide to visit Cicely, Alaska, as they were members of the Alaska Bar and thought it might be a good place to stimulate some legal business. First they see Maurice, who wants to buy some acreage and also quitclaim his interest in a condominium. "I can take care of both those things," says Al, even though he has never done any property law. He does not ask if Maurice has other representation, nor does Maurice ask him for legal help or advice.

Kelly is visiting the Brick, the local bar, when Shelly comes in. "I was just in an accident," she says, and then collapses on the floor. Kelly goes over and helps Shelly's hand sign a contract for legal services. "Bundy & Bundy to the rescue," she proclaims.

Peg is talking with Marilyn, the physician's secretary, and she tells Marilyn that her client, Noot Greenrich, had privately confessed to a murder. Marilyn's husband works for the FBI.

Paralegal Bud runs into Chris. Chris asks all kinds of questions about First Amendment law because of his work at the radio station. "I can tell you all about the law and what you should do to protect yourself," Bud tells him.

Al is talking with Ed, a local filmmaker. Ed tells Al that he wants to sue Nike because one of his shoes exploded, causing him to break his ankle. Despite the fact that Al has previously represented Nike as a client, Al tells Ed he will be glad to take the case.

It is the end of the day. "I like this place," says Al. "It's a lot easier to get legal clients than it is to sell a pair of shoes."

Model Rules for Professional Conduct, called "the Rules." States model their ethical rules on either the Code or the Rules; many feel that the Rules are more straightforward, easier to apply and understand, and more pragmatic than the Code. An easy way to tell the difference between these two sets of guidelines is to realize that the Code is divided into canons, ethical considerations, and disciplinary rules, whereas the Rules are direct statements followed by comments. If you look at state ethical guidelines, and you see a section called "ethical considerations," you know that the state has adopted the Code rather than the Rules.

In addition to the Code and the Rules, the ABA has directly addressed the issues of legal assistant use by publishing its Model Guidelines for the Utilization of Legal Assistants (1991). These guidelines have two purposes. First, they are a model for states to use as they attempt to develop guidelines for the uses of legal assistants in their own jurisdictions. Second, they are intended to educate lawyers about the effective utilization of legal assistants and thereby encourage the use of legal assistants. The fact that the ABA has created and published the Model Guidelines is testimony to the integration of paralegals into the legal profession, as well as to the evolving professionalism of legal assistants.

Four basic areas of the ABA codes are directly relevant to paralegals:

1. The unauthorized practice of law
2. Confidentiality
3. Attorney-client privilege
4. Conflict of interest.

These four sections of the ABA guidelines, which are covered in both the Code and the Rules, directly impact the paralegal and are therefore of utmost importance for the paralegal to understand. Furthermore, these four sections are addressed by both paralegal associations, the NFPA and the NALA. It is also important that legal assistants understand and have a working knowledge of other ethical principles; these principles will be dealt with in your class on legal ethics. As a starting point, know and understand at least these four principles, for it is impossible to be an effective paralegal without knowing the ethical guidelines that define paralegal work.

The Unauthorized Practice of Law

The issue of the unauthorized practice of law concerns whether an unlicensed person can perform tasks or activities that by law are reserved to licensed attorneys. The essential purpose of this doctrine is the protection of the public through the licensing and regulation of practicing attorneys. However, the doctrine has come under attack from some quarters because it reserves an economic monopoly for lawyers. As mentioned earlier, a number of states are experimenting with exceptions to the unauthorized practice of law doctrine, which would allow nonlawyers such as paralegals to perform work previously reserved for attorneys. Nonetheless, it is vitally important for legal assistants to understand this doctrine so they can conform their behavior to its requirements.

Rules 5.3 and 5.5(b) of the ABA Model Rules both relate to the lawyer's obligation to prevent the unauthorized practice of law. Rule 5.3 is the provision that makes lawyers responsible for supervising nonlawyer employees and for ensuring that the nonlawyer's conduct is compatible with the lawyer's professional obligations—one of which is the prevention of unauthorized practice.

RULE 5.3 Responsibilities Regarding Nonlawyer Assistants

———— IIII ————

With respect to a nonlawyer employed or retained by or associated with a lawyer:

(a) a partner in a law firm shall make reasonable efforts to ensure that the firm has in effect measures giving reasonable assurance that the person's conduct is compatible with the professional obligations of the lawyer;

(b) a lawyer having direct supervisory authority over the nonlawyer shall make reasonable efforts to ensure that the person's conduct is compatible with the professional obligations of the lawyer; and

(c) a lawyer shall be responsible for conduct of such a person that would be a violation of the rules of professional conduct if engaged in by a lawyer if:

(1) the lawyer orders or, with the knowledge of the specific conduct, ratifies the conduct involved; or

(2) the lawyer is a partner in the law firm in which the person is employed, or has direct supervisory authority over the person, and knows of the conduct at a time when its consequences can be avoided or mitigated but fails to take reasonable remedial action.

The Comment following this rule requires attorneys to give nonlawyer personnel acting as assistants "appropriate instruction and supervision concerning the ethical aspects of their employment."

Rule 5.5(b), like Rule 5.3, requires lawyers to supervise and take responsibility for the work prepared by their nonlawyer employees.

RULE 5.5 Unauthorized Practice of Law

A lawyer shall not:

(a) practice law in a jurisdiction where doing so violates the regulation of the legal profession in that jurisdiction; or

(b) assist a person who is not a member of the bar in the performance of activity that constitutes the unauthorized practice of law.

A nonlawyer cannot represent a client in court. To do so would clearly constitute the unauthorized practice of law, as would accepting a case, but there are other "gray" areas where the distinction between authorized and unauthorized practice is not so clear. These areas might include going with a client to an administrative agency and informing him what steps need to be taken, or communicating to a client what would be the most likely next step in his case at times when the attorney is unavailable.

Fundamentally, the attorney is ultimately responsible for seeing that those who assist him or her do not engage in the unauthorized practice of law. However, you, as the paraprofessional, must do your part to ensure that you are not crossing into those aspects of the legal process that are specifically reserved for the licensed attorney.

The distinction between tasks that constitute practicing law and tasks that may be performed by nonlawyer staff members in a law firm is frequently categorized as ministerial versus exercising legal knowledge. Generally, *ministerial* applies to tasks that are essentially administrative in character, whereas *exercising legal knowledge* requires independent thought and judgment. In general, paralegal work can be characterized as that work that is essentially ministerial.

When it comes to actually applying these categories, it is sometimes difficult to decide which category an activity would fall into. However, common sense tells us that if the paralegal is making a judgment call as to what step should be pursued next or what action at law should be taken, this judgment is "practicing law," for it requires the paralegal to utilize legal acumen and independent judgment. A good analogy is the one for doctors. Like attorneys, doctors are ethically bound not to encourage the unauthorized practice of medicine. Just as a nurse would not provide a patient with a diagnosis or recommend surgery, a paralegal should not tell a client that her case is a breach of contract and that suit should be filed in the action prior to the expiration of the statute of limitations. In addition, the nurse cannot accept a person as a patient, just as a paralegal cannot accept a person as a client. So, if you are "diagnosing" a client's legal ailment or recommending a legal "cure," you are probably engaging in the unauthorized practice of law.

There are several disciplinary methods for ensuring that you do not engage in the unauthorized practice of law. First, it is a violation of ABA, NALA, and NFPA ethical standards. Second, in jurisdictions requiring certification, certification may be revoked for such actions. Finally, most states have criminal statutes forbidding the unauthorized practice of law; therefore, to engage in the unauthorized practice of law may be a criminal act subject to fines and/or imprisonment.

Case law interpreting this rule seems to indicate that paralegals may draft legal documents, interview witnesses, assemble data, and do legal research, so long as the attorney retains responsibility for their work and the work is prepared under the direction of the responsible attorney. (See Figure 14-2.) Tasks that are clearly forbidden for paralegals are:

FIGURE 14-2 It is a paralegal's job to research the law, but advising a client of her legal rights is strictly the responsibility of the attorney.

1. *Representing clients in court.* A paralegal cannot appear in state or federal court on behalf of a client, although some administrative agencies do permit paralegals to appear in court. An example of this situation is a § 341 hearing in bankruptcy court, where a paralegal representing a creditor can question the debtor. To be safe, do not represent a client in any legal proceeding, including depositions, unless the rules of a particular agency permit it.

2. *Giving legal advice.* A paralegal should not give legal advice to a client. Giving advice might include telling clients they need to file suit, need to incorporate, or need to take any specific legal action. It is wise, also, to refrain from telling clients the types of issues involved in their case; these tasks should be left to the attorney.

3. *Accepting a case.* A paralegal cannot accept a case and agree that the attorney she is working with will represent the client. Only an attorney can accept a case. Further, only attorneys can set fees or the billing arrangements for a case.

Under the ABA standards, then, paralegals can assist in the practice of law, but cannot practice law directly. Most state definitions of *law practice* are very broad and difficult to apply, but the ABA's definition seems to define *practicing law* as using professional judgment. If you are using judgment or discretion, you are probably practicing law.

Unauthorized practice is also a subject of NALA rules. Canon 1 of the NALA Code of Ethics and Professional Responsibility states, "A legal assistant shall not perform any of the duties that lawyers only may perform or do things that lawyers themselves may not do." Canons 2 through 6 of the NALA code also address the concept of unauthorized practice of law. Specifically, these canons state as follows:

Canon 2. A legal assistant may perform any task delegated and supervised by a lawyer so long as the lawyer is responsible to that client, maintains a direct relationship with the client, and assumes full professional responsibility for the work product.

Canon 3. A legal assistant shall not engage in the practice of law by giving legal advice, appearing in court, setting fees, or accepting cases.

Canon 4. A legal assistant shall not act in matters involving professional legal judgment as the services of a lawyer are essential in the public interest whenever the exercise of such judgment is required.

Canon 5. A legal assistant must act prudently in determining the extent to which a client may be assisted without the presence of a lawyer.

Canon 6. A legal assistant shall not engage in the unauthorized practice of law and shall assist in preventing the unauthorized practice of law.

The Affirmation of Responsibility of the NFPA also recognizes the need for paralegals to ensure that their conduct does not fall under the definition of *unauthorized practice of law.* The Affirmation states that "a paralegal shall demonstrate initiative in performing and expanding the paralegal role in the delivery of legal services within the parameters of the unauthorized practice of law statutes." Unauthorized practice, then, is an important issue in paralegal ethics; all three sources address it, and you might well find yourself in a situation where you face an ethical conflict revolving around unauthorized practice.

But, like the nurse who can bandage knees and take vital signs, the paralegal can assist a lawyer by interviewing witnesses or drafting documents. The nurse, however, cannot operate on a patient, and the paralegal cannot appear in court on behalf of a client. In order to practice law by giving legal advice, one must be licensed by the state as an attorney, and therein lies the difference between a paralegal's abilities and those of an attorney.

An exception to the principle of unauthorized practice of law is self-representation, known as *pro se representation*; a person can always represent herself in any civil or criminal matter, and this is not defined as practicing law. But the choice is limited to an attorney or oneself; one cannot have a friend act as representative.

Confidentiality

A second area that impacts paralegal behavior under the ABA guidelines concerns the confidentiality of communications between legal professionals and their clients. Communications between attorney and client are confidential and cannot be revealed to anyone unless the client has given the attorney permission to reveal the information. Client communications to paralegals and other legal personnel who are acting within the scope of their employment as agents of the attorney are also protected. Paralegals, like attorneys, cannot reveal information obtained in their work to anyone except those working on the case.

Confidentiality is covered in Rule 1.6 of the ABA Model Rules, which provides:

RULE 1.6 Confidentiality of Information

(a) A lawyer shall not reveal information relating to representation of a client unless the client consents after consultation, except for disclosures that are impliedly authorized in order to carry out the representation, and except as stated in paragraph (b).

(b) A lawyer may reveal such information to the extent the lawyer reasonably believes necessary:

(1) to prevent the client from committing a criminal act that the lawyer believes is likely to result in imminent death or substantial bodily harm; or

(2) to establish a claim or defense on behalf of the lawyer in a controversy between the lawyer and the client, to establish a defense to a criminal charge or civil claim against the lawyer based upon conduct in which the client was involved, or to respond to allegations in any proceeding concerning the lawyer's representation of the client.

The Rules designate more information to be confidential than does the Code, requiring only that the communication "relate . . . to the representation." This includes any information, whether acquired before or after representation, that relates to the subject of representation. In this respect, the Rules are broader than the Code. Thus, any and all information that the legal professional or her agents may gain relating to the representation of a client is covered and cannot be disclosed.

MELISSA D. EDWARDS
LEGAL ASSISTANT

DREW, ECKL & FARNHAM
880 WEST PEACHTREE STREET
P.O. BOX 7600
ATLANTA, GEORGIA 30357

TELEPHONE
(404) 885-1400
TELECOPIER
(404) 876-0992
TELEX
9102502675 DEF ATL

FIGURE 14-3 It is essential that you present yourself as a legal assistant, not a lawyer, to fulfill your ethical obligations.

KELLY A. HOWARD, Legal Assistant

DREW, ECKL & FARNHAM
880 West Peachtree Street
P.O. Box 7600
Atlanta, Georgia 30357
(404) 885-1400

The ABA Code provision providing for confidentiality is Disciplinary Rule (DR) 4-101, which states:

(A) "Confidence" refers to information protected by the attorney-client privilege under applicable law, and "secret" refers to other information gained in the professional relationship that the client has requested to be held inviolate or the disclosure of which would be embarrassing or would be likely to be detrimental to the client.

(B) Except when permitted under DR 4-101(C), a lawyer shall not knowingly:

(1) Reveal a confidence or secret of his client.
(2) Use a confidence or secret of his client to the disadvantage of the client.
(3) Use a confidence or secret of his client for the advantage of himself or of a third person, unless the client consents after full disclosure.

(C) A lawyer may reveal:

(1) Confidences or secrets with the consent of the client or clients affected, but only after full disclosure to them.
(2) Confidences or secrets when permitted under the Disciplinary Rules or required by law or court order.
(3) The intention of his client to commit a crime and the information necessary to prevent the crime.
(4) Confidences or secrets necessary to establish or collect his fee or to defend himself or his employees or associates against an accusation of wrongful conduct.

(D) A lawyer shall exercise reasonable care to prevent his employees, associates, and others whose services are utilized by him from disclosing or using confidences or secrets of a client, except that a lawyer may reveal information allowed by DR 4-101(C) through an employee.

DR 4-101 is a broad rule that is based on the need to give clients protection from information disclosure, and it is concerned with the voluntary (rather than forced) disclosure of information by an attorney or her agent. A fundamental principle in the attorney-client relationship is that the attorney will keep confidential information private. This principle is one of the axioms of legal representation. Without assurances that information will be kept confidential, it is very likely that many individuals would go without legal representation. Unless an attorney knows all of the facts concerning a particular situation in which the client is seeking representation—even embarrassing facts—the attorney will not be able to represent that client to the best of her ability. Keeping clients' secrets and confidences preserves the integrity of the profession and assures clients that they will receive good representation.

Canon 7 of the NALA Code of Ethics and Professional Responsibility provides that "a legal assistant must protect the confidences of a client, and it shall be unethical for a legal assistant to violate any statute now in effect or hereafter to be enacted controlling privileged communications." The NFPA Affirmation of Responsibility also provides that "a paralegal shall preserve client confidences and privileged communications." The ABA, NALA, and NFPA principles mandating that client confidences be preserved illustrate the principle that confidentiality is an elemental, essential aspect of legal representation.

The Attorney-Client Privilege

The attorney-client privilege complements the idea of confidentiality of communications between an attorney and her client. Communications between an attorney (and her agents) and her client are totally privileged and cannot be revealed unless the client waives the privilege. Although this rule is an aspect of ethical behavior by attorneys, it is really codified through the rules of evidence. The Federal Rules of Evidence give each state the ability to create an attorney-client privilege. This privilege is similar to the notion of confidentiality because it protects information given to the attorney by the client, but it is different in that it protects the compelled or involuntary disclosure of the information. It therefore applies to situations in which the attorney is questioned by the police or in court: if the privilege applies, the attorney or the paralegal may refuse to reveal the information.

Basically this rule means that if an attorney is representing a criminal defendant [named Mr. Brown], and the defendant tells the attorney that he murdered the victim [Mr. Green], the attorney is absolutely forbidden from revealing this information to anyone unless Mr. Brown gives the attorney permission to tell someone else. Therefore, if the attorney is called into court to testify through a subpoena and is asked, "Who killed Mr. Green?" the attorney would respond, "This information is protected by the attorney-client privilege."[1] The court could not then compel the attorney to reveal the information.

This privilege is created whenever an attorney represents a client, and it ends, when that representation ends. However, when the representation ends the attorney cannot reveal any information the client gave while the attorney represented him. For example, if Mr. Brown has told his attorney that he murdered Mr. Green, and later Mr. Brown fires the attorney and hires another attorney to represent him, the first attorney cannot reveal that Mr. Brown murdered Mr. Green unless Mr. Brown gives permission to reveal that information. However, if after Attorney One is fired Mr. Brown tells Attorney One that Mr. Green was murdered in the warehouse, Attorney One can reveal that fact to the police, because the information concerning where the victim was murdered was not obtained while Attorney One was representing Mr. Brown. However, this may be a close call, because if Attorney One revealed where the victim was murdered she might also be questioned about who murdered Mr. Green, and if so she may be very close to revealing the fact that Mr. Brown killed Mr. Green—a fact Attorney One is completely prohibited from revealing.

As a general rule, communications in the presence of a third party are not confidential or protected by the attorney-client privilege, because it is assumed that if the client wanted confidentiality he would not have "published" his

---

[1] Of course, if this situation occurred in the "real world," the attorney would attempt to quash the subpoena on the basis of attorney-client privilege so that she would not even have to testify.

idea to others. However, if the third person is an employee of the attorney, such as a paralegal, that person is part of the "privileged network" and is prohibited from revealing confidential information. Several ABA standards prevent a paralegal from revealing any of the information she obtained while working with the attorney. The applicable Rules are Rule 5.3(A) and (B); the Code addresses this issue in EC 4-5.

Rule 5.3(A) and (B) state as follows:

With respect to a non-lawyer employed or retained by or associated with a lawyer:

   (A) a partner in a law firm shall make reasonable efforts to ensure that the firm has in effect measures giving reasonable assurance that the person's conduct is compatible with the professional obligations of the lawyer;
   (B) a lawyer having direct supervisory authority over the non-lawyer shall make reasonable efforts to ensure that the person's conduct is compatible with the professional obligations of the lawyer.

EC 4-5 provides as follows:

A lawyer should not use information acquired in the course of his representation of a client to the disadvantage of the client and a lawyer should not use, except with the consent of his client after full disclosure, such information for his own purposes. Likewise, a lawyer should be diligent in his efforts to prevent the misuse of such information by his employees and associates. Care should be exercised by a lawyer to prevent the disclosure of the confidences and secrets of one client to another and no employment should be accepted that might require such disclosure.

Although these rules apply to attorneys and suggest that attorneys must attempt to ensure that employees do not reveal the confidences and secrets of clients, the practical application of this rule means that paralegals themselves must regulate their own conduct so as to prevent the possibility that any confidences or secrets of clients will be revealed. It is neither possible nor desirable for an attorney to monitor every action or statement a paralegal might make, so paralegals must continually be aware of the limitations imposed on their communications by this ethical principle.

It is important to remember, as mentioned earlier, that although most communications from a client to an attorney are privileged, some are not privileged and can be revealed to others. However, these exceptions are few and are clearly delineated by the relevant bar rules. They cover situations such as when a client reveals her intention to commit a crime or when the attorney needs the information to collect a fee from the client. Using the example of Mr. Brown, the attorney could never reveal that Mr. Brown killed Mr. Green unless Mr. Brown gives the attorney permission to reveal that information. However, if Mr. Brown told the attorney that he was going to rob the First National Bank of Centerville tomorrow at 10:00 A.M., under the ABA guidelines this information would not be protected by the attorney-client privilege.

One interesting issue concerning the disclosure of confidential information occurs when information has been inadvertently disclosed. This might occur when a fax is sent to the wrong number or, when providing discovery to the opposition, a piece of paper containing confidential information is accidentally included in the discovery materials. This situation, which is not directly addressed in the ethical guidelines, implicates several ethical areas for lawyers. On the one hand, one might argue that using materials received accidentally is a part of diligent, zealous, and competent representation, and that the antidote is increased care for attorneys and their staff. On the other hand, ethical guidelines prohibit unfair or deceitful conduct, or conduct that is prejudicial to the administration of justice. This side would argue that advocacy does not mean uncontrolled or unrestrained advocacy.

The ABA's Standing Committee on Ethics and Professional Responsibility addressed this issue in its Formal Opinion 92-368, indicating that the proper response on the part of the lawyer or paralegal receiving the documents in issue is to refuse to examine the documents, notify the sending lawyer, and abide by his instructions. Although each state must confront ethical issues like this on a continuing basis, this opinion gives some reasonable direction in the exercise of professional discretion when it comes to the mistaken release of confidential information.

Conflict of Interest

Conflicts of interest are situations and factors that prevent the attorney or paralegal from representing the clients' interests to the fullest extent possible. Essentially, a conflict of interest may emerge when the attorney's loyalties are divided between two (or more) clients, or when client confidentiality is threatened. The relevant provisions of the Rules and the Code define the situations in which conflicts of interest exist, and they describe the proper responses to make when confronted with conflicts of interest.

In the Rules, the basic guidelines concerning conflicts of interest are described in Rule 1.7.

RULE 1.7 Conflict of Interest: General Rule

----------------------------------- IIII -----------------------------------

(a) A lawyer shall not represent a client if the representation of that client will be directly adverse to another client, unless:

(1) the lawyer reasonably believes the representation will not adversely affect the relationship with the other client; and

(2) each client consents after consultation.

(b) A lawyer shall not represent a client if the representation of that client may be materially limited by the lawyer's responsibilities to another client or to a third person, or by the lawyer's own interests, unless:

(1) the lawyer reasonably believes the representation will not be adversely affected; and

(2) the client consents after consultation. When representation of multiple clients in a single matter is undertaken, the consultation shall include explanation of the implications of the common representation and the advantages and risks involved.

This rule is stricter than the requirements set forth in the corresponding Code section, DR 5-105(A). Unlike the Code, Rule 1.7 requires that an attorney not represent a client if representation of that client will be directly adverse to another client unless the client not only consents, but the attorney is also reasonably assured, apart from that consultation, that the lawyer's interests would not detrimentally affect the client. This imposes a higher burden on the lawyer, because client consent must be combined with an objective decision that the client's representation will not be impaired.

The second section of Rule 1.7 mandates that a lawyer not represent a client if the representation of that client may be materially limited by the attorney's responsibilities to another client or third person, or by the lawyer's own interest. The same two requirements—that the attorney reasonably believe the representation will not be adversely affected and that the client consent after full disclosure—must be met before the attorney can accept the new client.

The Comments to Rule 1.7 recognize that "[l]oyalty is an essential element in the lawyer's relationship to the client." This concept of loyalty prohibits undertaking representation adverse to the client's interests without the client's consent. Conflicts of interest impair this loyalty because the lawyer is unable to consider, recommend, or carry out an appropriate course of action for the client, because of the lawyer's other responsibilities or interests. Thus, anything that materially interferes with an attorney's independent professional judgment would be a conflict and should be avoided.

Following this general rule concerning conflicts of interest, the Rules define certain specific conficts of interest. This is the same approach the Code takes: first the general rule, then specific instances. By reading the Code's provisions for conflict of interest, you will get a feeling for the specific types of conflicts that may arise in legal representation.

DR 5-101 Refusing Employment When the Interests of the Lawyer May Impair His Independent Professional Judgment

———— IIII ————

(A) Except with the consent of his client after full disclosure, a lawyer shall not accept employment if the exercise of his professional judgment on behalf of his client will be or reasonably may be affected by his own financial business, property, or personal interests.

(B) A lawyer shall not accept employment in contemplated or pending litigation if he knows or it is obvious that he or a lawyer in his firm ought to be called as a witness, except that he may undertake the employment and he or a lawyer in his firm may testify:

(1) If the testimony will relate solely to an uncontested matter.

(2) If the testimony will relate solely to a matter of formality and there is no reason to believe that substantial evidence will be offered in opposition to the testimony.

(3) If the testimony will relate solely to the nature and value of legal service rendered in the case by the lawyer or his firm to the client.

(4) As to any matter, if refusal would work a substantial hardship on the client because of the distinctive value of the lawyer or his firm as counsel in the particular case.

DR 5-102 Withdrawal as Counsel When the Lawyer Becomes a Witness

(A) If, after undertaking employment in contemplated or pending litigation, a lawyer learns or it is obvious that he or a lawyer in his firm ought to be called as a witness on behalf of his client, he shall withdraw from the conduct of the trial and his firm, if any, shall not continue representation in the trial, except that he may continue the representation and he or a lawyer in his firm may testify in the circumstances enumerated in DR 5-101(B)(1) through (4).

(B) If, after undertaking employment in contemplated or pending litigation, a lawyer learns or it is obvious that he or a lawyer in his firm may be called as a witness other than on behalf of his client, he may continue the representation until it is apparent that his testimony is or may be prejudicial to his client.

DR 5-103 Avoiding Acquisition of Interest in Litigation

(A) A lawyer shall not acquire a proprietary interest in the cause of action or subject matter of litigation he is conducting for a client except that he may:

    (1) Acquire a lien granted by law to secure his fee or expenses.

    (2) Contract with a client for a reasonable contingent fee in a civil case.

(B) While representing a client in connection with a contemplated or pending litigation, a lawyer shall not advance or guarantee financial assistance to his client, except that a lawyer may advance or guarantee the expenses of litigation, including court costs, expenses of investigation, expenses of medical examination, and costs of obtaining and presenting evidence, provided the client remains ultimately liable for such expenses.

DR 5-104 Limiting Business Relations With a Client

(A) A lawyer shall not enter into a business transaction with a client if they have differing interests therein and if the client expects the lawyer to exercise his professional judgment therein for the protection of the client, unless the client has consented after full disclosure.

(B) Prior to conclusion of all aspects of the matter giving rise to his employment, a lawyer shall not enter into any arrangement or understanding with a client or a prospective client by which he acquires an interest in publication rights with respect to the subject matter of his employment or proposed employment.

DR 5-105 Refusing to Accept or Continue Employment if the Interests of Another Client May Impair the Independent Professional Judgment of the Lawyer

(A) A lawyer shall decline proffered employment if the exercise of his independent professional judgment in behalf of a client will be or is likely to be adversely affected by the acceptance of the proffered employment, or it would be likely to involve him in representing differing interests, except to the extent permitted under DR 5-105(C).

(B) A lawyer shall not continue multiple employment if the exercise of his independent professional judgment on behalf of a client will be or is likely to be adversely affected by his representation of another client, or if it would be likely to involve him in representing differing interests, except to the extent permitted under DR 5-105(C).

(C) In situations covered by DR 5-105(A) and (B), a lawyer may represent multiple clients if it is obvious that he can adequately represent the interest of each and if each consent to the representation after full disclosure of the possible effect of such representation on the exercise of his independent professional judgment on behalf of each.

(D) If a lawyer is required to decline employment or to withdraw from employment under a Disciplinary Rule, no partner or associate, or any other lawyer affiliated with him or his firm may accept or continue such employment.

DR 5-106 Settling Similar Claims of Clients

(A) A lawyer who represents two or more clients shall not make or participate in the making of an aggregate settlement of the claims of or against his clients, unless each client has consented to the settlement after being advised of the existence and nature of all the claims involved in the proposed settlement, of the total amount of the settlement, and of the participation of each person in the settlement.

DR 5-107 Avoiding Influence by Others Than the Client

(A) Except with the consent of his client after full disclosure, a lawyer shall not:

(1) Accept compensation for his legal services from one other than his client.

(2) Accept from one other than his client anything of value related to his representation of or his employment by his client.

(B) A lawyer shall not permit a person who recommends, employs, or pays him to render legal services for another to direct or regulate his professional judgment in rendering such legal services.

(C) A lawyer shall not practice with or in the form of a professional corporation or association authorized to practice law for a profit, if:

(1) A non-lawyer owns any interest therein except that a fiduciary representative of the estate of a lawyer may hold the stock or interest of the lawyer for a reasonable time during administration;

(2) A non-lawyer is a corporate director or officer thereof; or

(3) A non-lawyer has the right to direct or control the professional judgment of a lawyer.

In a detailed study of ethics, you will learn more about these specific conflict-of-interest situations. For now, a general understanding of conflict of interest will suffice.

Certain conflicts of interest are clear. If, for example, a lawyer's family was in the asbestos business, and a client wanted to sue the lawyer's family for injury from asbestos, the lawyer's loyalties would clearly be divided, and he would be unable to represent his client zealously. This would be a clear conflict of interest. Similarly, if a firm were suing a bank on behalf of a client, and a paralegal working for the firm was the majority stockholder in the bank, there would arguably be a conflict of interest. On the other hand, if the firm is handling a case, and your ex-spouse is opposing counsel, it is unclear whether there is a conflict of interest. The same would be true when a paralegal is working on a case in which her client is suing one of the paralegal's former employers.

A new source of conflict of interest arises when a husband and wife are working on opposing sides in a case. Although several jurisdictions have determined that this is not a per se conflict of interest, it would probably be wise to avoid a situation such as this, which has the appearance of impropriety. In general, it is safest to avoid any situation that you believe may put you in a compromised position. If you find yourself in a situation that might be unprofessional, consult with your supervising attorney (see Figure 14-4). You will surely want to avoid any situation that might jeopardize your career or your firm's integrity and reputation.

FIGURE 14-4 If you are faced with an ethical dilemma, ask your supervising attorney for advice.

Although the areas of unauthorized practice, confidentiality, and conflict of interest are of primary concern for legal assistants, they are not the only ethical provisions applicable to and relevant for paralegals. It is also important to understand ethical guidelines relative to advertising and solicitation, zealous representation of clients, handling client funds, and competence. You will learn about these other aspects of legal ethics in a class in legal ethics and/or in training programs provided by your employer.

State Bar Ethical Rules

The ethical rules for the various states usually closely track the ABA rules. However, they can be detailed and specific because they address and reflect the ethical issues and situations that jurisdiction has addressed. It is advisable to check with the state and local bar associations in any locale prior to practicing to determine if there are any special regulations. Some states may even require that paralegals be licensed. The safest approach is to check with the state bar or local bar association in an effort to make sure that you comply with the relevant regulations and requirements.

NFPA Standards

As previously discussed, the National Federation of Paralegal Associations has created ethical standards specifically for paralegals, called the Affirmation of Responsibility. There are six parts to the affirmation. These parts are as follows:

I. Unauthorized practice of law.
II. Highest standard of ethical conduct.
III. Competency and integrity.
IV. Preservation of client confidences and privileged communications.
V. Provide quality legal services.
VI. Promotion of the development of paralegal profession.

As you can see from these six parts of the affirmation, all but three of the sections are aspirational in character; that is, they describe not the rules that you must follow in your behavior, but the goal of professional conduct for paralegals. The three parts, I, III, and IV, which can be interpreted to be binding and not merely aspirational, parallel the ABA standards and state the same principles as the ABA standards previously discussed.

NALA Standards

The National Association of Legal Assistants (NALA) also has ethical standards, which are called the Code of Ethics and Professional Responsibility. NALA's ethical standards are divided into 12 canons, which are elaborations on the ABA standards. Canons 1, 2, 3, 4, 5, and 6 concern the unauthorized practice of law. Canon 7 is parallel to the ABA standard regarding the protection of client confidences. Canons 8, 9, 10, and 11 are general canons designed primarily to be aspirational in nature. It is also interesting to note that Canon 12 of the NALA standards states that a legal assistant is governed by the ABA Code of Professional Responsibility; the NFPA Affirmation does not.

These three areas—the unauthorized practice of law, conflict of interest, and confidentiality—represent the three ethical areas most directly applicable to paralegals. They will affect your work on a daily basis, and your understanding of these areas and the importance of legal ethics in general are essential components of your professional responsibility.

Professionalism and Client Relations

The previous sections of this chapter outlined the major sources of rules governing the professional responsibilities of paralegals and discussed the major ethical issues that a paralegal faces. Ethics, however, have a practical impact in the practice of the law because they relate to the issue of client satisfaction. In this section, you will learn how professional behavior can contribute to the creation and maintenance of client satisfaction.

The client is the "customer" necessary for the business of practicing law. Unlike almost any other business, the law business has obligations to three entities: (1) the client, (2) the court, and (3) the bar. Sometimes legal professionals tend to forget that clients are the reason lawyers have a business. In addition, most ethical and malpractice claims arise when a breakdown in client relations has occurred. The need for good client relations cannot be overemphasized.

When it comes to interactions with clients, we cannot overemphasize the importance of understanding and acting in conformity with the prohibitions against the unauthorized practice of law. Successful paralegals must undertake client relations in ways that avoid the risk of performing unauthorized activities. Specifically, paralegals must be wary of responding to questions or issues if they believe they are giving legal advice or answering substantive questions about the law. This applies even if the paralegal knows or believes he knows the answer the client is seeking. For example, a client asks a paralegal what the statute of limitations is on a personal injury case. The paralegal might know that it is two years. However, the paralegal should not answer this substantive question, because the client might not have categorized the legal problem correctly. If the problem was the negligent leaving of a foreign object in the body by a doctor, for example, the case would be classified as a medical malpractice action, with a one-year statute of limitation. When dealing with clients, you must be extremely sensitive to the unauthorized practice doctrine. By recognizing the limitations on paralegal behavior, you will be in the best position to perform client relations functions in an appropriate and ethical manner.

The following key ideas will help you to create and maintain good relationships with clients.

1. Let the client know what is going on.
2. Do not overestimate the success of a client's case.
3. Explain the process to the client.
4. Meet deadlines that have been promised.
5. Take telephone calls, or at least return them promptly.
6. Do not send bills with only an amount written on them. Detail the work you have done and the charges for each item.
7. Realize the pragmatics of the legal process; a client does not want to spend $500 in legal fees and expenses to collect $200.

8. Document conversations that you have had regarding the case, and put these in the file.
9. Communicate effectively with your client.

The following discussion of each of these items will help you understand how to achieve client satisfaction through ethical behavior.

Let the Client Know What Is Happening

Many times the disciplinary section of the bar association is called and asked to contact a client's attorney to ask what is going on in a case. This problem arises when clients are not fully informed about the progress of their cases, and can easily be avoided by merely sending the client a copy of all documents that go out of the office pertaining to her case. If nothing is happening on the case, a status letter every month or so would be appreciated and would alleviate this problem. Remember that one of the most frustrating things for a client is to feel that she is in the dark about her own case. It is definitely worth the few extra minutes it takes to keep clients informed of the status of their cases.

Like people in general, clients prefer knowledge and information over uncertainty. Sometimes, you may want to communicate by mail or telephone with the client just to make contact, even though there have been no developments in the case. (See Figure 14-5.) Nurturing clients, and making them feel that they are in capable, secure hands, is not merely common sense and considerate—it is also good business. Both attorneys and paralegals can participate in the important process of keeping the client informed, as long as the paralegal is not pressured into giving legal advice.

FIGURE 14-5 Effective communication with clients is critical in creating and maintaining positive client relations.

Do Not Overestimate the Value of the Client's Case

Many clients assume that their case should be taken to the Supreme Court and is probably the "best" case the attorney has ever handled. Do not try to deflate their egos, but it is important not to encourage them inappropriately or unnecessarily. For example, in a personal injury suit, a client may have slipped and fallen in a major grocery store chain and suffered a bruised knee. The attorney handling the case will advise the client that the damages (compensation) that could be received from a lawsuit would be nominal for a bruised knee and that it would not be practical or cost-effective to institute a lawsuit, because the costs of filing suit far outweigh the chances of recovering any money damages.

If this happens, the client may be disappointed or frustrated, and might well contact the paralegal and ask what she thinks about the case. Remember that paralegals are not allowed to "diagnose" a client's case, for that constitutes practicing law. It is best to defer to the judgment of the attorney, because the client is paying for the attorney's professional judgment, gained in law school and through experience. Do not second-guess the attorney, especially in front of a client. Remember that, for many people, most exposure to the legal process is from television, through "Perry Mason" or "Matlock," and that in many instances clients have inflated expectations of what they can receive. It is your job to be as realistic as possible, but under no circumstances should you question the attorney's judgment to the client. If you do not understand an attorney's decision, ask the attorney in the privacy of your office.

Explain the Process to the Client

Most clients have not been involved in the legal process before. They are usually scared and do not understand the reasons for various documents or steps. Although some actual legal advice, such as whether to file in state or federal court, should be left to attorneys, a paralegal can explain that in a lawsuit the opposing party must be served before a court date is set. Explaining this simple step can alleviate a lot of unnecessary telephone calls from irate clients. Let clients know what you are doing and, most importantly, why you are doing it. Tell them what to expect next. For example, if a particular motion is filed, explain to the client that the court will not rule on the motion until several things happen, such as the opposing party having the statutory time to respond and possibly the court hearing oral argument on the case. Just letting clients know what to expect will save you, the client, and the attorney time, and it will help you maintain a good relationship with the client.

Meet Deadlines that Have Been Promised

Nothing will erode client relations more quickly than failing to meet deadlines. If a client is promised a will on Tuesday, he expects the will to be ready on Tuesday. Remember the fundamental principle of law—it is a business. If the dry cleaners continually promised your laundry on Tuesday and did not provide it until Thursday, you would be likely to choose another dry cleaner. The same logic applies to the business of practicing law.

The way to avoid this problem is to be realistic. Do not make promises that cannot be kept; realize that it is better to allow too much time and have a grateful client than to allow too little time and have an infuriated client.

However, if there is a good reason that you cannot meet a deadline, contact the client immediately, prior to the deadline, and explain the situation. The client will be grateful for your honesty and will most certainly understand. This, however, is a worst-case scenario; do not do this on a regular basis. By meeting deadlines, the paralegal heightens her professional image and contributes to client satisfaction.

Take Telephone Calls from Clients

All people who have worked in the legal process have dealt with clients whom they would prefer to avoid. Difficult clients and the hectic pace of a busy law office can both contribute to the habit of not returning phone calls. However, remember that practicing law is a business, and all businesses have good and bad clients. Even if you do not have any information to relay to a client, take her calls and at least explain that nothing is happening in the case, or that she should contact the attorney. If the client does need to speak to the attorney, let the attorney know by memo.

We all occasionally need quiet time to work on an especially important project, and have to have messages taken. This is fine; however, return those phone calls. During especially hectic times, it is easy to put off the task of returning telephone calls until you have more time. However, if you are always busy clients will become more and more upset. The best way to avoid this problem is to set up a specific time each day to use for returning telephone calls.

Practice Professional Billing Procedures

As you know, clients must be billed, or the business of law would not survive. Many firms have developed the unprofessional practice of billing clients for the total hours spent on their work, such as preparing a will, rather than breaking the bill down into smaller units. As discussed in Chapter 6 on law office accounting, the better practice is to document all work that went into preparing the will or other legal document. For example, rather than sending a bill for a total of 6.3 hours, it is far more professional to send a bill that details the work expended, as was illustrated in the materials on billing and accounting.

A client will pay more quickly and be more satisfied if the bill reflects all of the work done and the work is broken down into segments. Further, indicating what portion of the work was completed by paralegals and what work was completed by attorneys will demonstrate to the client that the firm is cost-conscious.

Realize the Pragmatics of Practicing Law

A client does not want to spend $500 in legal fees to collect a $200 debt. Different cases have different limitations. If, for example, your firm is defending a multibillion-dollar lawsuit for Exxon, you may be able to use couriers more readily than if you have a $200 collection case. Sometimes filing deadlines in litigation cases come into play. If the deadline for the Supreme Court brief is due today at 5:00 and it is 1:00 P.M., the expense of flying someone to Washington to file it would probably be prudent. However, if that same brief is due next week and it is completed, using an overnight delivery service would be most practical.

Essentially, when it comes to being cost-conscious, use your common sense; do the job well and professionally, but do it using the most economical means. In federal court and in some states, civil lawsuits can be served by first-class mail. This approach would be the least expensive means and would be the best way to serve a lawsuit, especially if fees and expenses need to be kept at a minimum. Always be aware of the goal of the client and the bottom line.

Document Conversations and Keep Them in the File

Often paralegals are called upon to contact a particular court or administrative agency and determine how to file a specific document. The court or agency will tell you what size paper is required and how many copies should be made. Or the district attorney calls to discuss a pending plea arrangement. Or a co-defendant's counsel calls with new ideas about trial strategy. Or another firm's paralegal calls with questions about a mortgage held by your firm's client. No matter whether you deem this information important or insignificant, you must communicate it effectively to your supervising attorney. To maintain accurate records, it is a good idea to document all such information and put it in the correspondence portion of the main file for that client or case.

This approach is especially important when specific information must be relayed to a certain individual. For example, if a deposition is canceled, and the attorney tells you to notify all parties, it is probably a good idea to write down who you called and what time you spoke to them. This simple step will prove its worth if opposing counsel files a motion to compel, claiming he was not notified of the cancellation, and requests attorney fees. Your documentation of your telephone call to him will be invaluable when your attorney must respond to the motion.

To document conversations effectively, you need an appropriate method or form. This will help you avoid having to later recreate telephone conversations from memory or search for that elusive scrap of paper where you made some quick notes. The telephone log in Figure 14-6, developed by Atlanta attorney Cathy Alterman, is a good example of a form that provides a quick yet comprehensive approach to documenting conversations.

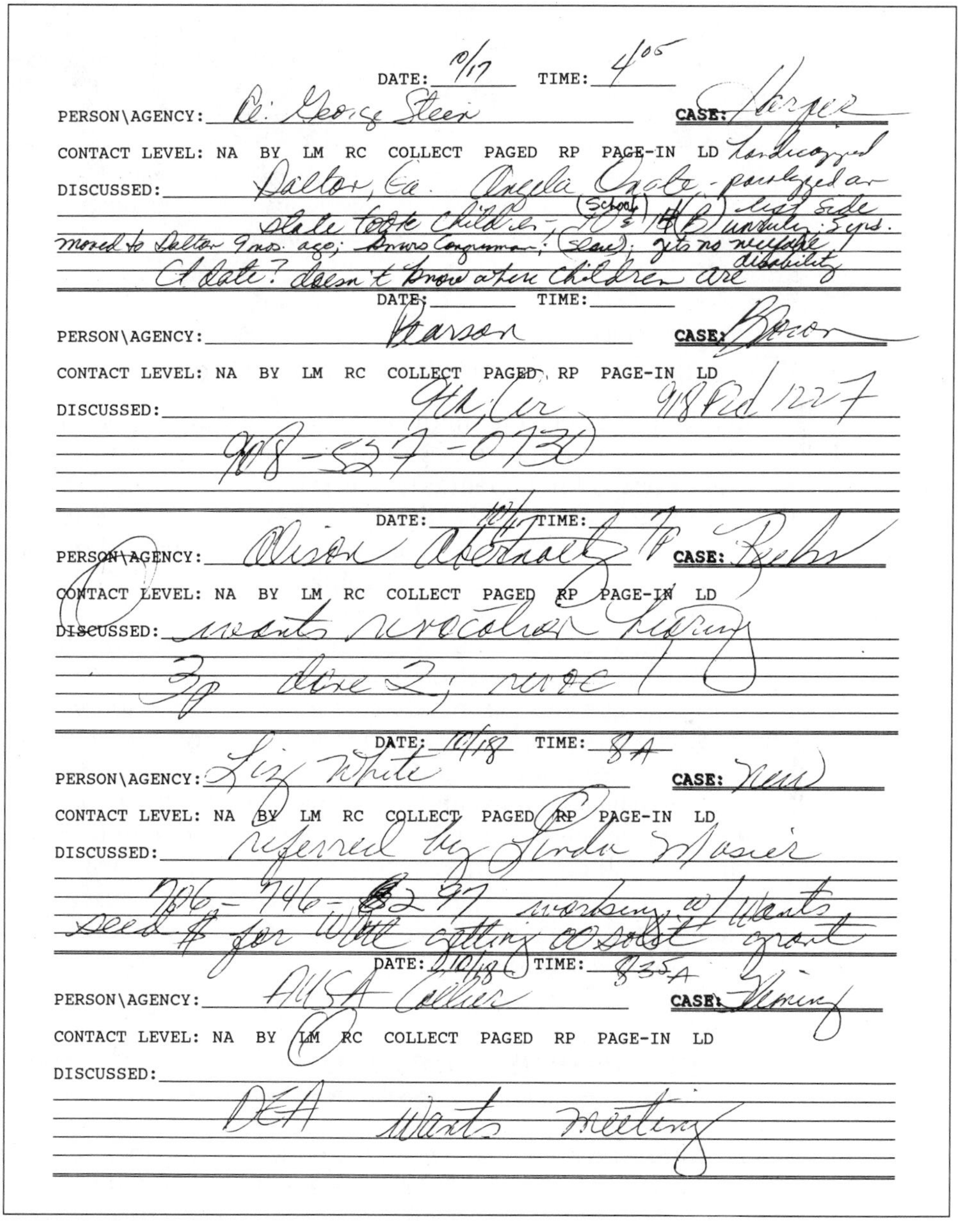
DATE: 10/17 TIME: 4:05
PERSON\AGENCY: Dr. George Steen CASE: Harper
CONTACT LEVEL: NA BY LM RC COLLECT PAGED RP PAGE-IN LD
DISCUSSED: Dalton, Ga.

DATE: TIME:
PERSON\AGENCY: Pearson CASE:
CONTACT LEVEL: NA BY LM RC COLLECT PAGED RP PAGE-IN LD
DISCUSSED: 9th Cir.
908-527-0730

DATE: TIME:
PERSON\AGENCY: CASE:
CONTACT LEVEL: NA BY LM RC COLLECT PAGED RP PAGE-IN LD
DISCUSSED:

DATE: 10/18 TIME: 8A
PERSON\AGENCY: Liz White CASE: New
CONTACT LEVEL: NA BY LM RC COLLECT PAGED RP PAGE-IN LD
DISCUSSED: referred by Linda Mosier

DATE: 10/18 TIME: 8:35A
PERSON\AGENCY: AUSA Collier CASE:
CONTACT LEVEL: NA BY LM RC COLLECT PAGED RP PAGE-IN LD
DISCUSSED:
DEA wants meeting

FIGURE 14-6 A quick and comprehensive approach to documenting telephone conversations.

ON
POINT

THE CASE OF HELPFUL HANNA

Paralegal Hanna is extremely distressed over her best friend's impending divorce, and she has told her friend to call on her for anything. As an experienced domestic relations paralegal, Hanna knows the ins and outs of divorce proceedings. Her friend asks Hanna where she can get the best representation at the most reasonable price. Hanna, who wants to be helpful, offers to prepare all of the necessary documents for her friend. To make things look good, Hanna uses her firm's stationery and puts the attorneys' names on the pleadings. She also signs her name to the documents without designating herself as a paralegal. She files the documents with the court for her friend and asks the sheriff to serve the estranged husband with the papers. Has Hanna's help created any possibility for a claim of malpractice?

Communicate Effectively with the Client

Excellent personal communication skills are an important aspect of professionalism. The importance of getting your ideas across and understanding the ideas of others is fundamental to success as a paralegal. The keys to good personal communication skills are simple. First, use clear, concise, standard English. Do not be tempted to use the latest slang terms. Nothing can destroy your credibility more quickly than not using standard English. Second, pronounce words correctly and use words in their proper context. If you are unsure about how to pronounce a word or the definition of a word, do not use it until you have looked it up in a dictionary. *Ballentine's Legal Dictionary and Thesaurus,* published by Lawyers Cooperative, is an excellent resource for this purpose. Third, when you are receiving information from someone else, listen. Although this idea may seem logical and almost second-nature, too many people have lost the art of listening. Listen to what people are telling you, and do not think about what you are going to have for lunch. Essentially this means giving the person your full attention. When people are involved with the legal process, sometimes with major issues at stake, they want and deserve to feel that you are attending to them as fully and completely as possible.

Professional Responsibility: A Summary

In this chapter, you have been introduced to the idea of professionalism as it is applied to the practice of law, and you have learned about the parameters for ethical behavior in the practice of the law. Legal ethics is such an important area that you will undoubtedly study it in depth before you begin working in the law, for ethical violations will affect not only your career and reputation but also those of the lawyers and firm for whom you are working. By understanding the sources for ethical behavior and the guidelines by which to judge your own actions and activities, you have taken an important step in understanding professional responsibilities as a paralegal.

Key Terms

attorney-client privilege	confidentiality	professionalism
client relations	conflict of interest	unauthorized practice of law

Problems and Activities

1. Read through the following list. For each situation, ask yourself if there is an ethical problem and, if so, what should be done to resolve it.

   a. A client confesses that he did not in fact kill the victim, but killed the victim's sister, who was found next to the victim. The client is on trial for the victim's murder. You, the paralegal, are subpoenaed to testify at the client's murder trial.

   b. You, the paralegal, sign a letter on the firm's letterhead to the court, without indicating that you are not a lawyer.

   c. A client in a civil case says that he is going to commit perjury on the stand.

   d. You are in an interview with a client in a divorce case, and the client reveals juicy information about her deviant sex life with her estranged husband, which violates the sodomy statutes in your jurisdiction. You immediately call your best friend and tell her about the conversation. She swears not to repeat the story.

   e. Your firm represents a client in an automobile accident, the client's insurance company is paying the legal bills. The insurance company wants to settle, but the client does not want to. Should the firm settle the case?

   f. The firm you work for calls itself "Torts Are Us" and lets paralegals go to trial with clients.

CHAPTER 15

THE ART OF COMMUNICATION

OBJECTIVES

By the completion of this chapter, you should:

- understand how communication is central to the work of being a paralegal;
- understand how the sender, the receiver, and the message work together to create effective communications;
- understand the specific types of communication used by paralegals; and
- learn how to avoid miscommunication.

Effective Communication: An Introduction

Communication is a fundamental skill that you must master to be a successful paralegal. Through communicating, individuals convey information to one another, and, in the work of the law, a tremendous amount of information must be conveyed on a daily basis. Formulating, presenting, listening, understanding, relating, synthesizing, conveying: all these communicative activities are of fundamental importance to the paralegal.

People communicate primarily through three communication channels: verbal, nonverbal, and written. A paralegal utilizes verbal communication skills when he has a conversation with clients, attorneys, co-workers, or other individuals; when he dictates; when he converses on the telephone; when he is tape-recorded or videotaped. Nonverbal communication skills are used simultaneously with verbal skills. These skills refer to the way a person looks: facial expressions and body language. Nonverbal behavior must complement verbal behavior. If you say you are interested in an assignment, and you also look enthusiastic, you are giving a consistent message. If, however, your nonverbal behavior contradicts your verbal behavior, it causes confusion for the listener. Written communication skills come into play when the paralegal drafts documents, writes a letter or memorandum, summarizes a deposition, or generally whenever thoughts are reduced to paper or the computer. To become a successful legal assistant, you must learn to master all these means of communication.

The communication process in all of these types of communications involves three elements, each of which is both an opportunity for effective communication and an area where miscommunication can occur. These three elements are the sender, the message, and the receiver. Whenever there is a breakdown in communication, it occurs in at least one of these three areas.

The *sender* is the person who initiates the communication (Figure 15-1). An example of a sender is a paralegal giving a speech or relaying information to an

---

_O ON
POINT   *CAROL THE CLUMSY COMMUNICATOR*

As Paralegal Carol walks into the law office one sunny morning, she is greeted by
her supervising attorney, who informs her that the interrogatories she is going to send
should be delivered via overnight mail to the opposing counsel's Rome office. Unsure
of whether he meant Rome, Italy, or Rome, Georgia, Carol sent them to Italy, figuring that
it was the more likely destination. When she sees the attorney, she informs him
that the interrogatories are in the mail, and asks if there is anything else she might do.
The attorney tells her to look up the evidentiary rules concerning impeachment relative to the Jameson case, but Carol did not clarify whether the Jameson case was being
tried in federal or in state court, so she figured it couldn't hurt to find out both sets of
rules. The attorney also asks her to summarize a deposition, but she did not ask
whether the deposition summary was to be used at trial or merely as an overview. She
decides to use the page-line format in lieu of the paragraph format, which results in a
30-page summary of a 60-page deposition. In reality, the attorney had wanted to contain costs on this case and merely wanted a three-page summary. As the morning
comes to a close, Carol's supervising attorney tells her to prepare the necessary documentation to have documents produced at trial. Carol is unsure whether to prepare a request for production of documents or a notice to produce. Since she had a form
for request for production of documents readily available, she decided to use it, which
resulted in the documents not being produced at trial. It's noon and time for lunch.
Carol thinks to herself, "Thank goodness I'm such a good communicator; this job
would really be rough if you didn't communicate well."

---

attorney. The sender needs to be aware of other elements in the communication process to convey the idea effectively. If she does not understand that
effective communication involves all three elements linked together, she cannot be an effective communicator. As a humorous and true example, consider
the attorney who asked his client on the witness stand, "Is your appearance
this morning pursuant to the subpoena served on you by my office following
your deposition?" and the witness who replied, "No, this is how I dress for
work every day."

The *message* is the idea that you are communicating. It is difficult, however,
to convey meaning to another person; people attach their own interpretations
and meanings to words. For example, when an attorney asks a paralegal to find
out building code regulations for water heaters, the attorney might be thinking
of new, electric water heaters, but the receiver might think of water heaters as
gas water heaters. Any message can be interpreted in several ways, and it is up
to both the sender and the receiver to anticipate potential problems the other
party might have in decoding the message. Breakdowns in messages occur
when incorrect vocabulary is used, when the message is redundant, when the
message is unnecessary, when the message contains incorrect or inappropriate
legal terminology, or when the sender frames the message in such a way that
the receiver is likely to be misled.

FIGURE 15-1
The sender
initiates the
communication
process.

Additionally, remember that the work of the law uses a specific vocabulary, and words in the legal context may have different meanings than when used in their usual context. A case that is dismissed "with prejudice," for example, has nothing to do with racial discrimination. Whether a defendant in a defamation case had "actual malice" does not have to do with his bad feelings for the plaintiff, and to have "consideration" in a contract has nothing to do with being polite to the other party. Consider as an example a conversation overheard by Robert L. Caummisar and Delores Woods in a Carter County courtroom. The defendant was an elderly man, faced with a divorce petition, who had dismissed his attorney so that he could plead his own case. When the judge asked the man if he knew that his wife was asking for "maintenance," the man replied that she did not need maintenance. He explained, "There wasn't a thing wrong with that house when I left it." When you communicate in legal work, your message must be accurate and precise if others are to understand it. Among other things, that requires an excellent understanding of the vocabulary used in the law.

The *receiver* is the individual to whom the message is sent. To make sure that the receiver understands the message, it is imperative that you understand the expectations of the listener, who the listener is, and the level of the listener's understanding. (See Figure 15-2.) For example, your way of asking the managing partner in a law firm to join you for lunch would be very different than your manner of asking a co-worker to lunch. If you had a question about a deposition, you could certainly assume that a lawyer knows what a deposition is. But if you were telling your courier to pick up a copy of a deposition, you should perhaps explain what it will look like. By understanding these subtle differences, you will become a much more effective communicator.

The three components in the communication process do not exist in isolation from each other. Rather, communication is a joint venture that links the

FIGURE 15-2 It is important to receive information accurately to be an effective communicator.

characteristics of a system; when one part fails, the entire venture fails. Each part exists only in relation to the other parts.

As an example of how the components of the communication process continually interact, consider the memo in Figure 15-3, which appears to be deceptively simple but is actually a complex piece of communication. As you can see, Penny Paralegal is reporting in writing on an oral phone conversation. Penny was primarily a receiver in the phone conversation, so she had to understand the information presented to her, asking relevant questions when appropriate. In this memo, she is the sender. Penny has had to choose the appropriate mechanism for conveying, here choosing a written memo. (She might also have sent this on e-mail if her firm had that capability.) Note that she has used certain shortcuts in her writing: she has used the pi symbol to mean plaintiff, which is a common abbreviation, and she has referred to a "depo," which is a common abbreviation for *deposition*. Note that the memo must be read and understood by Attorney Tom Freelance (for example, he must know who Milton Maddox is), because he must now communicate back to Penny to let her know about scheduling the deposition.

Each of these aspects of the communication process contains the possibility for miscommunication, which can be both embarrassing and expensive. So, the next time you see or partake in a communication that seems simple, remember that even the simplest communication requires that all the components of the communication process be fulfilled effectively. It takes a lot to achieve effective communication between people. You must possess a thorough understanding and appreciation of the communication process and its complexity, as well as a genuine desire to communicate effectively with others, to be an effective communicator in both simple and complex communications.

OFFICES OF

DREW, ECKL & FARNHAM
808 West Peachtree Street
Atlanta, Georgia 30309
(404) 885-1400

Date: 1-15-95   ☒ Telephone Conference

To: Tom Freelance   ☐ Office Conference

From: Penny Paralegal   ☐ Research

Client: Friendly Ins.   ☐ File Review

RE: Fire v. Sleet   ☐ Interoffice Memorandum

 Spoke w/ Milton Maddox re π 's depo on 1-14-95. Maddox would prefer it to be held at his offices. He also wants to take depo of her husband at same time (immediately after).

 Please let me know how to schedule - Tx

                                         PP

FIGURE 15-3 Even the simplest communication requires that all the components of the communication process be fulfilled effectively.

Effective Communication in the Law Office

 Applying the model of sender, message, and receiver to your communication skills in the law office will make your attempts to communicate much more meaningful and successful. (See Figure 15-4.) The keys to successful communication in the law office require that you learn and apply the following effective communication practices.

1. Brevity—be as brief as possible while still conveying all necessary information. As we have already seen, time is money in the law office.

2. Clarity—make certain that you are using correct vocabulary, grammar, and terminology. If you do not know if the word you want to use means what you want it to mean, look it up in the dictionary. Also, some legal assistants make the mistake of believing that using 20-syllable words with numerous dependent and independent clauses in their oral and written work will make them look good. Not true. The good communicator uses plain English and uses as few words as possible to convey her ideas. "Legalese" and flowery language should not be used, because they generally hinder the communication process. Remember also that the law has specific meanings for words and that you should learn and use them correctly; in the law, a "legitimate state interest" is not the same thing as a "compelling state interest," and you will need to get used to using words precisely and correctly.

3. Appropriate mechanism for conveying—if the message you are conveying is important and will be referred to in the future, put it in writing via either a memo or a handwritten note to the file. If the information is only important for a specific period of time, and you do not need a record for later, give it to the receiver orally. Other factors that should influence your decision about whether to convey the message orally or in writing include whether the receiver is available, whether there are multiple receivers, and whether documentation will be required in the future. Again, use your common sense, as well as established firm procedures, when deciding what channels should be used for conveying your messages.

4. Look the receiver in the eye—the principle applies not only literally to oral communication, when you actually must look the receiver in the eye instead

FIGURE 15-4
Communication
is a joint venture.

of looking at the floor or ceiling, but also metaphorically to written communication. Looking the receiver in the eye for written communication means getting to the point, rather than rambling on, and using language actively and accurately to convey your ideas.

5. Make a good impression—this principle applies to making sure you have good personal grooming habits as well as being certain that you do not have any annoying habits, such as smoking when talking to someone in their office, pulling your hair, playing with your jewelry, and so on. It is also applicable to written communication skills. Your impression in written communication is determined by the vocabulary you use, whether there are "typos" or misspelled words, or whether the paper is messy. An unprofessional personal appearance, or the unprofessional preparation of documents, will reflect poorly on you and can sabotage your efforts to communicate effectively.

6. Effective preparation—plan what information you are going to relay and how you are going to relay it. This preparation will ensure that you are aware of the purpose of your communication so that your actual communication can be more effective.

7. Just the facts, ma'am—it is tempting when relaying information, especially about a case or client, to give your opinion or judgment rather than stating what happened. Remember that the mark of a successful attorney is the ability to see things that others might have overlooked. Do not eliminate factual information when you communicate with attorneys, and do not give conclusions instead of the information that led you to that conclusion. Finally, remember the words of Joe Friday in your attempt to relay information objectively and effectively: "Just the facts, Ma'am."

Communication in the Law Office

The following areas represent specific situations in which a paralegal needs to demonstrate effective communication skills. The hints supplied in each area will help you master each of these forms of communication.

Telephone Skills

Paralegals spend a lot of time on the telephone. (See Figure 15-5.) Hints that will help you become a more effective communicator on the telephone include the following:

1. Always identify yourself when answering your telephone. Do not just say, "Hello." Rather, say, "Harry Norvell."

FIGURE 15-5
Excellent telephone
skills are essential
in the law office.

2. When calling someone who is out of the office, leave a detailed message. Do not just leave a message that you called. If you leave a detailed message about why you called and what you need, the caller will be able to gather necessary information prior to calling you back.

3. In an effort to avoid "telephone tag," ask when a person is expected to return, speak to that person's secretary, and ask if someone else may be able to help you.

4. Know the technical capabilities of your phone system, and be able to use it effectively and efficiently.

Client Communication Skills

Always, always, always, let the client know that you are a legal assistant and not a lawyer! Keep the conversation short and get to the heart of the matter so that the client will not think that his money is being wasted with longer-than-necessary telephone calls. However, if you sense that the client needs to talk, and if billing is not an issue, you may have to take your time. In either situation, you must be sensitive to the client's needs and expectations. Always address attorneys as Ms. or Mr., and remember that you are working for the client, so be sure to communicate respect for his needs. Even though your office may be casual, it is best to err on the side of formality when communicating with clients. It is also important to stay informed about your clients and their cases, so that when they do call you are current with their situations. This will make them feel that their work is in good hands.

Dictation

When dictating, speak clearly and spell out any difficult or unusual words. Do not eat or chew while dictating. Try to isolate yourself from any outside noises. Most importantly, do not mumble, and do speak deliberately and clearly into the microphone. (See Figure 15-6.)

FIGURE 15-6
When dictating, speak clearly and deliberately.

To help the person who will be transcribing the dictation, you might want to begin the dictation by stating what it is you are dictating and giving instructions. You will also want to gather all of your materials before beginning to dictate and spell any difficult or unusual words for the transcriber. If the dictation will be long, consider outlining the main points of the dictation at the beginning to help the listener. Finally, use tapes to record and listen to information as a means of transforming dead time into productive time.

RULES FOR DICTATION

Your work area will be equipped with a dictation unit. You are encouraged to dictate your memos and documents. Although this may seem awkward at first, your efforts to master the art of dictating will eventually be rewarded by the production of better quality work in a shorter period of time. The following tips for dictating may be helpful.

BASIC DICTATING PROTOCOL

1. Have your ideas or notes organized prior to starting your dictation. Jot down key words or phrases so that your dictation will flow more smoothly from one thought to the next. Know in general which citations you wish to include.

If the matter being dictated is rather long and complex, it is often helpful to do a quick outline of points to be covered, and the sequence of the material.

Avoid the natural tendency to write everything out in longhand or in elaborate outline form prior to dictation. You will become a good dictator more quickly if you force yourself to work from the key words and phrases which you have jotted down in advance.

2. Begin your dictation by telling the typist the style of document you are dictating (letter, memo, motion for summary judgment, etc.) and the approximate length. If the material to be dictated is lengthy and it is critical that you receive the typed draft quickly, you might put the dictation on several tapes so that more than one secretary can work on it simultaneously.

3. *Always* put instructions at the *beginning* of your dictation:
   a. Rough draft only
   b. Carbon/photocopies to (list names)
   c. Other special instructions: double- or single-space, legal- or letter-sized paper, etc.

4. Indicate on the tape, or when giving the secretary the material, the deadline for its completion. BE REALISTIC!

5. Give your secretary the file or other material that goes with the dictation. If this is impossible, give her all the information that will be needed, such as the client/matter number, the full name and address on a letter, or the case style on a pleading.

6. If, in mid-dictation, you think of something you have omitted or a particular phrase you want to remember for later use, depress the "cue" button on your microphone and proceed with special instructions, or say the typist's name and call his attention to a break in content. Then ask him to make a note of the thought within brackets. After noting to the typist that you are returning to the text you were dictating, resume dictation.

7. To indicate capitalization, say "Cap 'borrower,'" for example. Once you have capitalized a word or phrase that will be used frequently throughout a document, it is not necessary to say "Cap '_____,'" each time thereafter. Only indicate when you will *not* want the word or phrase capitalized.

8. Indicate the following during dictation:

All caps	Colon
Center	Paragraph
Underline	Indent for quotation
Period	Paren (parentheses)
Comma	Bracket or list
Semicolon	Section mark (§)

9. You do not need to dictate citation punctuation or underlining. For example, 123 F.2d 569 (5th Cir. 1973) should be dictated as "one twenty-three F second five sixty-nine fifth cir. 1973."

10. Identify the end of your dictation—"End of Tape," "End of Memo," etc.—so that the secretary knows there is no more material to follow. Do *not* rewind the tape when finished.

EDITING DICTATED MATERIAL

1. Use a red pen on typewritten material, unless it is a final copy with small typos such as transposition of letters. These can be corrected neatly, and the need for retyping eliminated. On such small errors, use light pencil markings with a checkmark indicating the line on which the error occurs. Do not circle errors.

2. Take a few extra minutes before submitting a corrected draft to your secretary to make sure you have noticed everything that needs correcting or changing.

3. When making insertions, write them in the margin or on a separate page identifying them as "Insert A," and "Insert B," and so on. Make the same marks on the original copy, indicating with an arrow where the insertions should go.

4. If insertions are long or if you have done major revisions of the draft, it may be much easier for you and your secretary if you redictate that portion of the material.

5. If you are handwriting any revisions, make sure to write legibly.

6. Even though the word processing system makes it easy for the secretaries to make corrections on your work, please try to keep the number of drafts they must produce to a minimum.

OTHER HELPFUL SUGGESTIONS

- Try to avoid lengthy pauses on the tape while you are thinking. Use the "Stop" button.
- Occasionally listen to what you have been dictating, especially if it is a long document. Listening will help you hear the tape as your secretary will be hearing it.
- Avoid dictating with noise or other distractions in the background.
- Be conscious of speaking distinctly, especially so with words that may sound similar—e.g., "in," "an," "end," "and."
- When reading material is dictated, be sure not to read so rapidly as to blur the distinction between the words. Again, articulate carefully.
- Consider asking your secretary from time to time for constructive criticism of your dictation habits. He may have suggestions useful to both of you.
- Photocopy and give to the typist long quotes you are including in your dictation. This allows your secretary to type the material exactly as it appeared in the original document, which makes proofreading easier and reduces the chances of major errors.
- When dictating numerous and/or repetitive cites, write them out on a piece of paper or dictate them at the beginning of the dictation for the secretary, identifying them as "Cite number 1," "Cite number 2," etc., and refer to them as such while dictating.
- Spell any unusual word or one that might be spelled several ways, such as "S-t-e-v-e-n" or "S-t-e-p-h-e-n." Spell or enunciate carefully such things as plural possessives, etc.
- You may wish to have one special tape onto which you can dictate memos to a file, entries in your black book, etc. and have that tape transcribed when it is full. Do not put anything on this tape which is critical or will be needed soon; restrict it to material of a more routine nature.
- When dictating, hold the mike two or three inches from your mouth. When you hold it closer, certain sounds tend to be overstated to the typist. When you hold it further away, distracting sounds are easily picked up.
- Use standard proofreaders' corrections, or at least make sure that you and the secretary use and understand all of the same proofreading symbols.
- Do not chew gum or eat food while dictating.

Written Memos

Use the memo form that your firm prefers. Write or type neatly and accurately. Like the tips just given on written communication, keep memos short and simple. Give only the facts without a lot of unnecessary information. Always reference the file name on the memo. (See Figure 15-7.) Also pay attention to the physical appearance of your written memos; your work reflects on your competence and professionalism.

Letter Writing

Most people, in today's video- and telecommunications-oriented society, do not use the letter as a primary means of correspondence. In the law firm,

---

MEMORANDUM

TO: Donna Masinter, Senior Partner

FROM: Theresa White, Paralegal

DATE: February 23, 1995

RE: Status Report
          Smith v. Jones

Pursuant to your instructions, I have made arrangements with opposing counsel for the deposition of Dr. Willard on March 3, 1995, in his office at 8:30 a.m. Sue Morse will be the court reporter.

I have reviewed the plaintiff's deposition and have identified all past employers and physicians named by the plaintiff. I am in the process of drafting Requests for Production of Documents to those employers and physicians.

The medical records received from Dr. Chase last week do not relate to the plaintiff's back injury. However, according to the Medical History included with the records, the plaintiff indicated he had problems in the past with his knees, but the treating physician was not named.

I have contacted opposing counsel regarding his responses to our Second Interrogatories, which are now two weeks late. He has promised the responses will be mailed tomorrow.

/raa

342415

FIGURE 15-7 A legal memo should be written.

however, letters are both common and important because they create a permanent record of all types of communications. It is extremely common, for example, for a paralegal to have a telephone conversation with an insurance adjustor and then follow that conversation with a letter reviewing the points discussed.

One of the trademarks of a successful paralegal is the ability to write clear, effective letters. All letters should be written on the appropriate stationery (indicating your status as a legal assistant), in standard English and in acceptable business letter format as recommended by your firm. Letters should be clear and to the point, and should be written to maximize the reader's understanding. (See Figure 15-8.) Also remember that even a seemingly small item such as a letter is an indication to others of the quality of your work and your professionalism, so make sure that every letter that goes out with your name on it is a document you can feel proud of.

Achieving Professionalism Through Effective Communication

In your quest to develop yourself and your career, it is essential that you present yourself in a professional manner. The way people know—and evaluate—you is through their perception of you, which comes primarily from your communications. This includes your appearance, your words, and your actions. By paying attention to and improving your abilities as a communicator, you will take a huge step toward achieving professionalism in your work. Effective communication is a key to superior job performance, and most positions of greater responsibility entail greater communications as part of the work.

Additionally, the other aspects of professionalism covered in this section of the book are all affected by communication. Ethical problems can generally be avoided by effective communication. The stress that accompanies the effects of miscommunication can be avoided by using effective communication, and good communication skills are essential in the process of obtaining a position as a paralegal and developing career opportunities for the future. By learning and using effective communication skills, you will lay the foundation for your professional identity.

Communication and Conflict Management

One of the realities of all offices—a reality that may be especially true of law offices—is that conflicts exist. If conflicts are not handled well, they can poison the entire work environment and impede work and productivity.

DREW ECKL & FARNHAM

ATTORNEYS AT LAW

880 WEST PEACHTREE STREET

P.O. BOX 7600

ATLANTA, GEORGIA 30357-0600

(404) 885-1400

CHARLES L. DREW
W. WRAY ECKL
CLAYTON H. FARNHAM
ARTHUR H. GLASER
JAMES M. POE
JOHN A. FERGUSON, JR.
THEODORE FREEMAN
JOHN P. REALE
STEVAN A. MILLER
H. MICHAEL BAGLEY
HALL F. McKINLEY III
G. RANDALL MOODY
B. HOLLAND PRITCHARD
T. BART GARY
DAVID A. SMITH
KENNETH A. HINDMAN
PAUL W. BURKE
DANIEL C. KNIFFEN
JOHN C. BRUFFEY, JR.
BENTON J. MATHIS, JR.
JOHN G. BLACKMON, JR.
DENNIS M. HALL
J. WILLIAM HALEY
DONALD R. ANDERSEN
ANN BISHOP BYARS
GARY R. HURST

STEPHEN W. MOONEY
KEVIN P. O'MAHONY
ANNE M. LANDRUM
NENA K. PUCKETT
NICOLE D. TIFVERMAN
JERRY C. CARTER, JR.
PHILLIP E. FRIDUSS
L. LEE BENNETT, JR.
CHRISTOPHER J. CULP
KATHERINE D. DIXON
WILLIAM T. MITCHELL
J. ROBB CRUSER
PHILIP W. SAVRIN
LUCIAN GILLIS, JR.
PETER H. SCHMIDT II
BROOKS B. POWERS
APRIL RICH
MAUREEN M. MIDDLETON
ROBERT L. WELCH
JULIE Y. JOHN
JEFFREY B. GRIMM
SUZANNE V. SANDERS
LEIGH LAWSON REEVES
BRUCE A. TAYLOR, JR.
DOUGLAS T. LAY
DOUGLAS M. BAKER

DAVID R. BERGQUIST
CHARLES L. NORTON, JR.
NANCY F. RIGBY
PETER A. LAW
DOUGLAS G. SMITH, JR.
TERRENCE T. ROCK
PHILLIP COMER GRIFFETH
MARIAN S. SINGER
STEVEN D. PRELUTSKY
JULIANNE L. SWILLEY
PAUL G. PHILLIPS
CARTER ALLEN
MARY H. HINES
LISA A. KELEHEAR
A. BRADLEY DOZIER, JR.
B. GREG CLINE
TRICIA R. STEVENS
C. LAWRENCE MEYER
E. JANYCE DAWKINS
PHILIP G. POMPILIO
ROBERT J. MOYE III
GREGORY S. ESSLINGER
SEÁN W. CONLEY
MARY ANNE ACKOUREY
BEVERLY POWELL SISK

FACSIMILE (404) 876-0992

WRITER'S DIRECT DIAL NUMBER
(404) 885-6211

February 3, 1995

Mr. Robert Richards
BNK Davis Ltd.
409 North Suffolk
London, England

Dear Mr. Richards:

I am writing to you at the suggestion of Caroline Kushner, following my referral of a potential physician-client to your health care group for a practice valuation. A recent letter from Bob Davis to Michael Kartt of this law firm, outlining your health care group's services for physician-clients, has also been brought to my attention.

As you may know, this law firm is a client of BNK Davis Ltd., and it has been suggested to me that some of your health care clients may, on occasion, need the type of legal advice and services that we provide on a regular basis for health professionals and institutions. In that regard, enclosed is a brief summary of the type of legal matters that we have handled for physicians, dentists, provider groups, and other health professionals in the past.

I would welcome the opportunity to discuss with you our respective services and client needs. Please let me know if you feel that such a discussion might be mutually beneficial.

Sincerely,

DREW ECKL & FARNHAM

Donna Masinter
Donna Masinter

Enc.

FIGURE 15-8 Letters are extremely common and important because they create a permanent record of all types of communication.

There are both preventive and reactive approaches to conflict management. All successful offices must engage in preventive conflict management, which means that the office develops policies and fosters attitudes that are least likely to create unnecessary conflict. They also must be prepared to react to and handle any conflicts that do emerge in an appropriate manner, because no organization is going to be conflict-free.

Additionally, remember that although conflicts might be difficult or uncomfortable, they are not necessarily bad. Some conflicts, such as disagreements over practice specialties in a growing firm, are the natural outgrowth of running a business and are part of the package. Other conflicts, although seemingly unnecessary or unproductive, can also be windows of opportunity to improve firm policies or group dynamics.

Ineffective communication practices are a frequent cause of conflict. Effective communication is the key to prevention of conflict as well as to the effective resolution of existing conflicts. Conflict prevention and resolution are achieved only through the development and maintenance of effective, open communication in the law office.

The following guest editorial provides an outstanding overview of conflict management, especially as it relates to the law office.

GUEST EDITORIAL

Resolving Conflict in the Firm

Joan Wagner Zinober

Joan Wagner Zinober, Ph.D., M.B.A., is president of Zinober and Associates, consultants to management, in Tampa, Florida. This article was reproduced by permission of the American Bar Association and the author.

The Nature of Conflict

Conflict is a real or perceived difference between two or more parties. It tends to polarize those involved, pushing them to increasingly opposite sides of an issue. Conflict also may be manifested as an apparent incompatibility of needs between two people or groups of people. Not all conflict is characterized by yelling or overt arguing. Some signs that there may be conflict in your practice are:

Distorted, Absent or Insufficient Communication.

You may notice that people who once conversed freely and easily with one another no longer do so. There may be repeated episodes of conflicting information about any given situation. People may seem to be insufficiently informed about things involving their work or work-life.

Increased Emotionality. Employees or lawyers may seem to overreact to seemingly minor occurrences. The reaction to a given situation may seem to be more emotional than would be objectively warranted. Lawyer meetings may be characterized by increased antagonism, including overt or covert attacks by some lawyers against other lawyers.

Feeling of Tension in the Air. While this is difficult to describe, it is usually recognized by those experiencing it. There is a heightened sense of stress and uneasiness accompanied by an increased level of discomfort.

Decline in Trust. This may be manifested in one or more of a variety of ways. Lawyers or employees may begin checking up on things they always took on faith before. Small groups of people may be overheard discussing one or more other people in a negative way. Rumors may abound. People may suddenly want to have more things in writing. You may sense that some people are no longer as open about mentioning or discussing things and that they seem fearful of doing so. The equity of the compensation system may be questioned even more than in the past. Departments that used to spread the work around to other departments that were under budget may begin hoarding their work and keeping it all in their own unit.

Sources of Conflict in a Law Practice

Legal practices are rife with opportunities for conflict. The responsibility for major cases can be stressful. The stakes are high and mistakes can be costly both in terms of client good will and dollars. Continued stress can cause otherwise easygoing people to become argumentative and/or uncommunicative, both of which can lead to conflict. Lawyers rarely have any background or training in management—either of people or financial and business matters (other than those aspects of business that clearly relate to legal issues). These factors are compounded by the fact that many types of law practice are adversarial in nature and those who get rewarded in the short run are those who are good at being adversaries—not advocates or team builders.

An understanding of the source of conflict in your particular firm is helpful because it can point the way to the nature of its resolution. Some common sources of conflict and examples of each are:

Divergent Goals. Goals for both practice and self may vary widely within any given practice. For example, some lawyers may be more interested in generating a large-volume practice while others may be more interested in having one that is smaller but higher in quality or restricted to specific types of clients. Some lawyers may want the firm to specialize while others may want to be part of a full-service firm or even be generalists themselves. Some lawyers may be interested in expanding through mergers and acquisitions while others may prefer to be part of a smaller-sized firm restricted to one geographic location.

Individual Style Differences. Some attorneys are people-oriented and will focus on interpersonal issues, even at the expense of efficiency or

productivity. Others may be task-oriented and be more attentive to getting the tasks at hand completed than to ensuring positive interactions between people. Some lawyers are extroverts while others are introverted. One lawyer may focus on the big picture while another may be more detail-oriented.

Status Conflicts. It is not unusual to find attorneys who work together getting caught up in issues of "Who's more important?" or "Who has the most power?" Competitive people may always need to feel like they are on top.

Value Differences. Some lawyers in a firm may value earnings most while others may place their highest value on reputation in the community, or doing the most community service, or having sufficient time off to pursue outside interests. Younger and mid-level attorneys may place a higher value on a productivity (as opposed to a seniority) system of compensation than do their older counterparts.

Role Pressures. The law is indeed a jealous mistress. The pressure for billable hours productivity is often intense. Such work demands may at times interfere with other roles such as parent, spouse or community activist. When the stress of these pressures is not successfully handled, lawyers may become unpleasant to work with. Similarly, the stress of handling major cases with major clients can result in attorneys becoming moody, argumentative, distracted or otherwise difficult to deal with. Attorneys who hold important positions outside the practice may occasionally find themselves in situations where decisions that benefit the practice would be detrimental to their other responsibilities, or vice versa.

Dysfunctional Organizational Structures. Your firm may be administratively or organizationally set up in such a way as to promote conflict and dissention. Perhaps you have people spread too thin. Perhaps employees do not have a clear chain of command. Perhaps your clerical and business staff is not held responsible to your office manager/administrator, which may make coordination and equity among departments difficult. Perhaps there is no structure for assuring that new associates get the training and supervision they need to perform at the level expected of them. Multiple practice sites also may be a source of conflict when the staffing and chain of command for each site is not well organized and agreed to by all those involved.

Limited Resources. This is manifested by people fighting over who gets what in terms of equipment, space and associate time. Who gets access to the new high-tech equipment and on what schedule? Which employee gets to have the new computer? Who gets to go to out-of-town meetings and training sessions? If there are fewer large private offices than partners/shareholders, who gets them?

Unsatisfactory Communication. When communication is absent, erratic, incomplete, confusing or only one-way, conflict is inevitable. In practices without a strong and trusted managing attorney, communication and decision-making may become further complicated when each attorney sets policy without consulting with the others, or when every decision—no matter how small—requires the input of all partners/shareholders. This latter situation makes it difficult for the practice to be responsive or to deal with concerns in a timely fashion. Staff as well as attorneys may become frustrated or interpret this as a lack of caring about them and their concerns. Communication among busy lawyers is at least as much of a potential problem as is communication between lawyers and employees.

Avoiding Dealing with Conflict

Like death and taxes, some conflict cannot be avoided. Even in the best of practices, just as in the best of marriages, some conflict is inevitable. Recognizing this, it is important not to overreact to occasional minor disagreements or differences of opinion. Such overreaction can elevate an otherwise minor skirmish to the level of major warfare. However, when the conflict becomes repetitive or disruptive to the practice, makes work unpleasant, or causes absenteeism and turnover, it should be clear that you have passed the point where it is time to develop some effective mechanisms for resolving the issues at hand.

While overreaction is at one end of the poles with respect to dealing with conflict, avoidance is at the opposite end. It is important to note that both types of extreme reactions can escalate problems, sometimes beyond the point of no return. A common misperception of conflict is that if you ignore it, it will go away. Avoidance and procrastination are so common among lawyers that at times it may seem as if they are bona fide occupational qualifications. This may come from the nature of those who tend to go into law, from the nature of the work where continuances are commonly obtainable, or from experiences that lawyers have had where lawsuits that are ignored for awhile settle. Everyone has a bad day and an isolated incident may be best left forgotten. But repetitive conflict should not be ignored.

Another common misconception about conflict is that its presence means you have made a mistake. There are numerous potential sources of conflict. Thinking that conflict is the result of your personal mistake may be dangerous because it tends to precipitate a defensive reaction that escalates rather than mitigates the problem. There are bound to be honest differences of opinion. This doesn't necessarily mean there is a right and a wrong way. It may just mean there are equally valid but different perspectives. Taking the time to understand the other person's perspective can help smooth things over and prevent negative situations in the future.

Handled properly, most conflict can be reduced once it occurs, and most can be prevented when dealt with proactively. Nonetheless, the tendency to avoid dealing with conflict is not as unusual as one might think. Some of the reasons people avoid and fear conflict are:

- The need to be liked;
- Fear of getting out of control;
- Fear of others getting out of control;
- A preference for dealing with the devil you know over the devil you don't;
- Fear of being wrong or losing;
- Fear that the other person will be vindictive;
- Fear of lack of knowledge/skill in how to handle the problem;
- Societal expectations about being nice;
- Fear of making the problem worse;
- Inertia—it's easier to maintain the status quo.

Conflict

As a result of unresolved conflicts, morale tends to decline and productivity is reduced as time and energy are diverted from work to griping, rumor mongering and reacting to the conflict.

If you or others in your practice are leading a life of quiet desperation, it is likely that one cause is the tendency to avoid dealing with problematic issues, either proactively or as they arise. Failing to deal with your anger at someone can cause resentments to build up. What started out as a petty/minor annoyance may, over time, become a major battleground. Eventually, the anger/annoyance that was suppressed in the workplace may spill over and become displaced onto personal relationships at home. The poor unsuspecting family members may be taking the heat for problems they neither caused nor can remedy.

When unresolved resentments build up, they tend to infect an entire office. Increased tensions and undercurrents of stress become noticeable. Over time, there is likely to be an increase in bad mouthing, griping and general criticism. As things become distorted with the passage of days, weeks and months, the nature of the criticism and bad mouthing may be seemingly unrelated to the original complaint, but tracing it backward often leads to one little kernel that was allowed to pop because it got too much heat for too long.

Worksites with continued unresolved conflicts are unpleasant places. As a result, morale tends to decline and productivity is reduced as time and energy are diverted from work to griping, rumor mongering and reacting to the conflict. Absenteeism and turnover may increase if resolution does not occur. Some attorneys may even choose to defect rather than endure an aversive environment.

How to Handle Conflict Productively

If you recognize some of the symptoms described above, either in yourself, your colleagues or your practice, the time to do something about it is now. Waiting for someone else to initiate the healing process will only prolong the diseased state. If you are uncomfortable, it is probably safe to assume that others are, too.

Perhaps they, like you, didn't know where to begin or had previously experienced a negative outcome when they attempted to intervene and/or address undesirable situations. The first step is to recognize and really understand that the goal is productive resolution—not placing blame. Individuals rarely feel they are the cause of any given problem and are likely to react to accusations in a manner that promotes a negative rather than a positive outcome.

A good first step might be to acknowledge the problem in a group or one-on-one setting, depending on what is appropriate in your particular situation. The key is to state the problem without accusing anyone of wrongdoing. An effective way to do this is with the use of "I" messages rather than "you" messages. Examples of "you" messages are "You made a big mistake," "You really messed up when you _____ ," "It's your fault" and "You shouldn't have done that." The effect of "you" messages is to engender anger and hostility and to lower self-esteem in the recipient of the message. Since "you" messages place blame and lay fault, they make the receiver angry, hostile, resentful and resistive. Such messages stimulate a win/lose confrontation and an attitude of "I'll show you!" Thus, rather than stimulate positive action, "you" messages tend to yield negative behavior.

A viable alternative to the "you" message is the "I" message. Examples of "I" messages are "When you take a long lunch hour, I get upset because the staff complains to me that they are having to do your work"; or "When you criticize me in front of others, I feel hurt/angry because it undermines my self-esteem and future relations with these people." The form of "I" messages is "When you _____ (noncritical description of behavior), I feel _____ (my feelings as a result of the behavior), because _____ (effects of the behavior on the practice, the attorneys, the clients, the employees, etc.)." The difference between "I" messages and "you" messages should be clear. "I" messages preserve self-esteem in the receiver. They offer an objective description of the behavior and its consequences. They state the effect the behavior has on you and thereby demonstrate your role in the issue. Rather than proposing a dictatorial solution (which is likely to be resisted),

"I" messages allow others to find the solution or to ask for your opinion in a nonthreatening environment.

Preventive Conflict Management

In the best of all possible worlds, people do not wait to deal with conflict until after it occurs but, rather, set in motion those things likely to prevent or minimize its occurrence. Preventive conflict management involves:

Clarifying Relationships and Roles Fully and Openly. The key here is to reduce uncertainty as much as possible and to assure that everyone knows, understands and agrees to his or her responsibilities. With respect to employees, written, detailed job descriptions go a long way toward accomplishing this end. Try not to spring things like overtime on people unless the ground rules have been discussed and agreed to in advance.

Anticipating Problems and Dealing with Them Early on. If you think things through in advance, especially changes, it is likely you will be able to identify potential problems and pitfalls you could reduce or eliminate if you start early enough. If you can't reduce or eliminate them, you can at least prepare people for them so they will know their feelings were considered and will be able to take whatever steps they personally need to be more prepared to tackle the difficult times.

Keeping Communication Open. If you aren't meeting regularly as a firm, you are missing out on opportunities to share information, learn about potential problems, build a winning team and understand one another's perspectives. Meetings should be held at least quarterly with administrative staff and appropriate attorneys. Monthly meetings are usually appropriate for attorneys (either partners/shareholders only or all attorneys).

If you have already experienced a conflict, schedule a meeting to discuss it. Prior to the meeting, write down your ideas about the nature of the problem and what you are willing to do or give up in order to resolve it. This will help you to focus on the most important things and to feel prepared. During the meeting, be positive. Don't rehash old problems. Focus on the

here and now and how to move forward. Avoid being judgmental or placing blame. "I" messages can be helpful here. Be certain to be a good listener. There is always more than one side to any issue. Successful resolution may rest on the other person(s) feeling he or she is understood. Make concessions when they are appropriate. Others may need to feel you are giving something, too. It is especially important to be open-minded and flexible. You may learn new information that changes the picture considerably so that the solution you began with is no longer either the best or the most appropriate. If you fail to respond to this new information by rigidly adhering to your prior position, you may lose credibility and threaten the successful resolution of the problem. Build toward success by starting with low-risk, easy items first. Get agreement on the small things so by the time you have moved to the big things you have already had some positive interaction and experiences. Confine the discussion to the doable. Be sure resources and the bottom line are clear so you don't find yourself committed to something you can't deliver. When the discussion is over, be certain to summarize the agreements you've made to be sure you are all leaving the discussion with the same understanding of what was decided. A statement beginning with "It's my understanding we've agreed to ____" is a good start.

If conflict in your firm has gone on for a long time, you are uncertain as to its cause, or you have been unsuccessful in remediating the problem, it may be time to call in an outsider. An independent person who is objective and skilled in both diagnosing and treating organizational problems may be just the right prescription, provided that all firm members involved trust the person hired and are willing to make a good faith effort to improve the situation.

The Positive Side of Conflict

While most people tend to view the presence of conflict as a negative, conflict isn't all bad. On the plus side, it can open the door to positive change by:

- Stimulating problem solving;
- Causing a team to unite around an issue;

- Bringing problems out into the open;
- Encouraging the search for new solutions;
- Creating new learning opportunities;
- Forcing the prioritizing of issues, ideas and people;
- Preventing more serious conflicts, if dealt with early;
- Increasing mutual understanding.

When people allow themselves to be open, nondefensive and responsive, conflict can be the catalyst for significant improvements. Dissention can provide an opportunity to resolve problems/concerns that have been plaguing the firm for too long.   ▥

Avoiding Communication Breakdowns

The following hypothetical situations illustrate some communication breakdowns that commonly occur in the law office and suggest some solutions to these problems.

Jonathan is a paralegal with a firm that specializes in the defense of product liability lawsuits. The attorney with whom Jonathan works has asked him to obtain building standards for pool fences for the metropolitan area, which he needs for a lawsuit involving a child who drowned in a pool without a fence. Jonathan does some preliminary research and determines that the standards for pool fences are particular to city, county, and state standards. He wonders which standards he should get for the attorney.

Solution: Attorneys are not always able to be specific about what they need. It is your job as a paralegal to take the initiative to make this determination. In Jonathan's case, he can do one of two things. First, he can obtain copies of all standards. Second, he can dictate a memo to the attorney asking for further guidance and explaining what he has determined at this point.

Jean is a paralegal with a litigation firm and has been asked to summarize depositions in a case she is totally unfamiliar with. The attorney is leaving the country and will not be back for three weeks. The summaries must be completed by the time he returns.

Solution: The attorney did not inform Jean of the facts behind the case so that the deposition summaries will focus on the important details in the case. Thus, it is Jean's responsibility to review the file and determine the key issues from the pleadings. She also might want to locate another attorney in the firm who has worked on the case to confirm that her analysis is correct.

The attorney with whom Frank works is very impatient and not very good at explaining facts. Frank has just graduated from paralegal school and wants to impress his new boss. Frank is called into the office and asked to prepare a corporate dissolution for Jump Industries, Inc. The attorney says, "Any legal assistant worth his salt can prepare a corporate dissolution blindfolded. Can you do this for me?" Unwilling to admit he doesn't know how to draft a corporate dissolution, Frank says, "Yes."

Solution: Sometimes it is best to swallow your ego and ask questions. Remember that time is money in a law firm and having to do something over again when you could have gotten it right the first time is unacceptable. Frank should have said, "I agree, but before I'm willing to do it blindfolded, I'd like a form so that the dissolution will be to your liking."

A friend of yours at the firm tells you that another paralegal said you were incompetent. You decide to handle the situation by ignoring that person.

Solution: Go to the source. When you need to find out information, go directly to the person responsible. Doing otherwise is likely to result in hearsay being taken as truth.

Promoting Teamwork Through Effective Communication

Effective relationships in the law firm are founded on good communications as well as clearly defined job responsibilities. (See Figures 15-9 and 15-10.) Good communications means letting people you work with know what you are doing and why you are doing it. It also means expressing yourself in clearly defined terms. If you are upset about how a particular person treated you, confront the situation directly and go to that person. Nip problems in the bud; most people appreciate frankness and clarity.

FIGURE 15-9 The effective paralegal communicates effectively in both formal situations ...

FIGURE 15-10
... and informal
exchanges.

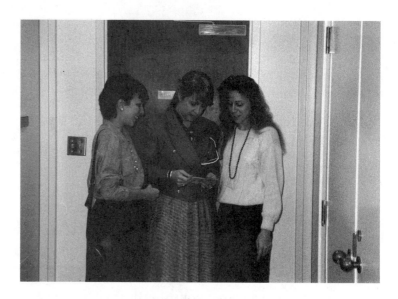

Paralegals are part of the legal team. The best way to develop successful relationships with the team is to act like a team member. The goal of the team is
to provide the best legal representation to the client in the most cost-effective
manner. Often this means that you will be assigned tasks or asked to assist on
projects that you view as clerical in nature. Remember that even attorneys have
to do clerical work at times. If you keep in mind that being asked to do this
type of work is not belittling your position, but rather complimenting you
on your role as a team member, relationships with other team members will
be good.

When beginning a job, ask the supervising attorneys if they have ever
worked with a paralegal before. If so, ask how they envision your position and
suggest additional skills that you can bring to the job. If not, give them a detailed explanation of your vision of the position.

One of the stickiest situations for the paralegal is the relationship between
the secretary and paralegal. Try to show the legal secretary that you are not in-
fringing on his work or position, but that you are there to make his job easier.
If the legal secretary has not worked with a paralegal before, the relationship
can be even more tenuous from the beginning. It might be a good idea to suggest that your supervising attorney sit down in a relaxed atmosphere with both
of you and clearly define your roles. If the legal secretary is to do only the attorney's typing and dictation, that should be clearly specified from the beginning.
However, if the legal secretary to the attorney is also responsible for your work,
you will need to help him prioritize assignments. This should be handled in a
very tactful way. Most legal secretaries consider the attorney's work to be the
first priority, no matter what. Try not to procrastinate about work and get it to
the secretary sufficiently ahead of time to have time to revise and edit the material without a frantic rush. If you do have to ask for a rush job, take a moment
and explain why it is a rush (i.e., you were given the assignment ten minutes

ago). Treating the legal secretaries with respect and taking time to explain things to them can go a long way in creating a professional and congenial environment in the law firm and among the legal team.

Communicating in a Multicultural World

One challenge that faces everyone in the contemporary world, and especially persons whose work involves interaction with many people, is to communicate effectively with those whose cultural, ethnic, or economic backgrounds are different from theirs. Changing population patterns have created a new American society, where diversity and difference are the norm rather than the exception. The reality is that, in the work of the law, you should expect to interact and communicate with people whose values, language, expectations, and attitudes may be very different from yours. One characteristic of the professional is to be comfortable in diverse situations and with people from diverse backgrounds; it is essential that you be aware of this multicultural phenomenon and be able to participate actively and effectively in it.

The first key to effective multicultural communication is a recognition that your cultural values are not universally accepted. Refuse to judge cultural values and behaviors as superior or inferior, and instead become interested in how others understand the human experience.

A second key is the desire to communicate effectively with all people. This desire will encourage you to learn about different cultures, and from this knowledge you will gain insight and understanding into both others and yourself as the products of culture and society.

The third key is to avoid stereotyping and to treat and respect each person as an individual. By freeing yourself from preconceptions and misperceptions of culturally diverse people, you will be in the best position to interact and communicate with them honestly and fairly.

The work of the law involves communication with a wide variety of people who come from tremendously diverse backgrounds. Lawyers and paralegals communicate every day with poor people and with wealthy people; with big corporate interests and with traffic accident victims; with African-Americans and Asian-Americans and Hispanics and Pakistanis; with wards of the state and with trust beneficiaries; with Jews and Buddhists and Christians and Seventh Day Adventists; with English professors and with those who have only a rudimentary knowledge of the English language. Some come from the country and some from the city; some wear suits and others wear blue jeans; some trust lawyers and some do not. All of them, however, come to you in your professional capacity with some very important things in common: they want to be listened to and understood; they want to be treated with respect; they want to be looked at as individual human beings; and they do not want to be judged by their differences, but want to be embraced for their common and shared humanity.

If you are going to be a successful communicator in the law office, you must be able to communicate effectively with all types of people from many diverse backgrounds in all types of situations. This ability to communicate successfully in the multicultural world of the 1990s, by embracing and appreciating, rather than rejecting and fearing, the cultural diversity of contemporary society, is a necessary quality of the modern paralegal. By developing the ability to handle the diversity of modern society, you will avoid the limitations that will naturally arise if you are only able to communicate in a shrinking monocultural environment.

Effective Communication: A Summary

If you had to describe the work of the paralegal in one word, that word might well be "communicate." Paralegals communicate in ways and with people far too numerous to mention here: formally and informally, with couriers and criminals, with networks and clients, with librarians and lawyers. Regardless, however, of the situation about which you are communicating, the environment in which you are communicating, or the people with whom you are communicating, you will need to be an effective communicator if you want to be a successful paralegal. By understanding the importance of effective communication and the causes of and solutions to communication breakdowns, you will be able to become a productive part of the communication process.

On Point

THE CONCERNED CLIENT

Ralph Cramdon, a client in the midst of heated, controversial litigation, calls his attorney one early evening, and his call is routed to you, the paralegal working on the case, because the attorney is unavailable. Ralph is obviously upset, and demands answers to his questions immediately. He asks the following questions. What is my potential liability on this case? Has any discovery been completed? Are my attorney's fees tax-deductible? What are my chances of winning? Have you deposed Alice Applegate yet? Do we have a court date? Should I settle this case for economic considerations? Do you think my attorney is competent to represent me?

How should you respond?

Key Terms

communication breakdowns
communication channels
communication process

conflict management
multicultural environment

Problems and Activities

1. Analyze your own communication style. How can you improve your verbal, nonverbal, and written skills?

2. List the three things that you believe contribute to communication breakdowns between people. For each, analyze how the miscommunication might be avoided.

3. The attorney for whom you work calls you into her office and says, "Could you please handle the deposition tomorrow in the McNair case for me?" Of course, you respond affirmatively. As you walk back to your office, you panic. ... did she want you to ask the deponent questions or merely take notes? What should you do?

4. An attorney in your office asks you to subpoena a witness in the Winston case. You immediately go to the forms files and pull a witness subpoena for trial. The day comes when the witness is supposed to appear for a deposition, and instead he calls the office screaming that his subpoena told him to appear in court that day, and not for a deposition. Why did this happen and what can you do to remediate the situation?

5. Compare the communication styles of males and females. How do these styles differ? Why is it important to understand the differences, and how might you apply this understanding in legal work?

CHAPTER 16

COPING WITH STRESS

OBJECTIVES

By the completion of this chapter, you should:

- understand the causes of stress;

- understand how to cope effectively with stress; and

- learn how to apply stress management techniques to increase your personal effectiveness.

Coping with Stress: An Introduction

One of your goals for your personal development in your work life should be to manage stress effectively. The pace of the modern world, the complexity of daily transactions, technological innovations, the hectic pace of law practice—all these contribute to a contemporary environment where everyone is vulnerable to being overwhelmed by stress. The modern world is stressful, and it is necessary for every person to learn how to operate effectively in the world. Additionally, the law office can be a particularly stressful environment, because of the different activities and time pressures that characterize each day.

Your personal effectiveness depends in large part upon your ability to effectively handle pressures and activities that are bound to come your way. Many people mistakenly believe that the way to handle stress is to find a perfect situation that causes no stress. To those in the law community, this is a fantasy; to those in the counseling community, this is an ineffective approach to stress because it makes your ability to handle stress dependent on the external conditions of your life. Although we all want and seek excellent circumstances and conditions, the effective person recognizes that life means being continually faced with challenges and difficulties. Rather than pinning one's hopes for sanity on the creation and maintenance of perfect conditions, the effective person and worker recognizes that the superior approach is to develop the capability to handle whatever situation is presented. Not only will this approach make you more independent emotionally, because you will be looking inside rather than outside for your solutions, but it will also make you stronger, because you will use what you formerly called stressful situations as opportunities for personal growth and strengthening. It is therefore vitally important for you to develop and implement a strategic plan to help you deal with stress. This chapter will help you achieve that goal by helping you understand the sources of stress and equipping you with effective strategies to cope effectively with stress.

LAW OFFICE STRESS

Ann Willingham could not believe it was only Tuesday; there were three more days left in the week, and she felt like she had already put in two months. The senior partner with whom Ann worked was getting ready for a huge jury trial starting Monday in India against one of the firm's major clients, Dirty Chemical Company. Ann was responsible for organizing the trial notebooks, making sure all of the witnesses were properly subpoenaed and served, making sure that all of the almost 500 trial exhibits were organized and copied, and summarizing last-minute depositions. All of these jobs absolutely had to be finished by Friday at noon because the flight to India was leaving on Friday at 3:00 P.M.

Ann had not even begun to pack for the trial, which would last at least three weeks, nor had she been able to make arrangements for child care for her two children, ages three and five. The computer system at the firm had gone down and was not expected to be up again until the next day. Another senior partner for whom Ann worked showed up in her office promptly at 8:30 that morning and demanded that she draft several discovery requests for his newest case. He also told Ann that the next time she was a half-an-hour late, as she had been that morning, she could plan on not even coming in.

Needless to say, Ann is stressed out beyond belief. So how can she handle the stress? First, Ann should realize that the worst thing that could happen to her is that she will not get everything accomplished that she needs to accomplish. Second, Ann should prioritize her tasks. For example, all of the material needed by Friday really cannot be done until the computer system is up, so this might be a good time for Ann to ask Senior Partner One for the afternoon off to deal with finding a babysitter and packing for the trip. Ann also needs to take this opportunity to discuss with Senior Partner Two that she is absolutely swamped and could not possibly draft the discovery he needs because she is preparing for a trial. He will probably understand. In order to clear the air, Ann should explain to Senior Partner Two that the reason she was late this morning was because she had to pick up copies of depositions from the court reporter.

Ann needs to sit back and breathe, take a hot bath or do whatever relaxes her. Once she has made her plan of attack, the stress level will surely have lessened.

Stress in the Law Office

Law offices are among the most stressful of all office environments. They do not merely create stress, they breed it. Working in a legal environment is demanding and stressful; it is also challenging and rewarding, but those rewards and challenges cannot be truly satisfying if you are overwhelmed and burned out. Stress management is really an issue of survival in a law office. To do your work and keep your sanity, you will need to develop and use effective stress management strategies and attitudes.

Many characteristics of legal practice directly contribute to making a law office a stressful environment:

- The adversarial and competitive nature of legal practice.

- Business pressures, such as managing growth or losing key clients.

- Clients who are more sophisticated and demanding than ever before.
- Technological advancements that require learning of new applications.
- Lack of empathy with support staff.
- The individualistic and demanding nature of many lawyers.
- The high stakes that are frequently involved with legal disputes.
- The emphasis on billable hours.
- The need to perform multiple simultaneous tasks.
- Serving two or more "masters" in your work and being responsible to several parties.
- The rising costs of practicing law.
- Poor communication.
- Support staff having an unclear sense of their responsibility or level of authority.
- Long hours. A day in a law office can be a full and exhausting day. It can also be a very long day. Lawyers may work 60 to 70 hours a week, and paralegals need to keep up with the work that is generated. (See Figure 16-1.)
- Frustration with clients. In the course of your work as a paralegal, you will be interacting with clients in a number of capacities. This may involve telephone contact. Clients act like all people: they miss appointments, give misinformation, do not appreciate your needs, and are very demanding. Naturally,

FIGURE 16-1 The quantity of work to be performed in law offices often causes stress.

this can be frustrating, especially when you are already pressured with other tasks and responsibilities.

- Frustration with management. As a worker in your law office, you will be subject to the policies and procedures of your organization. Some of these will be explicitly written in your office manual, but others will go unspoken. In the course of your work, you will undoubtedly come up against your share of conflicts and unfair policies, which will cause frustration.

- Frustration with money and status. Legal support staffs are frequently underpaid and underappreciated, and nothing fuels frustration with compensation like a stressful work environment.

Certainly this list is not exhaustive, but it suggests many possible sources of stress in a legal environment. In addition to these factors, consider the results of an extremely interesting and large study conducted by the St. Paul Fire and Marine Insurance Company in December 1992, entitled "American Workers Under Pressure." This study examined stress and burnout based on responses of more than 28,000 employees, and the findings seem especially relevent for employees in a law firm. The study suggested that the two chief workplace stresses were poor supervision and a lack of teamwork, and that improving these two work-related areas was critical to decreasing job burnout and stress. The study also found that those who cannot separate their work life and their personal life can be led into a downward spiral of stress—and stress, as we know, increases in response to negative lifestyle choices. To counteract these factors, the study suggested that firms develop flexible and "family-friendly" policies and implement programs such as Employee Assistance Programs (EAPs) to help employees balance their work and personal lives as well as their lifestyle choices. Law firms that address these issues will assist their employees in coping effectively with the stress that accompanies working in a law office. (See Figure 16-2 and 16-3).

In your quest to handle these and other stressful situations effectively, you will need to develop effective strategies to handle the situations that you know will occur. Although each person has her own way of handling stressful situations, general guidelines and strategies exist that can help you handle stress effectively, as well as minimize the creation of stress itself.

Stress Management Strategies

One approach to handling stress involves eliminating potentials for stress by using the systematized and structured administrative techniques discussed in the chapters on law office administration. Nothing contributes to stress as much as disorganization and poor work performance, and the systems approach will help you organize your work so as to avoid the stress that accompanies poor management techniques. Particularly important is using time-management techniques to maximize your productivity and feeling of control over your

FIGURE 16-2
Interruptions can be
a major source of
stress ...

FIGURE 16-3 ... as can competing priorities.

work. Additionally, you should avoid procrastination by dealing promptly with all work, accomplishing timely turnaround so you do not accumulate correspondence or requests in a pile on your desk.

Of course, your individual approach to work exists in the context of the environment in which you work. Employees in all types of organizations continually emphasize that management philosophy, supervisory approaches, and administrative policies all affect the amount of stress they experience, as well as their performance and their satisfaction with their work. Although stress is ultimately a personal issue, the environment in which you work surely affects the levels of stress you experience. Although all environments in which the work of the law is done are stressful to work in, you will be happiest if the environment in which you work is a good fit with your skills, attitudes, and expectations.

A second strategy for dealing with stress involves managing physical symptoms of stress. Because the stress response is a physical phenomenon that includes changes in your adrenaline, blood, and hormones, it can be eased by an appropriate physical response. You can eliminate the symptoms of stress through physical activity, and a regular program of exercise will definitely help you deal with stress.

Of course, you cannot leave your office and run five miles every time you are pressured, so you will also need to develop some responses that you can use on the job when stressful situations occur. On the job, it is important to develop your own relaxation response, where you can focus and avoid being overtaken by stress. One helpful approach is to focus on your breathing, counting your breaths as they go in and out. Even 15 seconds of this approach can be helpful. It is also helpful to have an escape plan, which may involve a quick trip to the restroom or to the water fountain, to help you focus your thoughts. (See Figure 16-4.)

Pursuing a healthy lifestyle and positive health behaviors is another method to help you deal effectively with stress. Contemporary research emphasizes the close connection between lifestyle choices and stress. It is common knowledge today that healthy eating habits, regular exercise (Figure 16-5),

FIGURE 16-4 A break can help you relax and refocus.

FIGURE 16-5 Exercise can help you manage stress successfully.

reduction of caffeine and nicotine, and regular sleeping habits are behavior patterns that can help us combat stress. Some research findings suggest an even stronger link between behavior patterns and stress. One experiment conducted by Professor Belloc with more than 7,000 adults showed that, out of seven positive health practices, those who practiced six or seven were twice as likely to live through the nine-and-a-half-year period being studied as were those who practiced three or fewer positive health practices. Given this dramatic relationship between health behaviors and mortality, it is easy to see how significantly positive health behaviors can help us effectively manage stress.

Effective communication is extremely important in preventing stress in a legal office. Paralegals must learn to be assertive and to request additional information when needed to complete a task. If you do not completely understand how to handle a project, it is important to get key instructions at the onset rather than waiting until the deadline approaches to obtain the information you need.

Do not fall into the common error of believing that others should know what you are thinking and feeling. Law office personnel are not mind readers, and should not be expected to be. If you have problems with someone, speak to that person; do not keep negative feelings bottled up. Should you have too much work, again, speak up, because only you can control your workload. It is better to let someone know you are not able to meet a deadline than letting the deadline come and go without meeting it.

One approach to handling the stresses of working in a law practice involves focusing on the client as a potential source of stress. Some clients, and some of the situations a client presents, are just not worth the time and energy they will take. No attorney takes every single case she is consulted about, and if the attorney is sensitized to the overly troublesome client or case, care can be exercised in the process of choosing which clients to take. Although paralegals are prohibited from accepting clients, they can surely give their input to the attorney, and perhaps save the attorney from a tremendously stressful situation.

The following guest editorial by attorney Lynne Z. Gold-Bikin, 1994 Chairperson of the ABA Section of Family Law, sugggests the kinds of clients that an attorney in a family law practice just might want to avoid.

GUEST EDITORIAL

Avoiding Troublesome Clients Can Make a Lawyer's Life Easier

Lynne Z. Gold-Bikin

The practice of family law lends itself to emotions and pressures generally not present in other areas of concentration. That fact can serve as a reminder to practitioners that life is too short to be brutalized by clients.

How, then, can lawyers in family law practice reduce the stress of their professional lives?

One approach is to carefully choose which clients to represent, especially avoiding certain "red flag" clients who are certain to make one's day longer and harder.

The initial interview is the best time to weed out those nightmare clients, who generally fit into one of the following categories:

The Peripatetic Client

These clients, who already have been represented by three or four other lawyers, appear at the initial interview with three cardboard boxes and a shopping bag full of files.

Counsel should not be swayed by such statements as "the other lawyers did not have your expertise"; "I know you can handle this"; or "well, I didn't pay their fees because they weren't worth it, but you are."

Find out the names of prior counsel and whether they have been paid. If three or four of your colleagues could not complete the case, you probably will be number four or five on a list of frustrated lawyers with a new receivable.

The Emotionally Upset Client

Many divorcing clients are depressed at the prospect of ending their marriages, and initial interviews are often devoted to allowing them to "vent."

It is helpful to refer such a client to mental health professionals who can assist them through the divorce process.

If a client is advised that the divorce process is emotionally difficult for everyone, he or she will be more likely to accept your suggestion of counseling.

If, on the other hand, the client resists that advice and also is unable to escape the depression stage, he or she will rarely be helpful to the lawyer in the litigation to come in the case.

These clients will either accept any offer (and blame counsel later) or they will be unresponsive to advice on how to protect themselves through the litigation.

The Vindictive Client

Although it is understandable that clients are angry for a period of time after their proceedings begin, beware of those for whom anger is an impediment to rational thinking and potential settlement.

When the client wants to "get even" at all costs or "just have my day in court" rather than accept a reasonable result, the case is headed for disaster.

The client who says, "I'd rather pay you than my wife," will probably pay neither of you.

The "Get It Over Fast" Client

"Pay her anything and just get this over with" or similar phrases are dangerous words for lawyers to hear.

In the passion of the moment, "getting it over with" may seem a priority to these clients, but when they have to pay excessive weekly checks or have to move out of the houses they built with their own hands, the blame for their unhappy state may become fixed on the lawyers who "allowed" this to happen.

The converse is the dependent spouse who agrees to a lesser settlement in the hope that, if he or she is reasonable and passive, the spouse will come back.

Counsel must advise these clients of the danger of accepting or offering far less or more than that to which they are entitled. Business reverses, a future marriage that does not occur, or even second thoughts after the agreement is signed are all potential problems for the lawyer who has permitted a client to enter into a one-sided settlement.

It is critical for counsel to put into writing their advice about the fairness of unreasonable offers and, if possible, to have their clients sign letters to acknowledge that they received this advice.

The emotional aspects of divorce are made more difficult by clients who will not take good advice when it is offered.

Stress in the office can be reduced by the recognition of which cases not to take. ▮▮

Stress: The Cognitive View

The previous sections have looked at the law office from the perspective of teaching you how to manage stressful situations effectively. In addition to those behaviors, you can employ mental, or cognitive, strategies to complement the strategies discussed earlier. We now turn to this cognitive understanding of stress.

When we experience stress—when the demands of the world overcome our abilities to deal with those demands—it certainly seems that those demands cause our stress. We might even think that if those events had not occurred or did not exist we would not be stressed out. This view suggests that stress is outside of us, and therefore happens to us.

Does an event really cause stress? On a well-known stress scale, Holmes and Rahe's Social Readjustment Scale, the death of a spouse is rated as the most stressful event a person can face, followed by divorce. But in a country where half the married couples get divorced, is it accurate to say that everyone experiences stress from a spouse's death or divorce? Might not some people feel relieved, perhaps even joyful?

Is losing your job stressful? Your answer probably depends on a number of factors. If you did not like your job, and knew you would have little trouble finding another job, it would not be as difficult as if you faced long-term unemployment and uncertainty.

Does an event really cause stress? The answer is yes and no. Yes, certain events make it easier for us to feel stress, but no, the event on its own does not make us feel any particular way. It is our perception of the event that really causes the stress. The event and our perception therefore work in unison. Imagine that the event is a plug and you (your thoughts and perceptions) are the outlet. Electricity, like feelings, can only happen when the two connect.

If we take an event (for instance, being reprimanded by your attorney for having made an error) on its own, it causes no emotional reaction. But when we combine that event with a thought or interpretation about that event, such as, "He'll never respect my work since I made that mistake," it causes one feeling; when we have another thought, such as, "Making mistakes in a new position is natural; the real issue is learning from them and not getting down about it," then we do not feel the same even though the same event has happened. It is therefore the combination of an event with our thoughts and perceptions about that event that truly cause our feelings.

It is easy to understand this approach to stress, which is referred to as the *cognitive approach,* by using Albert Ellis's famous theory of the A-B-Cs of Emotions. In this model,

A = the event (real or imagined)
B = your beliefs/perceptions/thoughts about A
C = your feelings.

Most people believe that A causes C, but, as we just saw, the same A can cause many Cs, depending on the B. Therefore, it is the B, activated by the A, which truly causes C, our feelings. In this paradigm, that which people refer to as *stress* is a C; it is the resulting feeling. And the feeling is not caused by the events (A), although there might well be a correlation between A and C. Rather, it is the B, the perceptions and beliefs of the person, that truly cause stress.

Certainly some life events are so difficult, or so traumatic, that it can fairly be said that they cause stress. Karen Calhoun's research on rape indicates that rape is an authentically stressful experience. Paul and Gerald Adams's research on stress experienced by the residents of Othello, Washington, which is near Mount Saint Helens, indicates that natural disasters are also authentically stressful. But these are extreme, negative, life events, such as the death of a child. The events that cause most people stress on a daily basis are not nearly as traumatic, although they might feel like it. It is hard to handle conflicting priorities, pressure-filled days with too much to accomplish, personal conflicts with co-workers, miscommunications, or losing a case for a client. These are the realities of life in an office, working with other people. Our goal should be to take these difficult situations and to solve our problems, wasting as little energy as we can on things we cannot change or things that are out of our control.

The simple truth is that difficult life events and difficult work situations will not disappear just because we want them to. For the effective paralegal, then, the key to managing stress is to realize that working in a law office is a demanding and draining experience, but to enjoy its challenges and rewards you will need to work on your abilities to handle events as productively as possible. In the framework of the A-B-Cs, the key is to work on the Bs. It is not that the As are not difficult, frustrating, or disappointing. They are. It is rather how one handles those difficult situations and experiences that defines one as a person who manages stress effectively or as one who becomes distressed and overwhelmed.

The cognitive approach to dealing with stress, which provides the most comprehensive approach to stress because it penetrates beyond the symptoms to the cause of stress, involves changing our perceptions and interpretations of events. It suggests that by restructuring our thoughts about our experiences we can change our feelings. It is therefore vital for you to recognize the kinds of thoughts that create stress, so that you can replace them with more effective thoughts. You will create unnecessary stress for yourself if you:

- Demand, rather than prefer, that things be the way you want

- Evaluate yourself or others as a whole person rather than evaluate your behaviors

- Are perfectionistic rather than quality-oriented

- Fail to see the humor in life

- Become so immersed in a situation that you cannot stand back from it

- Evaluate your performance based on things you cannot control

- Catastrophize difficult events, rather than take responsibility for potentially negative consequences

- See things in all-or-nothing terms

- Think that because things are difficult, they are also negative or stressful, rather than challenging.

These types of thinking patterns are the real causes of stress. As you examine your responses to situations, you will want to identify your own thinking patterns and cognitive responses that may be causing you unnecessary stress. By replacing these stress-producing thoughts with healthier ones, you will have taken a significant step toward developing strategies for overcoming stress.

ON POINT   *STELLA SIGNS UNDER STRESS*

It is 12:23, and it has already been a gruesome day in the law office of Barnaby Jones. Paralegal Stella has been completing a petition for certiorari to the United States Supreme Court to take with her on the 1:00 flight to Washington, D.C. Although Barnaby has reviewed the entire document and made the necessary changes, he is not back from his morning hearing by the time Stella has to leave for the airport. Rather than having an unsigned petition, she signs his name to the document. Any problems?

Coping with Stress: A Summary

One of the most important characteristics of a successful paralegal is the ability to handle stress effectively. There is no doubt that law offices can be extremely stressful work environments, just as the work of the law itself can be stressful. Faced with this reality, those who work in the legal process must develop effective strategies for dealing with stress. These strategies include but are not limited to developing systematic work habits, using physical activity to work out tensions, maintaining a positive attitude, pursuing a healthier lifestyle, and developing effective cognitive strategies. Both your work and your health will benefit if you can learn effective stress management techniques. Additionally, your ability to handle stress will help you in the future as you move into positions of increasing authority and responsibility and, yes, stress.

Key Terms

cognitive approach sources of stress stress management strategies

Problems and Activities

1. Bill Turner is a paralegal in a large metropolitan law firm. He is assigned to six attorneys in the real estate division. Three of the attorneys come to him within ten minutes of each other, each with a pressing matter that they say needs immediate attention. How would you suggest Bill handle this situation?

2. Actually, Bill has handled the situation rather poorly. When he sees the managing partner in the hall and is casually asked how things are going, Bill explodes at the managing partner, "This is the worst-managed firm I have ever worked in!" How can Bill recover from this faux pas?

3. What specific strategies should you use on a daily basis to help you deal with stressful situations? What behavioral or cognitive changes do you want to make to improve your ability to cope effectively with stress?

4. You have been assigned to a senior partner who is known as a brilliant attorney yet whose office and files are in disarray. As a result of the disorganization, it takes you three times as long as usual to complete your tasks, and your profitability level has substantially decreased. You like the attorney personally, but your work is suffering, and you are afraid that your poor productivity will put your job in jeopardy. What should you do?

5. You have a 4:00 appointment with a witness in your attorney's upcoming criminal trial. The witness must be interviewed and subpoenaed by the end of the day, because the trial starts at 9:00 tomorrow morning. As you are walking out the door for your 4:00 appointment, your child's day care calls and says your

child is very sick and must be picked up. How should you handle this situation? What strategic plans could you make to prepare for possible reoccurrences of this situation in the future?

6. Contact the committee of your local bar association that handles drug and alcohol problems for attorneys. Ask the committee members for information about their program and how they recommend that legal professionals handle drug and alcohol dependence.

CHAPTER 17

PROFESSIONAL DEVELOPMENT

OBJECTIVES

By the completion of this chapter, you should:

- understand the concept of professional development and how it applies to your career;

- learn how to obtain a position as a paralegal by developing the necessary foundations, learn how to present yourself in the job search, and learn how to identify job openings in your field of interest; and

- learn how to advance your career and meet your future career goals.

Professional Development: An Introduction

Professional development refers to the lifelong series of activities that begins with your initial preparation for your first position and ends only at retirement. It refers to the process of taking an active part in determining your work life and attempting to find work that you enjoy, do well, and fits your goals and interests. You will probably spend more time at work than at any other activity, and, by taking an active hand in the career development process, you will be able to develop the skills, abilities, and attitudes that will enable you to succeed in your career development.

Professional and career development are therefore based on the idea that people are happiest and most productive when their work is an outgrowth of their skills, interests, and passions. Both the employer and the employee benefit when there is a successful fit between the person, the organization, and the required work. Your task, therefore, is to learn about yourself and the world of work so that you can find work that fits your abilities and goals. Professional development refers to the entire series of activities that will enable you to achieve the goal of finding meaningful work and moving forward in your area of interest.

This chapter is divided into two sections. The first section teaches you about the process of obtaining a position as a paralegal. It will apply directly to the job search you will be conducting as you look for a position. The second section concerns activities that you can pursue to advance your career opportunities once you have a position. Together, these sections will give you a clear idea of what it will take for you to successfully define and achieve your career goals.

CASE STUDY　　　　　　**OBTAINING A POSITION AS A PARALEGAL**

Jonathan Englewood was a month from graduation from his paralegal program, and naturally a job search was on his mind. As he read through the want ads in the Sunday paper, he noticed the following:

WANTED: REAL ESTATE PARALEGAL

Drew, Eckl & Farnham, a medium-sized, AV-rated, insurance defense firm, is looking for a real estate paralegal. The ideal client should be knowledgeable in drafting pleadings and discovery documents as well as be able to actively participate in the litigation of cases. Our paralegals are on the front line and handle cases from start to finish. Candidates must have a degree from a certified program. Salary commensurate with experience. If you are looking for a challenging career in real estate, please send your résumé to: Donna Masinter, Director of Administration, 880 West Peachtree St., Atlanta, Georgia 30357. No phone calls, please.

Jonathan was attracted to the ad for several reasons. The job description seemed to offer the challenges he sought, and he had heard good things about the firm from another paralegal student. He decided to send a letter and a résumé, and he made a mental note to research the firm in *Martindale-Hubbell* when he was in the library later that afternoon.

His cover letter and résumé looked as follows:

JONATHAN J. ENGLEWOOD
6565 Rolling Hills Drive
Atlanta, Georgia 30305

(404) 351-5565

October 12, 1994

Ms. Donna Masinter
Executive Director
Drew Eckl & Farnham
P.O. Box 7600
Atlanta, Georgia 30357

Dear Ms. Masinter:

I am enclosing a copy of my résumé and a writing sample for your review in response to your advertisement for a real estate paralegal in the *Fulton County Daily Report*. As you can see from my résumé, I have been responsible for title searches, closing statements, and the firm docket system. I believe that my experience, coupled with my excellent academic credentials, make me an ideal candidate for the paralegal position at your firm.

Thank you for your time and consideration. I will contact you within the next few days so that we can set up a mutually convenient time for an interview. Should you need any additional information in the interim, please do not hesitate to contact me.

Sincerely,

Jonathan J. Englewood

Jonathan J. Englewood

/JJE

Enclosure

Jonathan J. Englewood
6565 Rolling Hills Drive
Atlanta, Georgia 30305   (404) 351-5565

OBJECTIVE	Seeking a career position as a paralegal
EDUCATION	**THE NATIONAL CENTER FOR PARALEGAL TRAINING** Lawyer's Assistant Program, Atlanta, Georgia; ABA Approved Specialty: litigation with training in corporations, real estate, probate, legal research and computer literacy **Certificate With Honors:** December, 1992
	UNIVERSITY OF NORTH CAROLINA at CHAPEL HILL Bachelor of Arts degree in Political Science, May, 1992
EXPERIENCE	**FORMAN, MARTH, BLACK AND ANGLE, PA**, Greensboro, NC Real Estate Paralegal, February, 1993–Present

- Search titles for an average of 45 closings per month
- Correct all title defects
- Complete knowledge of title insurance requirements and application
- Prepare closing statements and loan packages, when needed
- File firm pleadings in all courts
- Research court documents for all attorneys
- Manage firm docket system

WORK HISTORY	**ADIA**, Winston-Salem, NC Temporary Employee, June–August, 1992

- Performed general office duties, including switchboard tasks, for various companies assigned by the temporary agency

KRISPY KREME DOUGHNUT CORPORATION, Winston-Salem, NC
General Office Assistant, Summer: 1987, 1988, 1989

- Microfilmed company documents for entire fiscal year
- Assumed position as company receptionist as needed
- Investigated possible franchise opportunities for company expansion with population/territorial documentation

SKILLS	Proficient in WordPerfect 5.1 and SoftPro (real estate software) Working Knowledge of Lotus 1-2-3, WESTLAW and Microsoft Word for Windows
ORGANIZATIONS	Member of the Greensboro Paralegal Association
REFERENCES	Available upon request.

As you might imagine, Jonathan was very excited when he found the following letter in his mailbox a little over a week after having mailed his résumé and cover letter to Drew, Eckl.

DREW ECKL & FARNHAM

ATTORNEYS AT LAW

880 WEST PEACHTREE STREET

P.O. BOX 7600

ATLANTA, GEORGIA 30357-0600

(404) 885-1400

CHARLES L. DREW	GARY R. HURST	LEIGH LAWSON REEVES
W. WRAY ECKL	STEPHEN W. MOONEY	RICHARD B. MILLER II
CLAYTON H. FARNHAM	KEVIN P. O'MAHONY	BRUCE A. TAYLOR, JR.
ARTHUR H. GLASER	ANNE M. LANDRUM	DOUGLAS T. LAY
JAMES M. POE	NENA K. PUCKETT	VIRGINIA A. GREEN
JOHN A. FERGUSON, JR.	NICOLE D. TIFVERMAN	DOUGLAS M. BAKER
THEODORE FREEMAN	JERRY C. CARTER, JR.	ELIZABETH B. LUZURIAGA
JOHN P. REALE	PHILLIP E. FRIDUSS	DAVID R. BERGQUIST
STEVAN A. MILLER	L. LEE BENNETT, JR.	R. HAROLD MCCARD, JR.
H. MICHAEL BAGLEY	CHRISTOPHER J. CULP	CHARLES L. NORTON, JR.
HALL F. McKINLEY III	SCOTT T. BUSHNELL	NANCY F. RIGBY
G. RANDALL MOODY	KATHERINE D. DIXON	LORI V. WINKLEMAN
B. HOLLAND PRITCHARD	WILLIAM T. MITCHELL	PETER A. LAW
T. BART GARY	J. ROBB CRUSER	JOHN F. WOODHAM
DAVID A. SMITH	PHILIP W. SAVRIN	DOUGLAS G. SMITH, JR.
KENNETH A. HINDMAN	LUCIAN GILLIS, JR.	TERRENCE T. ROCK
PAUL W. BURKE	PETER H. SCHMIDT II	PHILLIP COMER GRIFFETH
DANIEL C. KNIFFEN	BROOKS B. POWERS	MARIAN S. SINGER
JOHN C. BRUFFEY, JR.	APRIL RICH	STEVEN D. PRELUTSKY
BENTON J. MATHIS, JR.	MAUREEN M. MIDDLETON	JULIANNE L. SWILLEY
JOHN G. BLACKMON, JR.	ROBERT L. WELCH	STEPHEN A. LISLE
DENNIS M. HALL	JULIE Y. JOHN	PAUL G. PHILLIPS
J. WILLIAM HALEY	JEFFREY B. GRIMM	CARTER ALLEN
DONALD R. ANDERSEN	KRISTEN K. DUGGAN	MARY H. HINES
ANN BISHOP BYARS	SUZANNE V. SANDERS	LISA A. KELEHEAR

FACSIMILE (404) 876-0992

WRITER'S DIRECT DIAL NUMBER

October 18, 1994

Mr. Jonathan J. Englewood
6565 Rolling Hills Drive
Atlanta, Georgia 30305

Dear Mr. Englewood:

Thank you very much for your letter of October 12, 1994, and the enclosed resume and writing sample. Your background appears to match quite well with a position which has become available in our Firm.

Please telephone my assistant, Brenda DeSimone, at your earliest convenience to arrange a time for an interview.

Best regards.

Sincerely,

Donna Masinter
Executive Director

DM:bd

Jonathan called and set up the appointment. Now to prepare for the interview. He read about the firm, reviewed his agenda of the items he wanted to get across in the interview, reviewed his materials in preparation for substantive questions on real estate procedures, and checked his wardrobe. Now he just had to wait.

Jonathan interviewed with the firm on October 24 and ended up spending several hours there, talking with various people and taking a tour of the office. He felt that he had come across well in the interview, and he was proud that he had spent a proper amount of time preparing for the interview. Now he hoped that the firm thought highly of him.

As a follow-up to the interview, Jonathan mailed the following letter the next day.

JONATHAN J. ENGLEWOOD
6565 Rolling Hills Drive
Atlanta, Georgia 30305

(404) 351-5565

October 25, 1994

Ms. Donna Masinter
Executive Director
Drew Eckl & Farnham
P.O. Box 7600
Atlanta, Georgia 30357

Dear Ms. Masinter:

I appreciated the opportunity to meet with you and several members of your Firm yesterday. Drew Eckl & Farnham is the type of active and progressive law firm with which I would like to be involved. Please allow me to take this opportunity to reiterate my interest in your Firm.

Should you require another writing sample or additional references, I will be delighted to provide them.

Sincerely,

Jonathan J. Englewood
Jonathan J. Englewood

On November 1, Jonathan's mail carrier delivered a letter that changed his life. This is what he found.

DREW ECKL & FARNHAM

ATTORNEYS AT LAW

880 WEST PEACHTREE STREET
P.O. BOX 7600

ATLANTA, GEORGIA 30357-0600

(404) 885-1400

CHARLES L. DREW
W. WRAY ECKL
CLAYTON H. FARNHAM
ARTHUR H. GLASER
JAMES M. POE
JOHN A. FERGUSON, JR.
THEODORE FREEMAN
JOHN P. REALE
STEVAN A. MILLER
H. MICHAEL BAGLEY
HALL F. MCKINLEY III
G. RANDALL MOODY
B. HOLLAND PRITCHARD
T. BART GARY
DAVID A. SMITH
KENNETH A. HINDMAN
PAUL W. BURKE
DANIEL C. KNIFFEN
JOHN C. BRUFFEY, JR.
BENTON J. MATHIS, JR.
JOHN G. BLACKMON, JR.
DENNIS M. HALL
J. WILLIAM HALEY
DONALD R. ANDERSEN
ANN BISHOP BYARS

GARY R. HURST
STEPHEN W. MOONEY
KEVIN P. O'MAHONY
ANNE M. LANDRUM
NENA K. PUCKETT
NICOLE O. TIFVERMAN
JERRY C. CARTER, JR.
PHILLIP E. FRIDUSS
L. LEE BENNETT, JR.
CHRISTOPHER J. CULP
SCOTT T. BUSHNELL
KATHERINE D. DIXON
WILLIAM T. MITCHELL
J. ROBB CRUSER
PHILIP W. SAVRIN
LUCIAN GILLIS, JR.
PETER H. SCHMIDT II
BROOKS B. POWERS
APRIL RICH
MAUREEN M. MIDDLETON
ROBERT L. WELCH
JULIE Y. JOHN
JEFFREY B. GRIMM
KRISTEN K. DUGGAN
SUZANNE V. SANDERS

LEIGH LAWSON REEVES
RICHARD B. MILLER II
BRUCE A. TAYLOR, JR.
DOUGLAS T. LAY
VIRGINIA A. GREEN
DOUGLAS M. BAKER
ELIZABETH B. LUZURIAGA
DAVID R. BERGQUIST
R. HAROLD MCCARD, JR.
CHARLES L. NORTON, JR.
NANCY F. RIGBY
LORI V. WINKLEMAN
PETER A. LAW
JOHN F. WOODHAM
DOUGLAS G. SMITH, JR.
TERRENCE T. ROCK
PHILLIP COMER GRIFFETH
MARIAN S. SINGER
STEVEN D. PRELUTSKY
JULIANNE L. SWILLEY
STEPHEN A. LISLE
PAUL G. PHILLIPS
CARTER ALLEN
MARY H. HINES
LISA A. KELEHEAR

FACSIMILE (404) 876-0992

WRITER'S DIRECT DIAL NUMBER

November 1, 1994

Mr. Jonathan J. Englewood
6565 Rolling Hills Drive
Atlanta, Georgia 30305

Dear Jonathan:

I enjoyed our conversation during your interview with our Firm on October 27, and I am delighted that you have accepted our offer of employment.

This letter will confirm our agreement, as follows:

1.   Your starting salary will be $28,000 annually, and you will begin employment on November 15, 1994.

2.   Performance reviews will be given on an annual basis.

3.   The Firm benefits are:

A.   all health, life and dental insurance premiums are paid in full on your behalf;

B.   you will be eligible and 100% vested in the pension plan at the conclusion of your second year of employment with the Firm;

C.   you will be eligible to participate in the 401K Plan at the conclusion of your first year of employment with the Firm;

D.   you will earn vacation at the rate of one-half (1/2) day per month from the date of your employment until the conclusion of the first year, thereby allowing you six (6) days of vacation during that period. When you have completed the

[continued]

first year of employment, you will then be entitled to ten (10) days vacation; an additional day of vacation is added each year until you reach the limit of fifteen (15) days. All vacation time must be used during the year and may not be carried forward unless you have received permission in advance to do so.

        E.   you will earn and accrue personal/sick time at the rate of three -fourths (3/4) day per month from your commencement date until your second anniversary. After your second anniversary, you will earn and accrue time at the rate of one (1) day per month. This time may be carried forward year to year.

    5.   On your first day of employment, you will spend your time in an orientation program and computer training class. You will also be given your security key card, which opens the security gates and employee entrance door.

    6.   As we discussed, there will be no charge for parking your automobile.

    7.   You may use our fitness center at no charge.

    We look forward to working with you. If ever I can be of help to you, please do not hesitate to call on me.

    Best regards.

        Sincerely,

        Donna Masinter
        Executive Director

DM:bd

Again as you can imagine, Jonathan was very excited. He was getting a chance to start his career with an excellent firm that offered great opportunities in real estate. Besides, they even had an exercise studio right in the law firm! But he did not let his excitement overtake his knowledge of proper job search procedures, so he typed the following acceptance letter:

JONATHAN J. ENGLEWOOD
6565 Rolling Hills Drive
Atlanta, Georgia 30305

(404) 351-5565

November 8, 1994

Ms. Donna Masinter
Executive Director
Drew Eckl & Farnham
P.O. Box 7600
Atlanta, Georgia 30357

Dear Ms. Masinter:

This letter will confirm my acceptance of the job offer set forth in your letter dated November 1, 1994. I am looking forward to working with Drew Eckl & Farnham and am eager to begin my employment on November 15, 1994. By that date, I will have satisfactorily completed all outstanding projects and commitments to my current employer.

If you should need to contact me prior to November 15, please feel free to telephone me at the number noted above.

Sincerely,

Jonathan J. Englewood

Jonathan J. Englewood

Jonathan was an excellent paralegal student who was eager to be successful in his work. He was also a highly organized and effective job seeker who approached his job search thoroughly and professionally, and he followed his established approach when applying for a position that had been advertised. It was this professional, systematic approach that helped him land the job.

Obtaining a Position as a Paralegal

The preceding case study illustrated many of the components of the job search in a narrative fashion. Now you will need to understand the job search process as it applies to you so that you can find a position that satisfies your professional and personal goals.

You will need to accomplish three groups of activities to obtain a position as a paralegal. The first group, laying the foundations for your job search, entails your developing skills, self-knowledge, and knowledge of work opportunities so that you can pursue a purposeful job search based on who you are and what you want. The second activity is developing skills in the two major areas where you will be presenting yourself to prospective employers, your résumé and your interview. The third activity involves learning about specific job search methods and pursuing the method that will best enable you to find the kind of position you want. The following discussion explains each of these activities in detail.

Laying Foundations for Your Job Search

Before you begin your actual job search, you will need to do some preparatory activities so that your job search will be focused and appropriate. If, for example, you were asked in an interview what part of the law was most interesting to you, and you could not answer because you had not thought about your interests, you would stand little chance of getting that job because the interviewer would probably feel that you do not have any career direction. If you do not have career goals and cannot articulate your interests to an interviewer, you will come across as unprepared, inept, and perhaps uninterested, and you will probably not get a job offer.

You need two types of foundational abilities to pursue a successful job search. These are knowledge of the skills you may use, including legal skills and career development skills, and market awareness, which involves knowledge of work opportunities.

Skills

The first thing you need to begin your professional development is skill. You need to master basic knowledge and procedures for an entry-level position, and these are generally learned in school or through work experience. These basic skills assure a prospective employer of your competency and suggest that you will be able to use those skills as building blocks for future knowledge and application. When you present yourself to prospective employers, therefore, you will want to emphasize your basic legal skills so that employers can see how you can make a contribution to their firm.

In addition to basic legal skills, you need career development skills. (See Figure 17-1.) A legal skill might be your ability to do research on LEXIS; a career-development skill is your ability to talk about your career goals or areas of interest. Career development requires four basic skills, which you must possess over and above your legal skills. First, you need to know yourself, to have assessed who you are, what you want to do, and how you can contribute to a law firm. Learning about yourself involves thinking about your experiences, choices, and interests so you can understand what motivates and interests you. Questions to help you assess yourself successfully might include the following:

Which areas of the law interest me the most?
Which paralegal courses or duties are most interesting to me?
What kind of working environment best suits me?
Do I prefer working alone or on teams?
Do I prefer working on lots of little cases or a couple of big cases?
Which of my values or ethics might affect my work choices?
What do I want out of the work part of my life?
How important is status/money to me?
How does work fit into the texture of my life?
What three adjectives best describe me?
What are my major strengths and weaknesses?

By thinking about questions such as these, you will begin to gain some insight into yourself and your career goals. Surely, you should also expect to talk about these things in an interview setting.

A second skill you need in the career development process, perhaps the most important skill of all, is the ability to communicate effectively. All stages of

FIGURE 17-1
The basis for career advancement is developing both your paralegal and career development skills.

the job search process involve effective communication. You will need to speak well in an interview, you will need to write effectively in your job search correspondence, you will need to read well to research firms or fields of interest, and you will need to listen effectively in interviewing, networking, and research. Additionally, effective communication is absolutely necessary for paralegal work, so this skill is of paramount importance in your quest for success.

A third skill you need is the ability to research effectively. Research is necessary to help you identify the kinds of situations and opportunities that exist. You will need to learn about firms in your field of interest, types of positions available with your skill profile, and ways of accessing your job targets. All of this information is available, but you will need skills to access it.

The final career development skill you need is really an attitude, that of assertiveness, professionalism, and appropriate confidence. This stance requires finding a midpoint between thinking too little of yourself and thinking too much of yourself, between being too formal and too informal, between being overly aggressive or overly passive in your self-presentation. The attitude you have toward yourself, your value, and others will permeate all of your career development activities, and you will be most successful if you become skilled in being assertive and professional in your attitude and presentation.

Market Research

The career development skills discussed previously require that you understand your role as the protagonist in the job search. Market research involves learning about your job targets so that you can identify the kinds of situations and opportunities that could use your skills. Equipped with both self-knowledge and market knowledge, you will be well prepared to find a situation that matches your career goals.

In the legal field, *market research* means learning about the kinds of environments in which the law is practiced and the kinds of specializations that are available to you. The preceding chapters in this book should have given you a start at identifying some of the alternatives available in legal work. You can gain information in a number of ways about work opportunities in the law. Your career counselor at school, and the career development library, are good places to start. You can talk to your teachers and other members of the legal profession to get their ideas and advice. Additionally, several publications will help you learn more about career opportunities in the law. *Martindale-Hubbell Law Directory* (Figure 17-2) is an excellent resource detailing law firms, their attorneys and orientations, and local official newspapers, such as the *Fulton County Daily Reporter,* and bar association newsletters can also help the job seeker learn about opportunities in legal practice.

One of the really great things about the law as a career field is that there is a tremendous variety of environments in which to do your work. As you know, law firms can be extremely different from one another in terms of the work they do, as well as the overall personality and culture of the firm. Working for

DREW, ECKL & FARNHAM

880 WEST PEACHTREE STREET
P.O. BOX 7600
ATLANTA, GEORGIA 30357
Telephone: 404-885-1400
Telecopier: 404-876-0992

General Civil Practice. Commercial and Corporate Litigation, Construction and Governmental Contracts, Environmental Litigation and Regulation, Insurance (Automobile, Casualty, Health & Accident, Fire and Allied Lines and Property), Labor and Employment Law (Title VII, NLRB, Wage-Hour, OSHA, ERISA, Immigration) Medical Malpractice, Municipal and Civil Rights, Products Liability, Self-Insured and Workers Compensation, and Sports Law. Trials in all State and Federal Courts.

MEMBERS OF FIRM

CHARLES L. DREW, born Atlanta, Georgia, April 23, 1931; admitted to bar, 1954, Georgia. *Education:* University of Georgia (LL.B., 1954). Phi Alpha Delta. Chairman, Governor's Legal Advisory Committee on Workmen's Compensation, 1973-1975. Member, State Board of of Workmen's Compensation Legal Advisory Committee, 1976-1978. *Member:* Atlanta and American Bar Associations; State Bar of Georgia; Lawyers Club of Atlanta; International Association of Defense Counsel; Defense Research and Trial Lawyers Association. [1st Lt., JAGC, Strategic Air Command, USAF, 1955-1957; Capt., 116 Fighter Interceptor Group, 1958-1964]. *Workers Compensation.*

W. WRAY ECKL, born Florence, Alabama, December 2, 1936; admitted to bar, 1962, Virginia and Alabama; 1964, Georgia. *Education:* University of Notre Dame (B.A., cum laude, 1959); University of Vienna, Vienna, Austria; University of Virginia (LL.B., 1962). Law Clerk, Chief Justice of the Supreme Court of Alabama, 1962. *Member:* Atlanta and American Bar Associations; State Bar of Georgia; Virginia State Bar; Alabama State Bar; Lawyers Club of Atlanta; American Board of Trial Attorneys; Trial Attorneys of America; Defense Research Institute; American Society of Hospital Attorneys; Georgia Society of Hospital Attorneys. [Captain, JAGC, U.S. Army, 1962-1965]. *Medical Malpractice, Products Liability, General Litigation.*

CLAYTON H. FARNHAM, born New Brunswick, New Jersey, August 18, 1938; admitted to bar, 1968, Georgia. *Education:* University of the South (B.A., 1961); University of Georgia (LL.B., 1967). Phi Delta Phi. Editor, Student Editorial Board, Georgia State Bar Journal, 1966-1967. Law Clerk to Hon. Newell Edenfield, U.S. District Judge, Northern District of Georgia, 1968-1969. Chairman and Author: "Arson for Profit: The Insurer's Defense," ABA National Institute, March, 1981. *Member:* Atlanta and American (Section of Tort and Insurance Practice: Member of Council, 1989—; Chairman, Property Insurance Law Committee, 1980-1981; Senior Vice Chairman, 1981—) Bar Associations; State Bar of Georgia; Lawyers Club of Atlanta; International Association of Defense Counsel (Chairman, Property Insurance Law Committee, 1987-1989); Defense Research Institute. [Lt., USNR, 1961-1964]. *Property Insurance Law, Mortgage Insurance Law.*

ARTHUR H. GLASER, born Jersey City, New Jersey, May 1, 1947; admitted to bar, 1973, Georgia. *Education:* Hampden-Sydney College (B.S., 1968); University of Virginia (J.D., 1973). Omicron Delta Kappa. Coauthor: "Jones v. State Farm, An Expensive Lesson," Georgia State Bar Journal, May, 1982. Speaker, "Duty to Defend, Declaratory Judgments, and Extracontractural Liability," State Bar of Georgia Insurance Law Institute, 1983. Lecturer, Georgia State Patrol Academy, 1974-1981. *Member:* Atlanta (Chairman, No Fault Insurance Seminar, 1984) and American Bar Associations; State Bar of Georgia; Lawyers Club of Atlanta; Defense Research and Trial Lawyers Association. *Commercial and Corporate Litigation, Construction and Governmental Contracts, Litigation, General Litigation, Medial Malpractice.*

JAMES M. POE, born Columbia, Missouri, April 14, 1949; admitted to bar, 1974, Georgia. *Education:* University of Virginia (B.A., with distinction, 1971); University of Georgia (J.D., 1974). Echols Scholar, University of Virginia. Member, The Order of Barristers. Member: Southern Moot Court Competition Winning Team; Team Region V National Moot Court Competition Winning Team; 1974 Law Day Competition Winning Team. Senior Editor, Georgia Law Review, 1973-1974. Recipient, Best Oralist Awards, 1973 Southern Competition. 1973 National Moot Court Regional V Competition; 1973 Law Day Competition. *Member:* Atlanta and American (Member, Tort and Insurance Practice Section) Bar Associations; State Bar of Georgia; Lawyers Club of Atlanta; Defense Research Institute. *Commercial and Corporate Litigation, General Litigation, Personal Injury and Products Liability.*

ASSOCIATES

DANIEL C. KNIFFEN, born Syracuse, New York, October 9, 1959; admitted to bar, 1984, Georgia. *Education:* Mercer University (B.A., 1981; J.D., cum laude, 1984). Member, 1982-1984 and Editor-in-Chief, 1983-1984, Mercer Law Review. Member, Moot Court Board. Editor: Supplement for Property Insurance Annotations--Fire and Extended Coverages, 1988; Supplement to Bad Faith and Punitive Damages Annotations, 1989. Co-Author: with Bagley and Blackmon, "Annual Survey of Georgia Law: Workers' Compensation," 41 Mercer Law Review 429, 1989; with Bagley, "Change in Condition v. New Accident: Old Problems Revisited," 40 Mercer Law Review 961, 1989. *Member:* Atlanta and American (Member, Property Insurance Law Committee, Section of Tort and Insurance Practice) Bar Associations; State Bar of Georgia (Member, Workers Compensation Section). *General Litigation and Self-Insured and Workers Compensation, Insurance.*

JAMES F. COOK, JR., born Atlanta, Georgia, December 1, 1953; admitted to bar, 1984, Georgia. *Education:* Georgia Institute of Technology (B.S., Industrial Management, 1975); University of Georgia (J.D., cum laude, 1984). Member: Moot Court Team, 1982-1983; Moot Court Board American Bar Association Coach, 1983-1984. Certified Arbitrator, Superior Court of Fulton County, 1986—. Member, 1985-1990 and Chairman, 1990, Atlanta Council of Younger Lawyers Scholarship Committee. *Member:* Atlanta and American Bar Associations; State Bar of Georgia; Atlanta Claims Association. [Major, U.S. Air Force Reserve]. *General Litigation, Products Liability, Municipal and Civil Rights, Commercial and Corporate Litigation.*

For significance of Fields of Law in biographical sketches, see Explanatory Notes on inside cover.

FIGURE 17-2 *Martindale-Hubbell* is an invaluable guide to law firms.

the government is different from working for a corporation, which is in turn different from working on your own as an independent paralegal. Because the legal field presents a wide variety of environments in which to work, you will want to look at yourself—your goals, ambitions, preferences, and personality—and attempt to make a match between you and the environment in which you work. Your market research should therefore be oriented to unearthing different possible environments that fit your skills, goals, and personality. You will then know not only what you want to do, but also where, and in what kind of a situation, you want to do it.

Once you have laid the foundation for your job search by doing effective self- and market analysis, you are ready for the second step, which is learning how to present yourself effectively in the job search.

Presenting Yourself in the Job Search

You present yourself in two major ways during the job search. These are through your résumé and through your interviewing skills. If you can develop an excellent résumé and superior interviewing skills, you will be well prepared to secure a position as a paralegal.

The Résumé

One of the most important items in the job search is the résumé. A *résumé* is a written document that gives the reader an overview of the person's skills, experiences, and general preparedness for the position. In many instances, your résumé will be the only document a prospective employer will use to determine whether to interview you for a position. Therefore, your résumé must present appropriate information in a way that is attractive and professional; both what your résumé says and how it is presented affect the reader's perception of you.

It is important to remember that the real goal of a résumé is to get an interview. It is highly unlikely that you will get a job based solely on your résumé; rather, prospective employers will evaluate résumés and choose the most promising applicants for personal interviews. Your résumé should therefore be the kind of document that will make employers want to learn more about you.

The information in your résumé will be presented in sections. As there is no single best way to write a résumé, you will have to decide which sections fit your experiences and present your abilities most effectively. Some must be there, such as your education or work experience, and some may be there, such as military experience or achievements. The following sections frequently appear in résumés. Once you have chosen the sections to include in your résumé, you will be able to complete your résumé by filling out each section.

The Sections of a Résumé

Identification Section

This section shows your name, address, and telephone numbers. Every résumé must have this section, as it will enable employers to identify and contact you.

Education

Your educational experiences should appear on your résumé. This section should include your paralegal training and may include other college or high school experiences. If educational achievements are one of your strong suits, you may want to make sure that this section gives relevant information, such as your grade point average or academic honors, for schools attended. A college degree prior to paralegal school should probably be mentioned, and you should think strongly about including other educational experiences, such as previous schooling, if they show you in a positive light.

Achievements/Awards

If you have significant or relevant achievements or awards, you will want them on your résumé. They might be a subsection of the education section, or they might constitute an entire section on their own. The more there are, and the more you want to emphasize them, the more you will want to consider having an entire section for them. If you are only listing a couple, they will probably fit better as a subset of another section.

Skills

Many employers like a skills section, in which you give an overview of your abilities and qualifications. This section also gives you the opportunity to emphasize your work and skill preferences. For example, if you were interested in becoming a real estate paralegal, you could create a subsection in your skills section where you could include abilities directly related to real estate, such as a real estate license or a summer job doing title searches. In this way, the skills section helps the employer understand your abilities and helps you tailor your résumé to your areas of interest and expertise.

Work Experience

This section is an opportunity for you to present what you have learned in your previous work experiences. If you have previous legal experience, describe it in detail, indicating what you have done and the legal skills you have obtained.

Military Experience

If you have military experience, it is frequently helpful to include it. Make sure to indicate your present status and your dates of service.

Interests and Hobbies

This section, if you choose to include it, enables you to present additional information about yourself. It may give the interviewer an ice-breaker for the beginning of the interview.

Final Preparation of Your Résumé

Once you have chosen and developed the sections of your résumé, you will need to go through some final procedures to develop it into a finished product. First, you need to look over each item in your résumé and make sure that you can speak intelligently about it if you are asked about it in an interview. Second, show it to a number of different people to get their feedback. Remember that you will be evaluated on your résumé, so you want it to present you effectively and conform to the needs and expectations of employers.

Once you have finished the final draft, you will need to have it printed. The two ways to print your résumé that will give you the most professional-looking document are typesetting and laser printing. Typesetting involves hiring a printer to set the type on a master résumé, and then ordering copies. It provides the most professional-looking résumé, but it does not allow you to vary your résumé for different openings. A computer-generated résumé, printed on a laser printer, can also provide a highly professional document, and this method offers the benefit of enabling the user to alter her résumé to fit different openings. Of course, you must have access to the equipment, and you must be able to use the software, but this is a less expensive, more flexible, and equally professional way to prepare the final form of your résumé.

Résumé Models

The following résumés (Figures 17-3 through 17-10) have been included to give you an idea of how other paralegals have constructed their résumés. These are intended to be models to stimulate your thinking; do not attempt to copy them, for your résumé, to be effective, must truly be your own.

LISA PHELPS HUGHES
702 Summerbrook Drive
Dunwoody, Georgia 30338
Phone: (404) 642-6442

CAREER OBJECTIVE To utilize my organizational and interpersonal skills to further my career as a paralegal.

EXPERIENCE ANALYSIS

Legal:

Contracts — Provided initial approval on corporate contracts. Reviewed supplements for contractual deficiencies. Drafted analysis memorandums.

Litigation — Drafted pleadings. Responsible for document control and retention. Assisted in all aspects of pretrial and trial preparation. Conducted factual investigations.

Collection — Responsible for establishing and maintaining over 300 collection files. Gathered all information to prepare file for legal action. Demonstrated ability to work effectively with large client base.

Research — Researched and drafted memorandums of law on variety of legal and personnel issues for region. Assisted in drafting corporate policy.

Administration:

Personnel — Interviewed and selected secretarial support. Provided input for yearly appraisals. Counseled employees in identifying areas of career development. Monitored daily workload of subordinates.

Computer — Trained secretarial staff on use of 3B2 computer with Unix software applications. Responsible for back-up and restore functions for all office users.

Library — Reviewed and ordered all literature for office library. Updated library on bi-monthly basis. Created and maintained inventory of library.

FIGURE 17-3

LORRI MEYER

10014 White Bluff Rd., Apt. 907
Savannah, Georgia 31406
Phone: (912) 236-2491 (w) or (912) 925-3786 (h)

QUALIFICATIONS:	Strong organizational and analytical skills and ability in planning. Experienced in writing summary and analytical reports. High comprehension level and above average communication skills. Interest in graduate work.
EDUCATION:	Cedar Crest College, Allentown, PA Bachelor of Science, May, 1985 Major: Business Administration Concentration: Public and Institutional Administration Certificate: Legal Assistance (Accredited by ABA) GPA: 3.1
	Lehigh County Community College, Schnecksville, PA Associates in Applied Science, May, 1982 Major: Secretarial Science/Legal
EXPERIENCE: Sept. 1985 – Present	Bouhan, Williams, & Levy, Savannah, Georgia *Paralegal/Information Coordinator* — Responsibilities include preparation of pleadings, discovery documents, trial materials and obtaining witness testimony and preparing deposition summaries. Procure and manage documents. Extensive computerized legal research and prepare memorandum on legal findings. Actively involved in implementing computer litigation support system. Manage daily operations of library.
June 1984 – May 1985	Air Products and Chemicals, Inc., Allentown, PA *Paralegal/Librarian* — Responsible for mechanics and recordkeeping of document production for an anti-trust suit and establish file system for specific cases. Perform general research and prepare legal memorandums. Administer daily operations of library.
Sept. 1980 – Sept. 1984	Merchants National Bank, Allentown, PA *ATM Clerk* — Monitor IBM 3604 and 3615 machines and oversee ATM network. Research and balance transaction journal and input on CRT and general clerical work.
EXTRA-CURRICULAR ACTIVITIES:	Active in church activities—plan special events, chaperon. Member of Georgia Association for Legal Assistants.
INTERESTS:	Enjoy hiking, camping, canoeing and bike riding.
REFERENCES:	Will be furnished upon request.

FIGURE 17-4

MELISSA DAWN EDWARDS

2053-F POWERS FERRY ROAD
MARIETTA, GEORGIA 30067
(404) 850-0548

OBJECTIVE

To obtain experience through a wide variety of paralegal opportunities.

CAPABILITIES

Strong organizational and managerial skills in the area of data collection and report production for legal professionals. Personal computer experience through the use of utility packages such as WORDPERFECT and BARRISTER WORD MANAGER.

EMPLOYMENT HISTORY

PARALEGAL (CONFIDENTIAL)   **6/88 – PRESENT**

Drew, Eckl & Farnham, Atlanta, Georgia

— Responsibilities include initiating and responding to all methods of discovery, summarizing and evaluating medical records and depositions, legal research in the areas of civil rights/employment discrimination, municipal liability and general insurance defense. Interface with clients and attorneys throughout all phases of litigation.

RIDESHARE COORDINATOR   **6/84 – 8/84**

Georgia Department of Transportation, Atlanta, Georgia

— **Governor's Internship Program** with the Bureau of Public Transportation. Responsibilities included sole monitoring of the Rideshare telephone, gathering and processing voluminous information forms in order to coordinate car pool programs throughout Metro Atlanta. Prepared status reports and newsletters regarding the progress of the Rideshare program.

EDUCATION

The National Center for Paralegal Training, June, 1988
Atlanta, Georgia
General Studies Program

Georgia Southern University, June, 1987
Statesboro, Georgia
B.S. in Political Science, International Studies Minor

ACTIVITIES

Georgia Association of Legal Assistants
National Federation of Paralegal Associations

FIGURE 17-5

KELLY ANN HOWARD
228 Club Place
Duluth, Georgia 30136
(404) 497-1126

OBJECTIVE

To obtain a position as a **Legal Assistant** where prior experience, training, and qualifications will be used.

EDUCATION

Lawyer's Assistant Program of The National Center for Paralegal Training, Atlanta, Georgia. ABA approved. Honor Graduate.
Courses in Civil Litigation, Debtor/Creditor Relationships, Family Law, Real Estate Law, Corporations, Computer Literacy, Legal Research, Criminal Law, and Estates, Wills, and Trusts.
October 1988 – June 1989.

University of Cincinnati, Cincinnati, Ohio.
Bachelor of Business Administration. Major: Marketing.
September 1980 – March 1985

EMPLOYMENT

A.C. Nielsen Company, Atlanta, Georgia.
Senior Marketing Research Representative.
Responsible for conducting comprehensive and detailed research on food, drug, and liquor products in the retail industry. Implement controlled store audits. Delegate assignments to subordinates. Gather causal data to track consumer trends. Analyze product effectiveness. Train, coach, and counsel temporary resources. Serve as a liaison between A.C. Nielsen Company and the retail market.
June 1985 – present

Shillito-Rikes (Lazarus), Cincinnati, Ohio.
Night Auditor.
Provided audit control and maintenance of cash flow. Balanced daily cash receipts from all branches. Resolved customer complaints and inquiries.
June 1984 – March 1985

Peachtree Bank and Trust (Trust Company Bank), Atlanta, Georgia.
Administrative Assistant, Accounting Department.
Assisted office personnel with duties performed throughout the banking system. Duties included accounting, personal and commercial accounts, credit references, and customer relations.
Holidays and Summers 1982 – 1984

Behavioral Sciences Lab, University of Cincinnati, Cincinnati, Ohio.
Work-Study Student.
Handled various clerical tasks. Aided supervisors with research projects.
September 1981 – June 1982

M.A.R.C. Inc., Atlanta, Georgia.
Telemarketing Representative.
Conducted interviews with consumers. Organized data for clients. Maintained quality control of final research.
March 1980 – August 1980

REFERENCES

Available upon request.

FIGURE 17-6

Brenda A. Paschal
1911 Oak Branch Way
Stone Mountain, Georgia 30087
(404) 972-4888

OBJECTIVE: Paralegal Position – Litigation.

QUALIFICATIONS:

- Two years of experience as a paralegal in complex litigation with increasing responsibilities for managing and evaluating personal-injury cases.

- Fifteen years of experience as a daily newspaper reporter, researching, investigating, interviewing, analyzing, writing and editing articles. Spent five years covering civil and criminal courts, observing hundreds of cases from the filing of complaints and warrants through trials, verdicts and sentencings. Won five awards in statewide competition sponsored by the South Carolina Press Association.

- Trained in WordPerfect 5.0, Inmagic and other software packages.

- Major strengths include:
  - Organizational skills.
  - Attention to detail.
  - Analytical abilities.
  - Oral and written communication.

PROFESSIONAL EXPERIENCE:

Litigation Paralegal
1988 – Present
Powell, Goldstein, Frazer & Murphy
Atlanta, Georgia

Newspaper Reporter
1971 – 1987
The Greenville Piedmont
The Greenville News-Piedmont Company
Greenville, South Carolina

Feature Writer (Summer Intern)
1970
The Atlanta Journal
Atlanta, Georgia

EDUCATION:

The National Center for Paralegal Training, Atlanta, Georgia.
ABA Approved. Honor Graduate with Litigation Specialty. 1988.

West Georgia College, Carrollton, Georgia.
Bachelor of Arts Degree in English. GPA 3.47. 1971.

REFERENCES AVAILABLE UPON REQUEST

FIGURE 17-7

JENNIFER LEIGH KETZLER
3071 Gant Quarters Circle
Marietta, Georgia 30068
(404) 977-2810

OBJECTIVE: Obtain a position combining my paralegal training in litigation and my degree in criminal justice.

EDUCATION: **The National Center for Paralegal Training**, Atlanta, Georgia
ABA Approved Lawyer's Assistant Program
Specialty in Civil Litigation
Certificate of Completion with Honors: September 1994

Texas Christian University, Fort Worth, Texas
Bachelor of Science, May 1993: Psychology and Criminal Justice
GPA 3.69/4.0

EMPLOYMENT: **Sales Associate**   09/93 – Present
Jennifer's Hallmark, Marietta, Georgia   05/91 – 08/91
Responsible for daily operations of store, including processing inventory, maintenance of stock and customer relations.

Research Assistant   02/93 – 05/93
Texas Christian University, Fort Worth, Texas
Reviewed, evaluated and encoded surveys. Performed research and analysis of various trends in juvenile institutions.

Research Coordinator   05/90 – 08/90
Hallmark Cards Inc., Southwest Regional Office, Atlanta, Georgia
Developed merchandise displays, evaluated product sales and revised card systems.

ACHIEVEMENTS: **Dean's List**—5 semesters
TCU Scholar—3 semesters (4.0 GPA)
Delta Sigma Pi—Business Fraternity
Pi Beta Phi—Social Fraternity
Psi Chi—Psychology Honor Society; Historian
Golden Key National Honor Society
Programming Council—Homecoming, Parents' Weekend
Student Government—Academic Subcommittee
Student Ambassador—New Student Recruitment

COMPUTER: Familiar with DOS 5.0, Windows 3.1, WordPerfect 5.2, Lotus 1-2-3, dBase III+, INMAGIC Plus, and WESTLAW.

References Available Upon Request

FIGURE 17-8

Michelle Binning
152 Lablanc Way, N.W.
Atlanta, Georgia 30327

404-352-7322

Education:	The National Center for Paralegal Training ABA approved. Paralegal certificate with focus in Business Transactions February 1994. Expected to graduate with honors.
	Lewis and Clark College Portland, Oregon Bachelor of Arts, June 1992 Majors: Communications & English G.P.A. 3.2
Work Experience:	Drew, Eckl & Farnham Records Clerk Performed conflict avoidance checks for all new matters. In addition, entered data and updated various records tracking databases. Responsible for entering new matters in DEF Daily, the firm newsletter. Emphasis on accuracy, detail and organization. October 1992 – Present
	Westland Investment Company File Clerk Clerical duties such as filing, typing and light bookkeeping December 1991 – April 1992
Experience:	Senior English Thesis Utilized English Legal History as the basis for interpreting Shakespeare's Richard II. Project required extensive literary research and analysis, as well as research of Renaissance statutes. March – June 1992
	Tutor/Note Taker Women's History tutor and note taker for a dyslexic student. Ensured that student understood concepts presented in class. January – March 1992
Computer Skills:	WordPerfect, Conflicts Database, Summation. DBase III, Lotus, Inmagic will be covered in class.
	Professional References Furnished Upon Request

FIGURE 17-9

NANCY ELLIOTT
597 East Paces Ferry Road
Atlanta, Georgia 30305
(404) 841-0963

EDUCATION:

Lawyer's Assistant Program of The National Center for Paralegal Training,
Atlanta, GA
Specialty in Litigation with training in Legal Research, general practice skills
in Real Estate, Probate, Corporations, and Computer Literacy.
Certificate: December, 1993

University of Georgia, Athens, GA
Bachelor of Arts Degree in Psychology: August 1993

EXPERIENCE:

Athena Management Group, **Leasing Assistant**, Athens, GA
Provided information to prospective tenants and assisted with completion
of leases. Handled general office administration assignments including
typing, filing and answering phones. Gained exposure to landlord-tenant
and dispossessory procedures.
January – September 1993

Social Expressions, **Cashier**, Atlanta, GA
Monitored and maintained inventory, and arranged merchandise displays.
November – December 1992

Three Dollar Cafe, **Waitress**, Atlanta, GA
May – August 1991

ACTIVITIES:

American Cancer Society, 1989–1993
Assisted with fundraising efforts

Psychology Club, 1992–1993
Visited patients at state mental facility

Delta Delta Delta, 1989–1993

COMPUTER SKILLS:

Working knowledge of WordPerfect.
Familiarity with LEXIS, WESTLAW, InMagic, Windows, DOS, Lotus 1-2-3,
and dBase III.

REFERENCES AVAILABLE UPON REQUEST

FIGURE 17-10

Interviewing

The interview is the culmination of the preparatory steps you have already taken in your job search; it is your opportunity to speak directly with a potential employer. It is the most powerful opportunity you have to present yourself and your skills for consideration, and you should take full advantage of this chance.

You should prepare for the interview by developing an interview agenda, relating your skills and abilities to the needs of the firm, and practicing interview responses. These three activities will enable you to present yourself professionally and effectively.

Developing an agenda refers to the process of thinking through what you want to convey in an interview so that you use the questions to reveal your strengths and abilities. Many interviewees go into an interview and say what they feel that day. Like an attorney preparing to give closing arguments, the interviewee will appear more professional if his or her answers are intelligent and thoughtful, giving the interviewer relevant information. Many interviewers, for example, begin an interview with the question, "Tell me a little about yourself." If you have thought through your interview strategy as part of your interview preparation, you will be prepared to answer this question with appropriate information, such as your training, legal experience, or areas of work interest. Without an agenda, it is easy to ramble on, presenting yourself as a candidate who is not really serious about a career position. Before your interviews, therefore, plan what you want to communicate in the interview, and then look for opportunities to get your points across. This will enable you to present yourself confidently and professionally.

A second important practice in preparing for interviews is to relate your skills and abilities to the needs of the prospective employer. (See Figure 17-11.) When firms interview for positions, they generally have needs that they want filled, not just needs in the present, such as for a litigation paralegal, but needs for the future, such as the ability to learn technical applications quickly. It is important that you identify the potential employer's needs and use the interview as an opportunity to explain how you can fill those needs. For example, if you have experience working effectively in stressful situations, you should emphasize this ability, as you know that legal practice is stressful and that you will need to handle stress effectively to be a successful paralegal. It is also helpful for you to bring up key issues, rather than waiting for an interviewer to ask about them. Do not wait for the interviewer to ask you, for example, whether you work well under stress. Seek opportunities to bring up your points. When you are asked about your major strengths, you can say, "One of my strengths, which I believe will really help me be successful as a paralegal, is the ability to work effectively under stress. While I was in college, I supported myself by working two jobs, which was a highly stressful situation, and I learned how to manage myself and my time without succumbing to the pressure. I know that working in a law office is stressful, and I am confident in my abilities to work

FIGURE 17-11
In an interview, it is important to relate your abilities to the needs of the firm.

productively even in stressful situations." If you can offer answers like this, the interviewer will be impressed, because you have directly related your abilities to their needs. You will also have demonstrated your preparation for the interview and your professional approach to the job search.

The initial preparation for interviews involves anticipating frequently asked questions. By thinking through potential responses to typically asked questions, you will help yourself make intelligent, thoughtful responses in the real interview. The following questions are frequently asked in interviews:

Tell me a little about yourself.

How did you get interested in the law?

What aspect of legal practice is most interesting to you?

What are your greatest strengths?

What are your major weaknesses?

Why should I hire you?

How would others describe you? How would you describe yourself?

How would you describe your ethical standards?

What was your favorite class in paralegal school?

Why did you want to become a paralegal?

Are you considering going to law school?

What part of a paralegal's job do you enjoy most, researching or interviewing clients?

What skill is your best, writing or speaking?

Do you have a writing sample? Why did you choose this writing sample?

If you could create an ideal job, what would it be?

Would you prefer working on many different cases or a couple of large cases?

What does teamwork mean to you?

Remember that you will be evaluated not only on your answers but also on your appearance and overall demeanor. It is imperative that you dress appropriately for the interview by wearing conservative, professional clothing. It is also important that you be positive, energetic, and enthusiastic about your work; if you appear distracted or disinterested, you will probably not get a job offer.

Two recent American Bar Foundation surveys of hiring partners found that when interviewing potential associates, the partners looked for skills that were necessary to attract and to retain clients. These skills are good oral and written communication skills, good legal analysis, instilling confidence in clients, computer research skills, library research skills, and sensitivity to professional ethics and concerns. Although these surveys concentrated on what partners looked for in potential associates, the survey results also seem applicable to paralegals. In an increasingly competitive job market, good communication skills and self-confidence are the traits that could make the difference in winning that great job.

Finding a Position as a Paralegal

Once you have done all of the necessary preparation for your job search, as described previously, you are ready to pursue your actual job search. You can pursue a combination of the following activities to find a position.

1. Your school's graduate placement office may help students find positions. They might even have employers interview on campus. Check with your school's office and learn about the services they provide.

2. Classified ads in the newspaper are a valuable source of job leads.

3. *Networking*, the process of making contact with people who might be helpful to you in your job search, can be an extremely effective method of finding a position. Many positions are filled without being advertised, as when a paralegal with a firm knows that another paralegal is leaving and suggests that her friend apply for the position. By involving other people in your job search, and by attending career fairs, open houses, or association meetings, you can meet people whose knowledge or contacts might be extremely valuable to you in your job search.

4. *Prospecting* refers to the process of researching firms and writing to them, inquiring about job openings. If you were interested in being a real estate

paralegal, for example, you could identify the 50 firms in a city with the largest real estate practices and send out your résumé with a cover letter.

5. For government work, learn about and follow the established procedures, which are sometimes quite different than with private firms. Most government agencies require that all applicants fill out particular applications for jobs. Be certain that you have completed the required documentation.

The preceding portion of this chapter has described the process of obtaining a position as a paralegal, which requires doing the proper preparation, presenting yourself effectively, and actually pursuing positions. The following section addresses the issue of how to get ahead once you have obtained a position.

Career Advancement for Paralegals

Once you have obtained a position as a paralegal and gotten settled into your new job, you will want to begin thinking and planning for your continued growth and development. Career development does not end when you have accepted a position, but is a lifelong activity in which you think about and plan your work life so that you achieve both your present and your future goals. Therefore, once you have become integrated into your new position, you will want to spend some time thinking about your future and about the ways in which you can move forward to achieve your goals and aspirations.

HOW NOT TO GET AHEAD AS A PARALEGAL

---

1. When you do not understand how to do something, just wing it—do not ask for instructions.
2. Instead of looking things up in the firm's manual, keep asking the firm administrator, "May I ask you a question?"
3. Argue with an attorney about the proper procedure to take in a particular case.
4. Argue with an attorney generally.
5. Forget that you are not licensed to practice law.
6. Bring your personal problems to the office.
7. Compete with the associates.
8. Give clients legal advice.
9. Step outside the realm of "paralegaling" into the realm of "lawyering."
10. Be generally difficult, self-centered, offensive, or otherwise unpleasant in your attitude, work habits, or personal habits.

Advancement Through Excellence

The basis for all future growth is excellence in your present work. In addition to performing your required job functions well and demonstrating the interpersonal skills that make you easy to work with, you can be an excellent paralegal by being willing to take on new assignments and responsibilities. You will find it hard to move ahead if you are unwilling to expand your skills and abilities. You should read voraciously, act professionally, and become a valuable team member by making suggestions and maintaining your billable hour requirements. Ask for feedback; be willing to change; go beyond what is required; be meticulous and detail-oriented in your work. All of these will help you lay the foundations for future growth.

You should learn what your firm expects of you and strive to meet its requirements by understanding how your performance will be evaluated. Performance evaluations typically cover the following areas:

Legal ability, including knowledge of job, analytical ability, problem-solving ability, and client communication and interaction;

Work habits, including organization, accepting responsibility, working well with supervisors, meeting deadlines, and dealing with change;

Attitude, including interest in work and cooperativeness with others;

Job performance, including productivity analysis, quality assessment, and job knowledge;

Personal qualities, including reliability, professionalism, appearance, and creativity;

Professional development, including education and self-development activities;

Time management, including attendance, punctuality, and accurate time-keeping.

In addition to achieving excellence in your work, you will want to continue your education in preparation for your career growth. Certainly you will want to take advantage of learning opportunities offered by your firm. You may decide to return to college if you do not have a degree, or to take additional courses, pursue a graduate degree, or even pursue a law degree. You will also want to take advantage of continuing legal education (CLE) offerings. CLE credits are not presently mandatory for paralegals, as they are for attorneys, but possible future developments include requiring CLE credits for paralegals. Additionally, one important quality of an excellent paralegal is the desire to expand knowledge and ability through education, and taking CLE credits is a sure way to increase your skills and demonstrate your ability to handle increased responsibilities.

As paralegals have integrated themselves more fully into the legal profession, more attention is being paid to professional development through continuing education for paralegals. One excellent example is the expansion of offerings for paralegals by the Practising Law Institute, the oldest and largest national organization for continuing legal education. PLI's Continuing Legal Assistant Training Programs cover a wide variety of topics and are frequently presented in association with NALA or NFPA. Some PLI programs are offered live via satellite and are available at multiple locations across the country. Additionally, PLI will arrange for these seminars to be broadcast directly to an office if the office has an appropriate satellite dish. Seminars usually have a course handbook for participants, and the programs are generally available on audio- and videocassettes as well.

Participation in professional activities and firm activities will also help you gain skills and exposure that will open opportunities for you in the future. Frequently a professional organization of your peers, such as NALS, NALA, NFPA, or PLA, will provide the greatest opportunities for professional development and the best continuing legal education. Volunteer work and community involvement will also enhance your career development.

Finally, you will want to learn about other career opportunities in the field of law that might be available to you in the future if you develop additional skills. Opportunities exist in firm administration, personnel administration, consulting, management in private industry, and technical support for law firms. By complementing your paralegal skills with additional relevant skills, you can create opportunities that meet your career goals. Remember also that paralegal work provides excellent preparation for going to law school and becoming a lawyer. Your paralegal training, work ethic, and career development activities can therefore work together to provide you with boundless opportunities for personal and professional growth.

ON POINT

PAULA'S PERJURY

Paula is a paralegal in a jurisdiction that certifies paralegals and requires a minimum of five hours of continuing paralegal education. Because Paula did not complete this requirement, the Board of Paralegal Certification notifies her by phone that her certification is immediately revoked and that the formal revocation will be in the mail next week.

The next day, Paula, who has told no one, is called as an expert witness for a case involving paralegal malpractice. She is asked on the stand whether she is a certified paralegal in the jurisdiction, and she testifies in the affirmative. On cross-examination, she breaks down and reveals the truth. She is also forced to reveal that she had lied on the résumé that she used in her job search. Given the fact that she has revealed these things in court, how should she now handle this situation?

Professional Development: A Summary

Professional development refers to the activities that you will perform and the materials that you develop in your quest to take advantage of career opportunities in your field. Most paralegals are attracted to legal work because it is exciting and because it offers many opportunities. By actively pursuing your own career development, from your first job through your retirement, you will be able to take advantage of the varied opportunities that the legal profession has to offer.

Key Terms

career advancement
continuing legal education (CLE)
interview skills and questions
job search strategies

market research
Practising Law Institute (PLI)
professional development
résumé

Problems and Activities

1. Take a few minutes and analyze yourself using the methods set forth in this chapter. Write a one-page summary of what type of paralegal position you hope to attain.

2. Write a sample cover letter for your résumé in response to the advertisement in this section from Drew, Eckl & Farnham.

3. Make a list of your career development goals and how you intend to achieve them for the next five years.

4. Go through the entire list of interview questions in this chapter and plan a response to each, using examples where appropriate to sell yourself and your abilities.

5. Write two paragraphs on why you decided to become a paralegal and what you intend to do with the degree.

6. Plan a general idea of what you will say if an interviewer greets you, sits down, and says, "Tell me a little about yourself."

7. If you wanted to pursue a nontraditional paralegal position, what strategies would you use?

APPENDIX A

Standardized Filing Rules and Records Retention Rules

STANDARDIZED FILING RULES

I. BASIC INDEXING

A. Personal Names

Names of individuals are indexed starting with the last name as the Key Unit, the first name or initial as Unit 2, and the middle name or middle initial as Unit 3. When alphabetizing, the first letter of the key unit is used first, the second letter second, and so on.

Name	Key Unit	Unit 2	Unit 3
Flo J. Acre	Acre	Flo	J
Benny K. Day	Day	Benny	K
Samuel J. Peterson	Peterson	Samuel	J

B. Business and Organization Names

Names of businesses and organizations are indexed as separate units just as they are written. Abbreviations should be spelled in full.

Name	Key Unit	Unit 2	Unit 3	Unit 4
Jay Rush Textile Co.	Jay	Rush	Textile	Co
First State Bank	First	State	Bank	
Miss Popcorn	Miss	Popcorn		
State Car Association	State	Car	Association	

C. Newspapers and Periodicals

Names of newspapers and periodicals are indexed as separate units just as they are written. If two newspapers or periodicals have identical names that do not include the city name, use the city name as the last indexing unit. When necessary, the state name may be used following the city name.

From Arn et al., *Records Management for an Information Age* (Albany, N.Y.: Delmar Publishers Inc., 1991).

Name	Key Unit	Unit 2	Unit 3
Dallas Post	Dallas	Post	
Lawrenceburg Star	Lawrenceburg	Star	Illinois
Lawrenceburg Star	Lawrenceburg	Star	Indiana
Sunrise Post	Sunrise	Post	Chicago
Sunrise Post	Sunrise	Post	Orlando

II. MINOR WORDS IN BUSINESS NAMES

Prepositions, conjunctions, and articles are considered to be minor words in business names. Such words are considered a separate indexing unit. Symbols are spelled out with the first letter capitalized and used as an indexing unit. The word "and" is an exception; it is not capitalized. When the word "The" is used as the first word of a business or organization name, it becomes the last indexing unit.

Name	Key Unit	Unit 2	Unit 3	Unit 4
The Country Inn	Country	Inn	The	
Pratt & Ratt	Pratt	and	Ratt	
Save by the $	Save	by	the	Dollar

III. PUNCTUATION AND POSSESSIVES

All punctuation is disregarded when indexing personal, business, and organization names.

Name	Key Unit	Unit 2	Unit 3
The East-West Bank	EastWest	Bank	The
Jimmy's Design	Jimmys	Design	
Angel P. Tone	Tone	Angel	P

IV. SINGLE LETTERS AND ABBREVIATIONS

Initials, abbreviations. and nicknames of personal names are indexed as they are written. Single letters of business names are indexed as written.

Index abbreviations as one unit.

If necessary, cross-reference names that have been spelled out to their acronyms. For example: American Automobile Association SEE AAA.

Name	Key Unit	Unit 2	Unit 3	Unit 4
Thos. Iveal	Iveal	Thos		
J A Movers	J	A	Movers	
The LWT Florist Co.	LWT	Florist	Co	The
NBEA	NBEA			
P & H Grill	P	and	H	Grill
U.S.A. Tire Company	USA	Tire	Company	
Bob Vann	Vann	Bob		

V. TITLES

A. Personal Names

When personal titles are used in a name, consider it to be the last indexing unit. These titles include: Miss, Mrs., Ms., and Mr. Seniority titles, when used, are the last indexing unit. Numeric titles (II, III, IV) are filed before alphabetic titles (Jr., Sr.). Professional titles are also considered the last indexing unit and filed alphabetically as written.

Name	Key Unit	Unit 2	Unit 3	Unit 4
Miss Rose H. Brown	Brown	Rose	H	Miss
Chris Z. Downs	Downs	Chris	Z	
Chris Z. Downs II	Downs	Chris	Z	II
Chris Z. Downs III	Downs	Chris	Z	III
Chris Z. Downs, Jr.	Downs	Chris	Z	Jr
Chris Z. Downs, Sr.	Downs	Chris	Z	Sr
Dr. Herman M. Hicks	Hicks	Herman	M	Dr
Mrs. Susan A. Lide	Lide	Susan	A	Mrs
Clover R. Nelty	Nelty	Clover	R	CPA
Sister Mary	Sister	Mary		

Professional titles include: Dr., M.D., D.D.S., CPA. Royal or religious titles (Brother, Sister, Father) followed by a surname or a given name are used only as the key unit. When all indexing units are identical, including titles, addresses are used to determine the filing order.

B. Business Names

Titles within business and organization names are indexed as written.

Name	Key Unit	Unit 2	Unit 3
Doctor Pets	Doctor	Pets	
Mayor Vance Vaces	Mayor	Vance	Vaces
Miss Suzy's	Miss	Suzys	
Mr. Bob's Stylists	Mr	Bobs	Stylists
Mrs. Kelley's Donuts	Mrs	Kelleys	Donuts

VI. MARRIED WOMEN

File married women's names as written. Cross-reference all known alternate names.

Name	Key Unit	Unit 2	Unit 3	Unit 4
Mrs. Irma S. Dace	Dace	Irma	S	Mrs
x (Mrs. Kenneth Dace)				
Mrs. Robert S. Fields	Fields	Robert	S	Mrs
Ms. Judith Hunter	Hunter	Judith	Ms	
x (Mrs. Judith Krider)				
x (Mrs. Nick Krider)				
Mrs. Geri Wilson	Wilson	Geri	Mrs	

VII. ARTICLES AND PARTICLES

A foreign article or particle in a personal or business name is combined with the part of the name that follows it. This forms a single indexing unit. Disregard any space when indexing. Examples of articles and particles are: D', Da, De, Del, De la, Den, Dos, Du, El, Fitz, L', La, Le, Les, Lo, Los, M', Mac, Mc, 0', Per, St., Saint, San, Santa, Te, Ten, Ter, Van, Van de, Van den, Van der, Von, Von der.

Name	Key Unit	Unit 2	Unit 3
Rev. Henry DeBoard	DeBoard	Henry	Rev
LeCook Billing Co.	LeCook	Billing	Co
Janet A. Saint John	SaintJohn	Janet	A
San Diego Loan Co.	SanDiego	Loan	Co
Lucy Van Cleve	VanCleve	Lucy	
Van Cleve Tires	VanCleve	Tires	
Amanda Van Den Berg	VanDenBerg	Amanda	
Vandenberg Meat Shop	Vandenberg	Meat	Shop
Van Den Berg Olds	VanDenBerg	Olds	
Vanden Berg Ski Resort	VandenBerg	Ski	Resort

VIII. IDENTICAL NAMES

Identical names are filed in this order: (a) last name, (b) first name, (c) middle name, (d) cities, (e) states or provinces, (f) street names, and (g) house numbers or building numbers as the last unit.

Name	Key Unit	Unit 2	Unit 3	Unit 4	Unit 5
Erin S. Edwards Dallas, Texas	Edwards	Erin	S	Dallas	Texas
Erin S. Edwards Houston, Texas	Edwards	Erin	S	Houston	Texas
Clif J. Ingram, Jr. Humble, Texas	Ingram	Clif	J	Jr	Humble
Clif J. Ingram, Jr. Orlando, Florida	Ingram	Clif	J	Jr	Orlando
Lincoln Hotel Aurora, Illinois	Lincoln	Hotel	Aurora	Illinois	
Lincoln Hotel Aurora, Indiana	Lincoln	Hotel	Aurora	Indiana	

When numbered street names are used as filing units, they should be written as figures and placed together in ascending numeric order before alphabetic street names. Street names with compass directions are indexed as written.

Street names with numbers after compass directions are filed before alphabetic names. House and building numbers written as figures should be indexed in ascending order and filed before spelled-out building names.

Name	Key Unit	Unit 2	Unit 3	Unit 4	Unit 5	Unit 6	Unit 7
Massey Groceries 32-20 Street Memphis, Tennessee	Massey	Groceries	Memphis	Tennessee	20	Street	32
Massey Groceries 20-25 Street Memphis, Tennessee	Massey	Groceries	Memphis	Tennessee	25	Street	20
Massey Groceries 35 NW 26 Street Memphis, Tennessee	Massey	Groceries	Memphis	Tennessee	NW	26	35
Massey Groceries 348 Pine Street Memphis, Tennessee	Massey	Groceries	Memphis	Tennessee	Pine	Street	348
Massey Groceries 690 Pine Street Memphis, Tennessee	Massey	Groceries	Memphis	Tennessee	Pine	Street	690
Massey Groceries 12 NW Fifth Street Memphis, Tennessee	Massey	Groceries	Memphis	Tennessee	NW	Fifth	Street
Massey Groceries 76 Rome Drive Memphis, Tennessee	Massey	Groceries	Memphis	Tennessee	Rome	Drive	76

IX. NUMBERS IN BUSINESS NAMES

Spelled-out numbers in a business name are indexed as written. Those written as figures are indexed as one unit. Names with numbers written as figures as the key are filed in ascending order before alphabetic names. Arabic numbers should be filed before Roman numerals. Drop -th, -rd, and -nd on arabic numbers. Names with inclusive numbers, such as 55–57, are filed using the first number only. Names with numbers located in other than the first unit are filed alphabetically within the appropriate unit immediately before a similar name without a number.

Name	Key Unit	Unit 2	Unit 3	Unit 4
6th & Arch Garage	6	and	Arch	Garage
6th and Cypress Shop	6	and	Cypress	Shop
6 Bits Movie	6	Bits	Movie	
600–605 Bridge Drive	600	Bridge	Drive	
The 600 Bridge Market	600	Bridge	Market	The
The 1645 Bakery, Inc.	1645	Bakery	Inc	
The 16000 Condos	16000	Condos	The	
The Six Sands	Six	Sands	The	
The Sixth Week Club	Sixth	Week	Club	The
Six-Thousand Dairy	SixThousand	Dairy		
Star 6 Records	Star	6	Records	
Star 9 Records	Star	9	Records	

X. SEPARATED SINGLE WORDS

When a business, organization, or institution uses a space within a single word, each part is indexed as a single unit. When a name consists of two compass directions separated by a space, each direction is a unit.

Name	Key Unit	Unit 2	Unit 3
Sea Shore Inns	Sea	Shore	Inns
Seashore Inns	Seashore	Inns	
South East Railways	South	East	Railways
Southeast Railways	Southeast	Railways	

XI. GOVERNMENT NAMES

A. Federal

Index federal government agencies using this order: (1) name of the government unit as the key unit, and (2) name of the office, bureau, or department, as the second unit. If the words "Office of," and so on are needed for clarity and are in the official name of the office, bureau, or department, they are used as indexing units. "Of" should not be used as an indexing unit if it is not part of the official name. The first three indexing units for the federal government should always be United States government.

Name	Indexing
Farmers Home Administration	United States Government
Department of Agriculture	Agriculture Department of
U.S. Government	Farmers Home Administration

B. State and Local

State and local government agencies are indexed by their names. If needed for clarity and in the official name, words such as "State of," "County of," and "City of" may be used as indexing units.

Name	Indexing
Game and Fish Commission	Arkansas State of
State of Arkansas	Game and Fish Commission
Board of Education	Perry County of
County of Perry	Board of Education
Animal Shelter	Conway City of
City of Conway	Animal Shelter

C. Foreign

Foreign government names are filed as: (1) English name of the government as the key unit, (2) name of the branch, department, or division as the second unit, (3) name of the state, city, province, or other official division as the last unit. It may be necessary to cross-reference the written foreign name to the English name.

Name	Indexing
Department of Agriculture	China Republic of
Republic of China	Agriculture Department of
Beijing, China	Beijing China
Department of Tourism	Canada Government of
Government of Canada	Tourism Department of
Ottawa, Canada	Ottawa Canada

RECORDS RETENTION RULES

Type of Records	Retention Time
Accident reports/claims (settled cases)	7 years
Accounts payable ledgers and schedules	7 years
Accounts receivable ledgers and schedules	7 years
Audit reports	Permanently
Bank reconciliations	2 years
Bank statements	3 years
Capital stock and bond records: ledgers, transfer registers, stubs showing issues, record of interest coupons, opinions, etc.	Permanently
Cash books	Permanently
Charts of accounts	Permanently
Checks (canceled—see exception below)	7 years
Checks (canceled for important payments, i.e., taxes, purchases of property, special contracts, etc. Checks should be filed with the papers pertaining to the underlying transaction)	Permanently
Contracts, mortgages, notes, and leases (expired)	7 years
Contracts, mortgages, notes, and leases (still in effect)	Permanently
Correspondence (general)	3 years
Correspondence (legal and important matters only)	Permanently
Correspondence (routine) with customers and/or vendors	2 years
Deeds, mortgages, and bills of sale	Permanently
Depreciation schedules	Permanently
Duplicate deposit slips	2 years
Employment applications	3 years
Expense analyses/expense distribution schedules	7 years
Financial statements (year-end, other optional)	Permanently
Garnishments	7 years
General/private ledgers, year-end trial balance	Permanently
Insurance policies (expired)	3 years
Insurance records, current accident reports, claims, policies, etc.	Permanently
Internal audit reports (longer retention periods may be desirable)	3 years
Internal reports (miscellaneous)	3 years
Inventories of products, materials, and supplies	7 years
Invoices (to customers, from vendors)	7 years
Journals	Permanently
Magnetic tape and tab cards	1 year
Minute books of directors, stockholders, bylaws, and charter	Permanently
Notes receivable ledgers and schedules	7 years
Option records (expired)	7 years
Patents and related papers	Permanently
Payroll records and summaries	7 years
Personnel files (terminated)	7 years

Type of Records	Retention Time
Petty cash vouchers	3 years
Physical inventory tags	3 years
Plant cost ledgers	7 years
Property appraisals by outside appraisers	Permanently
Property records, including costs, depreciation reserves, year-end trial balances, depreciation schedules, blueprints, and plans	Permanently
Purchase orders (except purchasing department copy)	1 year
Purchase orders (purchasing department copy)	7 years
Receiving sheets	1 year
Retirement and pension records	Permanently
Requisitions	1 year
Sales commission reports	3 years
Sales records	7 years
Scrap and salvage records (inventories, sales, etc.)	7 years
Stenographers' notebooks	1 year
Stock and bond certificates (canceled)	7 years
Stockroom withdrawal forms	1 year
Subsidiary ledgers	7 years
Tax returns and worksheets, revenue agents' reports, and other documents relating to determination of income tax liability	Permanently
Time books/cards	7 years
Trademark registrations and copyrights	Permanently
Training manuals	Permanently
Union agreements	Permanently
Voucher register and schedules	7 years
Vouchers for payments to vendors, employees, etc. (includes allowances and reimbursement of employees, officers, etc., for travel and entertainment expenses)	7 years
Withholding tax statements	7 years

Source: Association of Legal Administrators, Vernon Hills, IL (1987). Reprinted with permission.

APPENDIX B

Sample Office Manual Table of Contents

CONTENTS

Flowers / 0
Handling of Salesmen, Equipment Vendors, Solicitors, etc. / 0
Housekeeper / 0
Librarian / 0
Lights / 0
Maintaining Neatness of Reception Area / 0
Notaries Public / 0
Relief Personnel / 0
Reporting Heating, Air Conditioning, Lighting, or Electrical Problems / 0
Scheduling of Conference or Deposition Rooms / 0
Telephone / 0

C-11.   MISCELLANEOUS GUIDELINES   0

Secretarial/Paralegal Guide / 0
    Citations / 0
    Filing Guidelines for Various Courts / 0
    Index of Medical Abbreviations / 0
    Legal Terminology / 0
    Letters/Correspondence / 0
    Quotations / 0
    Secretarial/Paralegal Duties / 0
    Words Often Confused / 0

D-1.   DEF FORMS FREQUENTLY USED   0

E-1.   APPENDICES   0

Appendix 1:   Description of Firm / 0
Appendix 2:   Current Partners / 0
Appendix 3:   Managing Partners / 0
Appendix 4:   Associate Liaison Committee / 0
Appendix 5:   Administrative Personnel / 0
Appendix 6:   Firm's Legal Practice / 0
Appendix 7:   Associate Sharing Arrangements / 0
Appendix 8:   Firm Meetings Calendar / 0
Appendix 9:   Ad Hoc Committees / 0
Appendix 10: Management Committee / 0
Appendix 11: Associate Compensation Committee / 0
Appendix 12: Associate Orientation Committee / 0
Appendix 13: Associate Review Committee / 0
Appendix 14: Associate Training/CLE Committee / 0
Appendix 15: Building Committee / 0
Appendix 16: DEF Journal Committee / 0
Appendix 17: Forms Committee—General Liability / 0
Appendix 18: Hiring and Recruiting Committee/ Coordinator / 0
Appendix 19: Marketing/Business Development Committee / 0
Appendix 20: Paralegal Review Committee / 0

INDEX

Presentation graphics, 281, 284, 288–89
Printing, word processors and, 282
Privacy. *See* Confidentiality
Privileges. *See also* Confidentiality
  attorney-client. *See* Attorney-client privilege
  work product. *See* Work product privilege
Pro bono work, 59, 246, 247–48
Pro se representation, 116, 349
Probate paralegals, 6–7
Procedures, in office manuals, 250, 252
Productivity, 112, 117, 150, 153, 191, 204
Professional corporations, 53
Professional development, 409, 418, 438. *See also* Continuing legal education
  career advancement, 435–37
  career goals, 417, 418, 432
  communication and, 418–19
  malpractice and, 49
Professional standards, 33
Professionalism, 24, 342, 343. *See also* Ethics
  client relations and, 360–66
  communication and, 381
Profitability, 153, 163–65
Programming, 75
Promotion, 136
Prospecting, 434–35
Public areas, 78
Publications, 93

Q

Quality. *See also* Total Quality Management
  improvement through paralegal use, 15

R

Rainmakers, 66, 103
Real estate paralegals, 7–9, 410
Realization rates, 153, 165, 184
Realization reports, 153
Receiver, 371
Records, letters as, 381
Records clerks, 214
Records management, 213–14, 234
  closing records, 213

destruction. *See* Records retention
filing systems. *See* Filing systems
malpractice and, 40–42
outsourcing, 163
Records managers, 213–14
Records retention
  destruction dates, 214, 227, 229
  destruction procedures, 41, 229
  laws re, 227, 229
Records retention rules, 446–47
Records storage, 213. *See also* File storage
Recycling, 116, 117, 229
Referrals, 97
Regulations, 239
Rehabilitation Act of 1974, 134
Reich v. Page & Addison, 17
Reports
  billing summary, 161–63, 179
  detail, 153, 155
  docket control, 208–9
  file status, 153, 154
  management, 152–56
  New Matter, 218, 219
  realization, 153
  timeslip delinquency, 153
  work-in-progress, 166, 168
Research, 236
  computerized, 237–38, 244, 253–54, 323
  court calendars, 207
  expenses, 180–81
  linking to word processing, 281
  market, 419, 421
  nonlegal information, 237, 241
Research skills, 419
Respondeat superior, 33
Résumés, 421–23
  models, 411, 424–31

S

Safes, 173
Salaries, 17, 143, 163
  paralegals, 18, 144
Sales representatives, 257
Satellite offices, 59
Scanning. *See* Imaging
Schedule, typical day, 198–201
Scrivener, 329

Secretaries, 6, 15, 76, 114
  cost of, 186–87, 390
  number of, 73
Security
  computer, 271–72
  files, 222, 223, 229
  office manuals, 252, 253
Self-representation, 116, 349
Seminars, 90, 93, 101, 103, 116
  CLE, 246, 437
  database use for, 292
  firm-sponsored, 246, 248–49
Sender, 369–70
Senior attorneys, 65
Senior partners, 65
Sexual harassment, 128, 132–34, 135
Small law firms, 57–58
Smoking, 82
Social committee, 69
Social responsibility, 116, 229, 246
Software, 266–67, 270
  graphics, 284–86
  legal, 315, 338
  litigation support, 324
  multimedia, 283, 284
  reviews, 331
  word processing, 280, 281
Sole practitioners, 54–56
Solicitation, 37, 88
Spell checkers, 282
Spreadsheets, 281, 282
Standard of care, 123
State laws
  attorney advertising, 89
  unauthorized practice of law, 347
Statutes, 239, 243
Stereotypes, 133, 391
Storage space, 225
Strategic planning, 106–9
Stress, 117
  cognitive approach to, 404–5
  malpractice and, 48
  sources of, 396–98, 403–4
  symptoms of, 400
  understanding, 403–5
Stress management, 395, 398–406
Strock v. Southern Farm Bureau Casualty Insurance Co., 327
Substance abuse, 48, 128–31, 133
Supplies, 55, 257, 311